A Dictionary of

London Place Names

A. D. Mills is Emeritus Reader in English, University of London and is a member of the Council of the English Place-Name Society and of the Society for Name Studies in Britain and Ireland. His previous books include *A Dictionary of English Place-Names* (Oxford University Press), *The Place-Names of Dorset* (English Place-Name Society), and *The Place-Names of the Isle of Wight* (Paul Watkins).

Oxford
Paperback
Reference

The most authoritative and up-to-date reference
books for both students and the general reader.

Abbreviations
ABC of Music
Accounting
Archaeology*
Architecture
Art and Artists
Art Terms*
Astronomy
Better Wordpower
Bible
Biology
Buddhism*
Business
Card Games
Chemistry
Christian Church
Classical Literature
Classical Mythology*
Colour Medical
Computing
Dance*
Dates
Earth Sciences
Ecology
Economics
Engineering*
English Etymology
English Folklore*
English Grammar
English Language
English Literature
English Place-Names
Euphemisms
Film*
Finance and Banking
First Names
Food and Nutrition
Foreign Words and Phrases
Fowler's Modern English
  Usage
Geography
Handbook of the World
Humorous Quotations
Idioms
Irish Literature
Jewish Religion
Kings and Queens of
  Britain*
King's English
Law
Linguistics
Literary Quotations

Literary Terms
Local and Family History
London Place Names*
Mathematics
Medical
Medicines
Modern Design*
Modern Quotations
Modern Slang
Music
Nursing
Opera
Paperback Encyclopedia
Philosophy
Physics
Plant-Lore
Plant Sciences
Political Biography
Political Quotations
Politics
Popes
Proverbs
Psychology*
Quotations
Sailing Terms
Saints
Science
Scientists
Shakespeare
Ships and the Sea
Sociology
Statistics*
Superstitions
Synonyms and Antonyms
Theatre
Twentieth-Century Art
Twentieth-Century Poetry
Twentieth-Century World
  History
Weather Facts
Who's Who in Opera
Who's Who in the Classical
  World
Who's Who in the
  Twentieth Century
World History
World Mythology
World Religions
Writers' Dictionary
Zoology

*forthcoming

A Dictionary of
London
Place Names

A. D. MILLS

OXFORD
UNIVERSITY PRESS

OXFORD

UNIVERSITY PRESS

Great Clarendon Street, Oxford OX2 6DP

Oxford University Press is a department of the University of Oxford.
It furthers the University's objective of excellence in research, scholarship,
and education by publishing worldwide in

Oxford New York

Athens Auckland Bangkok Bogotá Buenos Aires Calcutta
Cape Town Chennai Dar es Salaam Delhi Florence Hong Kong Istanbul
Karachi Kuala Lumpur Madrid Melbourne Mexico City Mumbai
Nairobi Paris São Paulo Singapore Taipei Tokyo Toronto Warsaw

with associated companies in Berlin Ibadan

Oxford is a registered trade mark of Oxford University Press
in the UK and certain other countries

Published in the United States
by Oxford University Press Inc., New York

British Library Cataloguing in Publication Data
Data available

Library of Congress Cataloging in Publication Data
Data available

ISBN 0-19-280106-6

1 3 5 7 9 10 8 6 4 2

Typeset in Swift by Kolam Information Services Pvt Ltd, Pondicherry, India
Printed in Great Britain by Cox & Wyman Ltd, Reading, Berkshire

Sweet Thames, run softly, till I end my Song

(Edmund Spenser, *Prothalamion*)

For SOLVEJG,
who has lovingly shared me with place names
through many happy years

Preface

Having lived in London and among its place names for some fifty years, I welcome the opportunity to celebrate their rich diversity and to share their intriguing origins and meanings with others. They are a fascinating part of our linguistic and cultural heritage and reflect many aspects of the long and complex history of London and its region over two millennia.

The place names of London and its surrounding towns and villages have of course been written about before, notably by Eilert Ekwall, John Field, and the editors of the English Place-Name Society, and I stand particularly indebted to all their earlier work on the subject. In preparing a list of names that sets out to be more inclusive and comprehensive than any previously published, and in seeking to take a fresh and up-to-date look at the etymologies and meanings of the names, I have naturally consulted numerous other specialized studies on onomastic and related topics, as well as scores of books on the history of London and its hinterland of districts and boroughs—far too many to mention individually, so I trust that the many authors and editors in question will accept this general acknowledgement for any insights they may have given me. I would also like to acknowledge the great help afforded me by the many librarians and archivists I have consulted in preparing the book, again too many to mention by name. They have without exception been most patient and helpful in responding to the questions I have bombarded them with.

My best thanks are also due to Victor Watts, Master of Grey College, Durham, in his capacity as Honorary Director of the English Place-Name Society, for giving permission to quote from the county surveys published by the Society, and to all my colleagues in English name studies, past and present, for our many useful discussions over the years. However I do of course take sole responsibility for the views finally proposed in the book, as well as for any errors or deficiencies remaining.

David Mills

WEST WICKHAM
MAY 2000

Contents

Introduction

London Place Names and their Meanings

London place names cannot fail to be intriguing. What London commuter or resident, or visitor to the London area, has not wondered at some time or another about names like **Cockfosters**, **Shepherd's Bush** or **Chipping Barnet**? How on earth did **Piccadilly** or **Soho** get their names? Why **Crouch End**, **Mincing Lane**, **Pratt's Bottom**, or **Whipps Cross**? What is the meaning of names like **Cheam** or **Chiswick**, **Cricklewood**, **Sidcup**, **Wapping**, or **Neasden**? Of course, we take them all very much for granted. However curious they may seem when we stop to think about them, they are just the old familiar labels for places we encounter every day on map or signpost or season ticket.

In fact all these names, very much part of our rich and fascinating cultural heritage, have etymologies and original meanings that are often not at all apparent from their modern forms. That is because most of our older place names are today what could be termed 'linguistic fossils'. Although they had their origins as living units of speech, coined by our ancestors as descriptions of places in terms of their topography, appearance, situation, use, ownership, or other association, most have become, in the course of time, mere labels, no longer possessing a clear linguistic meaning. This is perhaps hardly surprising when we consider the great age of many of the names and their composition from vocabulary that may have evolved differently from the equivalent words in the ordinary language, or that may now be completely extinct and obscure.

Of course some place names, even very old ones, have apparently changed very little through the many centuries of their existence, and indeed may still convey something of their original meaning if the words from which they are coined have survived in the ordinary language (even though the features to which they refer may have changed or be long disappeared). Thus names (date of first record in brackets) such as **Barnes** (1086), **Blackfen** (1240), **Blackheath** (1166), **Catford** (1240), **Greenford** (845), **Knightsbridge** (1050), **Strand** (1185), and **Woodford** (1062), are shown by their early spellings to be virtually self-explanatory, having undergone only minor changes in form and spelling over a very long period.

But even a casual glance at the alphabetical list of London place names will show that such instant etymologies are usually a delusion. The modern form of an older name can never be assumed to convey its original meaning without early spellings to confirm it, and indeed many names that look equally obvious and transparent prove to have quite unexpected meanings in the light of the evidence of early records. We find, for instance, that neither **Harefield** nor **Hare Street** are named from hares, nor **Cattlegate** from cattle, nor **Ratcliff** from rats, nor **The Hawk Wood** from hawks; that **Cannon Street** has nothing to do with cannons (or even canons); that **Snow Hill** has no connection with snow nor **Chalk Farm** with chalk; and that **Peckham Rye** has nothing to do with the cereal crop! The inevitable association of such names with well-known words in the ordinary vocabulary is understandable but quite misleading, for they all derive from old words which survive in contracted or fossilized form in place names but which are in some cases no longer found in modern English.

Old place names and street names then can never be taken at their face value, but can only be correctly interpreted after the careful scrutiny of the earliest attested spellings in the light of all the relevant linguistic, historical, and geographical factors. These fundamental principles of place-name etymology are best illustrated by comparing pairs of apparently identical names that prove to have quite distinct origins. Thus, the **Bromley** near Beckenham and the **Bromley** in Tower Hamlets contain quite different Old English words, the first *brōm* 'broom' and the second *bræmbel* 'bramble'. **Tottenham** and **Tottenham Court Road** have totally different etymologies, as do **Seething Lane** and **Seething Wells** and the two examples of **Watling Street**. The two City street names **Addle Hill** and **Addle Street** have little in common: the first is from Old English *ætheling* 'prince', the second from Old English *adela* 'dirty place'! On the other hand, an examination of the earliest spellings for a name can reveal how it comes to exist in two different versions, as with **Haringey** and **Hornsey**, **Rotherhithe** and **Redriff**, and **Wormwood** and **Wormholt**.

Scope and Arrangement of the Dictionary

This dictionary sets out to provide the most likely etymology and original meaning for the place names of the area of Greater London (as constituted in the reorganization of 1965), based on a careful consideration of the earliest spellings for each name and assessment of those spellings in the light of all the other available evidence.

A fresh look at the etymologies of London place names is certainly called for. Of course some explanations, once acceptable enough, have in recent years been much refined and modified by new research, and these need to be updated. But quite apart from this and more importantly, dozens of completely mistaken and misleading etymologies still trotted out in histories, guidebooks, and other reference works about London, stand in need of correction. Indeed it is rather alarming how many explanations founded on folk etymology and legend, or even on pure fancy and linguistic ignorance, still abound even in quite reputable current titles! It is naturally hoped that this book will provide an antidote to these by offering etymologies that are rather more accurate, soundly based, and reliable.

The alphabetical list at the heart of the book covers the names of places in the thirty-two Greater London Boroughs and the City of London: the names of all boroughs and districts, towns and suburbs, stations both overground and underground, villages and hamlets, as are marked on the maps and listed in the indexes of the latest standard comprehensive atlases of Greater London as produced by various publishers. To these have been added (drawing particularly on the 1:50,000 series of Ordnance Survey maps) a considerable number of other names—of rivers and streams, islands and creeks, mansions and farms, mills and bridges, woods and parks, and many other such features.

The list also includes a large and representative selection of the names of roads, streets, and squares in the Central London area (the City of London, Westminster, and the West End), chosen on the basis of their intrinsic historical, linguistic, or cultural interest, or because they are particularly well known and familiar. Of course, given the vast quantities of such street names in these parts of London alone (not to mention those in the surrounding suburbs), this selection is bound to be an arbitrary and subjective one, but it is hoped that it contributes significantly to the list of names. In any case, especially in the central areas, present-day streets are often named from old manors, buildings, places, streams, or other features (**Aldwych**, **Cornhill**, **Houndsditch**, **Norton Folgate**, **Strand**, **Tottenham Court Road**, **Walbrook**, **Whitehall**), or themselves become the names of districts or stations (**Goodge Street**, **Hare Street**, **Maida Vale**, **Mornington Crescent**, **Queensway**, **Turkey Street**). In addition, in the areas all around Central London, street names have often been included because they preserve the names of important early settlements or medieval manors (**Bensham Lane** in Croydon, **Durnsford Road** in Merton, **Mapesbury Road** in Brent, **Portpool Lane** in Camden).

The great majority of names can be satisfactorily explained with respect to the elements from which they are derived, although the precise shades of meaning of the individual elements or of particular compounds may not always be easy to ascertain. For some names the evidence so far available is not decisive, and explanations may be somewhat provisional (**Lessness**, **Marble Hill**, **Rainham**). A few remain doubtful or obscure or partly so, at least for the time being (**Camberwell**, **Hurlingham**, **Snaresbrook**). Alternative explanations have often been given for names where two or more interpretations seem possible. For instance, it is often difficult to say whether the first element of an old compound name is a personal name or a significant word, as in names like **Bethnal Green**, **Eltham**, **Houndsditch**, **Putney**, **Ruxley**, and **Twickenham**.

Up to four or five early attested spellings are cited for each name, including the earliest reliable spelling found, these providing the basis for the etymology proposed once other evidence of a linguistic, historical, or geographical kind has been taken into account. All spellings are dated as accurately as possible (with the occasional use of the abbreviation *c.* for *circa* 'approximately'), and those recorded in early sources of particular interest like the Domesday Book of 1086, or even older documents such as the Anglo-Saxon Chronicle or Anglo-Saxon charters or land grants of pre-Conquest date, are specified as to their source. Otherwise readers needing details of other documentary sources or more refined dating, or interested in a much greater range of early spellings for a particular name, should consult the excellent and detailed county surveys published by the English Place-Name Society or the other volumes and monographs noted in the Select Bibliography. Where a spelling from Domesday Book or another source is followed by '(*sic*)' (Latin for 'thus'), this indicates that the spelling is given as it appears in that source even though it is apparently rather erratic or corrupt (the Norman scribes in particular had difficulty with the pronunciation and spelling of many English names!).

Elements and personal names cited with an asterisk (*) are postulated or hypothetical forms, that is although there may be strong evidence for their assumed existence in the early language in question, they are either not recorded in independent use or are only found at a later date (examples are words like *bica 'pointed ridge' in **Bickley**, *cingel 'shingle' in **Chingford**, or the personal names *Berica in **Barking**, *Beohha in **Beckenham**). To avoid unnecessary complication, the terminology for the provenance of elements and personal names has been somewhat simplified: Old English stands for all dialects, including Anglian, West Saxon and Kentish; Old French includes Norman French and Anglo-Norman; and the term 'Celtic' is used for British, Primitive Welsh, and the other early Brittonic languages. Similarly the term 'personal name' is used of personal names proper as well as bynames formed in the early period. A full list of the words and elements that occur in the London place names and street names included in the alphabetical gazetteer is given in the Glossary of Elements at the end of the book. The abbreviations OE (Old English), ME (Middle English), eModE (early Modern English), ModE (Modern English), and OFr (Old French) are used in this Glossary, but have been avoided in the main body of the book.

Headwords (i.e. main place-name entries) in the alphabetical list are given in **bold**. The headword is followed by the name of the London Borough in which the place referred to is to be found. Cross-references to other place names in the alphabetical gazetteer are given in SMALL CAPITALS. Place names, river names, and street names no longer in current use, like the older spellings of current names, are printed in italics (for example *Hog moore lane* under **Gloucester Road**, *Ludeburne* under **River Wandle**, *Pinnesknol* under **Muswell Hill**).

The literal original meanings of names have been given as fully as possible, and some care has been taken to offer an appropriate and accurate translation for each name even though the modern English phrase may still lead to oversimplification or appear clumsy. Distinctions of gender among the personal names are always noted, and the translation phrases used take account of the various types of place-name formation in early times. Thus, a so-called folk name like **Barking**, originally the name of a family or tribal group rather than the place, has been rendered '(settlement of) the family or followers of a man called *Berica'.

Once a sound etymology for a place name has been established with reference to its early spellings and other evidence of a linguistic, historical, or geographical kind, its fuller significance can begin to be appreciated in a wider cultural context. In addition to the information provided in the individual entries, some of the ways in which the place names and street names of London and its surrounding suburbs and towns reflect the complex history and varied landscape of the region is explored in later sections of this Introduction.

The outline maps of the London boroughs (pages lv–lxiii) are intended as a guide to the whereabouts of some of the main towns and districts within the Greater London area as well as providing the boundaries established in 1965. Place names featured on the maps that are known to be, or likely to be, at least

900 to 1,000 years old are printed in **bold**. Historically, the five London boroughs east of the River Lea were part of the county of Essex (originally the kingdom of the *East Seaxe* 'the East Saxons'); the four boroughs in the south-east were mainly in the county of Kent (an ancient Celtic name, possibly 'coastal district' or 'land of the hosts or armies'); the other boroughs south of the Thames were formerly in Surrey (an Old English name, 'the southerly district', i.e. relative to Middlesex); and the rest (and largest group of boroughs) formerly comprised the old county of Middlesex itself ('the Middle Saxons'), although a part of the borough of Barnet was once in Hertfordshire.

The Chronology and Languages of London Place Names

It would take a book much larger than this one to explore at all comprehensively the relationship between London's names and the long and complex history of the City and its hinterland. But the following outline of the relative chronology and stratification of the names, and of the languages from which they are derived, together with the later sections on some of their various structures, aspects, and themes, will direct the reader to the alphabetical entries (cited in **bold** lettering) where more detailed information can be found.

Place names show an astonishing capacity for survival, as the dates alone of many of the early spellings cited in the dictionary testify, even though it should be remembered that almost every name will be older than its earliest occurrence in the records, often a good deal older. In general it will be seen from the alphabetical list, and from the outline maps of the boroughs on which old names are printed in **bold**, that very many of the major names in the London region are 900 to 1,000 years old. A few of course are much older than that. On the other hand, many names are of later origin, some dating from the medieval or Elizabethan period, others from the 18th or 19th centuries, and quite a number from relatively recent times. Indeed the chronological stratification of London's place names is complex, for they reflect the long history of London and its surrounding villages—the various early conquests and settlements, the development of commerce, industry, and transportation in and around the city, the exploitation of the landscape and its natural resources, and the growth of the agricultural economy in the region.

Pre-Celtic Names

It is appropriate that the two oldest names in this book, so ancient that they are still not fully understood, are **London** itself (earlier *Londinium*) and **Thames** (earlier *Tamesis*). They possibly belong to an unknown early Indo-European language that is neither Celtic nor Germanic. Such pre-Celtic names, sometimes termed 'Old European', may have been in use among the very early inhabitants of these islands in Neolithic times (more than four thousand years ago), and it is assumed they were passed on to Celtic settlers arriving from the Continent about the fourth century BC. A third name thought to belong to this small but important group is the river name **Colne**. And another may be a lost river name *Humbre*; there are several instances of this river name in England, one of which may enter into the name **Northumberland Heath** in Bexley.

Celtic Names

Also ancient are the Celtic river names **Lea** or **Lee** (incorporated into **Leyton**), **Brent** (found also in **Brentford**), **Cray** (giving its name to **Crayford** and the four **Cray** villages), and the lost river name *Hyle* (preserved in **Ilford**). The words behind Lea and Brent may also have been the names of deities, suggesting that there may have been a cult of river worship along these rivers in ancient times. The Iron Age Celts, peoples speaking various Celtic dialects often referred to as Brittonic or British, invaded and settled in the London region as elsewhere in these islands (hence 'Britain') during the last four centuries BC. So these river names are survivals from a period when this Celtic language was spoken over the whole of what is now England as well as further west (its modern form being of course Welsh).

Another name of Celtic origin is **Penge** in south-east London, which has the distinction of being the only purely Celtic name in the Greater London area that is not a river name. The survival of this particular name may have much to do with the status of the place in Anglo-Saxon times: it was then not really a settlement at all, but a woodland pasture attached to the manor of Battersea, part of an ancient system of transhumance whereby livestock (probably pigs) were driven some 5 miles in the summer months to feed in the woods. We have to assume that all of these Celtic names were learnt and borrowed by the Anglo-Saxons when they came to Britain from the late 4th and 5th centuries AD onwards. Their significance is that they suggest communication and contact took place between the Celts and the incoming Germanic invaders, and indeed, along with Saxon names like **Walbrook** (once the stream at the heart of the City), **Wallington** and **Walworth** (both like Penge south of the Thames), all of which contain the Old English word *walh* 'Briton', they may also suggest the survival in some areas of a native British element in the population well into the Anglo-Saxon period.

Roman Londinium

Although the Romans founded the settlement here on the north bank of the Thames soon after their invasion of Britain in AD 43, siting it where the two low gravel hills, indicated by later names such as **Ludgate Hill** and **Cornhill**, rose either side of the Walbrook stream above the otherwise marshy ground, and eventually creating the important Roman city known as *Londinium*, the name itself as we have seen must already have existed and is not of Roman (Latin) origin. Indeed, in spite of the abundant archaeological and historical evidence for its 400 years of Roman rule and for its role as a centre of provincial government and international trade, with its impressive public buildings (palace, basilica, forum, temple, and fort), its public baths and private stone-built houses, its surrounding wall with its gateways, and above all its bridge, no Latin names from this era survive. The Latin name *Augusta* bestowed on London as a kind of honorific title in the 4th century failed to catch on and eventually disappeared.

The great landward wall, originally about 6 metres high and built around the west, north, and east sides of Londinium in about AD 200, can in parts still be seen. It is recalled in the street name **London Wall** which closely follows its northern alignment. All six of the major gateways, built at about the same time where the wall was intersected by important routes in and out of the City, have names given them later, during the Saxon period. A route from the important Roman city of Colchester entered London at what later came to be called **Aldgate** ('the ale gate', recorded from 1108, earlier 'east gate' in 1052). A route from the north (**Ermine Street**) entered the City at **Bishopsgate** (recorded thus 1275). Routes from the west entered the city at **Newgate** (thus in 1275, earlier possibly 'the west gates' in 857) and **Ludgate** ('the back gate', thus from c.1170). A fifth Roman gateway, later **Cripplegate** ('the low gate', recorded from 1068) was originally an entrance into the fort at the north-west corner of the City built c.120. And the sixth, later **Aldersgate** ('Ealdrēd's gate', recorded from c.1000) was another entrance into the City from the north. Three other names in the London area recall the Roman road system in and out of the city, all of them derived from Old English strǣt, a borrowing from Latin (via) strata and used by the Saxons to denote a Roman road: **Stratford**, **Stratford Bridge**, and **Streatham**.

The Anglo-Saxon Period

After some four centuries of Roman presence and influence, the great city of Londinium seems to have faded and fallen into disrepair by the early 5th century, indeed there seems to have been a gradual decline in its prosperity as a trading centre even before Roman rule and administration came to an end in 410 and military support was withdrawn. The Saxons, along with the Angles and Jutes one of the Germanic tribes from Northern Europe who invaded Britain and settled here from the late 4th and 5th centuries onwards, seem largely to have avoided the City, at least to begin with, spreading instead up the Thames valley. The extent and concentration of some of their earliest settlements in the region are suggested by the important pagan cemeteries discovered to the south, east, and west of London. The earliest Saxon occupation in the London area is represented by the group of wealthy cemeteries, dating from the late 4th and early 5th centuries, in the **Croydon** area (the most important being **Mitcham**). Other pagan cemeteries, dating from the 5th to 6th centuries, occur at **Keston** and **Orpington** to the south-east of London, at **Rainham** to the east, and at **Hanwell**, **Northolt**, and **Twickenham** to the west. Some of the Celtic (British) population presumably remained in London itself in the post-Roman era (distantly reflected perhaps in the much later name **Walbrook** already mentioned), and according to the Anglo-Saxon Chronicle in the annal for 457 this was augmented after the crucial battle of *Crecganford* (**Crayford**) when after their defeat by the Jutish invaders 'the Britons forsook Kent and fled to London in great fear'.

In the City itself there are few archaeological traces of Saxon occupation before c.750, although the first **St Paul's** seems to have existed on the site of the present Cathedral by the early 7th century. But outside the City there is important archaeological evidence for an extensive 7th–9th-century Saxon trading settlement, no doubt the place recorded as *Lundenwic* in the Kentish laws of the 680s and also in 8th- and 9th-century sources, alternatively *vicus Lundonie* in Latin, from Old English *wīc* 'trading settlement or port'. This lay to the west of the City walls and also west of the marshy valley of the Fleet, in fact along the **Strand** in the area of what is now Covent Garden. It is very likely the settlement distantly recalled in the name **Aldwych** (appropriately 'the old trading settlement'), and is probably what Bede was referring to when (writing in 730) he called London not only the capital of the East Saxons (i.e. Essex) but also 'a market place (*emporium*) for many peoples who visit it by land and sea'.

Then in the later Saxon period (between the recapture of London from the Danes by King Alfred in 886 up to 1066), the City itself within the walls slowly grew into an important and well-populated Saxon town and trading centre with markets, harbours, and a network of streets. Indeed some of the old street names in the City may well date from the end of the Old English period (i.e. pre-date the Norman Conquest of 1066): these include **Eastcheap** and **Cheapside** (the two ancient markets for the east and west sides of the City), **Cornhill** and **Snow Hill**, **Walbrook** (originally a stream), and probably even names like **Bread Street**, **Milk Street**, and **Wood Street**, which refer to commodities produced or offered for sale and appear in records from the mid-12th century. Names dating from the Anglo-Saxon period in the area to the west of the City include, besides **Aldwych** already mentioned, **Westminster** itself, **Ebury**, **Charing Cross** and **Hyde Park** (the last three originally simplex names), **Holborn**, **Knightsbridge**, **Lisson**, **Paddington**, **Tyburn**, and probably also **Strand**.

The great majority of the old names of towns and villages in the London area are also of Anglo-Saxon (i.e. Old English) origin, that is they were coined by these English-speaking Saxon settlers (who of course gave their names to Essex and Middlesex, 'the East and Middle Saxons') in the period between the 5th and 11th centuries. Some of these names probably belong to the early phases of the Anglo-Saxon settlement, or at least to the first three centuries of the Anglo-Saxon period (up to the mid-8th century). Among these are some of the names containing the Old English elements *hām* 'homestead' (**Dagenham**, **Mitcham**, **Streatham**), *ēg* 'island of dry land' (**Battersea**, **Bermondsey**), *hamm* 'land in a river bend' (**Fulham**, **Twickenham**), *ford* 'river crossing' (**Brentford**, **Stratford**), *-ingas* and its possessive form *-inga* 'followers of' (**Barking**, **Ealing**, **Yeading**, **Bellingham**, **Mottingham**), as well as other elements like *hȳth* 'landing place' (**Erith**) and *hearg* 'heathen temple' (**Harrow**). Also relatively early are names coined from Old English elements which seem to have been borrowings from Latin, such as **Addiscombe** (containing Old English *camp* 'field', from Latin *campus*), **East Wickham** and **West Wickham** (with Old English *wīc-hām 'homestead at a *vicus*, an earlier Romano-British settlement'), **East Bedfont** and **Wansunt** (both from Old English *funta 'spring', a borrowing from Latin *fontāna*), and **Croydon** (from Old English *croh*, a loanword from Latin *crocus* 'saffron', a plant thought to have been introduced by the Romans). All these names reinforce the evidence for direct contact between Romano-Britons and Saxons at an early phase of the settlement, of the kind already envisaged in citing names like **Penge** and **Walbrook**, **Wallington** and **Walworth**.

Scores of other names were probably coined in the later part of the Anglo-Saxon period between the 8th and 11th centuries, as the Saxons consolidated and extended their settlements, established churches and parishes and hundreds, and exploited the countryside around London for agriculture, trade, and other purposes. In any case, as noted before, all names are older than their earliest recorded spelling, sometimes much older, so that names first mentioned in, for example, Domesday Book (1086) or even in a 12th-century source usually have their origins at some time in the Saxon period. Cases in point might be **Wansunt**, almost certainly a name of archaic type but not found in documentary sources until 1270, **Uxbridge** not recorded before the 12th century but containing an ancient tribal name, or **Enfield** (from Old English *feld* 'open land') first recorded in Domesday Book (1086).

All in all then, the Anglo-Saxon stratum of names is dominant in the London area, as it is in most other areas of England except Cornwall and parts of the North. It results from the political domination by the Saxons of the Celtic-speaking Britons and the gradual imposition of their language on them. Although the Celtic river names and rare names like **Penge**, plus the three Old English *Wal-* names, suggest some survival of the British population and contact between the two peoples, hundreds of new names were coined in Old English during the six centuries of the Anglo-Saxon period. These include the names of the counties, Essex, Middlesex, and Surrey (but not Kent, which is a Celtic name), all of which contribute some parts to what is now the Greater London area. Others are the so-called folk names of an ancient type formed with the suffix *-ingas* 'people of' and originally denoting family or tribal groups, later their settlements: there are up to seven examples of this interesting type in the Greater London area, that is **Havering**, **Seven Kings** (possibly), **Tooting**, and **Wapping** (possibly), besides the three already mentioned.

Much more common are Old English names of a habitative type, that is names that denoted habitations from the start, whether homesteads, farms or enclosures, cottages, hamlets, or other kinds of settlement. The important element *hām* 'homestead, village' has already been mentioned as often belonging to the early period of the Anglo-Saxon settlement. Other common habitative elements include *worth* 'enclosed farmstead' in names like **Harmondsworth** and **Wandsworth** (plus eight more examples), *wīc* 'specialized farm or trading settlement' in **Aldwych** and **Chiswick** (and ten other instances), and above all *tūn* 'farmstead, estate, manor' in **Acton**, **Sutton** and no less than fifty other names. Among these are the relatively frequent *-ington* type such as **Kensington** and **Paddington** which probably contain the personal name of the owner of the estate at the time the name was coined.

Old English topographical names form an even larger and more diverse group. These refer to physical features of the landscape, or to settlements named from those features, whether rivers and streams (**Holborn**, **Kidbrooke**), springs and pools (**Muswell**, **Stanmore**), marshes and heaths (**Wricklemarsh**, **Blackheath**), hills and downs (**Hendon**, **Cornhill**, **Pinner**), or valleys (**Croydon**). Also abundant in the London area are places named in Old English from words denoting woods and woodland clearings (**Norwood**, **Wembley**), harbours and landing places (**Chelsea**, **Putney**), and as already mentioned, fords (**Deptford**, **Romford**), islands of dry ground in marsh (**Ebury**, **Hackney**), and land in river bends (**East & West Ham**, **Petersham**). In addition to all these groups, there are names of Old English origin referring to countless other natural and man-made features, from monasteries (**Westminster**) and fortresses (**Southwark**) to weirs (**Edgware**) and fruit orchards (**Plumstead**). The full range and variety of the Old English vocabulary used in the naming of places can be best judged by a glance at the Glossary of Elements at the end of the book.

The Scandinavian Influence

There are only a few signs of Scandinavian influence on the place names of London and its region. Although Essex became part of the Danelaw in 886 (with the River Lea forming the boundary between Danish and Saxon territory), there are only slight indications of Danish influence and settlement in this county, and there are none in the parts of Essex now lying within the Greater London area. London itself was raided by Danish Viking fleets in 841 and 851, and was even occupied by the Danish 'Great Army' in 871, after which it may have remained in Danish hands until it was taken by Alfred the Great in 886. A century or so later the Scandinavian Vikings returned, and in a new wave of raids attacked London in 994, 1009, and 1013, but its defences held. However when the Danish King Cnut came to the throne of England in 1016, he made London his main military base and developed it as a port and trading centre.

It is likely that the Danish community centred on **St Clement Danes** dates from this period: this highly significant name would suggest that there may have been a settlement of Danish merchants and craftsmen here by the 11th century. Other church dedications also indicate a Scandinavian influence: the five churches in the City (only one remaining) and the one in Southwark (see **Tooley Street**) dedicated to St Olaf or Olave, the Norwegian Viking king who helped King Ethelred in 1014, probably dating from after his death in 1030, and that dedicated to St Magnus the Martyr in Lower Thames Street (in existence by 1128–33). The Scandinavian presence in the City is further evidenced by the Ringerike style memorial stone found in the churchyard of St Paul's, with its characteristic runic inscription and carved beast and serpent, dating from the early 11th century. Otherwise the Scandinavian influence is only slight and indirect. Two words of Scandinavian origin that were borrowed into Middle English, *biggin* and *wro*, are found in **Biggin Avenue**, **Biggin Hill**, and **Roe Green**. Some personal names that are ultimately of Scandinavian origin also make their appearance. The woman called Gunnhildr and the men called Brand and Finn who once held the manors of **Gunnersbury**, **Brondesbury** (along with **Brownswood**), and **Finsbury**, respectively, were probably of Anglo-Danish stock, and the same is true of the woman called Guthrún who gave her name (surprisingly enough) to **Gutter Lane** in the City.

The Norman French Influence

The Norman French influence on the place names of the London area is also relatively slight (as indeed it is in the rest of England), in spite of the far-

reaching effects of the Norman Conquest on English social and political life
and on the English language in general. It is clear that by 1066, most major
settlements and landscape features already had established names, but the
new French-speaking aristocracy often gave distinctively French names to
their castles as in the case of **Richmond** ('strong hill') in North Yorkshire which
was in turn transferred by Henry VII to his new royal palace at what had earlier
been called **Sheen** (an Old English name). Characteristic of the French
influence is the group of 'complimentary' names with the adjectival element
beau or *bel* 'fine, beautiful', as in **Beulah Hill**, **Belmont** (no less than four
examples, but none of them old), *Bewregarde* (for which, see **Sutton Court Road**),
Belsize, and **Belvedere**. Many names of a manorial type incorporate the
personal names or surnames of Norman barons or other powerful French
families, examples being **Barnsbury**, **Bloomsbury**, and **Bucklersbury** (all with
Middle English *bury* 'manor'), **Castle Baynard**, **Savoy**, and **Vauxhall** (with Old
English *hall*).

It should be borne in mind that the everyday language of many leading City
families, as of many manorial lords in the countryside round about, would
have been French up to the end of the 14th century, and the overwhelming
French influence on the vocabulary of Middle English is apparent in the great
number of words borrowed from French during the post-Conquest period.
Many such words (e.g. *forest*, *frere*, *grange*, *lodge*, *vale*) were quickly assimilated
into English and appear in medieval place names alongside older items of the
vocabulary. In other cases names were coined, possibly by French speakers,
from words that may not have yet become part of the general Middle English
vocabulary: examples might include **Barbican**, **Charterhouse**, **Garratt**,
Minories, **New Change**, **Old Bailey**, **Plashet**, and **Poplar**. Another indication of
the strong French influence on the language in this period is the appearance of
the French definite article *le* or *la* in the early spellings of some simplex names,
even though they are of much older English origin, for example, *la Bernet* 1235
for **Barnet**, *La Charryng* 1263 for **Charing Cross**, *la Lee* in 1278 for **Lee**.

The Middle English Period

Of course not all of the names on the modern map, even names of sizeable
settlements or well-known features, are as old as most of those so far
mentioned. Besides the Norman French names already noted, hundreds of
other names originated in the Middle English period, that is roughly between
the 12th and 15th centuries inclusive, as London itself and many of its
surrounding villages became more prosperous, farming communities and
manorial estates evolved, and small settlements and hamlets of all kinds
developed in the countryside and woodland areas around the capital.
Particularly characteristic of this period are the numerous names given to the
secondary settlements and new hamlets that grew up on the edges of older
villages (a kind of expansion that obviously continued into the modern period).
Many of these names incorporate words like *ende* (**Crouch End**, **Mile End**), *grene*
(**Barnes Green**, **Stroud Green**), and *strete* (**Green Street**, **Turkey Street**), all of
which seem to be terms used to describe outlying hamlets or clusters of

houses. Also common are manorial names, some of them derived from the word *bury* 'manor, manor house' already mentioned (**Canonbury, Ravensbury**), others originally consisting of the family surname of the feudal overlord or owner of the estate (**Bruce Castle, Clitterhouse, Parsloes Park, Swakeleys**). Most City of London street names and district names also date from this period (although, of course, many may have been in use long before their first recorded spellings). Examples might include **Addle Hill, Cannon Street, Chancery Lane, Fleet Street, Houndsditch, Paternoster Row, Pudding Lane, Seething Lane,** and **West Smithfield**. Other names probably coined during this period are as numerous and colourful as those of earlier periods, and include examples as diverse as **Bayswater, Bow, Clerkenwell, Cockfosters, Collier Row, Corbets Tey, Cricklewood, Eastcote, Forest Hill, Heathrow, Highgate, Leytonstone, Marylebone, Perivale,** and **Shooters Hill**.

The Early Modern Period

A good many names originate in the post-medieval or early modern period, that is to say from roughly the 16th through to the 18th century. As with the earlier periods the names display tremendous range and variety, but mainly reflect the growth of new hamlets and suburbs even though the area around London remained essentially rural. Among the names first recorded in the 16th century (although of course they may be older than their first occurrence in writing) are **Clayhill, Earls Court, Isle of Dogs, Pield Heath, Pimp Hall,** and **Squirrels Heath.** Names first noted from the 17th century include **Crook Log, Golders Green, Honor Oak, Nunhead, Pall Mall, Piccadilly,** and **Pimlico,** and among those recorded from the 18th century are **Camden Town, Elephant & Castle, Fairlop, Hither Green, Ladywell, Pratt's Bottom,** and **Strawberry Hill**. Many names, especially for streets and squares in Westminster and the West End, recall the great estates of the landed gentry who began to develop their land in the 18th century, among them the Grosvenors, Dukes of Westminster and the Russells, Dukes of Bedford (**Grosvenor Square, Russell Square, Bedford Square**). Numerous other squares and streets built from the 18th century on are named from other landowning families, as will be seen from the alphabetical list of names (**Berkeley Square, Cavendish Place, Portman Square, Portland Place,** and so on). Only a selection of names of this kind has been included in this book: for the many other London and Westminster street names associated with such families, often alluding to their titles, marriage connections, and country seats, readers should consult the English Place-Name Society's volume on *The Place-Names of Middlesex*, or one of the specialized dictionaries of street names, or other surveys, noted in the Select Bibliography.

Modern and Recent Names

Hundreds of names have of course been coined in the last two hundred years, for new hamlets and suburbs, streets and housing estates throughout the whole of the Greater London area. Some 19th-century residential estates built to house workers in the shipyards, factories, and docks established along the north bank of the Thames are named after the industrialists or builders who developed them (**Beckton, Canning Town, Cubitt Town, Silvertown**), and there are similar names in other areas, named from landowners or developers, which also incorporate the word *town* in this sense of 'newly developed residential district' (**Angell Town, De Beauvoir Town, Summerstown**). **Pentonville** is a similar kind of name, with *-ville* as an alternative ending to give it a kind of pseudo-French look.

The rapid development of the railway system from the 1840s was probably the single most significant factor in the naming of modern suburbs and residential districts. Many stations on the newly laid railway lines were given names during the late 19th and early 20th century which were then transferred to the surrounding districts as houses and streets were built (**Clapham Junction, Hadley Wood, Loughborough Junction, Queensbury, Raynes Park**). Sometimes much older names first became properly established as the names of districts with the opening of railway and underground stations (**Arnos Grove, Belsize Park, Lyonsdown, Northwood, Wealdstone**). Many names originating in this period recall landowning families (**Barnehurst, Holland Park, Petts Wood**), some commemorate notable individuals (**Grahame Park, Reedham, Ruskin Park**), some are named from a prominent tavern (**Angel, Jamaica Road, Royal Oak, Swiss Cottage**), some refer to other buildings, structures, or man-made features (**Archway, Crystal Palace, Mudchute**).

A distinctive element among the 19th- and 20th-century street names of London and its suburbs (as of other towns and cities) is the occurrence of groups or clusters of names with definite themes, no doubt bestowed on the whim of a particular developer or local authority. Figures from literature and art are among the favourite themes (thus the Chaucer Road, Milton Road, Shakespeare Road, and Spenser Road in **Herne Hill** or the Landseer Road, Leighton Road, Millais Road, and Poynter Road in **Enfield**). Other suites of names commemorate figures from ancient history, birds, English counties, foreign places, military leaders, musicians, prime ministers, Shakespearian characters, and so on. For coverage of these, the reader is directed to the specialized treatments noted in the previous section, or to local publications on the street names of particular suburbs and districts.

A few modern names have been artificially created, inventions produced by committees or even resulting from newspaper competitions (**Bakerloo, Newham, Queensbury**). Some names for new residential developments have clearly been invented to sound attractive and to appeal to the rural idyll of the middle class suburbanite (**Falconwood, Forestdale, Thamesmead**), an earlier example of this being **Vale of Health**. For similar reasons some names of residential suburbs contain the word *Park*, not because this is earlier parkland, but to add an extra touch, perhaps a certain pretension of refinement (**Motspur Park, Raynes Park**). All in all, as with the names of earlier periods, modern names provide great variety, ranging from the exotic to the down-to-earth, some of them commemorating significant historical events in far-flung places (**Waterloo, Maida Vale, Cyprus**), others named from local fields (**Clam Field, Whyteleafe**), dialect words (**Anerley**), or even a Cockney delicacy (**Eel Pie Island**). At the time of writing, three of the most recent additions to the London scene are The Millennium Bridge, The Millennium Dome, and The Millennium Wheel (already nicknamed 'the London Eye'). Obviously, the two last are to be thought of as only temporary structures and therefore we would not expect their names to persist—but look at what happened to **Crystal Palace**, now the permanent name of a district in South London a century and a half after the original building so called was removed from Hyde Park and over sixty years after its successor burnt to the ground!

Some Different Place-Name Types and Structures

Some possible classifications or groupings of early place-name types have already been mentioned: folk names (**Barking**, **Ealing**), habitative names (**Dagenham**, **Wandsworth**), topographical names (**Croydon**, **Wembley**). Further comments on the different structures and formations found in London place names, with examples chosen mainly from among the older names, most of them formed during the Old English period, may be of interest.

Compound and Simplex Names

From the structural point of view, the vast majority of Greater London place names, as in the rest of England, are 'compounds', that is they consist of two elements, the first usually qualifying the second. The first element in such compound names may be a noun (as in **Catford**, **Finchley**, **Morden**, **Wormwood**), an adjective (**Cricklewood**, **Hendon**, **Deptford**, **Romford**), a river name (**Brentford**, **Ilford**, **Leyton**), a personal name (**Fulham**, **Gunnersbury**, **Harmondsworth**, **Wimbledon**), or a tribal name (**Uxbridge**, **Uxendon**). There are of course other kinds of early place-name composition, one of the most frequent being the use of the medial connective particle -ing- in Old English names like **Addington**, **Kensington**, **Orpington**, and **Paddington**. There are over twenty examples of this type in the Greater London region, all of them describing settlements associated with the particular named Saxon individual (whether *thegn* or *ceorl*, nobleman or free peasant farmer) who either owned, or had once owned, or had once been granted, the farmstead or estate in question, **Paddington** for instance being best explained as 'estate associated with, or called after, a man named Padda'. Far less common are the so-called 'triple compounds', consisting of three elements, such as **Bandonhill**, **Benhilton**, **Carshalton**, **Edgware Bury**, and **Peckham Rye**. In fact it will be seen that in all these cases the third element has been added later to an already existing compound.

However some place names, known as 'simplex', consist of one element only, at least to begin with (other words are often added at a later date). Examples include names like **Barnes** ('the barns'), **Coombe** ('the valley'), **Downe** ('the hill'), **Hale** ('the nook'), **Ham** ('the river-bend land'), **Hook** ('the spur of land'), **Lee** ('the woodland clearing'), **Nash** ('the ash tree'), **Roke** ('the oak tree'), **Sheen** ('the sheds'), and **Wyck** or **Wyke** ('the specialized farm or building'). Presumably such names must have been given in the first place to secondary settlements or features of mainly local importance, so that the need for a qualifying word was not so immediately felt. It will be noted that the French

definite article occurs in many of the medieval spellings of these names, thus
emphasizing the local character of the places at the time. Many such simplex
names later take on another element. One example is **Ebury**, the ancient
Westminster manor which was at first simply *Eye* 'the island' until the word
bury 'manor' was added in the 14th century. Another is **Charing Cross**,
originally simply *La Charryng* ('the bend') until an Eleanor Cross was placed
here at the end of the 13th century.

Names with Affixes

So-called 'double-barrelled' names, usually originating as ordinary simplex or
compound names but later having an affix added (often in the 13th or 14th
century) to distinguish them from similar or identical names, are not as
common in this region as in some other parts of England, except for those
which refer to the geographical position of a place in relation to its neighbours
or other places with the same name (**High Barnet**, **East Bedfont**, **North
Ockendon**, **South Harrow**, **West Drayton**, **Upper Norwood**). However there are
some of the manorial type, in which the affix is the name of a land-owning
family or the lord of the manor (**Cowley Peachey**, **Norton Folgate**, **Tooting
Graveney**), or alludes to early ownership of the manor or estate by a religious
foundation (**Friern Barnet**, **Monken Hadley**, **Tooting Bec**). Others refer to some
important nearby building or feature (**Chipping Barnet**, **Havering-atte-Bower**)
or to some aspect of construction (**Stoke Newington**). In a few names,
distinguishing affixes used in medieval times have since been dropped; thus
Coombe in Kingston was earlier *Cumbe Nevill*, with a manorial affix from a
family so called, and **Stratford** was once *Stratford Langthorne* to distinguish it
from *Stratford atte Bowe* (now simply **Bow**).

Reduction and Other Sound Changes

Many old place names, especially compounds, have undergone some degree of
reduction or contraction in the long period since they were first coined. Some
old compound names have been reduced to the point that they now resemble
simplex names in form (**Chalk Farm**, **Cheam**, **Kew**). These and names like
Brixton, **Isleworth**, **Roxeth**, and **Sipson** have been considerably reduced by
centuries of use in speech, although others like **Bermondsey**, **Harmondsworth**,
and **Rotherhithe** still retain more conservative spellings in spite of old local
pronunciations that represent the reduced forms (contrast the spelling of
Rotherhithe with the local street name **Redriff Road**). This discrepancy
between naturally worn-down spoken forms and officially preserved or
artificially revived written forms explains the existence of the curious pair
Hornsey and **Haringey/Harringay**, surprisingly enough alternative versions of
the same name. Similar reductions to these are found in street names too: a
nice example is **Cannon Street** which was originally 'candle-wright street'.

A common characteristic of early compound place names, and one which
often helps to disguise their origin, is the shortening of original long vowels
and dipthongs, as in compound words in the ordinary vocabulary. Just as *holi-*
and *bon-* in the compounds *holiday* and *bonfire* represent *holy* and *bone* with their

historically long vowels, so in compound place names Old English elements like *āc* 'oak', *bān* 'bone', *bēan* 'bean', *brōm* 'broom', **cīese* 'cheese', *dēop* 'deep', *fūl* 'foul', *gōs* 'goose', *hǣth* 'heath', **pēac* 'peak', *stān* 'stone', and *strǣt* 'street' occur with shortened vowels in names like **Acton**, **Bunhill**, **Bandonhill**, **Bromley**, **Chiswick**, **Deptford**, **Fullwell**, **Gosbury**, **Hadley**, **Peckham**, **Stanmore**, and **Stratford**. This tendency for long vowels to be shortened in compound place names, together with weakening of stress at the end of names, resulted in some originally distinct elements coinciding in form and pronunciation. Once shortened, the important Old English habitative element *hām* 'homestead, village' (Modern English *home*) came to sound like the quite separate topographical term *hamm* 'enclosure, land in a river bend'. As a result, without definite evidence of one kind or another, it is sometimes not possible to be sure whether a number of place names, such as **Beckenham**, **Clapham**, **Eltham**, and **Sydenham**, originally contained *hām* or *hamm* (in such cases both elements will usually have been cited in the entries for these names as possible alternatives). The same factors lead to the confusion of *-ton* from Old English *tūn* 'farmstead', *-don* from Old English *dūn* 'down' and *-den* from either *denu* 'valley' or *denn* 'swine pasture' in names like **Chessington** (from *dūn*), **Croydon** (from *denu*), **Harlesden** (from *tūn*), **Islington** (from *dūn*), **Morden** (from *dūn*), **Neasden** (from *dūn*), **Turpington** (from *denn*), and **Willesden** (from *dūn*). There are similar reasons for the replacement of historical *-mere* (from Old English *mere* 'pool') by *-more* (usually from Old English *mōr* 'moor') in the names **Stanmore** and **Widmore**; for the different endings of **Northolt** and **Southall** (even though they both contain Old English *halh* 'nook'); and for the various reduced spellings in names containing Old English *hȳth* 'landing place' (contrast **Chelsea** and **Putney** with **Lambeth** and **Rotherhithe**).

Of course certain place names, like many words in the ordinary vocabulary, have been subject to other kinds of sound development, often resulting in significant changes in spelling and pronunciation, and these will usually have been noted in the alphabetical entries: **Ickenham** was once *Tickenham*, **Motspur** was *Motes Firs*, **Tokyngton** was *Okington*, **Whipps Cross** was *Phippes Cross*, **Wimbledon** was *Wymendon*, and **Yiewsley** was formerly *Wewesley*. Sometimes a modern spelling has been influenced by that of a foreign place, thus disguising its original form: **Hainault** was once *Hineholt* until it was falsely associated with the Belgian place. One of the most interesting transformations is that of **Tooley Street**, which was once *Saint Olaves Street*: in popular speech the final *-t* of the word *Saint* was taken to be the initial letter of the name, exactly as with the word *tawdry* derived from *St Audrey*.

Some Archaic Grammatical Features

Archaic grammatical forms embedded in place names are still spoken by thousands of Londoners as they go about their business! Although the site of the well or spring that gave **Clerkenwell** its name now lies deep beneath the offices of the *New Statesman*, the name itself is in the form used in the 12th century, *clerken* having an old possessive plural inflection which disappeared generally from the ordinary language of London by the 14th century. This same

Middle English plural ending also survives in **Friern Barnet** and **Fryent Fields** (both 'of the friars') and in **Monken Hadley** ('of the monks').

Quite a number of older London names which go back to the Anglo-Saxon period still contain archaic grammatical features of the pre-Conquest language. Old English was a highly inflected language, and although certain grammatical endings of Old English nouns, adjectives, and personal names disappeared from the ordinary spoken language by the 11th or 12th centuries, they have left their permanent mark on a good many place names. Thus, the genitive (i.e. possessive) case singular of the so-called 'weak' declension of nouns and adjectives (Old English *-n*) survives as medial *-n-* in some twenty different names including **Dagenham** (Old English *Dæccan hām* '*Dæcca's homestead*', **Hackney**, **Kemnal**, **Putney**, and **Twickenham**. The same ending appears in slightly disguised form in **Becontree**, **Chessington**, and **Hillingdon**.

Other bits of fossilized grammar are also to be found. The old dative singular ending of the 'weak' adjective (Old English *-an*) is preserved as *-n-* or *-ing-* in **Hendon** and **Newington**, the old 'weak' noun plural form survives in **Sheen**, and **Cranham** ('hill-spurs of the crows') apparently contains two different ancient inflections. Dating from the medieval period are the names **Nash**, **Noak Hill**, **Nower**, and **Roke**, all of which contain remnants of Middle English phrases containing *atten* or *atter* 'at the' (originally from dative phrases in Old English). A particularly charming survival of this old phrase forms the affix of **Havering-atte-Bower** ('at the bower or royal residence'), found also in the earlier name for **Bow** (*Stratford atte Bowe*).

Old English Personal Names: 'a man called Hílda'

It will already have been seen that the personal names in use during the Anglo-Saxon period are quite a different set to the ones we are familiar with, most of which were introduced into England after the Conquest. Indeed relatively few of the Old English personal names have survived (or been revived) in use (though Alfred, Edgar, Edith, and Edward are among them). It might also be noted here that many of the shorter Old English names for men, in use during the Anglo-Saxon period and incorporated into place names, especially those ending in *-a*, actually resemble names used for women in more recent times. For this reason particular care has been taken in the explanations of place names in the alphabetical list to indicate the gender of the person involved, thus avoiding possible misunderstandings! The Hilda who gave name to **Hillingdon** and the Cylla in **Kilburn** were certainly men. Other instances of old masculine personal names liable to be misinterpreted by the modern reader include Abba (in **Abchurch**), Babba (in **Baber Bridge**), Cyssa (in **Keston**), Hana (in **Hanworth**), Inga (in **Ingrebourne**), and Lill (in **Lisson Green & Grove**).

To a more limited extent the opposite may also be true, that some old names for women may now have rather a masculine look. In fact relatively few early names refer to female ownership or occupation, but **Homerton** takes its name from a woman called Hūnburh, and other women represented among the names include the Lēofrūn of **Leather Lane**, the Gunnhildr of **Gunnersbury**, and the Guthrún of **Gutter Lane**.

Folk Etymology

There are numerous instances among London place names of the workings of a process sometimes known as 'folk etymology' or 'popular etymology'. This is a tendency for a name to be rationalized or reinterpreted once its original meaning has been obscured or lost—because words have gone out of use, or because the person commemorated in the name has been forgotten, or because of changes in pronunciation or spelling. Thus, the first element of **Chadwell Heath**, reduced from Old English *ceald*, Middle English *chald* 'cold', was taken to be the saint's name *Chad*, resulting in the dedication of the church here to St Chad and the name of nearby **St Chad's Park**! Somewhat similar is the case of **Petersham**, where the Old English personal name *Peohtrīc* which lies behind the first part of the place name was taken to be the saint's name *Peter*, hence also the church dedication here. These names, which as it were each produce a saint, contrast nicely with the name **Tooley Street** already mentioned where the local transformation of *St Olaves Street* in the spoken language caused another perfectly genuine saint to disappear!

Two old names in the City of London, both referring to gateways originally built by the Romans, have been subject to folk etymology. **Cripplegate** ('the low or creeping gate') was already by the 11th century associated with cripples, resulting in the dedication of the nearby church to St Giles, their patron saint. **Ludgate** ('the back gate'), interpreted by the 12th-century chronicler Geoffrey of Monmouth as referring to a legendary King Lud who was also said to have given his name to London itself, established a charming myth that has persisted almost up to the present day. Also in the City, **Gracechurch Street** was originally *Graschirchestrete* with a first element *grass*; its conversion to *grace* seems wonderfully appropriate!

Other instances of the workings of folk etymology include **Cambridge Heath**, **Clitterhouse**, **Eel Brook Common**, **Ravensbourne** and **Ravensbury**, **Seven Kings**, **Turkey Street**, and **Whipps Cross**. As with Cripplegate and Ludgate, popular interpretation of some of these original names is accompanied by the growth of colourful legends and traditions. **Seven Kings**, possibly an Old English folk name of the same type as Barking, is said to have been the meeting place of seven Saxon kings, and **Whipps Cross** (named from a local family) has been thought, predictably enough, to have been named from a whipping post for punishing lawbreakers! The first element of **Mortlake** is *mort* 'young salmon', but the name has been connected with pits for burying plague victims on the false assumption that it contains the French word *mort* 'death' or 'dead'!

Some of these folk etymologies are undoubtedly the creations of early antiquarians, and it is sometimes possible to catch them at work. The place-name **Welling** near Bexley was often spelt (unhistorically but understandably) *Well end* in the 18th century, from which Edward Hasted in his *History and Topographical Survey of Kent* (1797) rationalizes and extrapolates as follows: 'Welling...more properly Wellend, which name was given it from the safe arrival of the traveller at it, after having escaped the danger of robbers through the hazardous road of Shooter's hill hither'. It is probable that all such folk etymologies involve a little creative thinking of this kind, either that of an individual or of a more collective popular kind. One of the most creative (and persistent) popular legends surrounds **Battle Bridge** (the old name for the district around King's Cross), originally *Bradeford* 'the broad ford'. Progressive reduction to *Batford* and then *Battle* led to the wonderful legend that this was the site of a battle between Queen Boudicca of the Iceni and the Romans: it is known that she burned the new Roman town to the ground in 60 AD, but the notion of a battle here is pure moonshine!

Back-Formation

Folk etymology sometimes results in a process known as 'back-formation', a phenomenon that accounts for a good many modern river names. Once the original meaning of a place name was forgotten, there was sometimes a tendency for antiquarians and others to try to reinterpret it as if it contained the name of the river or stream on which the place was situated. Thus, **Crane** came to be the name of the river at **Cranford** because the village name (historically 'ford of the cranes or herons') came to be understood as 'ford on the stream called Crane'. Other examples of river names resulting from back-formation include **Beam** from **Beam Bridge**, **Beck** from **Beckenham**, **Ching** from **Chingford**, **Graveney** from **Tooting Graveney**, **Pinn** from **Pinner**, **Rom** from **Romford**, and **Wandle** from **Wandsworth**. Most of these streams or rivers had earlier names which were simply replaced and forgotten: **Crane** was once *Fyssheburn* 'fish stream', **Beam** was *Markedyke* 'boundary ditch', **Pinn** was simply *le Broke* 'the brook', and **Wandle** was once *Ludeburne* 'the noisy stream'. The back-formation **Beck** from Beckenham seems especially fortuitous since of course *beck* is a word for 'stream' (if only in northern dialects). Perhaps the most delightful of these new river names is **Moselle**. First recorded in 1600, and clearly influenced by its famous European namesake, this is simply an inspired back-formation from **Muswell Hill** through which the stream flows!

Names Transferred from Foreign Places

Botany Bay, **Bunker's Hill**, **Cyprus**, **Maryland**, **Picardy**, and **Severndroog** are all to be found within the Greater London area. There are various reasons for the appearance of these transferred names in their new locations. Some are commemorative, others topical for their time, others rather more whimsical, but they certainly add an exotic touch to the London map!

Some transferred names go back to medieval times, such as **Savoy** (from the French region, once an independent kingdom), **Syon** (from the hill of Zion in Jerusalem, originally affixed to the name of a monastery), and **Petty France** (perhaps named from French merchants). Many of the later examples commemorate famous battles or other historical events in which the British were generally deemed to have come out on top: **Bunker's Hill**, **Cyprus**, **Maida Hill & Vale**, **Portobello Road**, **Severndroog Castle**, **Trafalgar Square**. Others were originally given to large houses by owners or families with connections abroad, such as **Castelnau** (from a place in France) or **Trent Park** (from Trento in Northern Italy). The name of **Olympia** was transferred from the famous place in the Peloponnese where the Olympic games were first held. **Canada Water**, **Canary Wharf**, **Greenland Dock**, and the **East & West India Docks** recall the heyday of the London docklands when ships docked here from all over the world.

A few transferred place names may be whimsical or ironical. **Botany Bay**, the name of an early Australian convict settlement near Sydney, was bestowed *c*.1800 on a remote spot in the middle of Enfield Chase. This name, with its wry implications of solitariness and hard labour, is found elsewhere in England from about the same date, so the irony was no doubt topical at the time. Other somewhat whimsical names may be **Little Venice** (from its fancied resemblance to the real thing) and **Picardy** (apparently from its low-lying marshy nature). A name transferred from America is **Maryland** in Stratford, so named from that place in the 17th century when it was still a colony. A more unusual name from the same part of the world is **Pimlico**, also dating from the 17th century and likely to be of native American (Indian) origin. For a name of a fashionable district bordering on Belgravia and Westminster, you can't get more exotic than that!

Irony, Whimsy, and Some Unusual Formations

There are a number of somewhat less conventional formations among the names. **Adelphi** is of wholly Greek derivation (from *adelphoi* 'brothers'). **Bakerloo** is a 'portmanteau' concoction (from **Baker** Street and Water**loo**), apparently sneered at when it first appeared but now presumably thought perfectly acceptable. **Newham** is an artificial invention of the 1960s to describe the **new** London borough comprising East and West **Ham**. (One is tempted to slip in the equally artificial but purely fictional 'Walford', setting for the TV soap *East Enders*, a convincing enough portmanteau formation presumably based on **Wal**worth and Strat**ford**!)

A name of rather a different kind is **Belgravia**, an apparently self-conscious if not pompous pseudo-classical formation, paralleled by another early 19th-century name for a similar fashionable West End development, *Tyburnia* (see **Tyburn Way**). It is interesting that the newfangled and pretentious nature of these coinages was recognized at the time, judging by Thackeray's allusion in his *Vanity Fair* (1847–8) to 'Belgravia . . . . a sounding brass, and Tyburnia a tinckling cymbal'. It is also noteworthy that even the name **Tyburn**, the earlier name for **Marylebone** but also long associated with the dreadful gallows site where public executions still took place until 1783, could be thus prettified with a Latinate ending: but perhaps this is why the name did not last. The more recently coined **Fitzrovia** (apparently the inspiration of writers drinking at the *Fitzroy* tavern) is clearly a deliberately tongue-in-cheek and playful imitation of the type!

Some names seem to be 'complimentary', that is they describe places in favourable and flattering terms (not necessarily undeserved), among them those composed with the Old French adjective *beau* or *bel* 'fine, beautiful' (**Beulah**, **Belmont**, **Belsize**, **Belvedere**), and others such as **Fortune Green**, **Happy Valley**, **Honor Oak**, and **Vale of Health**. But even an outwardly complimentary name like **Mount Pleasant** may be deceptive. At least some of the several examples of this name in the London area refer after all not to 'pleasant mounts' but to 'refuse heaps' of various kinds! Lord Byron seems to have sensed something of this when he describes the hero of his poem *Don Juan* (1819–24) as riding into London 'through prospects named / Mount Pleasant, as containing nought to please / Nor much to climb'! The obviously ironical intention of the name is here rather emphasized by the exotic Frenchified vocabulary and phrasing (found without irony in a recent name like **Park Royal**).

Names that are more straightforwardly derogatory also occur. Among these may be included **Addle Street** ('dirty place'), **Chalk Farm** ('cold cottages'), **Coldharbour** ('cold shelter'), **Fetter Lane** ('false beggars, layabouts'), **Fullwell** and **Fulwell** ('foul or filthy spring or stream'), **Laystall Street** ('muck heap'), **Pudding Lane** ('entrails, offal'), **Puddle Dock** ('small dirty pool'), **Scadbury** ('thieves' fort'), **Sherborne Lane** ('shithouse'), **Shernhall Street** ('dirty stream'), and **Starveall Bridge** ('poor infertile ground'). Of course some of these may have been less intentionally derogatory than straightforwardly descriptive (calling a spade a spade): **Laystall Street** may simply be a non-ironical parallel to **Mount Pleasant**, the allusion in **Sherborne Street** may be a completely literal one, and the references to filthy streams remind us that sewage arrangements were not refined in medieval times (in any case sensitivities to dirt and squalor were no doubt a little different to ours).

There are many other names of a seemingly whimsical kind, where the various measures of humour, jocularity, and irony that may be involved are difficult to gauge. Surely *la Gidiehall* 'the giddy or crazy hall' raised an eyebrow (or a smile) in the 13th century when the name was first applied (see **Gidea Park**)! Was the name *Pickadilly Hall* a bit of a joke when it was first applied in the early 17th century (see **Piccadilly**), likewise other house names from the same period like *Chopped Straw Hall* (*see* **Strawberry Hill**), **Buckskin Hall** and **Coney Hall**? Is there wry humour in figurative names like **Neckinger** ('hangman's noose') and **Seven Sisters** (referring to seven elms)? Was the name **Rotten Row** a little mischievous and jocular? Is **Little Britain** in Cowley a humorous nickname for a tiny insignificant place, and is this also the case with **Lillyputts** (or is this simply a literary allusion)? It is more certain that **Botany Bay** (a transferred name from the notorious Australian convict settlement) and **World's End** are humorous allusions to their perceived remoteness and inaccessibility: the former lies in the middle of Enfield Chase, whereas **World's End Passage** in Chelsea is named from a 17th-century tavern at the once remote western end of the old village! As for the name **Isle of Dogs**, that remains something of an enigma. Is it jocular, derogatory, ironical, or does it make whimsical allusion to the Canary Isles? It would certainly be a nice enough irony if in the 16th century this flat damp marshy peninsula previously known as *Stepney Marsh* were to be called after a hot dry volcanic island off the north-west coast of Africa famous for its exotic birds and expensive wines!

There are many instances where good old names, once perfectly acceptable, come to be considered insalubrious or lacking in propriety. A change of name may then seem desirable, and indeed sometimes takes place as a result of these sensitivities: **Aldersbrook** in Redbridge was once *Nakedhall* ('bare or naked hall'), **Belmont** in Sutton was once *Little Hell* (probably only 'little hill' but it sounded all wrong), **Hogsmill River** was once *Lurtebourne* ('mucky stream'), **Marylebone** was formerly *Tyburn* (it is said that the name was changed because of the unpleasant association of the latter with the notorious place of execution here, see **Tyburn Way**), and the area now **Sloane Square** was once *Great Bloody Field*. Similar deliberate name changes for prudish or decorous reasons are also found among the street names: **Globe Road** was earlier *Theven lane* ('thieves' lane'), **Gloucester Road** was once *Hog moore lane* ('pig moor lane'), **Milton Street** was *Grubbestrete* in medieval times, **King Edward Street** was renamed from *Stinking Lane* (an allusion to local slaughterhouses), and **Middlesex Street** and **Petticoat Lane** were earlier *Hog Lane* ('pigs' again!). Fortunately most of the old names have remained, however mangled their modern forms compared to their originals. One old City name that is much the same as it was eight centuries ago, **Houndsditch** ('dog's ditch'), was threatened with change in 1927 for its perceived unpleasant connotations, but thankfully survived!

The Wider Significance of London Place Names

It will of course already be apparent that there is far more to a place name than its etymology. The interest of a name does not stop at its meaning and derivation, although these provide the basic and essential starting point for the fuller appreciation of its significance in a wider linguistic, historical, sociological, or geographical context. The place names of London and its surrounding towns and villages reflect many aspects of life in the capital and its region in the different periods of their history, and many of these have already been touched upon in the preceding sections. Although the scope of the present book does not allow for a full exploration and appraisal of how all the names relate to the long and complex history of London and the Greater London area, a few other aspects will be examined here, with reference as before to the entries for individual names where more information is usually provided.

London Town: The City's Names
The ancient street names of the City certainly require detailed study and scrutiny to do them any sort of justice, and it has been possible to include only a selection in this book. The reader is therefore directed to some of the volumes listed in the Select Bibliography for fuller coverage and treatment of these.

The names given by the Saxons to the six gates in the wall surrounding the Roman city have already been discussed, as have several of the other Saxon names that probably pre-date the Norman Conquest (see the sections above on 'Roman Londinium' and the 'Anglo-Saxon Period'). **Cheapside** and **East Cheap** represent London's two main ancient markets, one for each side of the City, and **Bread Street**, **Milk Street**, and **Wood Street** are just three of the old streets which specialized in the sale of particular products at an early date (all three are on record by the mid-12th century). Many other old names of lanes, rows, and streets in the City refer to the sale of certain foodstuffs and other goods, among them **Distaff Lane**, **Fish Street Hill**, **Garlick Hill**, **Giltspur Street**, **Lime Street**, **Old Seacoal Lane**, **Petticoat Lane**, and **Poultry**. Other such names, used in medieval times, have since been lost or replaced (see, for instance, the entries for **Cordwainer** and **Pancras Lane**). The name **Cornhill**, on record as early as c.1100, may have been named from the cultivation of corn here at a very early date within the City wall, or from a grain market. Also related to trading are **Pudding Lane** (named from the offal carted down to the river from the Eastcheap meat market) and **Seething Lane** (where corn was threshed and winnowed ready for sale). Some streets make reference to the actual specialist craftsmen or traders: **Billiter Street** (bellfounders), **Cannon Street** (candlemakers), **Pasternoster Row** (makers of rosaries). Along the riverside, the names **Billingsgate**, **Dowgate**, and **Queenhithe** refer to ancient wharves and landing places for goods, and **Puddle Dock** refers to a wharf of somewhat later medieval date.

Many City street names recall the once numerous ancient churches (for instance **Abchurch Lane**, **Bartholomew Lane**, **Bow Lane**, **Clements Lane**, **Fenchurch Street**, **Gracechurch Street**) or the medieval monasteries and other religious communities (**Blackfriars**, **Crutched Friars**, **Mincing Lane**, **Minories**, **The Temple**). Three small lanes near the ancient cathedral of St Paul's, **Amen Corner**, **Ave Maria Lane**, and **Creed Lane**, probably take their names from the prayers recited during the processions of the clergy round the precincts.

A small but significant number of City names refer to topography. **Moorfields**, **Moorgate**, and **Moor Lane** refer to the marshy ground which once lay to the north of the City wall, whereas **West Smithfield** and **Smithfield Street** are named from an area of level ground just outside the wall on the north-west side. **Cornhill**, **Ludgate Hill**, and **Snow Hill** describe rising ground within the City. The important river which once flowed through the centre of the old City gives its name to the street called **Walbrook**, and **Fleet Street** is named from the **Fleet** river which also flowed into the Thames, just west of the City at Blackfriars. The mighty river itself gives name to **Thames Street**, the longest street in the City because it follows the line of the old riverside wall built by the Romans in the mid-4th century.

Several early City places and streets are named from manors, tenements, or other properties once owned by powerful individuals or influential families (**Basinghall Street**, **Bevis Marks**, **Billingsgate**, **Bucklersbury**, **Little Britain**, **Lothbury**, **Throgmorton Street**). Others take their name from important officials (**Aldermanbury**, **Chancery Lane**), from princes (**Addle Hill**, **Watling Street**), from knights (**Knightrider Street**), or from their association with foreign financiers and merchants in medieval times (**Jewry Street**, **Old Jewry**, **Lombard Street**). One refers to the arms of one of the many medieval guilds (**Threadneedle Street**). Fortifications and towers added to strengthen London's defences after the Norman Conquest, apart from the great **Tower** itself, give name to **Barbican**, **Castle Baynard Street**, and **Old Bailey**. Many other buildings or former buildings in the City have given their names to streets or stations (**Bank**, **Leadenhall Street**, **Mansion House**, **New Change**).

In spite of these classifications, many City names remain difficult to categorize. **Gresham Street**, renamed thus in 1845 after the great financier, was *Cattestrete* 'street frequented by cats (or prostitutes)' in medieval times. **Love Lane** may allude to the innocent dalliance of lovers, or may also refer to prostitution. **Houndsditch**, referring to part of the moat that once bounded the City wall, was probably 'ditch frequented by dogs'. **Vine Street** recalls an 18th-century vineyard. **Fetter Lane** is so named from the false beggars who once hung out there. **Addle Street** had a muck-heap, and **Sherborne Lane** a well-known privy. The sheer range and diversity of these names is striking, and together they reflect something of the many-sided bustle and vibrancy of this ancient City and its citizens in Saxon and medieval times.

London Country: Place Names and the Landscape

Much of the area around London, now part of the sprawl of Greater London, was still relatively rural at the beginning of the 19th century, as the earliest maps of the Ordnance Survey show. During medieval times the old Roman and Saxon City had expanded a little beyond its walls and to the west the new City of Westminster had begun to take shape, but otherwise development had been mainly along the routes into London from outlying parts. The great urban expansion of London and its suburbs, relatively rapid and unplanned, took place during the last two centuries, a result of many economic factors including of course the arrival of the railway system centred on the capital. London's population grew sevenfold during the 19th century, and suburban growth has continued since.

In many ways it is surprising how relatively recent much of this suburbanization is. Typical suburbs like **Catford**, **Hackney**, or **Stockwell** were small rural villages until the 1800s, the open land at **Chalk Farm** was still being farmed in the early 19th century, there were working farms in the area of **Shepherd's Bush** in the late 19th century, and there were still stretches of woodland at **St John's Wood** and acres of farmland at **Dagenham** until the early 1900s. It is important to remember the crucial economic relationship between the city and its surrounding countryside: specialized farming, woodland management, and market gardening continued to thrive in and around London in order to provide food and other supplies to an ever-increasing population, and these economic forces are reflected in the names, as the following sections will show. But no matter how many of the villages and hamlets around London have now become suburbs, or how much of the countryside has been swallowed up by the urban sprawl of streets and houses (and of course great stretches of countryside still remain in the outer suburbs), the place names of the region recall and reflect its original earlier landscape strongly and distinctly. Our early ancestors made use of a vast range of topographical words, applied with precision in different periods and localities to every undulation and type of terrain, and to all the natural and man-made features they depended upon for their survival, subsistence, and prosperity. The extensive swathes of original forest which once lay both to the north and to the south of London and the Thames, the marshy valleys of the great river itself and its several tributaries, the large tracts of heathland and the areas of higher ground—these are all described and recalled in the region's place names.

Woodland and Heath

The once densely forested areas north of London, historically part of the counties of Essex, Hertfordshire, and Middlesex, are still partly represented by what remains of **Epping Forest**, **Waltham Forest**, and **Enfield Chase**. The vast royal hunting forest that once covered the south-west corner of Essex, originally Waltham Forest and later Epping Forest, is on record from the 13th century and once extended as far south as **Leytonstone** and **Wanstead**. It takes its early name from Waltham, just outside the Greater London area, which actually means 'forest settlement'. Many other names within the area recall the former extent of the old forest and suggest its importance in the local economy (among them **Aldborough Hatch**, **Chase Cross**, **Chingford Hatch**, **Collier Row**, **Forest Gate**, **Hainault (Forest)**, **Queen Elizabeth's Hunting Lodge**, and **Woodgrange Park**).

   Enfield Chase, another hunting area created as early as the 12th century out of the extensive woodland of this north-east part of Middlesex, is of course named from **Enfield**, an old name that describes a tract of open land cleared of trees at an early date. Several names in the vicinity relate to the Chase, among them **Cattlegate** and **Southgate** marking its northern and southern entrances, **West Lodge Park** referring to one of its three medieval lodges, and **Cockfosters**, probably so named because it was the estate of the chief forester.

   One of the main forest areas to the south of London and the Thames seems to have been that called 'the north wood' (hence the district name **Norwood**), a large tract of woodland that lay to the north of **Croydon** and which still partly remained until the early 19th century. Other significant names in the area referring to the early woodland here include **Penge** and **Forest Hill**.

   Elsewhere in the Greater London region, both north and south of the river, there are individual names, or clusters of names, that indicate early woodland areas. Among the large and specialized topographical vocabulary in Old English for describing woods and woodland clearings of various kinds, the most significant terms include *lēah* 'wood or woodland clearing' (as in **Bexley**, **Bromley**, **Finchley**, **Wembley**, and some twenty other early names), *wald* 'forest' (**Harrow Weald**, **Wealdstone**), *wudu* 'wood' (as in **Brownswood**, **Cricklewood**, **Harold Wood**, and **Woodford**), *holt* 'wood, especially of a single species of tree' (as in **Hainault**, **Kensal**, **Ruckholt**, and **Wormwood**), *hyrst* 'wooded hill' (**Chislehurst**, **Pickhurst**, **Selhurst**), *fyrhth(e)* 'sparse woodland' (**Frith Manor**, **Hamfrith**, **Monkfrith**), *hangra* 'wood on a steep slope' (**Hanger Hill**, **Pitshanger**), and *hǣs(e)* 'land overgrown with brushwood' (**Hayes**, **Heston**). Another very important early element, often used for settlements in old woodland areas, is the element *feld* 'open land', probably indicating land cleared of trees. It appears with this sense in several old names like **Chelsfield**, **Enfield** (see the comment on Enfield Chase above) and **Harefield**. The element *denn* 'woodland pasture, especially for swine' is chiefly found in the Weald of

Kent and Sussex, so not unexpectedly it occurs only in the south-east corner of the Greater London area, in names like **Hockenden** and **Tubbenden**.

There were also great expanses of heath both north and south of the Thames, and the Old English word *hǣth* is used to describe these (as in **Blackheath**, **Chadwell Heath**, **Hampstead Heath**, **Putney Heath**). The same word is found as the first element of the old names **Hadley** and **Hatton**, as well as the much later **Heathrow**.

Hills and Valleys

Many places take their names from their situation on or near hills or relatively higher ground. Several important names of Old English origin, going back to the Anglo-Saxon period, contain the element *dūn* 'hill' (the Modern English word *down*). Some of these are named from the crops or plants growing there (**Bandonhill** 'beans', **Waddington** 'wheat', **Waddon** 'woad'), others from some nearby feature or some characteristic of the hill itself (**Hendon**, **Neasden**, **Stickleton**, **Willesden**), others from personal names (**Chessington**, **Coulsdon**, **Islington**, **Wimbledon**). There are several simplex examples ('the hill'), including the village name **Downe** and the medieval names lying behind **Down Barns** and **Duntshill**.

Other Old English words for various kinds of hill or rising ground include *ōra* 'flat-topped hill' (**Nower Hill**, **Pinner**), **pēac* 'peak' (**Peckham**), *hrycg* 'ridge' (**Totteridge**), *beorg* 'mound, hill', also 'barrow, tumulus' (**Farnborough**, **Roxborough**), and of course the word *hyll* 'hill' itself (as in **Cornhill**, **Notting Hill**, and many other medieval and later names).

There seem to be fewer places in the Greater London area named from valleys. Only one major name of an early settlement (**Croydon**) contains the important Old English word *denu* (used especially of relatively long narrow valleys), and there are only a few instances of Old English *cumb* (often applied to shorter, broader valleys), such as **Coombe** and **Westcombe**. The names **Bollo** and **Kemnal** contain Old English *hol* 'a hollow'. A rarer Old English word, *dēope* 'a deep place', occurs in the early forms of **Colindale**. Other words meaning valley like *botm* 'valley bottom' (as in **Pratt's Bottom**) and *vale* (as in **Perivale**) are found in a few medieval or later names.

Rivers, Springs, Pools, and Marshland

Many old names refer to settlements by rivers, streams, springs, pools, and other watery features of the landscape. The importance of river valleys for early settlement, providing fertile soils and a good water supply, is reflected in the number of places named from the rivers or streams on which they are situated. Among these are names derived from Old English *brōc* 'brook' (**Aldersbrook**, **Cranbrook**, **Kidbrooke**) and *burna* 'stream' (**Holborn**, **Kilburn**, **Marylebone**), as well of course as those named from the even older names of the rivers themselves (**Brentford**, **Crayford**, **Leyton**). Several early names contain the Old English word *w(i)ell(a)* which could mean either 'spring', 'well', or 'stream' (**Camberwell**, **Clerkenwell**, **Muswell Hill**, **Stockwell**, **Willesden**), and one refers to a 'river spring' (**Carshalton**). Two old names contain an interesting early Old English word *funta 'spring' (**East Bedfont**, **Wansunt**). Such names describing early springs reflect the distinctive geology of their locations. Three early names from Old English *mere* refer to pools (**Merton**, **Stanmore**, **Widmore**), and others contain the word *dīc* 'ditch' (**Mardyke**, **Shoreditch**) or *water(ing)* 'stream, ditch' (**Bayswater**). Three other elements meaning 'small stream' are *lacu* (**Mortlake**), *rīth* (**Peckham Rye**, **The Wrythe**) and *rīthig* (**Beverley Brook**).

The names of places along the banks of the River Thames are particularly interesting. One of the most important elements used for early settlements in marshy ground was Old English *ēg* 'an island of dry ground in a marshy area', and there is a significant series of no less than six names containing this word in the low-lying areas along the river: **Battersea**, **Bermondsey**, **Ebury**, **Hackney**, **Horselydown**, and the lost *Thorney*, the old name for the site of **Westminster**. Also referring to their situation relative to the Thames are five old names containing the Old English element *hamm*, here used in the sense 'land in a river bend': **Fulham**, **Ham**, **Hampton**, **Petersham**, and **Twickenham**. All of these places lie in or near great loops in the course of the river. A third significant element characteristic of names for places situated along the Thames is of course Old English *hȳth* 'a landing place, a harbour', found in **Chelsea**, **Erith**, **Lambeth**, **Putney**, **Rotherhithe**, and **Stepney** (see also later section on 'Communications and Trade'). In addition to these, inlets and creeks along the river give name to the **Fleet** river and to **Barking Creek**, **Counters Creek**, and others, and the various stretches of the river known as 'reaches' are individually named (as in **Limehouse Reach**). Early settlements named from the actual river bank or shore of the Thames are **Strand** and **Strand on the Green** (from Old English *strand* 'shore') and **Ratcliff** (from Old English *clif* 'cliff, bank'). Later riverside names include **Bankside** and **Millbank**, both from the Middle English word *banke* itself, as well as **Blackwall** and **Millwall** which refer to stretches of river wall. The small islands in the Thames are named from the word *eyte* or *ayte* (as in **Chiswick Eyot**, **Isleworth Ait**).

Various names throughout the Greater London area refer to the marshy nature of the ground. The Old English word *mōr* (Modern English *moor*) often denoted 'marshy ground' in early names, and occurs in **Moorgate** and **Morden** among others. Old English *fenn* (Modern English *fen*) gives name to **Blackfen** and **Fenchurch Street**. The Old English word *mersc* 'marsh' itself is found in the early name **Wricklemarsh** and is also applied somewhat later to the marshland areas along the lower Thames (**Rainham Marsh**, **Wennington Marsh**, and so on). Old English *strōd* describes 'marshy land overgrown with brushwood', found in the two examples of the name **Stroud Green**.

Land Use and Agriculture

Besides those already mentioned, many other names relate to the utilization and development of the land around London for agricultural purposes in the Saxon and medieval periods. Given the nature of the economy in early times (and indeed right up to the 19th century), it is not surprising that a considerable number of significant terms evidenced in place names refer to different aspects of land use in the subsistence agriculture of our ancestors, where woodland had to be cleared, arable land had to be broken in to produce crops, meadowland produced hay, and pastures and enclosures were needed for animals. Several important terms used in early name-giving for different kinds of farming settlement have already been noted, among them *tūn*, *wīc* and *worth*, *lēah*, *feld* and *dūn*, *ēg*, and *hamm*. Another early term more difficult to categorize is Old English *halh* 'a nook or corner of land', found in names like **Bethnal Green**, **Northolt**, **Southall**, and **Tottenham Court** (named from a manor first recorded *c.*1000). Other terms for various kinds of enclosure or cultivated land, though usually appearing in somewhat later names from the medieval period, include *æcer* 'cultivated plot' (**Long Acre**), *ersc* 'ploughed land' (**Sundridge**), *hæg* 'enclosure' (**Gooshays**), *haga* 'hedged enclosure' (**Well Hall**), *læs* 'pasture' (**Oxleas Wood**), *land* 'cultivated or arable strip' (**Maylands**), and *tēag* 'small enclosure' (**Corbets Tey**).

Among the many Greater London names referring to specific cultivated crops are early names like **Bandonhill** and **Benhilton** ('beans'), **Barwell** ('barley'), **Cornhill** ('corn'), and **Waddington** ('wheat'); and **Croydon** may be named from the early introduction of saffron. The cultivation of the saffron crocus in later times is referred to in **Saffron Hill**, vineyards give name to **Vine Hill** and **Vine Street**, and lavender was once grown at **Lavender Hill**. **Worton** had a herb or vegetable garden, and a few names probably refer to fruit production, as in **Aperfield** ('apples'), **Plumstead** ('plums'), and **Purley** ('pears'). Several important early names (**Barnes**, **Berwick**, **Norbiton**, **Surbiton**, **West Barnes**) contain old words describing barns and other farm buildings where crops may have been stored, as does **Woodgrange** from a slightly later date. Some names refer to the character of the soil in the vicinity (**Chalk Wood**, **Chislehurst**, **Claybury**, **Erith**, **Sanderstead**, **Sands End**). A number of names refer to livestock, among them **Bollo** ('bulls'), *Hog Lane*, the earlier name for **Middlesex Street** and *Hog moore lane*, the earlier name for **Gloucester Road** ('pigs'), **Horselydown** ('horses'), **Lampton** ('lambs'), **Oxgate** ('oxen'), and **Rammey** ('rams'). **Osterley** contains an old word *eowestre* 'a sheepfold'. The rather later (17th century) name **Shepherd's Bush**, if as seems likely also a reference to sheep farming, speaks for itself!

Natural History

The natural history of the London region is also abundantly represented among its place names, often of course describing things as they were in much earlier periods when the area around the City of London was still essentially rural (several names date back to the Anglo-Saxon period, well before the Norman Conquest). At least a dozen different species of tree are evidenced (in names as various as **Acton**, **Aldersbrook**, **Bexley**, **Elmstead**, **Poplar**, **Selhurst**, **Thornton**, and **Widmore**). Some as already noted refer to fruit trees, and possibly therefore to orchards rather than to trees growing wild (**Aperfield**, **Plumstead**, **Perivale**, **Purley**). In any case most trees had some sort of particular use and value, and places would have been named with this in mind.

Several old place names incorporate the names of plants and vegetation, usually no doubt that characteristic of the locality in early times but also of course put to economic use whenever possible: **Bentley** ('bent-grass'), **Bromley** near Beckenham and **Brompton** ('broom'), **Bromley** in Tower Hamlets ('bramble'), **Carshalton** ('cress'), **Dulwich** ('dill'), **Farnborough** ('fern'), **Feltham** ('mullein or similar plant'), **Furzedown** ('furze'), **Rushey Green** and **Rushett** ('rushes') and **Waddon** ('woad', possibly a cultivated crop). Green vegetation generally is referred to in **Greenford** and **Greenwich**: the reference could be to either grasses or water plants. **Gracechurch Street** is so named from the once grassy situation of the ancient church here, or from its turf roof.

Among the references to wild animals in Greater London names, beavers are evidenced in **Beverley Brook**, badgers in **Broxhill** and possibly in **Brockley** and **Brockwell**, wildcats in **Catford** and **Cattlegate**, foxes in **Foxgrove** and **Foxley**, martens (possibly) in **Marble Hill**, and rabbits in **Coney Hall**. Badger setts are referred to in **Brockley Hill** in Stanmore, and **The Burroughs** in Hendon also allude to the burrows of either badgers, foxes, or rabbits. There are also several references to birds among the names. **Cranbrook** and **Cranford** are named from their cranes or herons, **Cranham** and **Croham** from their crows, **Dowgate** from its pigeons or doves, **Finchley** from its finches, **Hanwell** from its cocks (of wild birds), **Kidbrooke** from its kites, **Roehampton** and **Ruckholt** from their rooks. Fish are referred to in two names that originally described streams, **Mortlake** ('young salmon') and **Pinkwell** ('minnows'). The old name of the River **Crane**, dating in fact from the early 8th century, is *Fiscesburna* 'the fish's stream'. An abundance of frogs is attested to by the name **Frognal** found in both Hampstead and Sidcup, not to mention **Frog Island** near Rainham. And **Wormwood (Scrubs)** is named from its snakes.

Communications and Trade

London has always been, from the Roman period on, a great trading centre, and many of the older names contain elements which reflect the importance of communications and trade in the early economy of the City and its hinterland. The great River Thames and its many tributaries provided not only good settlement sites with fertile soil and good water supplies, but also important routes for trade and transport by water. The places named from the various early harbours and landing places on the Thames form a particularly interesting group. No less than seven names outside the City contain as final element Old English *hȳth* 'landing place on a river', representing early settlements that grew up around these landing places. Of these, three are upriver from the City (**Chelsea**, **Lambeth**, and **Putney**) and four downriver (**Erith**, **Rotherhithe**, and **Stepney**, with the fourth, Greenhithe, just outside the Greater London area). Looked at in another way, their distribution is again remarkably symmetrical: **Chelsea** and **Stepney** are on the north bank of the Thames on either side of the City, and of the five situated on the south bank, two lie to the west and three to the east of the City. The first elements of these *hȳth* names are also interesting. Although **Putney** and **Stepney** may be derived from Old English personal names, and **Erith** (like Greenhithe) perhaps refers to the character of the landing place itself, three of them refer to the goods or products shipped ('lambs' at **Lambeth**, 'cattle' at **Rotherhithe**, 'chalk or limestone' at **Chelsea**). In the City itself, as might have been expected, there are several other early *hȳth* names. **Queenhithe** was one of medieval London's most important landing places, and others now lost include *Garlickhith* and *Tymber Hithe* ('landing places for garlic and timber', see entries for **Garlick Hill** and **High Timber Street**). In addition to these, **Billingsgate**, **Dowgate**, and the lost *Rederesgate* (for which, see **Pudding Lane**), all from Old English *geat* in the sense 'entrance to a wharf', also refer to ancient wharves and landing places.

Also significant for what they tell us about early trading in and around London are the names containing Old English *wīc*, a word that seems to have been used for a trading or industrial settlement, and in some cases for a port or landing place. Clearly, for the places derived from this element that are situated on or near the river, these two functions may well have been combined; they are **Aldwych** ('old', probably recalling the very early trading settlement of *Lundenwic* west of the City, for which, see section above on 'The Anglo-Saxon Period'), **Chiswick** ('cheese'), **Greenwich** ('grassy'), and **Woolwich** ('wool'). The references to the goods produced and perhaps shipped, cheese and wool, are particularly interesting. Also significant are the two names **Hackney Wick** (on the River Lea) and **Hampton Wick** (on the Thames), both originally simplex names ('the Wick') and both convenient landing places for goods passing in and out of these two manors.

The Pool of London, the most important reach of the Thames for shipping from early times up to the end of the 19th century, is recorded from 1258. Ships and shipbuilding on the Thames during the later medieval period are represented by names like **St Katharine's Dock** (on record from the early 15th century) and the **Royal Naval Dockyard** at Deptford (founded in 1513 to build and service Henry VIII's navy). Docks first recorded in the 17th century include **Puddle Dock** in the City and **St Saviour's Dock** in Southwark. And of course the mighty 19th-century docks (**East India** and **West India**, **Royal Albert** and **Royal Victoria**, **Greenland** and **Surrey Docks**), all now closed but some converted to other uses, remain as local names to recall the great shipbuilding era of the past and London's status as a major international port.

The road network into and around London was just as important as the river for communications and trade and is reflected in many names. The great Roman routeways (among those named are **Watling Street**, **Ermine Street**, and **Stane Street**) gave name to early Saxon settlements at **Stratford**, **Stratford Bridge**, and **Streatham**. The district name **Hare Street** in Romford is also named from a Roman road, that leaving the City at **Aldgate** towards Colchester; the same Old English term *here-strǣt* 'military road', hence 'wide highway', is used of **Oxford Street** in the mid-10th century. Other ancient roads are referred to in names like **The Ridgeway** and **Holloway**. Some names recall medieval tolls (**Highgate**) or later turnpikes (**Turnpike Lane**) set up on busy routes (there was once a tollgate at **Hyde Park Corner**, where the main road from the west entered Westminster: there is plenty of precedent in medieval London for road charging!). Causeways sometimes had to be constructed where roads crossed marshy ground and these are referred to in **Risebridge** near Romford and **Newington Causeway** (on the line of the Roman **Stane Street**). The dragging of loads down slopes or across marshy ground to rivers is referred to in **Drayton Green** and **West Drayton**. Important crossroads and road junctions are recalled in names such as **New Cross** and **Four Wantz**.

The large number of ancient names in the Greater London area containing the Old English element *ford* confirms the vital part played by river crossings for communications and trade in early times. Such places where land routes crossed river routes, with all their strategic, economic, and commercial potential, were clearly prime sites for early settlement, and there are no less than twenty major names for towns and districts named from this word in the region. Many of them were on Roman roads or other ancient routes (**Brentford**, **Crayford**, **Romford**, **Stratford**, **Stratford Bridge**), though others may have been of mainly local significance linking one village to its neighbours. As already noted, some of them are named from the Roman road itself (**Stratford**, **Stratford Bridge**), others describe the soil condition or character of the river crossing (**Battle Bridge**, **Chingford**, **Longford**, **Romford**, **Stamford Bridge**, **Stamford Brook**), some are named from an early owner (**Loxford**) or nearby feature (**Whitford**, **Woodford**), some from birds or animals seen in the vicinity (**Catford**, **Cranford**). Like **Brentford** and **Crayford**, **Ilford** incorporates the ancient name of the river crossed, and **Twyford** is named from a 'double ford' on the River Brent.

London Bridge, on the site of by far the oldest bridge across the Thames probably first built by the Romans *c*.100 AD, was clearly always crucial for communications and trade from the very beginning of London's evolution as a great trading city. Even in medieval times, and right up to 1750, the only other bridge crossing these reaches of the Thames was upriver at **Kingston**, which of course gave that place enormous strategic importance. However, before **Westminster Bridge** was built in 1750, the old horse ferry operated across the Thames between Lambeth and Westminster, giving name to **Horseferry Road**.

The coming of the railways from the 1840s, with the rapid development of a whole network of lines, has already been mentioned. The new railway system, both overground and later underground, had an enormous impact on the growth of London and its surrounding suburbs, and resulted in new hamlets and residential districts which were either given new names (**Queensbury**, **Raynes Park**) or (more frequently) old names put to new uses (**Northwood**, **Wealdstone**).

Local Industries and Occupations

It will already be apparent that many names in London and its region recall the crafts, occupations, and industries of earlier times. In the old City itself of course, goods and products of all kinds were grown, manufactured, and sold, from Roman times into the Saxon and medieval periods, and some of the many early City place names and street names that reflect the range and bustle of this activity have already been noted (see earlier section on 'London Town: The City's Names').

Outside the area of the old City, there was lime-burning at **Limehouse**, chalk-quarrying at **Chalk Wood** (compare **Lime Street** in the City and **Chelsea** 'landing place for chalk'), brick-making at **Brick Lane**, and tile-making at **Tylers Common** (though not all necessarily during the same historical period). There must have been an important hammer smithy or forge at **Hammersmith** from at least the 13th century. There are numerous places named from mills (such as **Mill Hill, Millwall, Temple Mills, Turnmill Street**). Some of these refer to mill sites at a very early date. For instance names like **Abbey Mills** and **Mill Meads** in Stratford are in an area that was already industrialized by the 11th century: there are no less than eight mills recorded on the River Lea and its tributaries in the Domesday Book entry for *Ham* (i.e. **West Ham**). In the old forested areas, there was charcoal burning at **Coldfall Wood, Collier Row**, and **Colliers Wood**. Other names incorporating references to woods and trees may refer to timber production (for example **Acton** and **Elmstead**). In addition to these, it can be assumed that cheesemaking was important in **Chiswick** and that fishing took place at **Edgware** and **Mortlake**!

Place Names with Religious Associations
The Christian Church was of course a powerful institution and landowner in medieval times and numerous names recall the possession of manors and estates by churches, abbeys, monasteries, hospitals, and other religious foundations (there were at least twenty different religious communities in the City alone in medieval times).

Only one particularly interesting old name seems to have pagan associations, apparently pre-dating the conversion of the heathen Saxons to Christianity in the 7th century, and that is **Harrow**. This is first recorded as *Gumeninga hergae* in 767, that is 'heathen shrine of the tribe called the *Gumeningas*' (of whom nothing more is known). Of course the occurrence of the name does not necessarily imply that the hilltop site was still used for pagan practices at this date, but the name is nevertheless a significant and very early one.

Many names refer to actual Christian churches, among them **Hornchurch, Marylebone, Oldchurch, St Martin in the Fields, St Pancras, Upminster, Whitchurch**, and several in the City including **Abchurch Lane, Fenchurch Street, Gracechurch Street**, and **St Paul's** itself. Others refer to monasteries (**Blackfriars, Charterhouse, Westminster**), to priories (**Holywell Lane**) and friaries (**Crutched Friars**), to nunneries (**Minories**, and possibly **Mincing Lane**), to chapels (**Chapel End, Whitechapel**), and to hospitals set up by religious foundations (**St Bartholomew's, St Giles, St James's, St Katharine's, St Thomas's**). Another name that probably has a religious connotation is **Walthamstow**, since the final element *stōw* often meant 'holy place'.

Numerous names refer to the estates, lands, or woodlands once in the possession of churches, abbeys, or other religious bodies in early times. Some refer to former ownership by abbeys (**Abbey Mills, Abbey Wood, Covent Garden, Hainault, Monken Hadley**) or priories (**Priors Farm, Spitalfields**). Others once belonged to bishops or priests (**Bishopswood, Parsons Green, Preston, Priests Bridge**), or to canons (**Canbury, Cann Hall, Cannon Hill, Canonbury, Canons Park**). The religious order of the Knights Hospitallers of St John held an area of woodland within the manor of *Lylleston* (see **Lisson Green & Grove**) in the late

13th century (hence **St John's Wood**), and another medieval order, that of the Knights Templars had various possessions (including **The Temple**, **Temple Fortune**, **Temple Mills**). Among the references to ancient crosses are **Charing Cross**, **Crouch End**, and **Malden**, and the district name **Ladywell** (like **Holywell Lane**) refers to a holy spring.

Place Names and Social History

The place names of London and its region reflect many aspects of social history, some illustrating the structure of society, others providing fascinating glimpses into the everyday social life of the people, into their customs, pastimes, superstitions, and beliefs, at different periods. Various ranks of society are represented among the earlier names: kings and queens (**Kensal Green**, **Kingsbury**, **Queenhithe**), countesses and earls (**Counters Creek**, **Earls Court**), aldermen and other important officials (**Aldermanbury**, **Chancery Lane**), even the Anglo-Saxon freeman or peasant (**Charlton**).

In addition to these, many hundreds of named persons and families, often important, wealthy, and influential in their time, are recalled and commemorated in London's place names, as the alphabetical entries reveal. Of course nothing more is known about some of the individuals in the very early place names from the Old English period (such as the *Beohha of **Becontree**, the Ēadhelm of **Edmonton**, the *Fulla of **Fulham**, the Heremund or Heremōd of **Harmondsworth**, the Hygerēd of **Harlington**, the *Wemba of **Wembley**, or the *Wynnmann of **Wimbledon**) other than what the names themselves tell us: some may have been important overlords or chieftains, but most were presumably thegns who had been granted their estates by kings or bishops at some time between the 7th century and the Norman Conquest. However, many other persons and families mentioned in medieval and later names are well documented in local and national records, and of course some are particularly important and famous. **Harold Wood**, for instance, is named from Harold, King of England in 1066. Names ranging from **Vauxhall** and **Barnsbury** to **Leicester Square**, **Regent's Park**, and **Sloane Square** are among the very large number associated with well-known historical figures or powerful families at different periods of history.

Many other places are named from smaller landowning families of local importance, each name indicating the ownership or tenancy of a holding or estate at a particular date (such as **Clitterhouse**, **Corbets Tey**, **Figge's Marsh**, **Goodmayes**, **Petts Wood**, **Pickett's Lock**). In later periods some places are named from developers or builders (**Agar Grove**, **Baker Street**, **Cubitt Town**) or commemorate famous people (**Byron Recreation Ground**, **Ruskin Park**, **Whittington Stone**). Perhaps not surprisingly, only a few names seem to refer to the humbler sort (**Rayners Lane**, and perhaps **Shepherd's Bush**).

Several names allude to ancient boundaries, or to boundary stones and boundary marks (**Barnet Gate**, **Bevis Marks**, **Burnt Oak**, **Keston** and **Keston Mark**, **Mardyke**, **Mare Street**, **Markfield**, **Marks Gate**, **Wealdstone**). **Brixton** is probably so named from a standing stone which once marked the meeting place of one of the ancient hundreds of Surrey. Similarly, **Becontree** is named thus from a prominent tree on the heath here, once the meeting place of an Essex hundred, and **Hounslow** is named from the mound at which an old Middlesex hundred met. **Tothill Street** refers to an old lookout hill or mound, as perhaps does the name **Tooting**. The traditional Rogationtide ceremony of beating the bounds is referred to in the name **Gospel Oak**.

The diverse pleasures and pastimes of the past are also referred to in London place names. Places specifically associated with play or sport are recalled in the two instances of the name **Plaistow** (in Bromley and Newham), both recorded in medieval times. From the same early period, **Clerkenwell** alludes to a place where young people gathered, and **Knightsbridge** may have a similar connotation (it would seem that wells and bridges have always been popular as meeting places).

The mainly aristocratic sport of deer hunting, once practised in the vast wooded reserves of Waltham Forest and Enfield Chase as well as in other woodland areas, gives name to **Chase Cross** and **Chase Side**, and perhaps **Shooters Hill**. Several of the old *Park* names allude to tracts of land enclosed for hunting in medieval times (for instance **Park Wood** in Ruislip and **Richmond Park**), and **Soho** recalls hunting in this area of Westminster in the 16th century. The cruel sports of bear-baiting and cock-fighting, neither banned until the 1830s, are referred to in **Bear Gardens**, **Cockpit Steps**, **Cockpit Yard**, and **Cockspur Street**. Archery was once practised at **The Butts** in Brentford and at **Newington Butts**, and riding in jousts or tournaments is probably alluded to in **Giltspur Street** and **Knightrider Street** in the City.

The glorious years of the Elizabethan theatre in the late 16th century are recalled in **Curtain Road** and **Rose Alley**. The game of *pallemaille*, introduced into this country in the 17th century from Italy and France, gave name to **Pall Mall** and **The Mall**. **Cherry Garden Pier** on the Thames at Bermondsey is named from a popular place of recreation during the same period. Further upriver the name **Eel Pie Island** recalls the boating parties arriving to picnic here in the 19th century. **Mayfair** is named from the great annual 'May Fair' held in the fields here from the late 17th century to the mid-18th century, and the name **Fairlop** also refers to an annual fair. **Hornfair Park** is named from the old 'Horn Fair' once held at Charlton, and the name of **Cuckold's Point** on the Thames at Rotherhithe is perhaps to be associated with the same event. **Maypole** is named from the May festivities once held here.

The springs discovered at various places such as **Acton**, **Beulah Hill**, **Dulwich**, **Hampstead**, and **Islington**, and often considered to have medicinal properties, gave rise to numerous spas, many of which had their heyday in the 18th and early 19th centuries (thus names like **Bermondsey Spa**, **Seething Wells**, **Spa Fields**). These are all relatively late names; a really ancient name referring to a spring (or stream) thought to have healing properties is **Botwell** in Hayes. Several names recall early taverns, among them **Angel**, **Elephant & Castle**, **Globe Town**, **Jamaica Road**, **Nunhead** (probably), **Royal Oak**, **Swiss Cottage**, **Welsh Harp**, and **White Hart Lane**.

A few names seem to refer to old superstitions and beliefs. Among the really ancient names, there may have been a cult of river worship associated with the

Rivers **Brent** and **Lea** in pre-Saxon times (see the earlier section on 'Celtic Names'). **Grim's Ditch** may refer to the pre-Christian Saxon god Woden (compare the pagan temple site indicated by the name **Harrow**), and an early spelling for **Barnet Gate** alludes to the man-eating monster Grendel who features in the 7th-century Old English epic poem *Beowulf*. Among names of much later date, two seem to refer to the Devil and were therefore perhaps bestowed on places considered to be haunted or cursed (**Devilsden Wood** and **Scratch Wood**), two are grim reminders of sites where gallows once stood (**Galley Farm** and **Gallows Corner**, see also **Tyburn Way**), and another alludes figuratively to a hangman's noose (**Neckinger**). **Bunhill Fields** were already named thus by the mid-16th century from the bones of human corpses deposited there.

Highwaymen, frequently mentioned in early sources as preying on vulnerable travellers as they crossed the large areas of open heath and dense woodland on the main routes into London, may be referred to in **Shooters Hill** and **Robin Hood Gate** (although the first name may refer to archers or huntsmen and the second may simply commemorate Robin Hood as a popular figure). A different legend, that of King Arthur, is alluded to in the name **Camlet Moat**, an old moated earthwork situated in the middle of Enfield Chase.

Place Names and the Language

Many linguistic aspects of London place names have of course already been looked at in earlier sections, especially those on 'Some Different Place-Name Types and Structures'. But a few other points of interest might still be mentioned, one being the important contribution made to our knowledge of the original vocabulary of Old English by the study of place names such as those in the Greater London area. Dozens of words once used in living speech may never have found their way into literary or historical writings before they went out of use, but such words often occur in place names formed in the early Anglo-Saxon period. This archaic vocabulary (customarily asterisked to show that it is only evidenced in place names and not otherwise recorded) includes words like **b(e)alg* 'smooth, rounded' (in **Balham**), **bica* 'pointed ridge' (in **Bickley**), **ceg* 'tree stump' (in **Cheam**), **c(i)erring* 'a turn or bend' (in **Charing Cross**), **clopp(a)* 'lump, hill' (in **Clapham** and **Clapton**), **ēan* 'lamb' (in **Enfield**), **hǣs(e)* 'land overgrown with brushwood' (in **Hayes** and **Heston**), **scēo* 'shed, shelter' (in **East Sheen**), **tēo* 'boundary' (in **Tyburn**), and many others.

Moreover many words are evidenced much earlier in place names than in the ordinary language. From their occurrence in early place-name spellings we know that words such as **bula* 'bull' (in **Bollo**), **cingel* 'shingle' (in **Chingford**), **mort* 'young salmon' (in **Mortlake**), **scēotere* 'shooter' (in **Shooters Hill**), and **scora* 'steep bank or slope' (in **Shoreditch**), also asterisked to show that they are only recorded in independent use in Middle English or later, are likely to date back to the Old English period. Many other old words, once part of the living language but now lost from the general vocabulary, survive in fossilized form in place names. Words such as Old English *bærnet* 'burnt place' (found in **Barnet**), *cēap* 'market' (in **Cheapside** and **Eastcheap**), *cīeping* also 'market' (in

Chipping Barnet), *cisel* 'gravel' (in **Chiselhurst**), *eowestre* 'sheepfold' (in **Osterley**), *hearg* 'heathen temple' (in **Harrow**), and *hȳth* 'landing place on a river' (in **Chelsea**, **Lambeth**, and **Rotherhithe**), are among the scores of examples listed in the Glossary of Elements at the end of the book.

Greater London place names often reveal characteristics of the medieval English dialects once spoken in this area. For instance the *e*-spellings found in the medieval and current forms of names like **East Bedfont**, **Bexley**, **Herne Hill**, and **Stepney** are typical of the Kentish dialect of Old English, whilst West Saxon dialect forms lie behind the early and current spellings of names like **Chadwell**, **Chelsea**, **Chipping Barnet**, **Chiswick**, **Harrow Weald**, **Wealdstone**, and **Willesden**. Numerous names of somewhat later date contain interesting old dialect words of various origins, among them **Anerley**, **Chohole Gate**, **Clam Field**, **Clink Street**, **Four Wents**, **Parson's Pightle**, **Quaggy River**, and **Spankers Hill Wood**.

It has been said that nothing betrays an outsider like a literal spelling pronunciation of a local place name, and it is of course the case that the current local pronunciation of some place names (for instance **Chiswick**, **Deptford**, **Erith**, **Greenwich**, **Holborn**, **Isleworth**, **Marylebone**, **Plaistow**, **Ruislip**, **Southwark**, **Streatham**, **Wapping**, **Woolwich** and **Yeading**) differs from what the modern spelling might lead us to expect (unless we are familiar with the places or otherwise initiated). The historical and linguistic reasons for these disparities (i.e. between spelling and pronunciation) are of some interest and will often be commented upon in the individual entries. In almost all cases, the name has continued to evolve in the everyday spoken language but its spelling in written form has lagged behind, so that in a sense spellings are often rather traditional and conservative. Nevertheless they nearly always reveal some interesting aspect of the name's etymology. The *-wich* and *-wark* of **Greenwich**, **Woolwich**, and **Southwark** represent closely the old words from which the names derive, as do the *Plai-* and *Streat-* in **Plaistow** and **Streatham** (compare 'play' and 'street'). And in the case of **Deptford**, it is in fact the now silent *-p-* that is historical (reflecting the etymology from the word that has become 'deep'), whereas the *-t-* is intrusive and relatively recent. Otherwise the conservative spellings of many place names (such as **Bermondsey**, **Harmondsworth**, and **Rotherhithe**), in contrast with their naturally worn-down spoken forms, have already been noted in the earlier section on 'Reduction and Other Sound Changes'. Where current pronunciations of names are particularly unexpected and interesting, they are given within parentheses in a modified form similar to that employed in the *BBC Pronouncing Dictionary of British Names*: thus 'Chizzick', 'Grinidge', 'Grinitch' or 'Grenitch', 'Holeburn' or 'Hoeburn', 'Marrylebon' or 'Marlibon', 'Plasstow', 'Rizelip' or 'Ryeslip', 'Yedding', and so on.

Postscript: Some Associations, Uses, and Applications of London Place Names

So many London names have strong associations, powerful vibes, rich overtones, and iconic connotations of all kinds, and so many others have become bywords or catchphrases, it seemed desirable to comment on a few matters that might be considered outside the scope of a book like this. Whatever their etymologies, their original meanings and their wider historical and onomastic significance (all subjects at the heart of this Dictionary), it is quite clear that place names and street names often function as much more than labels on maps and signposts, or familiar locations where we work and live. In fact they function in all sorts of other ways, and contribute a rich vein to contemporary life, language, and culture.

Who can mention **Carnaby Street** without thinking of 1960s boutiques and 'swinging London', or **Baker Street** without thinking of Sherlock Holmes, or **Downing Street** without thinking of No. 10, or **Notting Hill** without thinking of the great Caribbean carnival (or of the famous blue door in the film), or **Peckham** without thinking of 'Del Boy' Trotter? In well-known phrases like '**Bloomsbury** Group', '**Greenwich** Meridian', '**Camden Town** Group', place names feature as parts of concepts that far transcend the actual locations.

A number of London names lie behind the derivations of ordinary vocabulary words and phrases. The words *bedlam* 'scene of uproar', *mall* 'public walk', and *mews* 'courtyard' in current English have developed both their forms and their senses from the place names **Bethlem**, **The Mall**, and *The Muwes* (now **Trafalgar Square**). The word *billingsgate* 'foul language', an attributive use of the name **Billingsgate** found from the 17th century to denote the vituperative language heard at the famous wholesale fish market here, is (or was) another such transfer from name to word. The phrase *Grub Street*, often still applied adjectivally to any mean literary production, is from the former name of **Milton Street**. But it should be noted that the word *hackney* 'a horse for hire' (as in *hackney carriage* 'vehicle let out for hire' and the adjectival derivative *hackneyed* 'trite'), has nothing to do with the place name **Hackney**: the word comes from Old French *haquenée* 'an ambling nag'!

Place-name phrases containing a name chosen to represent a certain type, class, or segment of society, are much beloved by journalists, politicians, and social commentators. No doubt thought quite brilliant and apt when first coined, such phrases quickly become clichés, and yet the use of a specific place name somehow ensures that they retain at least a little of their original impact. 'The Man on the Clapham Omnibus', eventually used as a legal phrase meaning 'man in the street', is an early example: it is interesting that the first stage coach service into the City of London was established at **Clapham** in 1690, although the phrase probably refers to middle-class commuters living in this pleasant and prosperous 19th-century suburb, who benefited from the introduction of omnibuses in the 1830s. In the world of politics, a creature known as 'Basildon Man' was much talked about in the early 1990s (so called from Basildon in Essex, outside the Greater London area), just as in the 1970s 'Selsdon Man' had been (applied to 'a new type of Conservative' after the Tory Party Conference held at **Selsdon**). In more recent times, political commentators only need to write of '**Hampstead** liberals' or '**Islington** trendies' and (we think) we know what they mean. Of course these convenient phrases pick up on some of the characteristic (and ever shifting) mind-sets of these various London suburban types, so wittily exposed in the pages of *Private*

Eye (with some particular focus on **Neasden**) and in books such as Glenys Roberts's *Metropolitan Myths* (1982, based on her articles in the *Standard*).

One of the wittiest of such phrases is undoubtedly 'Sloane Ranger' (often abbreviated to 'Sloane'), a 1970s creation describing the stereotypical upper middle class young woman who might well live in or around **Sloane Square** and also have a place in the country (there is even an adjectival derivative *sloaney*). The phrase puns cleverly on the name *Sloane* and that of the *Lone Ranger* of TV fame (mainly 1950s), setting up a number of striking contrasts in terms of gender (rough, tough, horse-riding, middle-aged cowboy: smart, chic, probably horse-riding, young woman) and habitat (vast wild open prairies: trendy Kensington shops and parties). A far cry from Sir Hans Sloane, co-founder of the British Museum, after whom the Square was named in the 18th century!

Nearer to the heart of government and slightly more abstract and faceless are the '**Whitehall** sources', the '**Downing Street** advisers', the '**Westminster** spokesmen', and the '**Millbank** spindoctors' we often see quoted or berated in the media. Indeed the place names themselves, used elliptically, often say it all, so that for Westminster, Whitehall, and Downing Street we can simply understand 'the government', for 'the City' we can read 'the financial and business community', and of course newspaper headlines like 'Whitehall rejects compromise' are commonplace.

Outside the human arena, other London places have given their names to particular species of wild life (the 'Camberwell Beauty', a rare butterfly *Vanessa antiopa*, so named in the 18th century from its having been spotted in **Camberwell**; the 'Shirley Poppy', named from **Shirley** near Croydon), or to products (the 'Chelsea Bun', named from **Chelsea**, the original 'Chelsea Bun House', demolished in 1839, having flourished during the 18th century; the 'Black or Buff Orpington', breeds of poultry first raised by farmer William Cook of **Orpington** in the 1880s), or to a whole variety of other things (the '**Bloomsbury** Group', the '**Camden Town** Group' and the '**Greenwich** Meridian' already mentioned, and, somewhat less sublimely and to bring up the rear, the '**Dagenham** Cleavage', believed to be a current colloquial usage for what is usually known as 'builder's bum'!).

Particularly striking, but not entirely surprising, is the strong contribution made by London place names to that strange linguistic phenomenon, the curious secretive Cockney form of language known as rhyming slang. Some rhyming slang dates back to the early 19th century and some of it is now obsolescent (it tends to be rather ephemeral), but much of it is still current. A small selection of examples recorded from the 20th century and possibly in some cases still in use might include: *barnet fair* for 'hair' (often reduced to simply *barnet*, a reference to the September fair held at **Chipping Barnet**); *chalk farm* for 'arm' (often reduced to *chalk*, from **Chalk Farm**); *colney hatch* 'match' (often reduced to *colney*, from **Colney Hatch**); *hampstead heath* for 'teeth' (usually reduced to *hampsteads*, from **Hampstead Heath**); *hampton court* for 'salt' (from **Hampton Court** with Cockney pronunciation); *kennington lane* for 'pain' (from **Kennington**, often in combination with the next); *newington butts* for 'guts' (often reduced to *newingtons*, from **Newington Butts**); *peckham rye* for 'tie' (often reduced to *peckham*, from **Peckham Rye**); *piccadilly* for 'silly' (from **Piccadilly**); *westminster abbey* for 'cabbie' (from **Westminster Abbey**); *woolwich and greenwich* for 'spinach' and *woolwich ferry* for 'sherry' (from **Woolwich (Ferry)** and **Greenwich**).

The popular, unofficial, often ephemeral, nicknames given to places are often interesting. The great 19th-century radical journalist and traveller William Cobbett was apparently the first to call London 'the Great Wen' (perhaps with the implication that this rapidly swelling metropolis would soon burst), and 'the Big Smoke' is another 19th-century phrase particularly applied to London (although later used of other major cities like Sydney, Melbourne, and Pittsburgh which were also considered dirty and polluted).

Nicknames for particular areas or districts in London have also been gently disparaging, but at the same time quite humorous. In early times part of **Bankside** was known as 'Stew's bank' from its numerous stews or brothels. In the 1840s the centre of the notorious slums of *Agar Town* (see **Agar Grove**) was known euphemistically as 'La Belle Isle'. **South Acton** was known colloquially as 'Soapsuds Islands' in the late 19th century from the two hundred or so laundries situated there. **Surbiton** was for a time in the mid-19th century known as 'Kingston-on-Railway' after nearby Kingston (on Thames) had refused to accept the railway and it was routed through Surbiton instead. The Rugby Football Ground at **Twickenham** was nicknamed 'Billy Williams's Cabbage Patch' when first opened in 1907 after the man who bought the site. The **Waterloo–Bank** underground link with the City, opened in 1898, is still commonly referred to as 'The Drain' (an inspired figurative application of the word). The prison at **Wormwood Scrubs** is known colloquially by its short form as simply 'The Scrubs' (which somehow sounds about right). **Earls Court** is sometimes nicknamed 'Bedsit Jungle' or 'Kangaroo Valley' (from its numerous flat-dwellers, many Australian). And the area to the south and east of the Docklands Light Railway is known to some of its artist residents as 'Grotsville'.

Like 'The Drain' and 'The Scrubs', other nicknames too have become quite well known and firmly established: **Fitzrovia**, 'the Square Mile' (see the **City**), **Speaker's Corner**, 'The Old Lady of Threadneedle Street' (see **Bank**). Many are not at all disparaging, indeed they seem quite affectionate, like 'Bart's' for **St Bartholomew's Hospital** (just a handy short form), 'Ally Pally' for **Alexandra Palace** (a nice reduplicating compound), 'Biggin on the Bump' for the aerodrome at **Biggin Hill** (note the neat alliteration), 'Brixton Beach' for the lido at **Brockwell** (the implied comparison is no doubt between **Brixton** nearby and Brighton on the south coast), 'Chinatown' for the Chinese quarter of **Soho**, and more recently, 'Banglatown' for the Bengali or Bangladeshi community around **Brick Lane** in **Spitalfields**. One with a surprisingly historical basis is the jocular 'Buck House' for **Buckingham Palace**: before it became a palace it was in fact simply *Buckingham House* in the 18th century. Besides these well-known nicknames for familiar places, there must be lots of others that have only local or ephemeral currency. One such, no doubt beginning as a waggish joke, is the nickname for the estate at **Bushey Mead**: it is known as 'The Apostles' because it consists of twelve parallel roads!

It is apparent that in many of the foregoing examples of nicknames for places, a tongue-in-cheek, wry kind of humour is at work, perhaps somewhat similar to the mixture of whimsy, jocularity, and irony seen in the formation of some early place names such as **Piccadilly**, **Mount Pleasant**, **Isle of Dogs**, and **Botany Bay** (for which, see the earlier section on 'Irony, Whimsy, and some Unusual Formations'). It also seems to be the case that, quite irrespective of their origins, some names are perceived to have a funny side, that is they appear to look or sound humorous to some people. Since there is nothing quite as subjective as humour, this sort of thing is probably down to individuals, but then again, the news seems to get around, and some names become part of a kind of humour bank of folklore. Analysis is certainly difficult, but here goes.

It is probably the case that some of the perceived humour (and of course charm) in names like **Chalk Farm** and **Shepherd's Bush** comes from the seeming incongruity of rural-sounding name and urban location: of course it is surely also fascinating to know that only a century or two ago these rustic names were still appropriate to their farming localities. Some make mock of **Penge** (an unusual name but not a pretentious place) by pronouncing it superciliously to rhyme with 'blancmange'. Coincidental association between names and other words in the vocabulary is also sometimes likely to raise a smile. **Ratcliff** has nothing to do with rats (it is actually 'red cliff'), but it does happen to be beside the Thames so the false association seems somehow appropriate (see the earlier section on 'Folk Etymology'). **Mincing Lane** in the City is almost bound to be associated with a mincing gait, even though etymologically it refers to nuns!

Some have thought **Sidcup** funny, perhaps because of its sound combination of 'Sid' (as in 'Sidney') and 'cup' (as in 'cup of tea'). Others think **Neasden** a laugh, perhaps because the first syllable sounds like 'knees', so that the whole name becomes a kind of comic contrast to a 'knees up' (in fact the name's etymology, 'nose down', is in itself quite amusing!). Others have been tickled by **Crouch End**, **Elmers End**, **Newington Butts**, and **Pratt's Bottom**, perhaps because they remind us of other, equally ridiculous and slightly ruder, parts of our anatomy. Of course it is not surprising that Pratt's Bottom should be the butt of jokes (you see how easy it is), when the surname Pratt is one of those you would sometimes rather not have. It is said that a local entrepreneur wanted to turn the joke on end and market a brand of jeans with the village name on the logo! And as for **Spankers Hill Wood** and **Whipps Cross**—warped sense of humour or what—let them speak for themselves.

If some names (like the last) can look or sound amusing, others simply produce their own strange coincidences and ironies. The station master in charge of **Orpington** station in 1885 was, according to the records, a Mr Orpin! The surname *Orpin* is derived from a medicinal plant, the yellow stonecrop: of course it would have been even more bizarre if he had been a Mr *Orpet*, a surname from the personal name *Orped* actually incorporated into the place name a thousand years earlier! It always seems mildly ironic that, of all places,

Catford ('the cats' ford') in south-east London should be particularly well known for its dog racing stadium, or that **Heathrow**, now a vast international airport handling over 60 million passengers a year, should have such a tranquil rustic name ('row of cottages on the heath'), or that **Scratchwood**, now the site of a temple dedicated to the car-god, should once have been considered haunted by the devil! Of course any perceived irony or amusement in the last example is with the benefit of a knowledge of the name's etymology. Why not? If your attic flat in **Chalk Farm** is draughty, badly heated, and uncomfortable, think of the 'cold cottages' that gave the place its name! And if you are stuck in the thick traffic of a **Croydon** rush-hour you can always meditate on the fact that this is after all simply 'the valley where wild saffron grows'!

Of course London and its surrounding towns and suburbs are enormously rich in literary associations, and for these the reader should consult one or other of the specialized literary guides such as *The Oxford Literary Guide to the British Isles* (1980) or Ed Glinert's *A Literary Guide to London* (2000). It goes without saying that because so many works of fiction have London settings, many place names lead a kind of double life, functioning as real place names in the humdrum everyday world of maps and signposts and workplaces, but often having another identity, another life, in fiction. Chaucer's references to the *Tabard* inn, to *the wateryng of Seint Thomas*, to *Chepe*, and to *the scole of Stratford atte Bowe*, in his *Canterbury Tales* (*c.*1387) are early examples of perfectly ordinary places achieving a special kind of stardom (see **Tabard Street**, **Neckinger**, **Cheapside**, and **Bromley-by-Bow**). Of course similar references to places abound in the plays of Shakespeare, Jonson, and others, in the novels of Dickens, and in the work of dozens of other famous writers who either migrated to London to live or who were Londoners born and bred, most of whom in their different ways found London's many-sided vitality irresistible, and therefore made frequent allusion to its districts and streets.

There are striking examples in relatively recent times of London place names acquiring almost cult status by featuring as settings in works of fiction. The **Baker Street** of Sherlock Holmes, the brilliant sleuth created by Sir Arthur Conan Doyle in 1887, is known to an international audience, even down to the number of his residence at No 221B (which is often looked for by enthusiastic tourists but is found not to exist). **Holloway** is particularly associated with its fictitious resident Mr Pooter in the Grossmiths's *Diary of a Nobody* (1892). The **Wimbledon Common** setting for Elisabeth Beresford's series of children's stories (1968–78) led to the birth of 'wombling' and 'The Wombles', with their delightful echoes of primitive Germanic vowel mutations. Two other south London place names, East Cheam and Peckham, have also acquired this kind of status, at least on a national scale, by serving as the settings for successful comedy series. East Cheam (this part of **Cheam** is not marked on current maps but once existed, at least it did in the 13th century!) is the setting for *Hancock's Half-Hour*, the brilliant BBC Radio series (1954–9) transferred to television in 1956, starring the wonderfully lugubrious Tony Hancock as the doleful social misfit. **Peckham** is the setting for the equally outstanding television series *Only Fools and Horses* (1980s–90s), starring the inspired wheeling and dealing of

Derek Trotter (Del Boy) in and around this area (the logo on his van reading 'Trotters Independent Trading Co, New York, Paris, Peckham'). Cheam and Peckham can never be the same again!

These settings, anchored to a real place name, might be contrasted with the location of the long-running television soap *East Enders*, where *Walford* is an invented name (there is of course a long tradition for this too, witness Trollope's *Barchester*, Hardy's *Casterbridge*, not to mention *Brookside* and *Emmerdale*). As noted earlier, this seems to be a so-called portmanteau invention based on the real names **Wal**worth and Strat**ford**: it certainly somehow has a convincing enough East End flavour.

Actual names of London places are often put to use quite effectively in the titles of ballads, plays, and novels. Early examples include *London Lickpenny*, a 15th-century ballad in which the hungry and penniless Kentish hero wanders through London's streets marvelling at the abundance and variety of food and drink on sale; *The Beggar's Daughter of Bednall Green*, a ballad written in the reign of Elizabeth I and later turned into a play (see **Bethnal Green**); Thomas Nashe's *Isle of Dogs* (1597), a lost satirical play which caused a furore by exposing abuses and which met with trouble from the authorities (see **Isle of Dogs**); and Ben Jonson's *Bartholomew Fair* (1614), a play that depicts in lively fashion the entertainers, bawds, and tricksters who turned up at this popular annual event (see **St Bartholomew's Hospital**). Later instances of London place names more or less successfully incorporated into the titles of plays and novels include Douglas Jerrold's comic play *The Bride of Ludgate* (1831); Harrison Ainsworth's historical novels *The Tower of London* (1840) and *Old St Paul's* (1841); Somerset Maugham's first novel *Liza of Lambeth* (1897), in which his heroine's loss of honour is ascribed to a Bank Holiday outing to Chingford; Rudolph Bezier's play *The Barretts of Wimpole Street* (1930); Muriel Spark's novels *The Ballad of Peckham Rye* (1960) and *A Far Cry from Kensington* (1988), both of which titles have a nice lilt to them; Leslie Thomas's *Tropic of Ruislip* (1974); Brian Wright's *Penge Papers: Confessions of an Unwaged Metropolitan Househusband* (1985); and of course Martin Amis's novel *London Fields* (1989). A recent collection of new writing from London, amply demonstrating that the capital has lost none of its strange fascination for authors, is called *Does the Sun Rise over Dagenham?* (1998), after the title of one of the short stories by Doina Cornell. A nice exploitation of a place name in a book title of a different kind is the punning *Strawberries and Cheam* (1996), the second volume of Harry Secombe's autobiography (he and his family resided in **Cheam** for over thirty years).

Film titles too have sometimes incorporated the actual names of their settings. In a way, since London has long been the centre of the British film industry, and given the enormous number of films shot in and around it, it is perhaps surprising there are not more. But the recent *Notting Hill* (1999) is a prime example (adding to **Notting Hill**'s cult status as the venue for the annual Caribbean Carnival, Europe's greatest street party), and before that there are the classic Ealing comedies *Passport to Pimlico* (1949), based on the conceit of the declaration of independence by this Westminster district (see **Pimlico**), and *The Lavender Hill Mob* (1951), said to be one of the best ever Ealing productions (see

Lavender Hill). Here as in the titles of novels and plays, the use of a real place name, anchored in its real locality, is perhaps seen to have greater impact and immediacy than any made-up name might have had.

In addition to the 15th- and 16th-century balladeers already mentioned, numerous poets from Chaucer, Langland, and Shakespeare to Betjeman and Pinter have of course celebrated London and its streets, districts, sights, and characters. There is a rich tradition of poetry on London themes, including the famous panegyric to London (c.1501) attributed to William Dunbar ('London, thou art the flour of Cities all'), the traditional 17th-century nursery rhymes ('Oranges and Lemons' and 'London Bridge is falling down'), and poems by William Blake, John Dryden, Dr Johnson, Alexander Pope, William Wordsworth, and very many others (see, for instance, the excellent anthology *London in Verse* (1982) edited by Christopher Logue). Not surprisingly, here too London place names have an important role to play, as in Alfred Noyes's lyrical celebration of Kew ('Come down to Kew in lilac-time (it isn't far from London!)') or John Betjeman's amusing piece *Business Girls* which begins:

> From the geyser ventilators
> Autumn winds are blowing down
> On a thousand business women
> Having baths in Camden Town.

Some London place names are of course particularly associated with certain events, pastimes, and sports. They remain the familiar comfortable labels for the places where we work, rest, and play, but they achieve a much wider cultural status and almost iconic value too, well beyond the confines of the locality they describe. For instance, what musical reverberations some London names have! At the turn of the century *Burlington Bertie* was a favourite music-hall hit, and in the late 1930s the *Lambeth Walk* was a popular Cockney dance and song (see **Burlington Arcade** and **Lambeth Walk**). The title of the first Beatles album, *Abbey Road* (1969), is taken from the street of that name in St John's Wood where the EMI studios are situated (see **Abbey Road**), and the name of the late lamented popstar Ian Dury's first band in the mid-1970s was *Kilburn & the High Roads* (see **Kilburn**).

Sport in particular has brought many London place names into powerful prominence, both nationally and internationally, especially in the last half century when certain events and competitions have become big business. Names such as the following, once just denoting districts or locations within the London area, are now known worldwide, and speak for themselves: **Arsenal**, **Brentford**, **Charlton** (Athletic), **Chelsea**, **Crystal Palace**, **Fulham**, **Leyton** (Orient), **Lords**, **Marylebone** (MCC), **Millwall**, **The Oval**, **Queen's Park** (Rangers), **Tottenham** (Hotspur), **Twickenham**, **Wembley**, **West Ham** (United), **Wimbledon**, and so on.

Even a parlour game has participated in the same process. Through the long-lived popularity of the game of *Monopoly*, London names such as **Old Kent Road**, **Pall Mall**, **Strand**, and even the more obscure **Vine Street** in the English version have become known, nationwide and even worldwide, as properties to be valued, bought and developed, like a weird kind of rerun of the last few centuries of London history.

It is not difficult to think of other London place names that have acquired a special kind of status through powerful extra associations of a similar kind, and for the most diverse of reasons: **Balham** (never the same name or place once you have heard Peter Sellers's brilliant 1960s spoof on 'Bal-ham, Gateway to the South'); **Carnaby Street** (a fairly insignificant little road behind Regent Street which became the centre of Mod fashions in the 1960s); **King's Road** (a kind of catwalk for 'with it' fashion trends, with Mary Quant's 1960s shop leading the way). **Berkeley Square**, **Bow Lane**, **Covent Garden**, **Downing Street**, **Ealing**, **Holloway**, **King's Cross**, **Piccadilly**... there are clearly hundreds of such cases, where place names have this 'other life', where the associations, vibes, and overtones are rich, colourful, and powerful, far transcending their everyday function to describe a simple location. Of course this is mainly a subjective thing, for every place name is bound to have some of this extra meaning for someone somewhere.

Place names are clearly important. They are part of our rich cultural heritage. They link us with our past, but they are also a part of our present. They are in a way just words and yet they are so much more than that. They lie deep in our consciousness. They are daily used and abused by us all in everyday situations, but they also trigger emotions and memories. They can be the butt of jokes but also the stuff of poetry.

And so we can end up as we started, with the name **London** itself and with the spectacular city it refers to. Its own vibes and associations are the sum of all we have mentioned, and more. It is a truly incredible, mighty, place. What's in a name?

The Greater London Boroughs

Barking & Dagenham
Barnet
Bexley
Brent
Bromley
Camden
Croydon
Ealing
Enfield
Greenwich
Hackney
Hammersmith & Fulham
Haringey
Harrow
Havering
Hillingdon
Hounslow

Islington
Kensington & Chelsea
Kingston upon Thames
Lambeth
Lewisham
London, City of
Merton
Newham
Redbridge
Richmond upon Thames
Southwark
Sutton
Tower Hamlets
Waltham Forest
Wandsworth
Westminster, City of

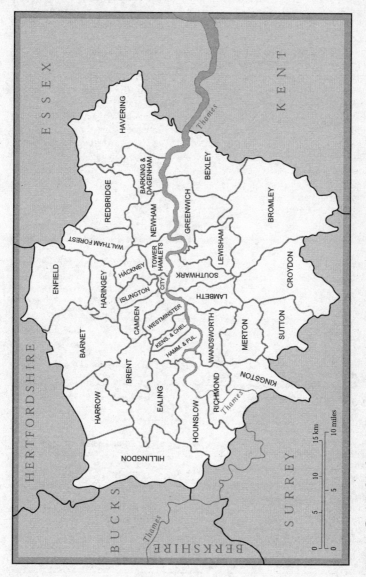

Map 1 Greater London

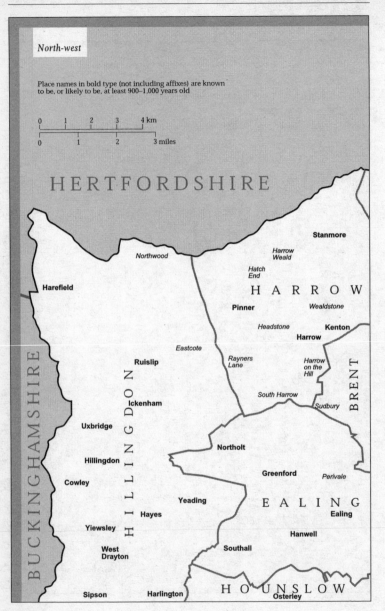

North-west

Place names in bold type (not including affixes) are known
to be, or likely to be, at least 900–1,000 years old

0   1   2   3   4 km

0   1   2   3 miles

HERTFORDSHIRE

BUCKINGHAMSHIRE

Harefield

Northwood

Stanmore

Harrow
Weald

Hatch
End

HARROW

Pinner

Wealdstone

Headstone

Kenton

Harrow

KENTON

Eastcote

Rayners
Lane

Harrow
on the
Hill

BRENT

Ruislip

Ickenham

South Harrow

Sudbury

HILLINGDON

Uxbridge

Northolt

Hillingdon

Greenford

Perivale

Cowley

EALING

Yeading

Hayes

Ealing

Yiewsley

Hanwell

**West
Drayton**

Southall

Sipson

Harlington

HOUNSLOW

Osterley

Map 2

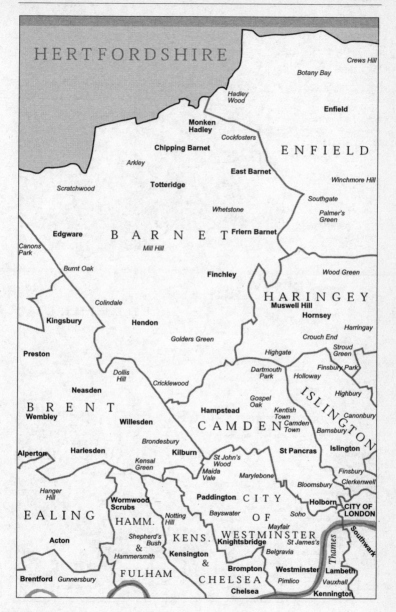

Map 3

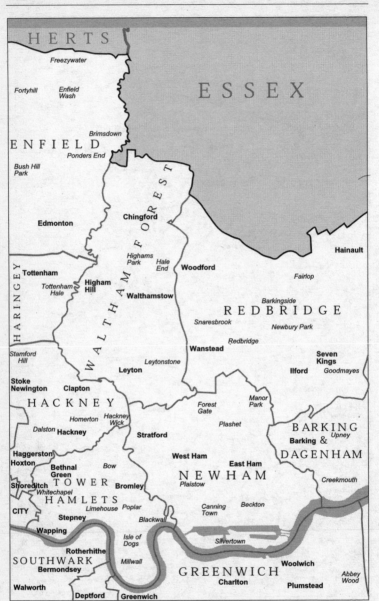

Map 4

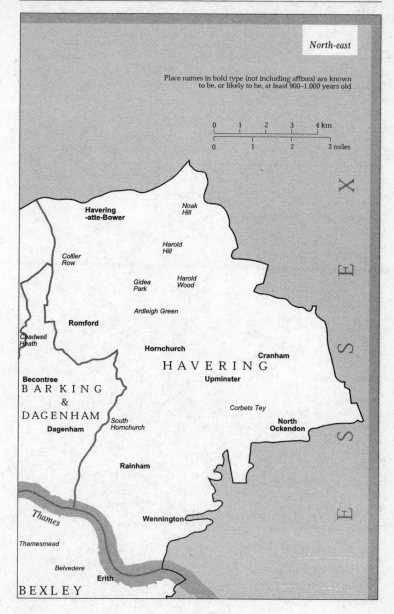

North-east

Place names in bold type (not including affixes) are known
to be, or likely to be, at least 900–1.000 years old

Map 5

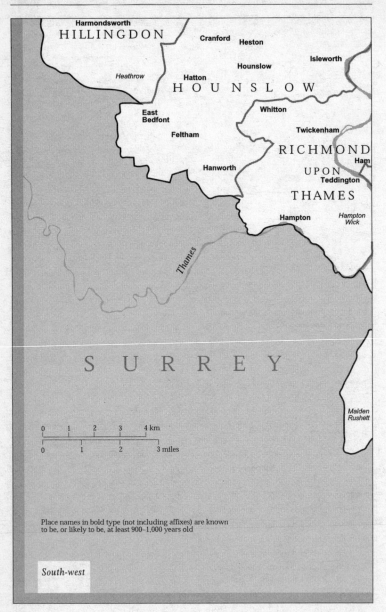

Map 6

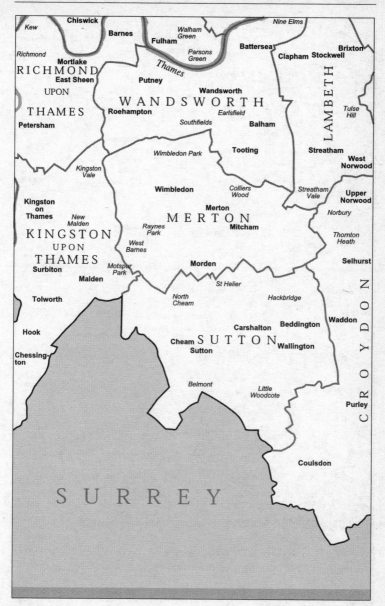

Kew
Chiswick
Barnes
Walham Green
Fulham
Nine Elms
Richmond
Mortlake
RICHMOND
East Sheen
UPON
THAMES
Petersham
Parsons Green
Battersea
Clapham Stockwell
Brixton
Putney
WANDSWORTH
Roehampton
Wandsworth
Earlsfield
Southfields
Balham
Tulse Hill
LAMBETH
Wimbledon Park
Tooting
Streatham
West Norwood
Kingston Vale
Wimbledon
Colliers Wood
Streatham Vale
Upper Norwood
Kingston on Thames
New Malden
MERTON
Merton
Mitcham
Norbury
Thornton Heath
KINGSTON
UPON
THAMES
Surbiton
Malden
Raynes Park
West Barnes
Motspur Park
Morden
St Helier
Selhurst
Tolworth
North Cheam
Hackbridge
Waddon
Hook
Carshalton
Beddington
CROYDON
Chessington
Cheam
SUTTON
Wallington
Sutton
Belmont
Little Woodcote
Purley
Coulsdon
SURREY

Map 7

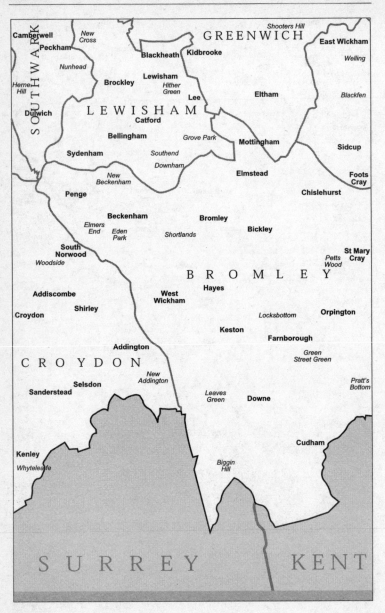

 Map 8

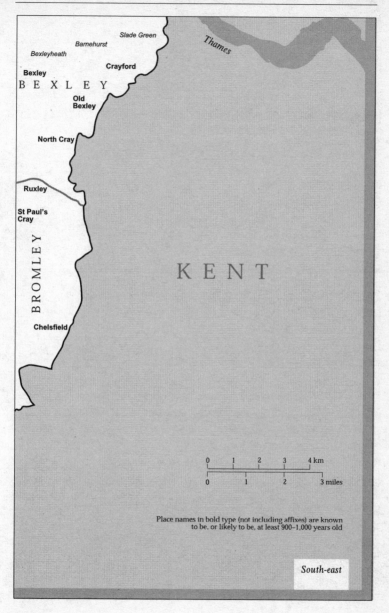

Place names in bold type (not including affixes) are known
to be, or likely to be, at least 900–1,000 years old

South-east

Map 9

A

Abbey Mills (at Stratford) Newham. Now the name of a Victorian pumping station built in 1865, but once the name of a watermill here, recorded as *Wiggemulne* 1312, *lez Abbey Milles* early 16th century, *Wiggen Mill otherwise The Abbey Mill* 1607, that is 'mill of a man called Wicga', from an Old English personal name and *myln*, later 'mill(s) belonging to the abbey', this referring to the former Abbey of *Stratford Langthorne* (*see* MILL MEADS and STRATFORD).

Abbey Recreation Ground & Road Merton. Recall the large Augustinian Priory of Merton which lay in this area in medieval times, some of its foundations being under the recently built Merantun Way. Although it was never more than a *priory*, the name Merton Abbey was sometimes used for this area from the early 19th century, *see* MERTON.

Abbey Road (in Barking) Barking & Dagenham. Recalls the important medieval nunnery here, *see* Barking Abbey, *under* BARKING.

Abbey Road (in St John's Wood) Camden/Westminster. Developed in the early 19th century from an earlier track, and so named from the medieval priory at KILBURN to which it led. Chiefly famous of course as the name of the 1969 Beatles album recorded here at the EMI studios!

Abbey Street (in Bermondsey) Southwark. Recalls the medieval abbey here, *see* BERMONDSEY.

Abbey Wood Greenwich. Residential area (marked *Abbeywood* on the Ordnance Survey map of 1888) developed from the end of the 19th century, so called from the extensive woodland known as *Abbey Wood* that once belonged to the monks of Lesnes Abbey (*see* LESSNESS HEATH), the remains of which are still to be found in Lesnes Abbey Woods.

Abbey Wood (near Rainham) Havering. Near *Abbey House* which is marked on the Ordnance Survey map of 1883, both referring to land once belonging to Barking Abbey (*see* BARKING).

Abchurch Lane & Yard City. *Abechirchelane* 1274, *Abbechirchelane* 1292, named from a 12th-century church replaced by the present St Mary Abchurch (built by Wren in 1686). The medieval church is recorded as *Habechirce c.*1200, *Abbechurche* 1211, that is 'church of a man called Abba', from an Old English personal name (perhaps of a priest or the founder of the church) and Old English *cirice*.

Abney Park Cemetery (at Stoke Newington) Hackney. Named from Sir Thomas *Abney*, Lord Mayor of London in 1700–1, who held the manor of STOKE NEWINGTON in the early 18th century and whose town house stood here (built 1676, demolished in the 1830s).

Acton Ealing. *Acton* 1181, *Aketon* 1211, *Chirche Acton* 1347, *Churche Acton* 1551, that is 'farmstead or village by the oak tree(s)', or 'specialized farm where oak timber is worked', from Old English *āc* and *tūn*, formerly with the affix *Church* to distinguish the main village from the separate hamlet of **East Acton**, which is *Estacton* 1294, *Estactongrene* 1474. In medieval times Acton was an important producer of firewood for London. The residential district of **South Acton** was developed from the late 1800s, **North Acton** and **West Acton** during the 20th century. **Acton Green**, another suburb south of Acton, is marked thus on Cary's map of 1786 and on the Ordnance Survey map of 1876–7. There was a popular spa at Acton during the 18th century, named as *Acton Wells* on Rocque's map of 1754.

Addington Croydon. *Eddintone* 1086 (Domesday Book), *Adingeton* 1203, *Adinton* 1219, *Adington* 1247, that is 'farmstead or estate associated with a man called Eadda or Æddi', from an Old English personal name with Old English medial connective *-ing-* and *tūn*. If the name of the Saxon landowner was *Æddi*, ADDISCOMBE (some 2 miles north-west) may refer to the same man. **Addington Hills** were earlier *hill of Pripledeane* 1552, *hill called Prible Dean (called Adington Hills)* 1756, that is 'gravel valley', from early Modern English *preble* 'gravel' and *dene*, note nearby Gravel Hill. **Addington Palace**, built *c.*1770 and much altered and extended *c.*1900, was the country residence of the Archbishops of Canterbury during much of the 19th century. **New Addington** is a residential development begun *c.*1935 by the First National Housing Trust on earlier farmland.

Addiscombe Croydon. *Edescamp* 1229, *Adescompe* 1279, *Addescompe* 1416, *Addescombe* 1456, that is 'enclosed land of a man called Æddi', from Old English *camp* and an Old English personal name. The same man *Æddi* may have given name to ADDINGTON.

Addle Hill City. *Adling Hill* 1596, earlier *Adhelingestrate* 1244, *Athelingestrate* 1280, *Adlingstreet* 1591, that is 'street of the prince or princes', from Old English *ætheling* (genitive case singular *-es* or plural *-a*) and *strǣt*, *compare* WATLING STREET (also in the City).

Addle Street City. *Adelstrete* 1537, *Addelstrete* 1557, earlier *Addelane* 1304, *Adellane* 1360, from Old English *adela* 'a dirty, muddy place'. The contrast between the origins of this and the previous name is to be noted.

Adelphi Westminster. The unusual name given to this imposing riverside development is from Greek *adelphoi* 'brothers', to commemorate the four famous brothers who designed and built it in the late 18th century—John, Robert, James, and William Adam. Streets within the district include Adelphi Terrace, Robert Street (named after the most gifted of the four), and John Adam Street.

Agar Grove & Place Camden. Recall the former district of *Agar Town*, a squalid shanty town developed in the 1830s by William *Agar*, an eccentric and miserly lawyer who had leased the land some years earlier. It was mostly swept away in the 1850s and 1860s when the railway stations at ST PANCRAS and KING'S CROSS were built. The dreary and impoverished locality at the centre of *Agar Town* was once known euphemistically as *La Belle Isle*.

Albany Westminster. Named from Frederick, Duke of York and *Albany*, second son of George III, who lived here at the end of the 18th century. He also gives his name to **Albany Street** (on the east side of REGENT'S PARK), but is perhaps more poignantly commemorated in the familiar nursery rhyme as 'the grand old Duke of York' on account of his inglorious career as Commander-in-Chief of the English army fighting the French in the Netherlands.

Albany Park Enfield. Created *c.*1902, like nearby Albany Road probably so named to commemorate Leopold, Duke of *Albany*, youngest son of Queen Victoria, who died in 1884. **Albany Park** in Bexley is more recent, a 1930s estate giving name to the station in 1935 and 'The Albany' public house in 1937.

Albert Bridge (Road) (in Battersea) Wandsworth. Bridge built in 1871–3, named after Prince *Albert*, see next names.

Albert Embankment Lambeth. Riverside road between LAMBETH and VAUXHALL constructed in 1866–70 after the embanking of the river, so named in honour of Prince *Albert*, *compare* VICTORIA EMBANKMENT.

Albert Hall & Memorial (near Knightsbridge) Westminster. The Hall was built 1867–71, the Memorial 1872–6, as national memorials to Prince *Albert*, Queen Victoria's consort, who died in 1861.

Albyns Farm (near Rainham) Havering. Marked as *Albyns* on the Ordnance Survey map of 1888, earlier *the land of Albyn* 1385, a manorial name from the family of Walter *Albyn* 1257; the farmhouse itself dates from the 16th century.

Aldborough Hatch Redbridge. Marked thus on the Ordnance Survey map of 1883, earlier *Aldborough Hacche* c.1490, *Aberryhatche* 17th century, *Abury Hatch* 1805, probably a manorial name from the *Alborgh* or *Albourgh* family mentioned in 14th- and 15th-century records, with Old English *hæcc* 'a hatch gate' (originally giving access to Hainault Forest, *see* HAINAULT). *Aberry* or *Abury* represent the old local pronunciation of the name.

Aldermanbury City. Street named from an ancient manor recorded as *Aldremanesburi* c.1124, *Aldermanesbury* c.1194, *Aldermannebur* 1279, *Aldermannebury* 1336, that is 'manor of the alderman', from Old English *ealdormann* and *burh* (dative case *byrig*). The person referred to may have been an *alderman* in the post-Conquest sense 'chief officer of a City ward', but the word here may have the older sense 'nobleman of the highest rank'. Indeed if the name is rather older than the earliest spellings, it is possibly a reference to Æthelred, son-in-law of Alfred the Great and *Ealdormann* (i.e. 'underking') of Mercia who was for some time, from 886 until his death in 911, also governor or overlord of London, *see* QUEENHITHE.

Aldersbrook Redbridge. *Aldersbroke* 1535, *Aldersbrook* 1805, 'brook where alders grow', from Middle English *alder* and *broke*. The original brook was a small tributary of the River RODING. The earlier name for the farmstead here seems to have been *Nakethalle* or *Nagethalle* 1383, *Nakedhall Hawe or Alderbroke* 1531, literally 'naked hall', from Middle English *naked* (in one of its senses 'bare, exposed, unoccupied or unfurnished') and *hall*, with *hawe* 'hedge, enclosure'.

Aldersgate Street City. *magnus vicus de Aldredesgate* ('great street of *Aldredesgate*') 1266, *Aldresgatestrete* 1303, named from *Ealdredesgate* c.1000, that is 'gate associated with a man called Ealdrēd', from Old English *geat* and an Old English personal name. *Aldersgate*, originally constructed by the Romans in the 2nd to 3rd century when the City wall was built, was an entrance into the City from the north; the road through it may have linked up with WATLING STREET. The gate probably acquired its name in the late Saxon period, and was finally demolished in 1761. It gave name to one of the ancient wards of the City.

Aldgate City. Street earlier known as *Alegatestrete* 13th century, *Aldgate Street* 17th century, named from the eastern gateway into the City first built by the Romans *c*.200. The gate itself was first referred to by the Saxons as *Æst geat* 1052, that is 'east gate', from Old English *ēast* and *geat*. However in 1108 it is referred to as *Alegate*, this being the usual spelling in medieval times from which the modern name is derived. The meaning is 'ale gate', from Old English *ealu* and *geat*, probably denoting a place where ale was sold and consumed. Weary travellers from Essex were no doubt in need of refreshment on entering the City! Certainly by the early 15th century there was a tavern here referred to as the *Saresyneshede withynne Algate* ('Saracen's Head inside Aldgate') in 1423. It should be noted that the -*d*- in the modern spelling *Ald*- is intrusive and unhistorical, appearing only from the 17th century. Aldgate is also the name of one of the ancient wards of the City.

Aldwych Westminster. Crescent-shaped street created in 1903 and named after the medieval settlement in this vicinity (just outside the City) recorded as *Vetus vicus* (Latin) 1199, *Aldewic* or *Aldewich* 1211, *Oldewiche* 1393, *Aldewyche* 1398, that is 'the old trading settlement', from Old English *ald* and *wīc*, *see* DRURY LANE. This is a particularly interesting and significant name, since it probably refers to the extensive commercial settlement known as *Lundenwic* which flourished in this area between the 7th and 9th centuries, *see* Introduction: 'The Anglo-Saxon Period'.

Alexandra Palace & Park Haringey. Marked thus on the Ordnance Survey map of 1877, named in honour of *Alexandra*, the Danish princess who married Edward Prince of Wales in 1863 and who became Queen when he came to the throne as Edward VII in 1901. The Palace itself, known colloquially as 'the Ally Pally', was opened in 1873. In its chequered history this vast exhibition building has been rebuilt twice after being ravaged by fire (in 1873 and 1980), it has served both as a barracks for British soldiers and a prison for German prisoners of war (1914–18), and it has housed the world's first television transmitter and the BBC studios (1936–56).

Allfarthing Lane (in Earlsfield) Wandsworth. Preserves the name of the old manor of *Allfarthing* or *Half Farthing* (as it is marked on the Ordnance Survey map of 1816), earlier *Elverding* c.1230, *Alferthyng* 1268, *Halfefarthing* 1544, that is 'division of an estate consisting of half a fourth part', from Old English *healf* and *fēorthing*, *see* EARLSFIELD.

All Saints (in Poplar) Tower Hamlets. Station named from All Saints Church in East India Dock Road, built 1821–3.

Alperton Brent. *Alprinton* 1199, *Alpertone* 1282, *Alpurton* 1350, *Aperton alias Alperton* 1578, that is 'farmstead or estate associated with a man called Ealhbeorht', from an Old English personal name with Old English medial -*ing*- and *tūn*.

Amen Corner City. So called in 1661, earlier *Amen Lane* 1603. One of a small group of names near ST PAUL'S referring either to the writers of religious texts living in this vicinity or to the prayers recited during processions of the Cathedral clergy round the precincts, *see* AVE MARIA LANE and CREED LANE.

Anerley Bromley. Recorded thus on the Ordnance Survey map of 1904, named from the first house built on this hilly part of Penge Common (*see* PENGE) by a Scotsman William Sanderson in the mid-19th century, which he called by the Scottish word *anerly* 'solitary, lonely'.

Angel Islington. District and station named from a former coaching inn on the Great North Road called the *Angel* dating from the 17th century. The inn name is also preserved in nearby Angel Mews. The inn was rebuilt in 1819 and flourished throughout the 19th century, but there is now a bank on the site. The station is named on the Ordnance Survey map of 1904.

Angell Town (near Brixton) Lambeth. Residential district developed in the 1850s and named after the *Angell* family who owned land here from the late 17th century.

Angel Road (at Edmonton) Enfield. Station named from the street which is marked thus on the Ordnance Survey map of 1877, so called from an inn of that name.

Aperfield Bromley. *Apeldrefeld* 1242, *Appeldorefeld* 1253, *Apeldurfeud* 1270, *Apperfield* 1819, that is 'open land where apples trees grow', from Old English *apuldor* and *feld*.

Aquarius Golf Course (near Honor Oak) Southwark. Owned by the Metropolitan Water Board, so aptly named from the astrological sign of the zodiac meaning 'the water carrier'.

Archway Islington. Originally named from the 19th-century stone-built arched viaduct designed by John Nash to carry Hornsey Lane across the cutting (which became Archway Road) made through Highgate Hill (*see* HIGHGATE). This was demolished and replaced in 1897 by the present graceful iron arch designed by Sir Alexander Binnie.

Ardleigh Green Havering. Marked as *Hardley Green* on the Ordnance Survey map of 1883, earlier *Hadleygrene* 1514, *Hardey Green* 1777, named from *le Haddeleye* 1362, that is 'heath clearing, clearing where heather grows', from Old English *hæth* and *lēah*, with the later addition of Middle English *grene* 'village green'.

Arkley Barnet. Recorded as *Arkleyslond* 1332, *Arcleylond* 1436, *Arkeley* 1547. This is a difficult name, but taking into account a local field name *Erkefordemad* 1332, it looks likely that the first element of both names is Old English *(e)arc* 'an ark, a chest, a bin or other receptacle, especially perhaps one used when fishing' (it is the word found in the surname Arkwright 'a maker of arks'). Thus, Arkley would then be 'woodland clearing by the ark, or where arks are made', from Old English *lēah* with the addition of *land* 'cultivated ground', and the 14th-century field name would be 'meadow at the ark ford', with Old English *ford* and *mæd*. There are various streams in the neighbourhood, one of them crossed by **Arkley Lane** which is *Arcleylane* in 1436, from Old English *lane*.

Arnos Grove (at New Southgate) Enfield. Named from an estate called *Arnoldes Grove* 1551, *Arno's grove* c.1865, that is 'grove or copse of the *Arnold* family' (who are mentioned in local documents from the 14th century), from Old English *grāf(a)*. The house here, now called Southgate House, was built in 1723. **Arnos Park** nearby takes its name from the same family.

Arrandene (at Mill Hill) Barnet. Open space named from a mansion (built 1789) called *Arran Dean* (no doubt with reference to the Island of Arran) by its Scottish owner c.1868 (earlier known as *Rose Villa*). It is still marked as *Rose Villa* on the Ordnance Survey map of 1877, but appears as *Arran Dean* on the later map of 1904.

Arsenal Islington. Station named from the ground of Arsenal Football

Club nearby. The club moved here in 1913, having been founded in 1884 at the Royal Arsenal in WOOLWICH.

Ave Maria Lane City. *Ave-maria aly c.*1510, *Aue Mary lane* 1603, a reference to writers of religious texts who once lived in this area, or to the recitation of the *Ave Maria* (the Hail Mary) and other prayers during processions by the clergy of ST PAUL'S, *see* AMEN CORNER and CREED LANE which are both nearby.

Avenue Park (at Cranford) Hounslow. Once the grounds attached to the 18th-century *Avenue House* (demolished in 1949).

Avery Hill (near Eltham) Greenwich. Marked thus on the Ordnance Survey map of 1876, but called *Pollcat End* on the earlier map of 1805. The land here was called *Aviary* in 1839 and *Avery* in 1847, so it is possible the name refers to an earlier 'aviary'. The name Avery Hill was later given to the splendid Italianate mansion built in 1890 (from 1906 used as a teachers' training college and now part of GREENWICH University). **Avery Hill Park** was opened in 1903.

Ayletts (near Rainham) Havering. Marked thus on the Ordnance Survey map of 1883, earlier *Elliots* on maps of 1777 and 1805 and recorded as *Aylwards* in 1568, a manorial name from the family of John *Ayleward* 1339.

B

Baber Bridge Hounslow. Recorded thus on Norden's map of 1593, named from *Babbewrth* 1268, *Babbeworth* 1274, that is 'enclosed settlement of a man called Babba', from an Old English personal name and Old English *worth*. The bridge carries the old road to the west (now Staines Road, earlier *Stanes way* 1438 and *Brentford Great Road* 1652) over the River CRANE.

Bakerloo Line. A perfectly good portmanteau invention for the first underground railway to cross London from north to south, opened in 1906 to run between BAKER STREET and WATER*LOO*. At first the line proved to be rather a flop and the name, apparently coined by the *Evening News*, was frowned upon as vulgar and undignified!

Baker Street Westminster. Recorded thus in 1794, named after the builder William *Baker* who laid out the street in the second half of the 18th century on land leased from the estate in MARYLEBONE of Henry William Portman, *see* PORTMAN SQUARE. Remarkably enough, Baker Street's most famous resident (at No. 221B) was a purely fictional character, the detective Sherlock Holmes created by Sir Arthur Conan Doyle in 1887!

Balham Wandsworth. *Bælgenham* 957 (Anglo-Saxon charter), *Belgeham* 1086 (Domesday Book), *Balgeham* 1103, *Balam* 1472, probably 'smooth or rounded enclosure', from Old English **b(e)alg* (dative case *-an*) and *hamm*. Until the mid-19th century, Balham was still a rural hamlet, called *Balham Hill* on the Ordnance Survey map of 1816. The original settlement lay on STANE STREET, the Roman road from London to Chichester (now Balham High Road, the A24), so that in a sense it was a 'gateway to the south' long before Peter Sellers in the 1960s made the place familiar far beyond south London with his brilliant depiction of 'Bal-ham, Gateway to the South'! The local pronunciation of the name is of course 'Balam', without any hint of the medial -*h*-.

Ballards Farm Road, Ballards Plantation & Way (in South Croydon) Croydon. Preserve the old names *Ballardes Wood* 1544, *Ballards Farm*

1765, *Ballards* 1819, all from a family called *Ballard* recorded in this area as early as 1263.

Balls Pond Road (at Canonbury) Islington. Recorded thus in 1841, so called from a spot marked *Balls Pond* on the Ordnance Survey map of 1822. The large pond here (surviving until the early 19th century) was named from John *Ball* who lived near NEWINGTON GREEN in the 17th century.

Bandonhill Sutton. *Bandon* 1203, *Bandone* 1229, *Bendon* 1229, *Bandonhill* 1876, that is 'hill where beans are grown', from Old English *bēan* and *dūn*, with the later (strictly tautological) addition of *hill*. The beans in question would have been both 'horsebeans' and 'broad beans': in early times the latter were an essential element in the poor man's diet, *see also* BENHILTON some 2 miles west from here.

Bank City. Station named from the Bank of England, which was first established in 1694, although its first building on the present site was completed in 1734. The Bank's popular nickname, 'The Old Lady of THREADNEEDLE STREET' (from its situation in this street), dates from the beginning of the 19th century.

Bankhurst Road (in Catford) Lewisham. Preserves the name of the old manor of *Bankhurst* (recorded thus in 1809), earlier *Bankers maner* 1361, *Bankers* 1484, a manorial name from the *de Banquelle* or *Bonquer* family who possessed lands here from the 13th century.

Bankside Southwark. *the Banke syde* 1554, *Banckes syde* 1593, *the bank side* 1603, that is 'street or district alongside the bank of the Thames', from Middle English *banke* and *side*. In early times the area around this street was well known for its entertainments, which included bear-baiting, brothels, and (from the end of the 16th century) theatres like the *Rose* (built 1586–7), the *Swan* (1594–6), the *Globe* (1598–9), and the *Hope* (1613), *see* BEAR GARDENS and ROSE ALLEY.

Barbican City. Recorded as *Barbikan* c.1260, *Barbekan* 1295, *le Barbecan* 1307, *la Barbican* 1315, from Old French *barbacane* 'an outer fortification of a city or castle, usually with a watchtower'. It probably referred to a fortified tower built to keep watch on routes from the North entering the City at ALDERSGATE.

Barking Barking & Dagenham. *Berecingum* 731, *Berchinges* 1086 (Domesday Book), *Berking* 1193, *Barking* 1289, that is '(settlement of) the family or followers of a man called *Berica', from an Old English personal name with *-ingas*. This is therefore an Anglo-Saxon folk name of ancient type like EALING and HAVERING, each representing settlements of individual family or tribal groups in the early part of the Anglo-Saxon period. **Barking Abbey**, a great Benedictine nunnery founded in the 7th century (*c*.675), was demolished in 1535 with the dissolution of the monasteries. An indication of its prestige and importance in medieval times is that it included among its abbesses no less than three queens, two princesses, and the sister of Thomas Becket; its remains, near the magnificent 15th-century church of St Margaret, give name to ABBEY ROAD in Barking. Before the rapid growth of the town with the coming of the railway in 1854, the main industry in Barking was fishing, centred on BARKING CREEK; there were still over 200 fishing smacks here in the early 19th century. The London Borough of Barking & DAGENHAM was created in 1965.

Barking Creek (where the River Roding flows into the Thames at Barking). Recorded as *Barking Creek* in 1588, *Barking Creekes* or *le Fleete* in 1609, earlier referred to as *flēot* in an Anglo-Saxon charter of 958 (describing the bounds of EAST and WEST HAM), from Old English *flēot* 'an inlet or creek' later replaced by the synonymous Middle English *creke*. It gives its name to the area called CREEKMOUTH.

Barkingside Redbridge. Marked as *Barking Side* on the Ordnance Survey map of 1805, earlier *Barkingside* 1538, that is '(place) beside BARKING', from Middle English *side*, referring to its situation on the extreme edge of the old parish of Barking.

Barnehurst (near Crayford) Bexley. Residential district named from the station (marked thus on the Ordnance Survey map of 1905), so called because the land here belonged to Colonel *Barne* (who was also chairman of the BEXLEYHEATH Railway Company), *see* BARNES CRAY. This was formerly a wooded area; the Middle English word *hurst* indicates 'a copse or wooded hill'.

Barn Elms Richmond. *Barnes Elms c*.1540, *Bernelmes* 1580, *Barn Elms* 1876, 'the elm trees near BARNES', from Old English *elm*; the original spelling *Barnes Elms* is still found as late as the Ordnance Survey map of 1816. This was formerly the manor house of Barnes, demolished 1954.

Barnes Richmond. *Berne* 1086 (Domesday Book), *Bernes* 1222, *La Berne* 1244, *Barnes* 1387, that is '(place by) the barn or barns', from Old English *bere-ærn* (literally 'barley house'). The spelling *Berne* 939 sometimes cited is from a spurious charter. The manor was held in medieval times by the Dean and Chapter of ST PAUL'S. **Barnes Bridge** (built 1846–9) is marked on the Ordnance Survey map of 1876. **Barnes Common** is *le Comyn* 1469, *The Comon of Barnes* 1665. **Barnes Green** is *Berne grene* 1443, *Barnes Greene* 1608, from Middle English *grene* 'village green'.

Barnes, West Merton, *see* WEST BARNES.

Barnes Cray (near Crayford) Bexley. Marked thus on the Ordnance Survey map of 1876, earlier *Barns Cray* on the 1805 map, that is 'estate on the River Cray belonging to the *Barne* family', *see* CRAY. This family owned land here in the late 18th century, *see also* BARNEHURST.

Barnet (borough). The modern borough (created in 1965) is named from the ancient settlement, recorded as *Barneto c.*1070, *Barnet* 1197, *la Bernet* 1235, *La Barnette* 1248, that is 'the land cleared by burning', from Old English *bærnet*, referring to the clearing of this once densely forested area in early times. The three manors of **Barnet** were distinguished one from another at an early date, see following entries. CHIPPING BARNET and EAST BARNET were included in Hertfordshire because they were possessions of the Abbey of St Albans, whereas FRIERN BARNET was in the old county of Middlesex because it belonged to the Knights of St John of Jerusalem. **New Barnet** (marked thus on the Ordnance Survey map of 1887) and **Barnet Vale** are areas mainly developed from the end of the 19th century.

Barnet, Chipping Barnet. *Chepyng Barnet* 1321, *Chepinbarnet* 1347, that is 'the BARNET manor with a market', the distinguishing affix being Old English *cīeping*. It was also known as *Westbarnet* 1449 (to contrast with EAST BARNET) and from the 16th century as *High Barnet*, as in *High Bernet* 1575, *Chipping Barnet alias High Barnet* 1628. A market was first granted here in 1199 by King John to the Abbot of St Albans, to whom the manor then belonged, and in 1588 a charter was granted for a horse and cattle market here by Queen Elizabeth I.

Barnet, East Barnet. Recorded as *Est Barnet c.*1275, *Estbarnet* 1294, 'the eastern manor of BARNET', the affix *ēast* distinguishing it from CHIPPING BARNET (earlier often called *Westbarnet*). Nearby **South Barnet** is a 20th-century development.

Barnet, Friern Barnet. *Frerennebarnethe, Frerenbarnet* 1274, *Frerenebarnet* 1294, *Freresbarnet* 1336, *Friern Barnet* 1535, that is 'the BARNET of the brothers', with distinguishing affix Middle English *freren* 'of the brothers', referring to the early possession of this manor by the Knights of St John of Jerusalem. The medieval manor house here, referred to as *Frerynbury* in 1428 (that is 'the brothers' manor', from Middle English *freren* and *bury*), was replaced in the 16th century by a new house called *Friary House* or the *Friary* which was given by Queen Elizabeth I to Sir Walter Ralegh, *see* FRIARY PARK. Friern Hospital was opened here in 1851; it was at first called *Colney Hatch* (*see* COLNEY HATCH) but was renamed in 1937.

Barnet, High Barnet. Now separately marked on maps but originally an alternative name, first recorded in the 16th century, for CHIPPING BARNET.

Barnet Gate Barnet. Marked thus on the Ordnance Survey map of 1822, referring to a former gate on the Barnet Road at the old county boundary between Hertfordshire and Middlesex. The site of the 'gate' is ancient, for it is recorded as *Grendeles gatan* in an Anglo-Saxon charter of *c*.975 describing the bounds of the north part of HENDON, later as *Greensgate* 1574 and *Grinsgate* 1754, that is 'Grendel's gate', an interesting reference to the man-eating monster slain by the hero in the Old English epic poem *Beowulf*!

Barn Hill (near Preston) Brent. Marked thus on the Ordnance Survey map of 1822 and recorded as *Barnhills* in 1800, no doubt self-explanatory, 'hill(s) with a barn'.

Barnsbury Islington. *villa de Iseldon Berners* 1274, *Bernersbury* 1406, *Barnersbury* 1492, *Barnesbury* 1543, that is 'manor of the *de Berners* family', from Middle English *bury*. William de *Berners* held land here in 1235; the surname is from Bernières in Calvados, France. In the 13th-century spelling, *Iseldon* is an early form of ISLINGTON.

Barons Court Hammersmith & Fulham. Name given to an estate built here by Sir William Palliser at the end of the 19th century, and no doubt inspired by nearby EARLS COURT. *Barons* may be a somewhat whimsical allusion to the 'court-baron', an old term for an assembly held by the lord of a manor, or it may be an allusion to the Margrave of Brandenburgh who had a house here *c*.1790 (marked as *Brandenburgh House* on the Ordnance Survey map of 1822) and whose wife Lady Craven gave name to Margravine Road & Gardens (the continuation of Barons Court Road).

Bartholomew Lane City. *Seint Bartilmew lane* c.1350, *saynt Bathellmuw lane* 1553, named from the former church of *St Bartholomew-by-the-Exchange* which is first mentioned c.1150 and which was taken down c.1840 to make way for the new ROYAL EXCHANGE (built to replace earlier London bourses so called, the first opened by Elizabeth I in 1570).

Barwell Court (near Chessington) Kingston. Marked thus on the Ordnance Survey map of 1819 and as *Burrel Court* on Rocque's map of 1765, named from *Berewelle* 1242, *Berewell* 1375, that is probably 'the barley spring or stream' (i.e. near which barley was grown), from Old English *bere* and *wella*, with the later addition of *court* 'manor house'.

Basinghall Street (off Gresham Street) City. Recorded as 'the street of *Basingeshawe*' in 1279, later *Bassings hall streete* 1603, so named from *Bassingshage* or *Bassieshaghe* late 12th century, *Bassingehawe* c.1220, that is 'messuage or enclosure of the *Basing* family', from Old English *haga*, hence also the name **Bassishaw** for this ward of the City. This wealthy and influential family, recorded in London from the 12th century, probably came from Basing or Basingstoke in Hampshire.

Baston Manor (near Hayes) Bromley. *Bestane* 1240, *Bestan*, *Bicstane* 1254, *Bastane* 1301, possibly from Old English **bæc-stān* 'a baking stone, a flat stone used for baking'.

Batsworth Road (in Mitcham) Merton. Preserves the old name *Battesworth* 1235, *Batisworth* 1485, *Battysworth* 1512, *Batchworth* 1840, that is 'enclosed farmstead of a man called **Bætti*', from an Old English personal name and Old English *worth*.

Battersea Wandsworth. *Badrices ege*, *Batrices ege* 693 (11th-century copy of Anglo-Saxon charter), *Patricesy* (*sic*) 1086 (Domesday Book), *Batriseye* 1366, *Battersea* 1595, that is 'island, or dry ground in marsh, of a man called Beadurīc', from an Old English personal name and Old English *ēg*, here referring to a settlement on higher ground in the marshland by the River Thames. **Battersea Bridge**, dating from 1886–90, replaces an earlier wooden bridge built in 1772. **Battersea Park**, opened in 1853, is marked thus on the Ordnance Survey map of 1876; it was developed from part of the area known earlier as *Battersea Fields* (thus on the map of 1816) which was already well known for its places of entertainment along the riverside and its Sunday fairs. The disused **Battersea Power Station**, opened in 1933 and closed fifty years later, remains as a distinctive landmark but still awaits its regeneration.

Battersea Rise is recorded thus in 1718, and is so named from a field called *le Ryse* 1605, *the Rise* 1656; this may be from Old English *hrīs* 'brushwood' with reference to an area once covered with shrubs and brushwood, or from the word *rise* in the sense 'rising or sloping ground'.

Battle Bridge Road Camden. This small street behind King's Cross station preserves the old district name *Battlebridge* (now KING'S CROSS). This was originally *Bradeford* 1207, then *Bradefordebrigge* *c.*1387, becoming *Battle Bridge alias Batford Bridge* 1625, that is '(the bridge at) the broad ford', from Old English *brād* and *ford* with the later addition of Middle English *brigge*. The ford and bridge were across the River *Holborn* (for which, *see* HOLBORN). The relatively late date of the corruption (or rather development) of *Bradeford* to *Battle* (via the intermediate form *Batford*) is to be noted. There is of course no truth in the legend that this was the site of a battle between Queen Boudicca and the Romans!

Bayhurst Wood (near Harefield) Hillingdon. Marked thus on the Ordnance Survey map of 1822, earlier *Baynhurste* 13th century, *wood called Bayhurst* 1522, probably 'wooded hill of a man called Bǣga', from an Old English personal name (genitive case *-n*) and Old English *hyrst*.

Bayswater Westminster. *Bayards Watering Place* 1380, *Bayards Watering* 1652, *Bayeswater* 1659, probably 'the watering place for horses', from Middle English *bayard* 'a (bay) horse' and *watering*. Alternatively, *Bayard* may be a surname (from the same word) bestowed as a nickname on an early landowner or even on some manorial officer who had charge of the watering place, which was where the road to Oxford crossed the Westbourne Brook (*see* WESTBOURNE GREEN). There were still only a few houses at this spot at the end of the 18th century.

Beam Bridge (near Dagenham) Barking & Dagenham. On the site of a medieval bridge called simply *la Beme* in *c.*1210, 'the beam of wood', *see* BEAM RIVER.

Beam River (flowing into the River Thames at Dagenham). Marked thus on the Ordnance Survey map of 1888, a late back-formation from BEAM BRIDGE or DAGENHAM BEAM BRIDGE both of which cross the river. The bridge names go back to medieval times, the first being *la Beme* in *c.*1210, the second *Dagenham Beem* in 1299, from Old English *bēam* 'a beam of wood', referring originally to a tree trunk laid across the stream to form a footbridge. The earlier name of the river itself is *le Markediche* 13th century, *Markedyke* 1301, that is 'boundary ditch' (because it forms the boundary between DAGENHAM and HAVERING), from Old English *mearc* and *dīc*, a name preserved in MARDYKE FARM.

Bear Gardens (near Bankside) Southwark. Named from the bear- and bull-baiting arena once sited here (briefly converted into the *Hope* theatre 1613–16). There is reference to this popular but barbarous entertainment at BANKSIDE as early as 1546, and up to 1670, after which year the bear gardens were closed. The site is approximately that of the reconstructed Shakespeare's Globe Theatre.

Beck, The (stream rising at Spring Park to flow through Kelsey Park into Pool River). A late back-formation from BECKENHAM; the existence of the northern dialect word *beck* (from Old Norse *bekkr* 'a brook') is a nice coincidence.

Beckenham Bromley. *Beohha hammes gemæru* 973 (Anglo-Saxon charter), *Bacheham* 1086 (Domesday Book), *Becheham* 1179, *Bekenham* 1240, that is 'homestead or enclosure of a man called *Beohha*', from an Old English personal name (genitive case *-n*) and Old English *hām* or *hamm*. The first spelling (from a description of the Anglo-Saxon bounds of BROMLEY) contains the Old English word *gemǽre* 'boundary'. An even earlier reference (in another Bromley charter dated 862) is the phrase *Biohhahema mearcæ* 'boundary of the people of Beckenham', from Old English *hǽme* 'dwellers' and *mearc* 'mark, boundary'. **Beckenham Place**, marked thus on the Ordnance Survey map of 1816, was built by John Cator (*see* CATOR PARK) in 1773; it gives name to Beckenham Place Park. **New Beckenham** is a station and suburb (developed from the late 19th century) north of the town. There is a stream here called the BECK, a late back-formation from the place name.

Beckton Newham. Marked thus on the Ordnance Survey map of 1904, a district developed in the late 19th century and named from Simon Adams *Beck*, governor of the Gas, Light and Coke Company which built a large works here opened in 1870. The main estate of *New Beckton*, built in 1881, was also known as CYPRUS.

Becontree Barking & Dagenham. *Beuentreu* (*sic*) 1086 (Domesday Book), *Beghentro* 12th century, *Bekentre* 1238, *Becontre* 1594, that is 'tree of a man called *Beohha*', from an Old English personal name and Old English *trēow*. This was the name of one of the ancient hundreds of

Essex, which had its meeting place on **Becontree Heath**, recorded as *Bekentre hathe* 13th century, *Bentrye Hethe* 1594, *Beacon Tree Heath* 1805, from Old English *hæth* 'a heath'. The original tree would have stood on the heath to mark the place where hundred meetings were held in early times. The Becontree Estate, built by the London County Council in the 1920s and 1930s, was the largest estate of public housing in the world, extending over 4 square miles of DAGENHAM and BARKING and providing nearly 27,000 homes.

Beddington Sutton. *Beaddinctune* 901–8 (Anglo-Saxon charter), *Beddintone* 1086 (Domesday Book), *Bedington* 1229, *Beddyngton* 1340, that is 'farmstead or estate associated with a man called *Beadda', from an Old English personal name with Old English medial connective *-ing-* and *tūn*. **Beddington Corner**, a hamlet so named on the Ordnance Survey map of 1819, refers to the north-west *corner* of the original parish. **Beddington Park** is also marked on the 1819 map, and is recorded earlier as *Ye Parke* 1579, *see* CAREW MANOR. **South Beddington** is so named on the Ordnance Survey map of 1905.

Bedfont, East Hounslow, *see* EAST BEDFONT.

Bedford Hill (in Balham) Wandsworth. Once a private road leading to a large mansion called *Bedfordhill House* (marked thus on the Ordnance Survey map of 1876), so named from the Duke of *Bedford* who owned an estate here.

Bedford Park (near South Acton) Ealing. Residential district built as a garden suburb in the 1870s, the first of its kind in London, named to commemorate the Russells, Dukes of *Bedford*, who had a residence here in the 17th century.

Bedfords Havering. Marked thus on the Ordnance Survey map of 1805, recorded as *Erles alias Bedfordes c.*1480, so called because part of an estate once held by the family of Robert *de Bedeford* 1285, earlier still by the *Earls* of Sussex. It gives name to **Bedfords Park**.

Bedford Square Camden. Laid out *c.*1775 and so named after the Dukes of *Bedford*, within whose estate this lay, *see* RUSSELL SQUARE.

Beech Hill Park (at Hadley Wood) Enfield. Marked thus on the Ordnance Survey map of 1822, named from a mansion called *Beech Hill* 1795, now a golf clubhouse.

Beech Street City. Recorded as *le Bechlane* in 1279, *Bechestrete* in 1285,

Bechelane in 1333, 'lane or street by a locality called *la Beche*'. There is reference to 'land in *la Beche*' in 1257; this is from either Old English *bēce* 'beech tree' or Old English *bece* 'stream'.

Belgravia Westminster. Fashionable residential district developed from the 1820s on land owned by Earl Grosvenor, later 1st Marquess of Westminster, and centred on **Belgrave Square**, so named from Belgrave in Cheshire where the Grosvenors had another estate, *see* GROSVENOR SQUARE & STREET. For the self-conscious and slightly pompous formation, compare *Tyburnia*, for which, *see* TYBURN WAY.

Bell Green (near Lower Sydenham) Lewisham. Marked thus on the Ordnance Survey map of 1816, but shown as *Sydenham Green* on 18th-century maps, *see* SYDENHAM. The origin of the later name is uncertain, but perhaps refers to an early inn here called The Bell.

Bellingham Lewisham. *Beringa hammes gemæru* 973, *Beringaham* 998 (Anglo-Saxon charters), *Belingeham* 1198, *Byllingham* c.1610, that is 'homestead or enclosure of the family or followers of a man called *Bera', from an Old English personal name with Old English *-inga-* (genitive case of *-ingas* 'followers') and *hām* or *hamm*. The earliest spelling (from a description of the Anglo-Saxon bounds of BROMLEY) contains the Old English word *gemære* 'boundary'. The early change of *Ber-* to *Bel-* is due to Norman influence.

Belmont (in East Barnet) Barnet. Named thus in 1811 and on the Ordnance Survey map of 1887, but earlier called *Mount Pleasant* in 1636 and on the 1822 Ordnance Survey map. Both of these are commonly found as 'complimentary' names and are almost synonymous, Belmont being 'beautiful hill' from Old French *bel* and *mont*.

Belmont (at Mill Hill) Barnet. An elegant 18th-century house, named as *Belmont House* on Greenwood's map of 1819, see previous name.

Belmont (near Stanmore) Harrow. Shown as *Bell Mount* on Rocque's map of 1754, and as *Belmount* on the Ordnance Survey map of 1822, another 'beautiful hill' from Old French *bel* and *mont*. There is a marked hill here of some 344 ft.

Belmont Sutton. Marked thus on the Ordnance Survey map of 1905 and so called from the early 19th century, *see* previous names. Earlier, for instance on Rocque's map of 1765, it appears as *Little Hell*, hence no doubt the change of name to something considered more desirable, although here *Hell* may be nothing more sinister than an old dialect form of the word *hill*!

Belsize Park Camden. Named from *Belsize House* (marked thus on the Ordnance Survey map of 1822), earlier *Belassis* 1317, *Belassize* 1360, *Belsise* 1593, that is 'beautiful seat or residence', from Old French *bel* and *assise*. The same complimentary name occurs in other English counties, e.g. Belsize in Hertfordshire. The splendid manor house here, rebuilt in the 17th century, was pulled down in 1854 and its extensive gardens and grounds built over in the following decades.

Belvedere (near Erith) Bexley. Marked thus on the Ordnance Survey maps of 1805 and 1888, originally the name of a mansion built *c*.1740 now demolished, 'the fine view', from Old French *bel* and *vedeir*.

Benhilton Sutton. Earlier *Benhull* 1392, *Benehill* 15th century, *Benehyll* *c*.1480, that is 'hill where beans are grown', from Old English *bēan* and *hyll*. It was still *Beenhill* or *Benhill* on the Ordnance Survey maps of 1819 and 1876 (surviving in Benhill Road & Recreation Ground), so the final -*ton* is only a recent addition in spite of its medieval look. The early cultivation of beans is also referred to in the name BANDONHILL some 2 miles east from here.

Bennet's Hill (off Castle Baynard Street) City. *St Benet's Hill* 1666, named from St Benet's Church (known as St Benet Paul Wharf, built by Wren *c*.1680 on the site of a 12th-century church). In medieval times the street was known as *Haggelane* 1202–4, *Haggen lane* 1260, *Haggenelane* 1279, 'lane of the hags', from Middle English *hagge*, a derogatory term for an old woman.

Bensham Lane (at Broad Green) Croydon. Preserves the name of the old manor of *Benchesham* 12th century, *Bennechisham* 1372, *Bensom* 1721, that is 'homestead or enclosure of a man called Bynic', from an Old English personal name with either *hām* or *hamm*.

Bentley Priory (at Stanmore) Harrow. Marked thus on the Ordnance Survey map of 1822, named from *Benetlegh* 1243, *Binttley* 1291, *Bentleye* 1315, that is 'woodland clearing where bent-grass grows', from Old English *beonet* and *lēah*. The priory here was founded in 1170, but the present building dates from 1777. The Battle of Britain was directed from here in 1940.

Berkeley Square & Street (near Piccadilly) Westminster. The Square was laid out *c*.1730, the Street *c*.1700, both taking their names from *Berkley House*, a mansion built on the north side of PICCADILLY in 1665 for the 1st Lord *Berkeley* of Stratton (the Royalist commander in the Civil War).

Bermondsey Southwark. *Vermundesei* (*sic* for *B-*) *c*.712 (13th-century copy of Anglo-Saxon charter), *Bermundesye* 1086 (Domesday Book), *Bermonsey*, *Barmesey* 1450, that is 'island site of a man called Beornmund', from an Old English personal name and Old English *ēg*, here referring to an 'island' of higher or drier ground amid marshland along the River Thames. The earliest spelling of the name is a scribal error. The second of the spellings dated 1450, *Barmesey*, represents the old local pronunciation of the name, contrasting with the current written form with its more conservative spelling. There was a Cluniac priory here in medieval times, founded in 1082; it became an abbey in 1399 (dissolved by Henry VIII in 1538) which gives name to ABBEY STREET. The dedication of the abbey is alluded to in the name of ST SAVIOUR'S DOCK. **Bermondsey Spa** (near Spa Road) recalls the chalybeate spring discovered here *c*.1770.

Berrylands (near Surbiton) Kingston. Mainly 20th-century development named like SOUTHBOROUGH from the medieval manor of *la Bergh* 1241, later *Barrow* 1819, that is 'the mound or hill', from Old English *beorg*. This area between SURBITON and HOGSMILL RIVER is still shown as agricultural *land* on the Ordnance Survey map of 1905.

Berry's Green (near Cudham) Bromley. Marked thus on the Ordnance Survey map of 1871 and as *Burys Farm* on that of 1819, preserving the name of the old manor of *Bertrey* found as *Berterye* 12th century, *Bertred* 1271, *Betred* 1292, *Bertre* 1316, the second element of which may be Old English **rede* 'clearing' with an uncertain first element.

Berwick Manor (Farm) (near Rainham) Havering. *Berwyk* 1361, *Berwyck* 1412, *Baruuyk* 1496, *Berwick* 1805, from Old English *bere-wīc*, literally 'barley farm' but often denoting 'an outlying part of an estate'. It gives name to **Berwick Pond** and **Berwick Ponds Farm** (this is *Ponds Farm* on the Ordnance Survey map of 1805).

Bethlem Royal Hospital (at Monks Orchard) Croydon. Preserves the ancient name of the Hospital of St Mary of *Bethlehem*, originally a priory founded in 1247 at BISHOPSGATE and recorded as *Bedleem* 14th century, *Bedlam* 1528. In the 14th century the priory became a notorious asylum for the insane, hence the word *bedlam* which is derived from this name. The hospital was moved to MOORFIELDS in 1676, then to a new building in LAMBETH in 1815 (now housing the Imperial War Museum), and eventually in 1926 to its present site.

Bethnal Green Tower Hamlets. *Blithehale* 13th century, *Blithenhale* 1341, *Blethenalegrene* 1443, *Bethnal Greene* 1657, that is probably 'nook of land of a man called *Blītha', from an Old English personal name (genitive case -*n*) and Old English *halh*, with the later addition of Middle English *grene* 'village green'. Alternatively, the first element may be an old stream name *Blīthe* meaning 'the gentle one'.

Beulah Hill (at Upper Norwood) Croydon. *Beaulieu Hill* 1823, named from *Beulestret* 1359, *Bewle* 1456, *Beawley* 1493, *Bulay* 1816, probably 'beautiful place' from Old French *beau* and *lieu* and therefore identical in origin with Beaulieu in Hampshire. In the early 19th century there was a fashionable spa here, centred on a mineral spring discovered in a wooded area called *Bewlys Coppice* at the south end of Beulah Hill and still recalled in the street name Spa Hill in Upper Norwood (*see* NORWOOD).

Beverley Brook (rises in Sutton, flowing through Richmond Park and into the River Thames at Barnes). Recorded as *Beferithi* 693 (in an 11th-century copy of an Anglo-Saxon charter), *Beverey* 1548, *Baveley Brook* 1822, that is 'small stream frequented by beavers', from Old English *beofor* and *rīthig*. The substitution of -*ley* for the more historical -*rey* is found from the 17th century. It gives name to **Beverley Bridge** where the Kingston–Wandsworth road crosses the brook at the south-east corner of Richmond Park (*see* RICHMOND), marked as *Baveley Bridge* on the Ordnance Survey map of 1816.

Bevis Marks (near Aldgate) City. This strange street name is recorded as *Bewesmarkes* 1405, *Bevys Marke* 1450, *Burysmarkys* c.1460, *Buries markes* 1603, apparently meaning 'boundaries (of estate) belonging to Bury' (referring to the Abbey of Bury St Edmunds), from Old English *mearc* 'mark, boundary'. The corrupt spelling *Bevis* seems to have arisen through confusion between the letters *v* and *r* in medieval scripts.

Bexley, Old Bexley (town and borough). *Byxlea* 814 (Anglo-Saxon charter), *Bix* (*sic*) 1086 (Domesday Book), *Bixle* 12th century, *Bexle* 1314, that is 'wood or clearing where box trees grow', from Old English *byxe* and *lēah*. **Bexley Park Wood** is marked thus on the Ordnance Survey map of

1876; it is *Bexley Park* on the earlier map of 1805. The London Borough of Bexley was created in 1965.

Bexleyheath Bexley. Residential area developed from the early 19th century, marked *Bexley Heath* on the Ordnance Survey map of 1876, earlier *Bexley New Town* on that of 1805, so called from the heathland originally lying to the north of BEXLEY.

Bickley Bromley. *Byckeleye* 1279, *Bykeleye* 1292, *Bikeleye* 1297, probably 'woodland clearing on or near a pointed ridge', from Old English **bica* and *lēah*. Bickleigh in Devon has the same origin.

Biggin Avenue (in Mitcham) Merton. Preserves the old name *La Bygg-ynge* 1301, *Biggen* 1587, *Begin* 1765, *Biggin Farm* 1876, that is 'the building', from Middle English *bigging*, *see* next name.

Biggin Hill Bromley. Marked thus on Bowen's map of *c*.1762 and on the Ordnance Survey map of 1871, earlier *Byggunhull* 1499, that is 'hill with or near a building', from Middle English *bigging* and *hull* 'hill'. The element *bigging* is much rarer in the South of England than in the North, since it derives from a Scandinavian word meaning 'to build' introduced by the Vikings. The aerodrome here, particularly famous for its vital role in the Battle of Britain during the Second World War, had already become known affectionately as 'Biggin on the Bump' by pilots and ground staff in the First World War.

Billingsgate Market City. Named from *Billingesgate c*.1000, 1229, that is 'gate of a man called Billing', from an Old English personal name and Old English *geat*. The 'gate' probably referred to the gap in the Roman riverside wall, giving access to the Thames, and also gave name to one of the ancient wards of the City. Cargoes of fish were among the goods landed here from early times, though Billingsgate did not become a specialized fish market until the late 17th century. The fish market was transferred to its new site on the ISLE OF DOGS in 1982.

Billiter Square & Street (off Fenchurch Street) City. The street is *Belthotereslan* (*sic*) 1282, *Belyetslane* 1298, *Belleyettereslane* 1306, *Belleyeter-estret* 1349, that is 'lane (later street) of the bellfounders', from Middle English *belleyetere*.

Birchin Lane (off Lombard Street) City. Recorded as *Bercheruere lane* 1193–5, *Berchervereslane* 1260, *Berchenereslane* 1300, *Birchenlane* 1386, possibly 'lane of the beard-cutters or barbers', from Middle English *berdcherver* and *lane*. The development of the name has been affected by the confusion between *u/v* and *n* in medieval manuscripts.

Birdcage Walk (St James's Park) Westminster. Marked *The Birdcage Walk* on Cary's map of 1808, named after 'The *Bird Cage* in St James Park' mentioned in 1683, this being an aviary for exotic birds originally built by King James I (1603–25) and enlarged by his grandson Charles II (1660–85).

Birkbeck (near Elmers End) Bromley. Station named from the *Birkbeck Estate*, a residential development begun in the 1870s and so called to commemorate the work of Dr George *Birkbeck* (1776–1841), physician, philanthropist, and pioneer in adult education, who was co-founder of Birkbeck College (University of London) in 1823.

Bishopsgate City. Recorded as *Bishopesgatestrete* 1275, *Busshoppes gate Strete c.* 1550, a street named from the main gate into the City from the North (*see* ERMINE STREET), originally built by the Romans *c.*200 and demolished in 1760. It is so called from the tradition that it was rebuilt in the late 7th century by Eorconweald, Bishop of London, and is referred to as *portam episcopi* ('gate of the bishop') in 1086 (Domesday Book). It gives name to one of the ancient wards of the City.

Bishop's Park Hammersmith & Fulham. Riverside park (opened to the public in the early 20th century) near Fulham Palace (*see* FULHAM), official residence of the *Bishops* of London (who were Lords of the Manor of Fulham) until 1973.

Bishopswood Road (at Highgate) Haringey. Preserves the old name *Bishops Wood* (marked thus on the Ordnance Survey map of 1822), earlier *Byssehopeswode c.*1387, that is 'the bishop's wood', from Middle English *bishop* and *wode*, this being part of the Bishop of London's manor in HORNSEY from the earliest times.

Blackbrook Lane Bromley. Preserves the old name *Blackbrook* (marked thus on the Ordnance Survey map of 1876), earlier *Blakebroke* 1278, *Blakebrok* 1327, that is 'the dark-coloured stream', from Old English *blæc* and *brōc*.

Blackfen Bexley. *Blakewenne* 1240, *Black Fen* 1805, that is 'the dark-coloured fen or marshy ground', from Old English *blæc* and *fenn*.

Blackfriars City. Named from a community of Dominicans or 'black friars' (so called from the black mantles worn over their white woollen habit), established originally in 1221 near LINCOLN'S INN but granted a site for a larger monastery on the river here in 1278. The existence of the monastery, dissolved in 1538, is still also recalled in local street-names like Blackfriars Lane & Passage and Friar Street. The first **Blackfriars Bridge** was built 1760–9.

Blackheath Lewisham. *Blachehedfeld* 1166, *Blakehetfeld* 1226, *Blakeheth* 1275, that is 'dark-coloured heathland', from Old English *blæc* and *hæth* (with *feld* 'open land' in the early forms). This was the name of one of the ancient Hundreds of Kent, the meetings of which were held here on **Black Heath**. Indeed the Heath has been an important place of assembly throughout the centuries, from Wat Tyler's gathering of his supporters in 1381 during the Peasants' Revolt to the annual fairs, the first held in 1689. Before the development of the village in the 19th century, the Heath was notorious for its highwaymen. The residential areas known as **Blackheath Park** and **Blackheath Vale** are also 19th-century developments.

Blackhorse Lane & Road (at Walthamstow) Waltham Forest. Recorded as *Black Horse Lane* in 1793, but as *Black House Lane* in 1822 and as *Black Horse or Black House Lane* in 1848. In spite of the early confusion (no doubt reflecting the pronunciation of the name in the local dialect), the streets are so called from *The Black House* which was on the site of the Clock House.

Blackwall Tower Hamlets. *Blakewale* 1377, *Blakwall* 1480, *Blackewall* 1561, self-explanatory, from Old English *blæc* and *wall*, referring to an artificial bank constructed to keep out the river in this low-lying area beside the Thames. **Blackwall Reach**, a stretch of the river marked thus on the Ordnance Survey map of 1822, recorded as *Blackwalle Reache* in 1588, was once used as a mooring place for larger vessels. It was from Blackwall in 1606 that Captain John Smith and his companions set sail to found Virginia, the first permanent English colony in America (named after the 'Virgin Queen', Elizabeth I). The **Blackwall Tunnel** under the Thames linking Blackwall with GREEN-WICH was built 1891–7. Blackwall Yard, closed in 1987, was an important early dockyard established by the East India Company in 1614, *see* EAST INDIA DOCKS.

Blendon Bexley. Marked as *Blenden* on Bowen's map *c.*1762 and on the Ordnance Survey map of 1805, earlier *Bladidun*, *Bladindon* 1240, *Bladindoune* 1327, *Bladyngdone* 1332, probably 'hill associated with a man called *Blæda', from an Old English personal name with Old English medial connective -ing- and *dūn*. *Blenden Hall* is marked on Bowen's map *c*.1762, *Blendon Hall* on the 1876 Ordnance Survey map.

Bloomsbury Camden. *Soca Blemund* 1242, *manerium de Blemund* 1274, *Blemondesberi* 1291, *Blomesburye* 1567, that is 'manor held by the *de Blemund* family', from Middle English *bury* (alternatively with Latin *soca* 'district under a particular jurisdiction' and *manerium* 'manor' in the early spellings). A William *Blemund* is mentioned in connection with the manor of *Totenhale* (*see* TOTTENHAM COURT ROAD) in 1202. The family name probably came from one of two places called Blémont in France. **Bloomsbury Square** (at first called *Southampton Square*) was laid out in the early 1660s by Thomas Wriothesley, 4th Earl of Southampton, to the west of his new house (*Southampton House*) which was built in 1657 and (having changed its name to *Bedford House*) was demolished in 1800, *see* SOUTHAMPTON BUILDINGS, PLACE & ROW. This district, already fashionable by the 18th century, gave its name in the early 20th century to the 'Bloomsbury Group', an association of artists and writers (among them Virginia Woolf, Vanessa and Clive Bell, and E. M. Forster) many of whom lived here.

Blythe Hill (near Catford Bridge) Lewisham. Marked thus near to *Blythe House* (built *c*.1830) on Bacon's map of 1888, possibly a transferred name or so called from the surname of some local person or family.

Bog Lodge (in Richmond Park) Richmond. Marked thus on the Ordnance Survey map of 1904, so called from a marshy area called *The Bog* which also gives name to Bog Gate.

Bollo Bridge Road, Bollo Lane (in Acton) Ealing. The bridge is recorded as *Bolebregge* 1229–39 and *Bolholbregge c*.1470, the lane as *Bolhollane* 1408, that is 'the bridge and lane at bull hollow', from Old English *bula and hol* with the addition of *brycg* and *lane*. The bridge was over STAMFORD BROOK which was referred to as *Boller Brook* in 1826.

Bond Street Westminster. Fashionable shopping street named after Sir Thomas *Bond*, Comptroller of the Household to Queen Henrietta Maria (widow of Charles I). The southern end known as **Old Bond Street**, recorded thus in 1754 and earlier as simply *Bond Street* in 1708, was developed (principally by Bond) *c*.1684. The northward extension to OXFORD STREET, now known as **New Bond Street** (recorded thus in 1732) was added in the 1720s.

Bonner Hall Bridge (near Victoria Park) Tower Hamlets. Named from *Bonners Hall* 1745, 1822, *Bishop Bonners Hall* 1808, earlier *Bisshops Hall* 1495, a former house of the Bishops of London, lords of the manor of Stepney, one of whom, Bishop *Bonner*, was here in the 16th century. The site of the hall, pulled down *c.*1800, was partly in what is now VICTORIA PARK. Note also the nearby street names Bishop's Way and Bonner Road.

Bonner Hill Road (in Norbiton) Kingston. Named from *Bonner Hill* 1575, earlier *Baneworth* 1342, *Bonworthe hill* 1550, that is 'enclosed settlement of a man called Bana', from an Old English personal name and Old English *worth*, with the later addition of *hill*.

Borough, The Southwark. District named as *Southwarke borow* in 1559, *the borough of Southwarke* in 1603, *Borough Southwark* in 1677, from the word *borough* (from Old English *burh*) in the sense 'suburb of a city (lying outside the wall)', so called in contrast to the 'City' just across LONDON BRIDGE, *see* SOUTHWARK. **Borough High Street** was itself called *Long Southwark* in 1603, *The Borough or Long Southwark* in 1682, later simply *(The) Borough* until the middle of the 18th century, *see* STANE STREET. **Borough Market** has its origins in medieval times, developing in the 13th century from a market at the southern end of LONDON BRIDGE.

Bostall Heath & Woods Greenwich. Named from *Borstall* 1254, *Borstalle* 1264, *Burstalle* 1354, that is 'place of refuge or protection', from Old English *borg-steall*. Borstal in Kent (near Rochester) has the same origin. The word itself survives in south-east dialects as *borstal* 'winding path up a steep hill'.

Boston Manor (House) (at Brentford) Hounslow. *Bordeston* 1377, *Burston* 1547, *Boston* 1593, *Boston Farm & House* 1822, possibly 'farmstead or estate of a man called *Bord', from an Old English personal name and Old English *tūn*. Alternatively the first element may be the Old English word *bord* in the sense 'border' (referring to its situation on an old parish and hundred boundary). The present manor house here dates from 1662. If the spelling *Bordwadestone* 1175–7 belongs here, the etymology would need to be reconsidered as containing a personal name or other elements of uncertain form and origin.

Botany Bay Enfield. Marked thus on Greenwood's map of 1819. This transferred name (from the site of an early Australian convict settlement in the late 18th century near what is now Sydney) was here as elsewhere bestowed on a spot considered rather remote and inaccessible. The hamlet is situated in the middle of ENFIELD CHASE, no doubt developing after the enclosure of the Chase in 1777.

Botolph Lane (off Eastcheap) City. *Seyntbotulfeslane* 1349, *Botulpheslane* 1432, named from the 12th-century church of *St Botolph Billingsgate* which was destroyed in the Great Fire of 1666. This was one of four medieval City churches dedicated to this saint: another St Botolph's church at ALDGATE gives name to **St Botolph Row & Street**.

Botwell Common Road, Botwell Lane (at Hayes) Hillingdon. Preserve the ancient name *Botwell* (marked thus on the Ordnance Survey map of 1816–22) which is earlier recorded as *Bote wælle* in 831 (Anglo-Saxon charter), *Botewell* 1266, that is probably 'the healing spring or stream', from Old English *bōt* 'remedy' and *wella*.

Bounds Green Haringey. *Boundsgrene* 1608, *Bounds Green* 1822, earlier *le Boundes* 1365, 'village green associated with the family called *Bo(u)nde*', from Middle English *grene*. John *le Bonde* and Walter *le Bounde* are mentioned in local records from the 13th century.

Bow Tower Hamlets. *Stratford* 1177, *Stratford atte Bowe* 1279, *Stratford at the Bowe* 1494, *Stratford the Bowe* 1543, *Stratford bowe* 1547, *Bowe* 1594, *Stratford le Bow* 1822, from Old English *boga* 'an arched bridge', originally the same name as STRATFORD (Newham) but called *Stratford atte Bowe* ('at the arched bridge') to distinguish this place (then in Middlesex) from the Essex Stratford on the other side of the river. The bridge itself, said to have been built in the 12th century by Queen Maud, wife of Henry I, and referred to as early as 1294, no doubt replaced the original ford here as well as the one at OLD FORD. **Bow Church** (a station name) refers to the church of St Mary first built as a chapel in 1311, the only relic of the former medieval village which once surrounded it. **Bow Common** is marked thus on the Ordnance Survey map of 1822. **Bow Creek** (the mouth of the River LEA where it joins the Thames and in fact earlier called *Luymudhe* 13th century, *Leymoth* 1547, from Old English *mūtha*) is so named on Rocque's map of 1754. **Bow Road** (a station name) is the name of a stretch of the old main road from London to Essex.

Bower House Havering. Marked thus on a map of 1777 and on the Ordnance Survey map of 1805. The house was built in 1729 near the site of *the Bowre* 1418, 'the royal residence' from Middle English *bour* (Old English *būr*), *see* HAVERING-ATTE-BOWER. When first built it was called *Monthavering* and later *Manor House*. Nearby **Bower Farm** and **Bower Wood** are also named from the former royal palace at Havering.

Bowes Park Haringey. District developed in the 1880s named from an old manor called *Bowes* 1396, marked as *Bowes Farm* and *Bowes (Manor)* on the Ordnance Survey maps of 1822 and 1877, respectively. This is 'estate of a family called *Bowes*'; one John *de Arcubus* (Latin for 'of the bows or arches') occurs in a local document from 1274.

Bow Lane (off Cheapside) City. *Bowlane* 1485, *Bowe Lane* 1537, so called from the 11th-century church of St Mary-le-Bow, which gets its name from the arches (Old English *boga* 'a bow or arch') in the Norman crypt. The famous 'Bow bells', destroyed in the Second World War, were associated with the belief that every true Cockney was born within the sound of their being rung.

Bow Street Westminster. Already so called in 1682, from its curved course, shaped like a *bow*.

Boxers Wood Croydon. To be associated with *Boxford* 1403, probably a manorial name from the family of a Robert *de Boxeford* mentioned in 1279. In 1461 there is mention of *Boxfordesmere*, that is 'boundary of the *Boxeford* estate' from Old English *mære*; Boxers Wood is on the old boundary between CROYDON and COULSDON.

Bread Street City. *Bredstrate c.*1165, *Bredstret* 1204, *Bred Strate* 1223, that is 'street where bread was baked and sold', from Middle English *bred* and *strete*. This was one of several specialized market streets near the main market of *Cheap* (for which, *see* CHEAPSIDE), and gave name to one of the ancient wards of the City.

Brent (borough). New borough created in 1965, uniting the former boroughs of WEMBLEY and WILLESDEN and named from the River BRENT.

Brent, River (rises near Totteridge in Barnet and flows into the Thames at Brentford). Recorded as *Brægente* 959 (Anglo-Saxon charter), *Brainte* 1202, *Breynte* 1347, *Brent c.*1540, a Celtic river name meaning 'holy one' from a word **brigantiā* which was also the name of a goddess (thus suggesting a cult of river worship in ancient times). It is known as DOLLIS BROOK in its upper course and is also fed by SILK STREAM.

Brent Cross Barnet. Named from the intricate crossroads and flyover near to the old hamlet of *Brent Street* in HENDON, which is marked thus on the Ordnance Survey map of 1822 and is earlier *Braynestreete* (sic) 1613, *Brent Street* 1710, that is 'hamlet by the River BRENT', from Middle English *strete*. Nearby **Brent Bridge** (*Braynt Bridge* 1662) and **Brent Reservoir** (created 1835–9 and marked thus on the Ordnance Survey map of 1877) are also named from the river, *see also* WELSH HARP.

Brentford Hounslow. *Breguntford* 705, *Bregentforda* 781 (Anglo-Saxon charters), *Breinford* 1222, *Brentford* 1593, that is 'ford over the River BRENT', from a Celtic river name (meaning 'holy one') and Old English *ford*. The ford was no doubt where the main road to the west crossed the river just above its junction with the River Thames. A bridge (replacing the ford) on the site of **Brentford Bridge** at the west end of the High Street existed at least as early as the 13th century and is recorded as *Braynford brigge* in 1463. **Brentford Ait** is an island in the Thames, from Middle English *eyte* or *ayte* 'small island'. **Brentford End** is a residential district developed in the early 20th century. **New Brentford** (formerly in the parish of HANWELL) is recorded as *Newe Braynford* 1521 and was earlier *Westbraynford* 1294. **Old Brentford** (formerly in the parish of EALING) is *Old Braynford* 1476, earlier *Estbraynford* 1294. There were notable battles at Brentford in 1016 (between King Edmund Ironside and Cnut) and in 1642 (in the Civil War between Royalists and Roundheads).

Brentham Garden Estate Ealing. Modern name for residential district developed 1901–15 on land once part of Pitshanger Farm (*see* PITS-HANGER PARK) near to the River BRENT.

Bretons (near Rainham) Havering. Marked as *Britons* on the Ordnance Survey map of 1805, earlier *Bretouns* 1359, *Breteynes* 1517, a manorial name from the family of Ralph *Briton* 1177; the house itself dates from the late 17th century.

Brick Lane (at Spitalfields) Tower Hamlets. *The Brick Lane* 1542, *Brickkill lane* 1622, that is 'brick or brick kiln lane', from the manufacture of bricks and tiles in this area from the 16th century.

Bride Lane (off Fleet Street) City. *vico* ('street') *Sancte Brigide* 1205, *venella* ('lane') *Sancte Brigide* 1279, *Bridelane* 1349, *Seintebrideslane* 1379, 'St Bride's lane', named from the church of St Bride or St Bridget. The present church, built by Wren *c*.1670, stands on the site of earlier churches dating back to Saxon and Norman times. A holy well near here dedicated to St Bride gave name to *Bridewell*, a palace built in 1515–20 by Henry VIII on the banks of the FLEET river, later given by Edward VI to the City for use as a workhouse and prison (demolished 1863–4). It is recalled in the street name **Bridewell Place** (off New Bridge Street).

Bridge Within & Without, wards of the City, *see* LONDON BRIDGE.

Brimsdown Enfield. *Grymesdoun* 1420, *Grymesdoune* 1441, *Grymes downe, Brymesdowne* 1610, *Grymsdown, Brymsdown* 1686. There has been a curious change of initial consonant in this name. Originally the first element seems to have been the surname *Gryme* (but perhaps *compare* GRIM'S DITCH), with Middle English *doun*, here 'slightly raised ground' (in low-lying marshy area beside River LEA).

British Museum, *see* SLOANE SQUARE & STREET.

Brixton Lambeth. *Brixiges stan* 1062 (Anglo-Saxon charter), *Brixiestan* 1086 (Domesday Book), *Brixistane* 1279, *Bryxston c*.1530, that is 'stone of a man called Beorhtsige', from an Old English personal name and Old English *stān*. This place gave its name to one of the ancient hundreds of Surrey, so that the 'stone' may well have been one marking the meeting place of the hundred. **Brixton Hill** is marked thus on the Ordnance Survey map of 1816; a gallows was erected here in the 1720s, specifically to deal with highwaymen who haunted this main route between London and CROYDON. **Brixton Prison** was opened in 1820 as a *Surrey House of Correction*.

Broad Green Croydon. Marked thus on the Ordnance Survey map of 1819, earlier *Brode grene* 1543, *Broode greene* 1573, self-explanatory, 'the broad village green', from Middle English *brode* and *grene*.

Broad & Little Sanctuary Westminster, *see* SANCTUARY.

Broad Street, Old & New City. Old Broad Street is *Bradestrate c*.1212, *Bradstrete* 1255, *Bradestrete* 1279, *Brodestrete* 1513, 'the broad street', from Middle English *brade* and *strete*. The street name became the name of a City ward in the late 13th century.

Brockley Lewisham. *Brocele* 1182–4, *Brokele* 1270, *Brockele* 1328, *Brookley* 1690, probably 'woodland clearing of a man called *Broca'*, from Old English *lēah* with an Old English personal name. Alternatively, the first element may be Old English *brocc* 'badger', giving a meaning 'badgers' clearing', or Old English *brōc* 'brook'. The area was still heavily wooded in the 18th century.

Brockley Hill (at Stanmore) Harrow. *Brokeley Hill* 1593, *Brockley hills* 1682, probably named from *Brokhole* or *Brokholes* 1277, *le Brocholes* 1354, 'the badger holes', from Old English *brocc-hol* with the later addition of *hill*. The soils of this area, with alternations of sand and loam known as Claygate Beds, would have provided favourable sites for badgers' setts. The site of the important Romano-British posting station and settlement of *Sulloniacis* ('estate of a man called Sullonios') was near here on WATLING STREET.

Brockwell Park (near Tulse Hill) Lambeth. Recorded thus on the Ordnance Survey map of 1904, formerly the grounds of *Brockwell Hall* which is so marked on the Ordnance Survey map of 1816. The present hall (damaged by fire in 1990) was built in 1813 on the site of an earlier house. If the name Brockwell is an old one, it probably represents 'badger stream', from Old English *brocc* and *wella*, in which case it might well be an earlier name for the River EFFRA which runs alongside the park. The open-air swimming pool in the park, the well-known Brockwell Lido which dates from 1937, is sometimes referred to as 'Brixton Beach'.

Bromley (town and borough). *Bromleag* 862, *Brom leage* 973 (Anglo-Saxon charters), *Bronlei* 1086 (Domesday Book), *Bromlega* 1178, that is 'woodland clearing where broom grows', from Old English *brōm* and *lēah*. This is the usual meaning of the name Bromley found in other counties like Essex and Hertfordshire, but compare the next name for a different etymology. The early charters cited give the bounds of Bromley in 862 and 973 during the reigns of Æthelberht (King of Wessex and Kent) and Edgar (one of the first Kings of all England). **Bromley College** was founded in the late 17th century as an almshouse for the widows of clergy. **Bromley Common** is marked thus on Bowen's map of *c.*1762 and on the Ordnance Survey map of 1819; there was a race course here in the 18th and 19th centuries, closed in 1874. **Bromley Palace** (now part of Bromley Civic Centre) was built in 1775 on the site of a medieval manor house belonging to the Bishops of Rochester who were lords of the manor of Bromley; in the grounds was a chalybeate spring known as *St Blaises's Well*, discovered in 1754 and once famous for its medicinal waters. **Bromley Park** is a district west of the town mainly developed from the end of the 19th century. The London Borough of Bromley was created in 1965.

Bromley Tower Hamlets. *Bræmbelege c.*1000 (Anglo-Saxon charter), *Brembellee* 12th century, *Brambeley c.*1128, *Bromlegh* 1274, that is 'woodland clearing where brambles grow', from Old English *bræmbel* and *lēah*. In spite of some early confusion of the first element with Old English *brōm* 'broom' (*see* previous name), spellings with -*a*- like *Brambeley* and *Bramley* are usual up to the end of the 16th century. **Bromley-by-Bow**, so called from its proximity to BOW, is so named in 1786. In medieval times there was a Benedictine convent at Bromley dedicated to St Leonard (hence St Leonard's Street), founded *c.*1100; this was no doubt the nunnery alluded to when Chaucer describes his Prioress as speaking French 'after the scole of Stratford atte Bowe' in the Prologue to the *Canterbury Tales*, *see* BOW. The residential district of **South Bromley** was still mainly farmland on the Ordnance Survey map of 1822.

Brompton Kensington & Chelsea. *Brompton* 1294, *Bromton* 1309, *Brumpton* 1380, *Brumeton* 1610, that is 'farmstead or estate where broom grows', from Old English *brōm* and *tūn*. **West Brompton** is marked as *Old Brompton* on the Ordnance Survey map of 1822. **Brompton Hospital** was founded in 1842. **Brompton Oratory** was built in 1879–84.

Brondesbury Brent. *Bronnesburie* 1254, *Brondesbury* 1291, *Brondesbiri* 1328, *Brundesbury* 1535, that is 'manor of a man called Brand', from an Anglo-Scandinavian personal name and Middle English *bury*. The *Brand* in question may have been the canon of ST PAUL'S of that name *c.*1200, *see also* BROWNSWOOD PARK. **Brondesbury Park**, not developed as a residential area until the early 20th century, is still marked as parkland on the Ordnance Survey map of 1904, and is earlier shown as *Brandsbury House* and *Brandesbury Park* on the maps of 1822 and 1876.

Brook Green Hammersmith & Fulham. *Brookegreen* 1616, *Brook Green* 1822, 'village green by a brook', from Middle English *broke* and *grene*. The brook here, referred to *c.*1420 as *le Brooke*, is now covered over. On the Ordnance Survey map of 1822, a neighbouring place just to the west has the delightful name *Cacklegoose Green*.

Brookmans (near Upminster) Havering. Marked thus on the Ordnance Survey map of 1883, no doubt a manorial name from a family called *Brookman*.

Brook Street (in Mayfair) Westminster. Marked thus on Rocque's map of 1746. The 'brook' referred to is the River *Tyburn* which once flowed here (its valley still marked by the dip in the street), *see* MARYLEBONE and MAYFAIR.

Broomfield House & Park (near Palmers Green) Enfield. *Broomfield House* is marked thus on the Ordnance Survey map of 1877, *Broomfield Grove* on the earlier map of 1822, though the house itself is shown on a parish map of the late 16th century. They are named from *Bromefeyld c.*1530, 'tract of land where broom grows', from Old English *brōm* and *feld*.

Broom Hill (near Orpington) Bromley. Marked thus on the Ordnance Survey map of 1819, self-explanatory.

Brownswood Park & Road (near Stoke Newington) Hackney. Preserve the name of the old manor of *Browns Wood*, earlier *Brandeswode c.*1250, *Brouneswode* 1291, *Broundeswode* 1450, 'wood of a man called Brand', from an Anglo-Scandinavian personal name and Middle English *wode*. The man in question may well be the same *Brand* who gave name to BRON-DESBURY, since both manors belonged to ST PAUL's in medieval times.

Broxhill Common & Road Havering. Named from Brox Hill, earlier *Brokisbourghe(s)hilles* 1542, that is 'hills at the badger's burrows', from Middle English *brok* and *borow* with *hill*.

Bruce Castle & Grove Haringey. *Bruce Castle*, marked thus on the Ordnance Survey map of 1877, takes its name from a manor called *Bruses* 1353, *Le Bruses in Totenham* 1375, *Breuses* 1487. This is 'estate of the *Bruse* family', the same powerful Scottish family who had earlier produced the famous Robert Bruce, crowned King of Scotland in 1306 and leader of the army that defeated Edward II at Bannockburn in 1314. The castle, an Elizabethan manor house rebuilt *c.*1670, is now a museum. **Bruce Grove** is named from the castle.

Brunel University (at Uxbridge) Hillingdon. Established here in 1966–7, having been originally founded as Brunel College of Advanced Technology at ACTON in 1957. It is named from Isambard Kingdom *Brunel* (1806–59), the famous engineer who was responsible for the Great Western Railway which went through Acton.

Brunswick Park Barnet. Residential district developed from the late 19th century, perhaps an allusion to the ducal house of *Brunswick*, see next name.

Brunswick Square (in Bloomsbury) Camden. Laid out 1795–1802 and named after Princess Caroline of *Brunswick*, whose disastrous marriage to the Prince Regent, later George IV, took place in 1795.

Buckingham Palace Westminster. The present Palace stands on the site of *Buckingham House* 1708, so named after John Sheffield, Duke of *Buckingham*, who had it built in 1702 (on land partly leased from the Crown) and whose heir sold it to George III in 1762. This building was rebuilt and much enlarged in the 1820s and 1830s according to the designs of John Nash and Edward Blore, becoming Queen Victoria's favourite town residence when she came to the throne in 1837. The site was earlier known as *Mulbury Garden feild* 1614, *The Mulberry garden* 1668, the walled garden having been planted with thousands of mulberry trees by James I who apparently had the grand idea of establishing a silk industry in London.

Bucklersbury City. Street named from a tenement called *Bukerelesbury* 1270, *Bokerelesbury* 1275, *Bokerelesberi* 1278, that is 'manor of the *Bukerel* family', from Middle English *bury*. This wealthy and influential family appears in London records from *c*.1100.

Buckskin Hall (in East Barnet) Barnet. Recorded as *Buckskyn Hall* in 1652. On the edge of ENFIELD CHASE and thought to have belonged to one of the keepers, so that this is probably a nickname for a house associated with the *buckskin* clothing worn while hunting.

Budge Row (off Cannon Street) City. Preserves the old name of *Bogerowe* 1342, *Bogerouwe* 1359, *Bugerowe* 1384, *Bouge Rowe* 1554, 'row of houses where budge (a kind of fur consisting of lambskin with the wool dressed outwards) was sold', from Middle English *bugee* or *boge* and *rowe*.

Bulls Cross Enfield. Recorded thus *c*.1580 and on the Ordnance Survey map of 1822, earlier *Bollyscrosse* 1540, 'crossroads associated with the family called *Bolle* or *Bull*' (who are mentioned in local documents from the 13th century).

Bullsmoor (Lane) Enfield. Marked as *Bellsmore* on the Ordnance Survey map of 1822, earlier *Bellesmore lane* 1619, *Belsmoor Lane* 1754, 'marshy ground associated with a family called *Bell*', from Middle English *more*. The modern spelling is due to influence from nearby BULLS CROSS.

Bunhill Fields (near Finsbury) Islington. *Bonhilles* 1544, *Bonhil Field* 1567, *Bunne Hill* 1615, *Bunhill Fields Burying Ground* 1799, that is 'fields with heaps of bones', from Middle English *bon(e)* and *hill* (here in the sense 'heap or mound'). It is recorded that human remains were brought here from ST PAUL'S charnel house in 1549, but the fields were clearly in use as a burial ground before that, and indeed continued in use, mainly by nonconformists, until 1854. Among the monuments here are those to John Bunyan (1688), Daniel Defoe (1731), and William Blake (1827).

Bunker's Hill (near East Finchley) Barnet. Named thus *c.*1840, commemorating the famous American battle of *Bunker Hill* Massachusetts, fought 17 June 1775, in which the colonial forces were defeated.

Burgess Park (in Walworth) Southwark. Created in the 1950s and 1960s by demolishing derelict houses and factories, it now extends to over 135 acres and includes London's largest post-war lake. It began as a small area known as *North Camberwell Open Space*, later (*c.*1965) becoming *St George's Park* and eventually (late 1960s) Burgess Park after a local councillor.

Burlington Arcade & Gardens, Burlington House, New & Old Burlington Street (near Piccadilly) Westminster. Burlington House in PICCADILLY, much rebuilt and enlarged over the years, was originally a mansion built by the 1st Earl of *Burlington* in 1665. The streets recall his estate in this area, *see also* SAVILE ROW.

Burnt Oak (near Edgware) Barnet. Marked thus on the Ordnance Survey map of 1904, area named from *Burnt Oak Close & Field* 1754, fields on the parish boundary no doubt so called from an oak tree that had been struck by lightning and was used as a boundary mark.

Burnt Stub (in Chessington) Kingston. A pseudo-Gothic mansion (now part of Chessington Zoo, *see* CHESSINGTON) built in the 19th century, but the name is older. It appears as *Burnt Stubb* on the Ordnance Survey map of 1819 and as *Burn Stub Farm* on Rocque's map of 1765, the original meaning being 'burnt tree stump', from Middle English *stubb*.

Burrage Grove, Place & Road (in Plumstead) Greenwich. Preserve the name of the old estate known as *Borowash maner* 1464, *Burgh Asshe* 1482, *Burwage* 1537, *Burrish-place* 1778, so called from the *de Burghersh* family (originally from Burwash in East Sussex) who had lands here in the 14th century.

Burroughs, The (at Hendon) Barnet. Recorded thus on the Ordnance Survey map of 1877, earlier *land called Borowis c.*1530, *Burrowes* 1574,

Burrows 1822, probably 'the animal burrows', from Middle English *borow*, with reference to holes made by badgers, foxes, or rabbits.

Bursted Wood (near Barnehurst) Bexley. *Burnes stede*, *Burnestede* 814 (Anglo-Saxon charter), *Borstede* 1301, *Burstede* 1334, that is 'stream place', from Old English *burne-stede*. This term may have been used for 'a bathing place' or for 'a watering place for cattle'. A small stream is shown on the Ordnance Survey map of 1876.

Bury Farm (near Edgware) Barnet. Named from EDGWARE BURY.

Bury Street (off Bevis Marks) City. *Burye street* 1508, named from the Abbey of Bury St Edmunds which possessed an estate here, *see* BEVIS MARKS.

Bushey Mead (at Raynes Park) Merton. Residential estate built from the 1890s, so named from fields called *Bushey Meadows* 1877 belonging to the Rayne family, *see* RAYNES PARK. The name is self-explanatory, but the estate also came to be known locally as 'The Apostles', with reference to its layout with twelve parallel roads.

Bush Hill (Park) Enfield. Recorded as *Bussheyhill* 1549, *Upper Bushhill* 1608, *Bush Hill* 1822, 'bushy hill, hill covered in bushes', from Middle English *busshi* and *hill*.

Bush Lane (off Cannon Street) City. *Le Busshlane* 1445, *Busshlane* 1511, named from *Le Busshetavern* 1445, 'tavern at the sign of a bush' (an ancient inn sign, originally consisting of a bunch of ivy hung up to indicate a place where wine was sold).

Bushy Park (at Teddington) Richmond. *Bushie Parke* 1650, *Bushey Parke* 1667, *Bushy Park* 1816, probably self-explanatory, 'parkland with bushes', from Middle English *busshi*. Like neighbouring Hampton Court Park (*see* HAMPTON COURT), it once belonged to Cardinal Wolsey and during the reign of Henry VIII was a royal hunting reserve. The elegant Diana Fountain was placed here by Sir Christopher Wren in 1713.

Butts, The (in Brentford) Hounslow. Square recorded with this name in 1664, named from Middle English *butte* 'an archery butt', no doubt because the place was used for archery practice in medieval times, *compare* Newington Butts, *see under* NEWINGTON.

Byron Recreation Ground (at Wealdstone) Harrow. Named to commemorate the poet Lord *Byron* who attended HARROW School in 1801–5.

C

Caledonian Road Islington. Station named from the road which was so called in 1861, from the *Caledonian Asylum*, an orphanage for Scottish children founded in 1815. The road, constructed *c*.1826, was earlier known as *Chalk Road*.

Camberwell Southwark/Lambeth. *Cambrewelle* 1086 (Domesday Book), *Cambyrwell* 1154, *Camerewelle* 1199, *Camberwelle* 1241, from Old English *wella* 'spring or stream' with an obscure first element, just possibly an Old English personal name **Cantbeorht* or **Cantmær*. **Camberwell Green** is recorded as *Camerwell grene* in 1572, from Middle English *grene* 'village green'; an annual fair was still held here up to 1855. **Camberwell Grove**, on the site of the once fashionable *Camberwell Tea Gardens*, is marked *The Grove* on the Ordnance Survey map of 1816. Camberwell was still a small rural village up to the end of the 18th century; the butterfly known as 'Camberwell Beauty' was seen and named here in 1748.

Cambridge Heath Tower Hamlets. *Camprichthesheth* 1275, *Cambridge Heath* 1596, possibly 'heathland of a man called **Cantbeorht*', from an Old English personal name and *hæth*. It is clear that through folk etymology the name was associated with the place name Cambridge at a relatively early date.

Cambridge Park (at Twickenham) Richmond. Named from *Cambridge House* (marked thus on the Ordnance Survey map of 1876), residence *c*.1750 of Richard Owen *Cambridge*.

Camden Park & Place (in Chislehurst) Bromley. Named after William *Camden* (1551–1623), the great antiquarian, who retired to live here in 1609; the mansion is marked as *Camden Place* on the Ordnance Survey map of 1805.

Camden Town Camden. Marked thus on the Ordnance Survey map of 1822, residential area so named in 1795 from Charles Pratt, Earl *Camden* of CAMDEN PLACE (*see* previous name), who died in 1794. He had come into possession of the manor of KENTISH TOWN through marriage, and in 1791 began to let this part of it for building development. In the early 20th century, it gave name to the 'Camden Town Group' of artists (including Sickert, Pissarro, and Augustus John). The London Borough of Camden was created in 1965.

Camlet Moat (near Trent Park) Enfield. Recorded as *(lodge of) Camelot* 1441, *Camelot Moat* 1658, and mentioned as *Camlet Moat* in Scott's novel *The Fortunes of Nigel* (1822), all with reference to the old moat and earthwork here. This is a name full of romantic association, since it clearly derives from the *Camelot* of Arthurian legend. Its situation in the middle of ENFIELD CHASE, a wilderness of clay and woodland in medieval times, is to be noted. By tradition it is also said to be the site of the ancient manor house of ENFIELD, but there is no real evidence for this.

Campden Hill (in Kensington) Kensington & Chelsea. Road and district named from *Campden House*, a mansion built *c.*1612 for Sir Baptist Hicks, created Lord *Campden* (of Campden, Gloucestershire) in 1628; it was rebuilt after a fire in 1862 but was finally demolished *c.*1900.

Canada Water Southwark. Station on the Jubilee Line Extension near **Canada Dock**, so named from the ships that once docked here from this part of the world (nearby streets are Canada Road and Quebec Way), *see* SURREY DOCKS.

Canary Wharf (on Isle of Dogs) Tower Hamlets. This grand commercial development with its massive 850-ft tower (the highest building in the country), begun in 1987, takes its name from a modest fruit warehouse! *Canary Wharf* was the name given to a warehouse built in 1937 for the Canary Islands and Mediterranean fruit trade of a company called 'Fruit Lines Ltd'. The name of the Spanish island of Canary (i.e. *Gran Canaria*, this giving its name to the whole group of 'Canary Islands') is of course also of interest: it is derived (through French and Spanish) from Latin *Canaria insula*, that is 'isle of dogs' (apparently with reference to the large dogs once found here), *see* ISLE OF DOGS.

Canbury Park Road & Canbury Place Kingston. Preserve the old name *Canonbury* 1375, *Canburystret* 1432, *Canbery Stret* 1503, *Canunbury* 1544, that is 'manor belonging to the canons', from Middle English *canoun* and *bury*, alluding to land here held in medieval times by the canons of MERTON priory.

Candlewick, an ancient ward of the City, *see* CANNON STREET.

Cann Hall (near Leyton) Waltham Forest. Marked thus on the Ordnance Survey map of 1883, earlier *Cann Halle* 1276, *Canon Hall c*.1510, *Canhall alias Cannon Hall c*.1580, that is 'hall or manor house of the canons', from Middle English *canoun* and *hall*. It belonged to the canons of *Holy Trinity Priory* within ALDGATE, an Augustinian foundation built in the 12th century and dissolved by Henry VIII in 1532.

Canning Town Newham. First recorded in 1848 and marked thus on the Ordnance Survey map of 1876, a new industrial estate probably named either from Sir Samuel *Canning*, an industrialist who had associations with the manufacturing firm of S. W. Silver & Co (*see* SILVERTOWN), or from George *Canning*, an engineer associated with the development of the docks and railways here.

Cannon Hill (Common) (near Raynes Park) Merton. *Canondownhyll* 1536, *Cannondoune Hill* 1611, *Cannon Hill* 1819, that is 'hill belonging to the canons', so called because the canons of MERTON priory had lands here, from Middle English *canoun* with *doun* 'down, hill' and further 'explanatory' *hill* (although the middle element has now been dropped).

Cannon Street City. Recorded as *Candelewrithstret* 1183, *Candelwrichstrete* c.1185, *Kandelwiccestrate* 1241, *Canwyke strete c*.1430, *Canyngesstrete* 1480, that is 'street of the candlewrights (chandlers or candle makers)', from Middle English *candelwricht* and *strete*. To complete the amazing transformation of this name, the modern form is not found until the 17th century, for instance in Pepys's Diary (1667). The already altered medieval spelling *Kandelwiccestrate* (with loss of *-r-* and change of *-cht-* to *-cc-* in the second syllable) gave name to the old City ward of **Candlewick**.

Canonbury Islington. *Canonesbury* 1373, *Canbury* 1544, *Canonbury alias Canbury* 1552, that is 'manor of the canons', from Middle English *canoun* and *bury*, referring to the canons of ST BARTHOLOMEW'S Priory, Smithfield who were granted land in ISLINGTON before 1253 (probably in the 12th century) by Ralph *de Berners* (*see* BARNSBURY).

Canons Park (near Stanmore) Harrow. Marked thus on the Ordnance Survey map of 1877, named from the estate known as *Canons c*.1525, *Cannons* 1593, *Canons* 1822, so called from the Augustinian *canons* of ST BARTHOLOMEW'S, Smithfield, who were granted 6 acres of land in Little Stanmore (*see* STANMORE) in 1331.

Capel Manor (near Bulls Cross) Enfield. Marked as *Capel House* on Greenwood's map of 1819 and on the Ordnance Survey map of 1887, earlier *Capels* c.1615, a manorial name, 'estate of the family called *Capel*', from Sir George *Capel* 1547.

Carew Manor (at Beddington) Sutton. Named from the *Carew* family, lords of the manor of BEDDINGTON from the 14th century. The original medieval manor house here was rebuilt several times, and the present house (now a school) dates from c.1860. The house was formerly known as *Beddington Park Place* or *House*, and the house and its grounds are recorded as *Ye Parke* 'the park' in 1579, *see* Beddington Park, *under* BEDDINGTON.

Carey Lane (off Gutter Lane) City. *Kyrunelane* 1234, *Kironeslane*, *Kyronlane* 1275, *Kery lane* 1603, possibly 'lane of a woman called *Cynerūn', from an Old English personal name and *lane*.

Carnaby Street (in Soho) Westminster. Street famous in the 1960s for its fashionable clothing boutiques, so named from a house called *Karnaby House* built in 1683 just before the street was laid out. The name is no doubt a surname, or a transferred name, from Carnaby in the East Riding of Yorkshire, 'village of a man called *Kærandi or *Keyrandi', from an Old Scandinavian personal name and *bý* 'village'.

Carshalton Sutton. *Aulton* 1086 (Domesday Book), *Kersaulton* 1218, *Cresaulton* 1235, *Carshaulton* 1279, that is 'farmstead by the river spring where watercress grows', from Old English *æwell* and *tūn*, with the later addition of Old English *cærse* 'cress'. Pre-Conquest spellings sometimes cited (*Æuueltone* 727, *Euualtone* 933) are from spurious charters. The reference is to one of the headsprings of the River WANDLE which feeds the town ponds. There are still watercress beds by the river, and these are mentioned as early as the 13th century. **Carshalton Beeches** and **Carshalton on the Hill** are 20th-century developments to the south of Carshalton on land formerly known as *Carshalton Fields* and *Carshalton Downs* (thus on the Ordnance Survey map of 1876). **Carshalton House** dates from the early 18th century. **Carshalton Park**, marked thus on the Ordnance Survey map of 1819, was once part of the grounds of a mansion called *Carshalton Place* now demolished. The pronunciation of the name is 'Car-shawlton'.

Carter Lane (off Cannon Street) City. *Carterestrate* 1295, *Cartereslane* 1349, *Carterelane* 1397, 'lane where carters lived', from Middle English *cartere* and *lane*.

Carthusian Street (near Barbican) City. Recalls the medieval Carthusian monastery of CHARTERHOUSE.

Castelnau (in Barnes) Richmond. Marked thus on the Ordnance Survey map of 1876–7, originally referring to *Castelnau Villas*, built *c*.1840 and named from Castelnau de la Garde near Nîmes in France where the Boileau family of MORTLAKE, who developed this area of BARNES, had their ancestral home.

Castlebar Hill, Castle Bar Park Ealing. Marked as *Castle Bear Hill* (near *Castle Bear Common*) on Rocque's and Cary's maps of 1741–5 and 1786, as *Castle Bear Hill* (near *Castle Hill*) on the Ordnance Survey map of 1822, and as *Castlebar Hill & Park* on that of 1876–7. They are named from *Castlebeare* 1675, *Castle Beare* 1680, which is from Middle English *castel* 'castle' with an uncertain second element, probably Old English *bær* 'woodland pasture'. The 'castle' in question may have been a 'fortified or castellated mansion', perhaps the house mentioned as being in existence here at least as early as 1641.

Castle Baynard Street City. Recalls the magnificent *castel* or fortified mansion built by the Duke of Gloucester in 1428, much used by Kings and Queens during the 15th to 17th centuries but largely destroyed in the Great Fire of 1666. This imposing building with its high walls and tall towers, situated by the River Thames just to the east of BLACK-FRIARS, took its name *Baynards Castle* or *Castle Baynard* from an earlier Norman military castle at the south-west corner of the City wall (to the south of LUDGATE on the site of what later became the monastery of BLACKFRIARS), built by *Baynard*, a Norman baron who came over with William the Conqueror. Castle Baynard is also the name of one of the old wards of the City.

Castle Green Barking & Dagenham. Residential district mainly developed from the 1930s, named from a former castellated mansion called *Ripple Castle*, built *c*.1800, *see* RIPPLE ROAD.

Catford Lewisham. *Catteford* 1240, *Cateford* 1254, *Katford* 1278, *Cateforde* 1311, that is 'ford frequented by wildcats', from Old English *catt* (genitive case plural *-a*) and *ford*. The ford was across the River RAVENS-BOURNE in what was once woodland. Catford was a small rural hamlet until the coming of the railway in 1857. **Catford Bridge**, now also the name of the station, is on the site of the original ford; the bridge is *Catsford Bridge* on the Ordnance Survey map of 1816.

Cator Park (at Beckenham) Bromley. Commemorates John *Cator*, a local benefactor who built Beckenham Place (*see* BECKENHAM) in 1773.

Cattlegate (near Crews Hill) Enfield. *Cathalgate*, *le Chathalegate* 1441, *Cattle Gate* 1605, *Cathellgate* 1636, named from *Cathale* c.1220, that is 'nook or corner of land frequented by wildcats', from Old English *catt* and *halh*, with the later addition of Middle English *gate* with reference to the northern entrance to ENFIELD CHASE.

Cavendish Place & Square, Old & New Cavendish Streets Westminster. All laid out during the 18th century and named after Lady Henrietta *Cavendish* Holles, wife of Edward Harley, 2nd Earl of Oxford, who inherited the manor of MARYLEBONE.

Chadwell Heath Barking & Dagenham. Marked thus on the Ordnance Survey map of 1805, earlier *Blackheth alias Chaldwell heth* 1609, and named from *Chaudewell* 1254, *Chadwellestrete* 1456, *Chauldwell* 1544, *Chardwell* 1574, that is 'the cold spring or stream', from Old English *ceald* and *wella*, with the later addition of Middle English *hethe*. This area, on the southern fringes of Hainault Forest (*see* HAINAULT), once had a reputation as a haunt for highwaymen and robbers; its older name is recorded as *Blakhethe* in 1440, that is 'dark-coloured heath', *compare* BLACKHEATH. The main hamlet of *Chadwell Street* (note the spelling from 1456) is still marked thus on the Ordnance Survey map of 1805, with *strete* used here in the sense 'hamlet'. Nearby St Chad's Park, together with the dedication of the modern church here to St Chad, are interesting examples of folk etymology, *see* ST CHAD'S PARK.

Chaffinch Brook (rising in Shirley, flows into Pool River at Cator Park). Recorded as *Chaffinch's River* in 1827, apparently a late name from the surname *Chaffinch*. It gives name to Chaffinch Avenue in MONKS ORCHARD and Chaffinch Road in BECKENHAM.

Chafford Heath (near Upminster) Havering. *Chafford Hethe* 1461, named from *Ceford* c.1075, *Ceffeorda* 1086 (Domesday Book), *Cheaffeworda* 1130, *Chaffewurth* c.1175, probably 'enclosure of a man called *Ceaffa', from an Old English personal name and Old English *worth*, with the later addition of Middle English *hethe*. This was the meeting place of the ancient Essex hundred of Chafford.

Chalk Farm Camden. Marked thus on the Ordnance Survey map of 1822, named from *Chaldecote* 1253, *Caldecote* c.1400, *Chalcote* 1593, *Chalk* 1746, that is 'the cold cottage(s)', from Old English *ceald* and *cot* (plural *cotu*). Names identical in origin to this one, usually still spelt Caldecote or Chalcote, occur in most English counties, but their precise significance is uncertain: they may refer to dwellings which are poorly built or which stand in exposed locations, or even to inhospitable spots to which malefactors were once banished. It will be noted that the 'worn-down' form *Chalk* appears relatively late; on the 1822 Ordnance Survey map the old form *Chalcott* still appears beside *Chalk Farm*, these representing the two farms known in the 17th century as *Upper & Lower Chalcot*. In 1822, just before much development took place, they are still both surrounded by open land. The soil here is clay, this emphasizing the fact that the transformation of the original name is due only to phonetic changes and folk etymology!

Chalk Wood (near North Cray) Bexley. Marked thus on a map of 1799, probably to be associated with earlier *Chelkehelde* 1301, 'the chalk slope', from Old English *cealc* and *helde*. This was probably a place where chalk, of great value to early farmers for marling soils, was once dug: there are ancient 'deneholes' (bell-shaped pits from which chalk was extracted) in the vicinity.

Champion Grove, Hill & Park (at Camberwell) Southwark. *Champion Hill* is so named in 1823, this and the other names all commemorating the family of Philip *Champion* de Crespigny who had an estate here and who died at *Champion Lodge* (now demolished) in 1765. The family is also recalled in the nearby street name De Crespigny Park.

Chancery Lane City/Westminster/Camden. *Chauncerylane* 1454, that is 'lane beside the chancellor's office', from Middle English *chauncerie* (a reduced form of *chauncelerie*) and *lane*. It was originally called *Newestrate* 1227, 'new street', then *Converslane* 1279 from a house for Jewish converts to Christianity founded here *c*.1231. When this building (demolished 1896) was later taken over in the 14th century for the use of the keeper of the rolls of Chancery, it came to be called *Chaunceler-eslane* 1338, 'chancellor's lane', before receiving its present name.

Chandos Recreation Ground (at Little Stanmore) Harrow. Named from the Duke of *Chandos* who owned the estate of CANONS PARK in the early 18th century.

Channelsea River (a small tributary of the River Lea at Stratford). Marked *Channel Sea River* on the Ordnance Survey map of 1876, named from an old bridge probably built in the 12th century and recorded as

Chaveresbregge 1302, *Chanelesbrigge* 1312, *Chanells Bridge* or *Charles Bridge* c.1540, from Middle English *brigge* with an uncertain first element, possibly a surname.

Chapel End (at Walthamstow) Waltham Forest. Marked thus on the Ordnance Survey map of 1805, earlier *le Chapellende* 1528, that is 'the part of the parish near the chapel', from Middle English *chapel* and *ende*, with reference to *Higham Chapel* 1521, one of the two chapels once belonging to the manor of Higham (*see* HIGHAM HILL).

Charing Cross Westminster. The first part of the name is recorded early, as *Cyrringe* c.1100, *Cherring* 1198, *La Cherryng* 1258, *La Charryng* 1263, that is 'the turn or bend', from Old English **c(i)erring*, with reference either to the bend in the River Thames here or (more probably) to the well-marked bend in the old main road from London to the West ('Akeman Street', *see* GREAT WEST ROAD) at this point (near to the site of the present TRAFALGAR SQUARE). The second part of the name refers to an 'Eleanor Cross' (the last of twelve crosses set up in 1290 by Edward I at the places where his Queen's coffin rested on its journey from Harby in Nottinghamshire to Westminster Abbey, *see* WESTMINSTER). This medieval cross (a modern replica of which stands in the forecourt of the railway station) is referred to as *The stone cross of Cherrynge* 1334, *La Charryngcros* 1360, from Middle English *cros*, and this gives the place its name. **Charing Cross Station**, built on the site of the former *Hungerford Market* (*see* HUNGERFORD BRIDGE), was opened in 1864.

Charlton Greenwich. *Cerletone* 1086 (Domesday Book), *Cherleton* 1275, *Cherlton* 1292, that is 'farmstead of the freemen or peasants', from Old English *ceorl* (genitive case plural *ceorla*) and *tūn*. This is a common English place name, found in most Southern counties (the Northern equivalent being Carlton). **Charlton House**, marked thus on the Ordnance Survey map of 1888, is a splendid Jacobean mansion built in 1612 (now a library and community centre); the family that owned the manor until 1925 gave their name to MARYON and MARYON WILSON PARKS. **New Charlton** is a mainly late-19th-century development. The somewhat notorious 'Horn Fair' was held at Charlton every October until closed down in 1872, *see* CUCKOLD'S POINT and HORNFAIR PARK.

Charterhouse (near Smithfield) Islington. *Le Charthous next Smythfeld* 1375, *Charterhous* 1385, an adaptation of Old French *chartrouse* 'a house of Carthusian monks'. The monastery here, founded in 1365 on the

site of a Black Death cemetery, gives name to **Charterhouse Square &
Street** and is also recalled in nearby CARTHUSIAN STREET. Having been
dissolved by Henry VIII at the Reformation, it became a school in 1614,
which then removed to Godalming in 1872; only a few of the old
buildings survive.

Chase Cross Havering. Marked thus on the Ordnance Survey map of
1883, 'cross or crossroads by the chase', from Middle English *chace*
'tract of ground for hunting' with reference to Hainault Forest (*see*
HAINAULT) which once extended as far east as this. An earlier spelling
Cheese Cross on a map dated 1777 is probably an error.

Chase Side Enfield. Marked thus on Rocque's map of 1754 and on the
Ordnance Survey map of 1887, 'hamlet beside the chase', with reference to ENFIELD CHASE.

Cheam Sutton. *Ceg(e)ham* 727, 967 (spurious Anglo-Saxon charters),
Ceiham 1086 (Domesday Book), *Chayham* 1226, *Cheyme* 1569, probably
'homestead or village by the tree stumps', from an Old English *ceg
and *hām*. **North Cheam**, marked thus on the Ordnance Survey map of
1876, is a relatively recent development. There was also a *Little* or
Lower Cheam, shown on the 1816 map. But the medieval manor was
already divided as early as 1225 into *Estcheiham* and *Westcheiham*.
Interesting that the 'East Cheam' made famous by Tony Hancock in
the 1960s actually already existed by the 13th century!

Cheapside City. Street name recorded as *Chapeside* 1436, *Chepe Side* 1479,
Chepseyde 1534, that is 'district by the side of *Cheap* ("the market")',
from Old English *cēap* and *sīde*. *Cheap* was the chief market of medieval
London, as well as a main thoroughfare, and the street itself was earlier called simply *Chepe* 1304, *le Chepe* 1377, or alternatively *Westchepe*
1249, *Westchep* 1286, to distinguish it from EASTCHEAP, another ancient market in the City. The market also gave name to one of the old
wards of the City, still known as **Cheap**. The old names of several
specialized market streets which run off Cheapside still survive: these
include BREAD STREET, HONEY LANE, MILK STREET, and WOOD STREET.

Chelsea Kensington & Chelsea. *Celchyth* 789, *Caelichyth* (*sic*) 801 (Anglo-
Saxon charters), *Chelchede* 1086 (Domesday Book), *Chelchuthe* 1300,
Chelsyth alias Chelsey 1556, that is probably 'landing place for chalk or
limestone', from Old English *cealc* (perhaps influenced by an *i*-mutated
derivative **c(i)elce* 'chalk place') and *hȳth*. The spelling *Cælichyth*

suggests early rationalization and confusion with a different word, Old English *cælic* 'cup, chalice'. Chalk, much valued as a commodity in early times for increasing crop yields as well as for building and limeburning, was probably shipped up the Thames from Chalk near Gravesend in Kent (*Cealca c*.975, *Celca* 1086) where there is a natural outcrop, then unloaded and transported (perhaps up WATLING STREET) for use on the clayey Middlesex fields as well as in the City, *see also* CHALK WOOD and LIMEHOUSE. There was formerly a hamlet called *Little Chelsea* (marked thus on the Ordnance Survey map of 1822 and recorded as *Little Chelcy* in 1655) at the west side of the parish on the Fulham Road. **Chelsea Bridge**, dating from 1934, replaced an earlier suspension bridge built in 1851–8. **Chelsea Creek** is a small inlet where the stream called COUNTERS CREEK enters the Thames. The road called **Chelsea Embankment**, made possible by the embanking of this stretch of the riverside, was opened in 1874. **Chelsea Hospital** (The Royal Hospital) was founded by Charles II and built in 1682–92 by Sir Christopher Wren as a home for veteran soldiers (which it still is); its grounds are the annual venue for the famous Chelsea Flower Show. The old borough of Chelsea was amalgamated with that of KENSINGTON to create The Royal Borough of Kensington & Chelsea in 1965.

Chelsfield Bromley. *Cillesfelle* 1086 (Domesday Book), *Chilesfeld* 1087, *Chele(s)feld* 12th century, *Chelesfeld* 1242, that is 'open land of a man called Cēol', from Old English *feld* and an Old English personal name. The original settlement around the 13th-century church is known as **Chelsfield Village**.

Cherry Garden Pier (in Bermondsey) Southwark. So called because it was once the landing stage for the *Cherry Garden*, a popular place of recreation in the 17th century.

Chessington Kingston. *Cisendone* 1086 (Domesday Book), *Chissendon* 12th century, *Chessingdone* 1279, *Chesyngton* 1563, that is 'hill of a man called Cissa', from an Old English personal name (genitive case *-n*) and Old English *dūn*. The spelling *-ton* (eventually replacing historical *-don*) is not found before the 16th century. **Chessington Zoo** was opened here in 1931, *see* BURNT STUB.

Child's Hill (near Cricklewood) Barnet. Marked thus on the Ordnance Survey map of 1822, earlier *Childes Hill* 1593, 'hill associated with a family called *Child*'; a Richard *Child* is mentioned in local records in 1321.

Chingford Waltham Forest. *Cingefort* (*sic*) 1086 (Domesday Book), *Chingeford* 1181, *Chingelford* 1242, *Chyngleford* 1440, that is 'shingle ford', from Old English *cingel and *ford*, referring to gravel or small pebbles. The word *shingle* is not recorded before 1578 but seems to have existed in Old English, as evidenced by this and other names. The original ford was probably where an old road to EDMONTON crossed the River LEA. The name has sometimes been interpreted as 'ford of the dwellers by the stumps', from an original Old English form *cægingaford (with a variant of the element *ceg found in CHEAM), mainly on the basis of the isolated spelling *Chagingeford* 1219. However, in spite of the discovery of the remains of pile-dwellings near the River LEA in the extreme south-west of the parish which might seem to corroborate this etymology, it is linguistically most unlikely. The River **Ching**, a small tributary of the River Lea, is a late back-formation from the place name; it was earlier called simply *the Boorne* 1562 or *the Brook* 1585, from Old English *burna* 'stream' and *brōc* 'brook'. **Chingford Green** is marked thus on the Ordnance Survey map of 1805, as is also **Chingford Hatch**, earlier *Chenkford Hache* 1525 and referred to in the surname of Simon *de la Hache* 1222, from Old English *hæcc* 'a hatch-gate' (giving access to EPPING FOREST). **Chingford Mount** and **South Chingford** are 20th-century developments to the south of the town, near to what was earlier called *Normanshire* (*see* NORMANSHIRE DRIVE).

Chipping Barnet, *see* BARNET, CHIPPING.

Chislehurst Bromley. *Cyselhyrst* 973 (Anglo-Saxon charter), *Chiselherst*, *Chiselhurste* 1158, *Chesilherst* c.1762, that is 'gravelly wooded hill', from Old English *cisel* 'gravel' and *hyrst*. The 'gravel' referred to in the name is still evident in the rounded black flints and pebbles found in fields and gardens here. **Chislehurst Caves**, the remains of ancient chalk mines, were used as air-raid shelters during the Second World War. **Chislehurst Common**, shown as *Chiselhurst Common* on the Ordnance Survey map of 1805, is the site of an old cockpit (a reminder that cockfighting was once a popular sport here as elsewhere until it was prohibited in 1834). **Chislehurst West**, an area mainly developed from the late 19th century, is marked thus on the Ordnance Survey map of 1905.

Chiswick Hounslow. *Ceswican* c.1000, *Chesewic* 1181, *Chiswyk* 1537, *Cheswyke* 1566, that is 'specialized farm or trading settlement where cheese is made', from Old English *cīese and *wīc*. The same name occurs with the same spelling in Essex and in the variant forms Cheswick in Northumberland and Keswick in Cumbria and Norfolk. **Chiswick Bridge**, crossing the Thames to MORTLAKE and the finishing point of the Oxford–Cambridge University Boat Race, was opened in 1933. **Chiswick House** (now belonging to English Heritage) is a splendid Palladian villa built in 1725–9 by the 3rd Earl of Burlington and once the home of the Dukes of Devonshire, *see* DUKE'S MEADOWS. **Chiswick Mall**, recorded from *c*.1800, is so named from PALL MALL. **Chiswick Park** station was so named in 1887. Chiswick is pronounced 'Chizzick'.

Chiswick Eyot Hounslow. A small island in the Thames near CHISWICK, marked as *Chiswick Ait* on Greenwood's map of 1819, from Middle English *eyte*, *ayte* 'islet'. It was earlier known as *Ye Twigg Eight* 1650, that is 'the islet with twiggy brushwood'.

Chobham Road (in Stratford) Newham. Preserves the name of the old manor of *Chabhames* 1412, *Chobhams* 1488, apparently so called from a family called *Chobham* (no doubt from Chobham in Surrey).

Chohole Gate (at south-east corner of Richmond Park) Wandsworth. So named *c*.1745, from a dialect word *chockhole* 'deep furrow or rut in a road'.

Church End (at Finchley) Barnet. So named in 1683 and on the Ordnance Survey map of 1877, 'district (of the parish) by the church', from Middle English *churche* and *ende*, referring to the parish church of St Mary which has 12th-century origins.

Church End (at Willesden) Brent. Recorded as *the Churchend* 1593, identical in origin with the previous name. It refers to the 13th-century church of St Mary here, marked as *St Mary's* on the Ordnance Survey map of 1876.

Church Hill (at East Barnet) Barnet. Recorded as *Church hyll* in 1553, so named from the 11th-century church of St Mary the Virgin.

City, The. The City of London, as defined by its ancient boundaries, is often referred to simply as 'The City'. This usage is found from the end of the 16th century, as in Shakespeare's 'Know you not the Citie fauours them?' (*3 Henry VI*, I.i.67, dated 1593). More particularly, 'The City' is used for the financial and commercial centre of London, hence also for the commercial and business community located here, a usage dating from the mid-18th century. In more colloquial usage, as banking and business centre the City is often known as 'The Square Mile' (with reference again to its ancient boundaries).

Clam Field Recreation Ground Greenwich. From the dialect word *clam* 'damp, cold and sticky'.

Clapham Lambeth/Wandsworth. *Cloppaham* c.880 (Anglo-Saxon Chronicle), *Clopeham* 1086 (Domesday Book), *Clopham* 1184, *Clapham* 1503, that is 'homestead or enclosure near a hill or hills', from Old English **clopp(a)* and *hām* or *hamm*. The two examples of Clapham in Bedfordshire and West Sussex are identical in origin. **Clapham Common** (earlier called *East and West Heath*) is so called in 1718 and on the Ordnance Survey map of 1816; from 1690 the Common was crossed by the first stage coach service into London and became notorious for its highwaymen. **Clapham Junction**, marked thus on the Ordnance Survey map of 1876, is named from the many lines that converged here after the coming of the railway in 1838. **Clapham Park** is so called on the Ordnance Survey map of 1876.

Clapton, Lower & Upper Hackney. *Clopton* 1339, *Clapton* 1593, that is 'farmstead or estate on a hill', from Old English **clopp(a)* and *tūn*. Clapton is situated on high ground descending steeply to the River LEA on the east side. Lower Clapton is marked thus on the Ordnance Survey map of 1822, Upper Clapton on that of 1877. **Clapton Park** is a residential district largely developed at the end of the 19th century.

Clarence House (near St James's Palace) Westminster. Built in 1825–8 for William, Duke of *Clarence*, later William IV.

Claybury Hall (near Woodford Bridge) Redbridge. Marked thus on the Ordnance Survey map of 1883, earlier *le Clayberye* 1270, *Cleyberye* 1566, *Claybury* 1805, 'manor with clay soil', from Old English *clǣg* and Middle English *bury*. It lies just to the north of CLAYHALL.

Clayhall Redbridge. Recorded thus in 1449 and on the Ordnance Survey map of 1883, named from *la Claie* 1203, *La Claya* 1239, 'the clay', that is 'clay soil district', from Old English *clǣg* with the later addition of Middle English *hall* 'manor house'. This area of clay also gives name to CLAYBURY just north of here.

Clay Hill Enfield. *Clayhyll* 1524, *Clayhillgate* 1636, apparently self-explanatory, 'hill with clay soil', with -*gate* no doubt referring to a gate of **ENFIELD CHASE**. However the local name **Claysmore**, earlier *Clayes More Grove* 1610, is to be associated with the family of William *atte Cleye* (that is 'at the clayey place') 1274, John *Clay* 1420, so that even the name Clay Hill may derive from the surname rather than from the word *clay*.

Clay Tye Farm (near Upminster) Havering. Marked thus on the Ordnance Survey map of 1883, earlier *Cley Tey* on that of 1805, probably the home of John *atte Tye* 1327, that is '(living) at the small enclosure', from Middle English *atte* and *tye* (Old English *tēag*), with the later addition of *cley* 'clay'.

Clement's Lane (off Lombard Street) City. Recorded as *vicus sancti Clementis* ('lane of St Clement') 1241, *Seint Clementeslane* 1348, so named after the church of St Clement Eastcheap (recorded by *c*.1100) at the south end of the present lane (which formerly extended further south), *see* **ST CLEMENT DANES** for another early church dedicated to the same saint.

Clerkenwell Camden/Islington. *Clerkenwell c*.1150, *Clerkenewella c*.1152, *Clerekenewelle* 1242, *Clarkynwell* 1551, that is 'well or spring of the scholars or students', from Middle English *clerc* (plural *-en*) and *welle*. In early Latin sources (from *c*.1145) the well or spring is referred to as *fons clericorum*. There is vivid corroboration of the etymology in William FitzStephen's account of London in 1174, in which he describes scholars and youths gathering at this and two other wells (for which, *see* **ST CLEMENT DANES** and **HOLYWELL LANE**) on summer evenings. Another such meeting place for young people in early times may have been **KNIGHTSBRIDGE**. The well site is now beneath the offices of the *New Statesman* in Farringdon Road (*see* **FARRINGDON**).

Clink Street Southwark. Recalls the London estate of the Bishops of Winchester in medieval times, known as the 'Liberty of the Clink', and the site of the notorious prison once belonging to the Bishops, recorded as *the Clynke* in 1524 (apparently much used to lock up those who misbehaved while frequenting the brothels at **BANKSIDE**). The slang word *clink* for 'a prison' is of obscure origin, but may derive from the sound made by clinking chains. The great palace of the Bishops of Winchester, known as *Winchester House*, once lay near here along the bank of the Thames.

Clissold Park (at Stoke Newington) Hackney. Named after the Revd Augustus *Clissold* who married (after much unpleasantness due to the

opposition of her father) the heiress of the Crawshay family, landowners in STOKE NEWINGTON in the 19th century. It was opened with
its present name in 1889; on the Ordnance map of 1877 it is called
Newington Park.

Clitterhouse Recreation Ground (near Cricklewood) Barnet. Preserves
the old name of *Clitterhouse Farm* (marked thus on the Ordnance Survey
map of 1877), earlier *Clyderhous* 1445, *Clitherhouse* 1535, *Clitter House*
1649, *Clutterhouse Farm* 1822, a manorial name meaning 'estate of the
Cliderhou family'; one Robert *de Cliderhou* (from Clitheroe in Lancashire)
is mentioned in local records in 1311. The change from *Clyderhou's* to
Clyderhouse is due to folk etymology.

Clock House (near Beckenham) Bromley. Named from the 18th-century
Clock House at BECKENHAM, a large red-brick mansion demolished in
1896 (so called from the large turret clock on the stable block).

Clock House (near Little Woodcote) Sutton. Suburb named from *Clock-
house Farm* in Woodmansterne, Surrey, compare previous name.

Cloisters Wood (in Stanmore) Harrow. Perhaps so called with reference
to BENTLEY PRIORY or to CANONS PARK, both nearby.

Cloudesley Estate Islington. Built from 1825 onwards on land called *the
Stoney Field* bequeathed to the parish of ISLINGTON by Richard *Cloudesley* in 1517; Stonefield Street (named from the field) is so called in
1735.

Cockfosters Barnet. *Cokfosters* 1524, *Cockffosters* 1610, *Cock Fosters* 1822,
that is 'the chief forester's (place or estate)', from early Modern
English *cock* and *for(e)ster*. The settlement was on the edge of the once
extensive ENFIELD CHASE, *see also* WEST LODGE PARK.

Cock Lane (off Snow Hill) City. *Cockeslane c.*1200, *Cokkeslane* 1311, *Coklane*
1543, probably 'lane where fighting cocks were reared and sold', from
Middle English *cocke* and *lane*.

Cockpit Steps Westminster, **Cockpit Yard** Camden, *see* COCKSPUR
STREET.

Cockspur Street (near Charing Cross) Westminster. Recorded as *Cock
spurr street* in 1753, no doubt so named because spurs for fighting
cocks were once sold here. There was a cockpit for this cruel sport
at WHITEHALL, and other sites are recalled in **Cockpit Steps** on

BIRDCAGE WALK and by **Cockpit Yard** near GRAY'S INN. Cockfighting was not finally banned until 1834.

Coldblow (near Old Bexley) Bexley. Marked thus on the Ordnance Survey map of 1905, no doubt so called from its exposure to cold winds in this location at the edge of Dartford Heath.

Coldfall Wood (near Fortis Green) Haringey. Marked thus on the Ordnance Survey map of 1877, named from *place called Colefall* 1599, probably 'woodland clearing where charcoal was burnt', from Old English *col* and **(ge)feall*. This name, like nearby HIGHGATE WOOD and QUEEN'S WOOD, are reminders that this was once a wooded area, part of 'the bishop's wood', for which, *see* BISHOPSWOOD ROAD.

Coldharbour Point (near Rainham Marshes) Havering. A pointed promontory on the Thames, named from *Coleherbert (sic) c.*1560, *Great & Little Coldharbour* 1777, *Great & Little Cold Harbor* 1805, that is 'cold or cheerless shelter', from Old English *cald* and *here-beorg*. This place out on the riverside marshes must always have been an inhospitable spot, and the name is no doubt a derogatory one. It was the site of a lighthouse on the Ordnance Survey map of 1904. There are several other examples of the name Coldharbour, all with the same origin, in the London area. **Coldharbour** in BLACKWALL (also on the Thames, at the north-west corner of the ISLE OF DOGS) is marked thus on a map of 1703 and is earlier *Coleharbor* 1617. **Coldharbour Road & Way** in CROYDON are named from *Cold Harbour* 1789. **Coldharbour Lane** in CAMBERWELL, mentioned as *Coal Harbour lane* in 1787, is named from *Coldherbergh* 1363. This last was probably transferred from the medieval tenement so called in the City, situated on the Thames just west of LONDON BRIDGE, recorded as *Coldherberghe* in 1317. This messuage was acquired at that date by Sir John Abel (who also came into possession of the Camberwell property). The magnificent riverside house built here by Sir John de Poulteney in the 1330s took its name from the messuage, and after his death in 1349, it passed through several noble and royal hands. It was pulled down by the Earl of Shrewsbury in 1590, and replaced by a tall tenement block (sometimes called *Shrewsbury House* but otherwise known by various forms of the older name, such as *Cold Harbrough* in Stow's *Survey* 1603). This came to be used as a sanctuary for debtors—thus giving new emphasis to the derogatory associations of the name and accounting for its frequent use as a transferred name in the 17th century—until it was burnt down in the Great Fire of 1666.

Coleman Street (off Gresham Street) City. *Colemanestrate* c.1182, *Colemannestrete* 1279, possibly 'street of the charcoal burners or sellers', from Middle English **coleman*. Alternatively, the first element may be the personal name *Col(e)man*; indeed the name may refer to the original dedication to St *Coleman* of the ancient church that once stood in this street, *St Stephen Coleman* (rebuilt by Wren in 1676 but destroyed by bombing in 1940). The street gave name to a City ward by 1224.

Cole Park (at Twickenham) Richmond. Like *Coles Bridge* (marked on the Ordnance Survey map of 1816), to be associated with a local family called *Co(a)le* recorded in the 17th century.

Colham Green Hillingdon. *Collamgrene* 1578, *Collume Green* 1670, named from *Colanhomm* 831 (Anglo-Saxon charter), *Coleham* 1086 (Domesday Book), *Colam* c.1180, that is 'enclosure or river meadow of a man called Cola', from an Old English personal name and *hamm*, with the later addition of *grene* 'village green'. This ancient manor in the parish of HILLINGDON was near to the River PINN.

Colindale Barnet. Marked *Collin Dale* 1877, *Colin Dale* 1904 on early Ordnance Survey maps, earlier known as *Collyndene* 1550, *Culling Deepe* 1584, *Collen Deep* 1675, *Colin Deep* 1822, 'valley associated with a family called *Collin*' (who are mentioned in 16th-century records). The word *dale* has replaced Old English *denu* 'valley' and Old English *dēope* 'deep place', although the latter is still preserved in **Colindeep Lane** (*Collin Deep Lane* 1584). The name refers to the valley of SILK STREAM; indeed the *-deep* seems, remarkably enough, to refer to the feature described as *deopan fura* ('the deep furrow') in an Anglo-Saxon charter of 957 describing a grant of land in the north part of HENDON.

College Hill & Street (near Cannon Street) City. Named from the College of St Spirit and St Mary founded here, together with an almshouse, by Richard Whittington, four times Mayor of London, in the early 15th century, *see* WHITTINGTON STONE.

College Park (near Kensal Green) Hammersmith & Fulham. Alluding to land here held by All Souls College, Oxford, like the two nearby street names All Souls Avenue and College Road in KENSAL GREEN.

Collier Row Havering. Marked thus on the Ordnance Survey map of 1805, earlier *Colyers rewe* 1440, *Colyer(s) Rowe* mid-15th century, *Colley Rowe* 1609, *Collirow* 1694, that is 'row of houses occupied by charcoal burners', from Middle English *colier* and *rewe* or *rowe*. This was originally a hamlet at the edge of Hainault Forest (*see* HAINAULT), and the production of charcoal was clearly once a local industry here.

Collier's Wood Merton. Named from a house so called built in 1777 (on the site of an earlier Elizabethan house) and marked thus on the Ordnance Survey map of 1816. The name, like the local field name *The Colliers Close* 1576, refers to woodland used or occupied by charcoal burners, from Middle English *colier*, and indicates the production of charcoal here in early times.

Colne, River (rises near Hatfield, flowing past Uxbridge to the River Thames at Staines). Recorded as *Colenea* in 785, *Colne* in 894, an ancient pre-Celtic river name of uncertain origin and meaning, identical with the River Colne in Essex. In the earliest form the ending *-ea* represents Old English *ēa* 'river'. It forms the historical boundary between the counties of Middlesex and Buckinghamshire.

Colney Hatch Barnet. *Colnehache, Colnehatche* 1492, *Coanie hatch* 1593, *Colney Hatch* 1822, from Old English *hæcc* 'hatch, hatch gate', referring either to a former gateway of ENFIELD CHASE or to a sluice on a nearby tributary of PYMMES BROOK. The first element is unexplained but may be a family name from Colney in Hertfordshire.

Coney Hall (near West Wickham) Bromley. 1930s residential estate named from a farm called *Coney Hall*, marked thus on a map of 1769 and on the Ordnance Survey map of 1819 but recorded from as early as the 17th-century. The first element is Middle English *coni* 'rabbit'; indeed 17th-century leases indicate that tenants of the farm had sole rights to 'catch coneys' on an area known as *Jacksons Heath*, part of WEST WICKHAM Common (hence also the Victorian mansion here known as The Warren).

Coombe Kingston. *Cumbe* 1086 (Domesday Book), *Combe* 1242, *Cumbe Nevill* 1260, *Coumbnevill* 1318, that is 'the valley', from Old English *cumb* (characteristically denoting a broad, shallow valley), with later manorial affix from the *de Nevill* family here in the 13th century. **Coombe Hill** is *Cumhulle* in 1279, from Old English *hyll* 'hill'. **Coombe Wood** is marked as *Combe Wood* on the Ordnance Survey map of 1816.

Coombe Farm, Lane, Lodge, Park & Wood Croydon. *Combe Farm* and *Combe Lane*, together with *Combe Hill* and *Combe House*, are marked thus on the Ordnance Survey map of 1819; they all take their names from *Combe* 1332, *Coumbe* 1403, that is 'the valley', from Old English *cumb*.

Copenhagen Street Islington. Named from the former *Copenhagen House* (marked thus on the Ordnance Survey map of 1822), earlier *Coopen Hagen* 1680, *Copenhagen* 1735. The house, demolished in 1853, was probably so called because it was occupied by the Danish ambassador during the Great Plague in 1664–5.

Coppermill Bridge & Stream (in Walthamstow) Waltham Forest. Named from the old *Copper Mill* on the River LEA which stood on the site of a medieval mill and which was used to strike copper coins during the Napoleonic Wars (1803–15).

Copse Hill (near Wimbledon) Merton. Marked thus on the Ordnance Survey map of 1876, self-explanatory.

Copse Wood (at Ruislip) Hillingdon. Marked thus on the Ordnance Survey map of 1880, but called *Ruislip Wood* on the earlier map of 1822. However the later name is probably to be associated with *Copshawe* 1436, from Middle English *copis* 'coppice' and *hawe* 'enclosure, tenement'.

Copthall (at Hendon) Barnet. *Copt Hall* 1574, *Copidhall* 1632, 'hall or manor house with a high peaked roof', from Old English *coppede* and *hall*.

Corbets Tey (near Upminster) Havering. *Corbinstye* 1461, *Corbynsty* 1514, *Corbettes Tye* 1588, *Corbettes Tey* 1777, that is 'small enclosure associated with a family called Corbin', from Middle English *tye* (Old English *tēag*). A family of this name is mentioned in local records from the 13th century: the surname *Corbin*, like its replacement *Corbett*, derives from an Old French word meaning 'raven'.

Cordwainer City. An ancient ward of the City, earlier *Cordwainer street ward* as in Stow's *Survey* of 1603, named from *Corueiserestrate* 1217, *Cordewanere-strete* 1230, *Corveyserestrate* 1260, *Cordewanerstrate* 1297, that is 'street of the shoemakers', from Middle English *cordewaner* (literally a worker in cordwain or cordovan leather), alternating in the early spellings with the synonymous term *corveiser*, and *strete*. The street referred to, running south from Cheapside to Upper Thames Street, is now called BOW LANE and GARLICK HILL. The Cordwainers' Company received their first charter in 1439.

Cornhill City. Street named from *Cornehulle* c.1100, *Cornhilla* early 12th century, *Cornhell* 1260, *Cornhulle* 1283, that is 'hill where corn was grown or sold', from Old English *corn* and *hyll*, this being the highest hill in the City. This old name may have arisen at a time when corn was still cultivated within the City wall, or it may indicate an early grain market here. Cornhill is also the name of one of the ancient wards of the City.

Cottenham Park (near Wimbledon) Merton. Recorded thus on the Ordnance Survey map of 1876, so called because *c.*1840–50 this was the estate and residence of Lord Chancellor *Cottenham*.

Coulsdon, Old Coulsdon Croydon. *Cudredesdune* 967, *Cuthredesdune* 1062 (Anglo-Saxon charters, the earliest spurious), *Colesdone* 1086 (Domesday Book), *Culesdon* 1235, *Coulesdon* 1346, that is 'hill of a man called Cūthrǽd', from an Old English personal name and Old English *dūn*, referring to a hill spur to the south of the town. **Coulsdon Common** is marked thus on the Ordnance Survey map of 1816.

Counters Creek (small stream entering the River Thames at Chelsea Creek). So called in 1826, it is named from a bridge called *Countesses-brugge c.*1350, *Contessesbregge* 1421, *Counters Bridge* 1612, that is 'the bridge of the Countess', possibly with reference to the *Countess* of Oxford (the Earl of Oxford gave his name to nearby EARLS COURT). Both the stream and the bridge were on the boundary between the parishes of FULHAM and KENSINGTON.

Cousin Lane (off Upper Thames Street) City. *Cosinelane* 1283, *la Cosynes-lane* 1306, *Cosineslane* 1338, *Cosynlane* 1379, so named from a family called *Cosyn* who owned property here from the end of the 13th century.

Covent Garden Westminster. Recorded as *Covent Gardyn* in 1491, *le Convent Garden* in 1537, that is 'the garden of the convent or monastery', from Middle English *convent* and *gardin*, with reference to a walled enclosure belonging to the monks of the Abbey of St Peter at WESTMINSTER. After the Dissolution of the monasteries in 1535–40, the garden was granted to the Earl of Bedford whose successor built a house here *c.*1590 (known as *Bedford House*, demolished in 1706). The square now known as Covent Garden was laid out in the 1630s as a Piazza on elevated ground adjoining the garden of *Bedford House*. The famous fruit and vegetable market at Covent Garden (since 1974 moved to a new site at NINE ELMS) began with just a few stalls in this Piazza in the 1650s.

Coventry Street (near Piccadilly) Westminster. Recorded thus in 1682, so named from Henry *Coventry*, Secretary of State during Charles II's reign, who had a house here in 1673.

Cowley Hillingdon. *Cofenlea* 959, *Cofanlea* 998 (Anglo-Saxon charters), *Covelie* 1086 (Domesday Book), *Couelegh* 13th century, *Cowelee* 1294, that is 'woodland clearing of a man called *Cofa*', from an Old English personal name and Old English *lēah*, see next name.

Cowley Peachey Hillingdon. *Couele Peche* 1358, *Coulepecche* 1371, *Cowleypechey* 1560, that is 'estate in COWLEY held by the *Pecche* family'. Bartholomew *Pecche* was granted land in Cowley and ICKENHAM in 1252.

Cranbrook (near Ilford) Redbridge. *Cranebroc* 1233, *Cranbroke* 1552, 'brook frequented by cranes or herons', from Old English *cran* and *brōc*. The brook itself (a small tributary of the River RODING) is still called **Cran Brook**, earlier *Cranbrook-rill* 1650, from *rill* 'small stream'.

Crane, River (flowing into the River Thames at Isleworth). The modern name, shown on the Ordnance Survey map of 1876 and appearing as *Cran Brook* in 1825, is a late back-formation from CRANFORD. Its earlier name is *Fiscesburna* 704 (Anglo-Saxon charter), *Fisseburn* 1275, *Fyssheburn* 1305, that is 'the fish's stream', or simply *le Borne* 1375, 'the stream', from Old English *fisc* and *burna*. The upper part of the stream is known as YEADING BROOK.

Crane Park (near Whitton) Richmond. Named from its situation along the River CRANE.

Cranford Hounslow. *Cranforde* 1086 (Domesday Book), *Craunforde* 1211, *Craneford* 1294, that is 'ford frequented by cranes or herons', from Old English *cran* and *ford*. The ford was where the Bath Road crosses the River CRANE; indeed the river name itself is a back-formation from Cranford. **Cranford Bridge** (on the site of the ford) is marked as *Craneford Bridge* on Norden's map of 1593. **Cranford Park**, once the grounds of the 17th-century *Cranford House* (demolished in 1945), was opened as a public space in 1935.

Cranham (near Upminster) Havering. *Craohv* (*sic*) 1086 (Domesday Book), *Crawenho* 1201, *Crauenho* 1241, *Crawenham* 1397, *Craneham* c.1490, that is 'spur of land frequented by crows', from Old English *crāwe* (genitive plural *crāwena*) and *hōh* (the later spelling perhaps reflecting the Old English dative plural *hōum*). In early times it was alternatively known as *Wochedunam* 1086 (Domesday Book), *Wokindon Episcopi* 1254, *Bishopp Wokyndon* 1343, that is 'Bishop's Ockendon' with reference to the possession of part of this manor by the *Bishop* of London, *see* NORTH OCKENDON. **Cranham Hall** was rebuilt in the late 18th century on the site of the old hall, referred to as *Crawehehalle* 1344, from Middle English *hall* 'large residence, manor house': General James Oglethorpe, founder of the American state of Georgia, lived here until his death in 1785. **Cranham Place** is marked thus on the Ordnance Survey map of 1883.

Cranley Gardens Havering. District of MUSWELL HILL so called from the street of this name built from *c*.1895.

Cray, River (rising in Orpington, joins the River Darenth to flow into the River Thames). Recorded as *Cræges æuuelma* 798, *Crægean* 814, *Craie* *c*.1200, an old Celtic river name from the British word **crei* 'fresh, clean', in the first spelling with Old English *æwelm* 'river spring, source'. The river gives its name to no less than six places: BARNES CRAY, FOOTS CRAY, NORTH CRAY, ST MARY CRAY, ST PAUL'S CRAY and CRAYFORD.

Crayford Bexley. *Crecganford* (*sic*) 457 (Anglo-Saxon Chronicle), *Creiford* 1199, *Craiford* 1202, *Crainford* 1322, that is 'ford over the River CRAY', from Old English *ford*. The ford was at the point where the Roman road from Dover to London (WATLING STREET) crossed the river. Indeed this was probably the site of the Roman town of *Noviomagus* (a Celtic name meaning 'new field', or perhaps 'new market'). The early spelling is an error for *Cræganford*; in this entry from the Anglo-Saxon Chronicle, Crayford is the site of an important battle between the invading Jutes and the native Britons of Kent, resulting in a decisive victory for the Germanic incomers.

Creed Lane City. *Crede Lane* 1548, *Creede lane* 1603, a reference to writers of religious texts who once lived in this area, or to the recitation of the *creed* during processions by the clergy of ST PAUL'S, *see* AMEN CORNER and AVE MARIA LANE which are in the same vicinity. In the 14th and 15th centuries it was called *Sporyer Rowe*, that is 'row of houses occupied by spurriers or makers of spurs'.

Creekmouth Barking & Dagenham. Marked thus on the Ordnance Survey map of 1888, earlier *Fletesmouthe de Berkingge* 1323, *Barking*

Creeks Mouth 1805, that is 'mouth or estuary of BARKING CREEK', from Old English *mūtha* 'mouth' with Middle English *creke* 'creek' (replacing Old English *flēot* which had the same meaning).

Crews Hill Enfield. Named from its association with the *Crew* family, mentioned in local records in the mid-18th century.

Cricklewood Barnet/Brent. *le Crikeldwode* 1294, *Crikeledewod* 1321, *Crykyll Wood* 1509, *Krickle Wood* 1754, that is 'the wood with indented outline', from Middle English **crikeled* and *wode*. Even today the large open space here has a very irregular shape.

Cripplegate Street City. Named from one of the City gates built by the Romans (in fact originally leading into the fort at the north-west corner of the City built *c*.120), referred to as *Cripelesgate c*.1000, *Cripelesgata* or *Crepelesgate* in 1068, later *Crepulgate* 1423, *Creplegate c*.1560, from Old English *crypel-geat* 'a low gate in a wall' (literally 'a gate for creeping through'). The gate was situated in WOOD STREET and was finally demolished in 1760. It gave name to one of the ancient wards of the City. Not surprisingly, the name was associated at an early date with *cripples*, and indeed the nearby church of St Giles without Cripplegate, founded in the 11th century, is dedicated to the patron saint of cripples. There is an old street name in Worcester which is identical in origin and meaning.

Crofton Bromley. *Crop tunes gemæro* 973 (Anglo-Saxon charter), *Croctvne* (*sic*) 1086 (Domesday Book), *Crofton* 1240, that is 'farmstead on a rounded hill', from Old English *cropp* and *tūn*. The first spelling (from a description of the bounds of BROMLEY) contains the Old English word *gemǣre* 'boundary'. Remains of a Romano-British villa have been found here.

Crofton Park Lewisham. Name of recent origin for the southern area of BROCKLEY (near the house marked as *Brockley Hall* on the Ordnance Survey map of 1876) not developed until the late 19th century. It first appears in 1892 as the name of a new railway station on the Shortlands and Nunhead Railway.

Croham Hurst Croydon. Marked thus on the Ordnance Survey map of 1876, earlier *Cromehurst* 1605, the first part of which is *Craweham* 1225, *Crouham* 1282, *Crome Farm* 1819, that is 'homestead or enclosure frequented by crows', from Old English *crāwe* and *hām* or *hamm*, with the later addition of *hyrst* 'wooded hill'.

Cromwell Road Kensington & Chelsea. So called from *Cromwell House* (demolished *c.*1850), earlier known as *Hale House* 1606, *Hale House commonly called Cromwell House* 1820, so named from a tradition that Henry *Cromwell*, son of Oliver Cromwell, once lived here (he was certainly married in KENSINGTON, in 1653). The older name is from a lost place called *le Hale* 1400, that is 'the nook or corner of land', from Old English *halh* (dative case *hale*).

Crook Log (in Bexleyheath) Bexley. District and stretch of main road (earlier WATLING STREET) named from land called *Crook Log(g) alias Taylehangers* in 1654 and 1681, later (early 19th century) transferred to 'a common beer shop just outside the Turnpike Gate' known as *Ye Olde Crook Log*. The name no doubt originally referred to the crooked or twisted branch of a felled or dead tree, from the adjective *crook* 'crooked, bent' and *logge* (the early alternative name *Taylehangers* is obscure, but may represent an occupational term 'tile hangers').

Crossharbour (on Isle of Dogs) Tower Hamlets. Station named from a bridge (shown on the Ordnance Survey map of 1904) which crosses Millwall Inner Dock, *see* MILLWALL.

Cross Ness (near Thamesmead) Bexley. Marked thus on the Ordnance Survey map of 1888, a promontory on the River Thames, from Old English *næss* or *ness* 'a piece of land round which a river flows to form a headland', *see* HALFWAY REACH. Perhaps there was once a standing cross on the river bank here.

Crouch End Haringey. *Crouchend* 1465, *Crowchende* 1480, *the Crouche ende* 1482, *Crutche Ende* 1553, that is 'the district around the cross', from Middle English *crouch* and *ende*. It was no doubt the home of Stephen *atte Cruche* and Geoffrey *atte Crouche* (that is 'at the cross') mentioned in local records from the late 14th century. There must once have been a wayside cross at the junction of roads here where the hamlet developed. Nearby **Crouch Hill** (in Islington) is named from this place.

Crowlands (near Romford) Havering. Marked thus on the Ordnance Survey map of 1883, earlier *Crowland* 1514, probably land belonging to the family of John *Crowland* 1480.

Crown Farm (west of Romford) Havering. Marked thus on the Ordnance Survey map of 1904, but called *Pigtail Farm* on earlier maps of 1777, 1805, and 1883. This may refer to a stream or piece of ground thought to resemble in shape the tail of a pig (there is a place called Pigtail on the Isle of Wight which has this origin), but alternatively it may be from Middle English *pightel* 'a small enclosure', with alteration of the form through folk etymology.

Croydon (town and borough). *Crogedene* 809 (Anglo-Saxon charter), *Croindene* 1086 (Domesday Book), *Croienden c.*1150, *Croindone* 1229, *Croydone c.*1240, that is 'valley where wild saffron grows', from Old English *croh* (alternating with an adjectival form **crogen*) and *denu* (the valley referred to is that of the River WANDLE). The Old English word *croh* from Latin *crocus* refers to the plant *Crocus sativus* which may have been introduced into this country (along with the word) by the Romans who used it for dyeing. Croydon was still a relatively small market town in the early 19th century (its market dates back 700 years, the present Surrey Street being recorded as *Le Bocherrowe* in 1549, that is 'butchers' row'). *Croydon Palace* (probably first built in the 13th century and recalled in Old Palace Road & School) was the manor house of the Archbishops of Canterbury who were Lords of the Manor and who used it as their summer residence until 1780, *see* WHITGIFT HOSPITAL & SCHOOL. **Croydon Airport**, opened in 1915, was made London's airport in 1920 and remained important until the late 1940s, finally closing in 1959. The residential district of **South Croydon** was developed from the end of the 19th century. Croydon first became a borough in 1886, but the new London Borough of Croydon was created in 1965.

Crutched Friars (near The Tower) City. Street recorded thus in 1666, earlier *Crouchedfrerestrete* 1405, *Crouched Freres* 1424, *the Cruchydffrers* 1551, that is 'street of the Friars of the Holy Cross', from Middle English *crouched* 'bearing or wearing a cross' (a derivative of Middle English *crouch* 'cross') and *frere*. This order of friars had a small friary here in medieval times, founded *c.*1298.

Crystal Palace Bromley. Marked thus on the Ordnance Survey map of 1876, district named from the spectacular building, originally created in HYDE PARK for the Great Exhibition of 1851 but moved here to this high spot overlooking London later that same year. After functioning for some 85 years as a popular venue for concerts, exhibitions, and other entertainments, it was destroyed by fire in 1936. The structure was first dubbed *Crystal Palace* by the magazine *Punch* on account of its large areas of glass.

Cubitt Town (on Isle of Dogs) Tower Hamlets. Marked thus on the Ordnance Survey map of 1876, district developed during the 1840s and 1850s by the well-known Victorian builder William *Cubitt* (Lord Mayor of London in 1860–1) to house workers at the nearby shipyards, factories, and docks.

Cuckold's Point (in Rotherhithe) Southwark. Recorded thus in 1757, earlier *Cuckolds haven* 1588, a promontory on the bank of the Thames, where at *Cuckold's Point Stairs* otherwise known as *Horn Stairs* a maypole surmounted with a pair of horns was apparently set up in 1562, no doubt as a mockery or warning to cuckolded husbands. Indeed there is probably a connection with the popular 'Horn Fair', held at nearby CHARLTON until 1872 (*see* HORNFAIR PARK), to which visitors with horns on their heads flocked, many arriving by boat (a ferry across the Thames is still shown here on the Ordnance Survey map of 1876). According to local tradition, a miller was granted an estate hereabouts by King John as a kind of recompense for having cuckolded him by seducing his young wife!

Cuddington Golf Course (near Cheam) Sutton. Named from the old village of Cuddington near Ewell, Surrey, *Cotintone* 727, Cudintone 933 (spurious Anglo-Saxon charters), *Codintone* 1086 (Domesday Book), that is 'farmstead associated with a man called Cuda', from an Old English personal name with Old English medial connective *-ing-* and *tūn*. The village was cleared in the early 16th century by Henry VIII to make room for his palace and park of Nonsuch, *see* WORCESTER PARK.

Cudham Bromley. *Codeham* 1086 (Domesday Book), *Cod(e)ham* 1226, *Cudeham* 1278, *Codam* 1458, that is 'homestead or enclosure of a man called Cuda', from an Old English personal name and Old English *hām* or *hamm*.

Curtain Road (in Shoreditch) Hackney. Recorded as *The Curtain Road* in 1682, so called from the Elizabethan theatre known as *The Curtain* which was built here in 1577 and which fell into disuse about 1625. The very first playhouse in London, called simply *The Theatre*, was also opened near here in 1576 (only to be taken down in 1598 and re-erected as *The Globe* in Southwark). Plays were probably performed in both playhouses by the company known as The Chamberlain's Men, which included William Shakespeare himself. The two theatres were near to the famous *Pimlico* alehouse at HOXTON, for which, *see* PIMLICO.

Curzon Street & Place (in Mayfair) Westminster. So named *c*.1710 from the *Curzon* family. The Derbyshire baronet Sir Nathaniel *Curzon* came into possession of *Greate Brooke feilde* (the site of the 'May fair' that gave its name to MAYFAIR) in 1699, and development began soon after.

Custom House Newham. District and station (opened in 1855) named from the Custom House at ROYAL VICTORIA DOCK; it developed as a residential area in the late 19th century.

Cyprus Newham. Alternative name given to *New Beckton*, part of the late 19th-century estate of BECKTON near the ROYAL ALBERT DOCK, apparently to commemorate the surrender of this Mediterranean island to British administration in 1878.

D

Dagenham Barking & Dagenham. *Dæccanhaam* c.690 (8th-century copy of Anglo-Saxon charter), *Dakenham* 1261, *Dagenham* 1274, *Dagnam* 1499, that is 'homestead or village of a man called *Dæcca', from an Old English personal name (genitive case -*n*) and Old English *hām*. **Dagenham Breach**, marked thus on the Ordnance Survey map of 1888 and giving name to *Breach House* 1805, is what remains of a lake formed when a 400-ft *breach* in the Thames wall (which had occurred in December 1707) was repaired in the early 18th century. **Dagenham Dock** station is named after a tidal basin constructed in 1887. **Dagenham Heathway** station is named from Heathway, a main street running north towards the heathland of Becontree Heath (*see* BECONTREE) and CHADWELL HEATH. The old village of Dagenham largely retained its rural character until the early 1900s, after which date its industries rapidly developed: perhaps the best known of the firms established here, the Ford Motor Company, began production at their Thames-side works in 1931. The London Borough of BARKING & Dagenham was created in 1965.

Dagenham Beam Bridge Barking & Dagenham. On the site of a medieval bridge called simply *Dagenham Beem* in 1299, from Old English *bēam* 'beam of wood' (used as a footbridge), *see* BEAM RIVER. By 1427 the bridge here was one made of stone.

Dagnam Park (near Harold Hill) Havering. Marked thus on the Ordnance Survey map of 1805, named from an estate called *Dakenham* 1378, *Dagenhams* 1384, *Dagnams* 1495, this having originally been land belonging in the early 14th century to William *de Dageham* or *de Dakenham* (from DAGENHAM).

Dalston Hackney. *Derleston* 1294, *Dorleston* 1388, *Darleston* 1581, *Dalston* 1741, that is 'farmstead of a man called Dēorlāf', from an Old English personal name and Old English *tūn*. The current local pronunciation of the name is 'Dorlston' (compare the 1388 spelling). For **Dalston Kingsland**, *see* KINGSLAND.

Danson Park (near Welling) Bexley. Marked thus on the Ordnance Survey map of 1805, preserving the old name *Danson* found as *Dansington* 1284, *Densinton* 1301, *Danston* 1327, *Danson* c.1762, possibly 'farmstead associated with a man called *Denesige', from an Old English personal name with medial connective *-ing-* and *tūn*. The Palladian villa here built c.1765 stands in grounds landscaped by 'Capability' Brown who also created the large artificial lake.

Dartmouth Park Camden. Residential district developed from c.1870, named from the Earls of *Dartmouth*, owners of the estate here during the 18th and 19th centuries.

Dawley Parade & Road (at Hayes) Hillingdon. Preserve the name of the old manor of *Dawley*, recorded as *Dallega* 1086 (Domesday Book), *Daulee* 1199, *Dalleye* 1311, *Dawley* 1592, possibly 'woodland clearing at a hollow', or 'woodland clearing held in common', from Old English *dæl* 'pit, hollow' or *dāl* 'share, portion' and *lēah*.

Deans Brook (at Edgware) Barnet. Marked thus on the Ordnance Survey map of 1887, named from *Denes* 1574 and **Dean's Lane** (*Dinns Lane* 1685), probably from a family called *Dene*. The old name of the brook was *Heybourne* 1574, earlier *Yburnan* c.975 (Anglo-Saxon charter), probably 'yew-tree stream' from Old English *īw* and *burna*.

De Beauvoir Town Hackney. Estate developed c.1840 by the *de Beauvoir* family from Guernsey. When they acquired the land in 1687 it was known as *Bammes* or *Baumes*, so named from a family called *Bamme* found in London records from the 14th century.

Denmark Hill Southwark/Lambeth. Named thus on the Ordnance Survey map of 1816, said to be so called from the hunting lodge of Prince George of *Denmark*, husband of Queen Anne whom she married in 1683.

Deptford Lewisham. *Depeford* 1293, *Depford* 1313, *Deppeford* 1314, *Depford* 1334, that is 'the deep ford', from Old English *dēop* and *ford*. The ford was across the River RAVENSBOURNE at the point (now **Deptford Bridge**) where it widens out into **Deptford Creek** to join the River Thames. The medial *-t-* spelling in the modern form, found from the 15th century, is quite unhistorical, but no doubt reflects a change of pronunciation in the name at that date (still currently 'Dettford'). This former fishing village was chosen as the site of a large naval dockyard by Henry VIII, *see* ROYAL NAVAL YARD. The two parishes of St Nicholas and St Paul were otherwise known as *Lower* and *Upper Deptford* (the latter marked thus on Bowen's map of *c*.1762).

Derry Downs (near St Mary Cray) Bromley. So named in 1885 and marked thus on the Ordnance Survey map of 1904, perhaps so called from the surname *Derry* of some local family.

Devilsden Wood Croydon, *see* HAPPY VALLEY.

Distaff Lane (off Cannon Street) City. *Distavelane* 1200, *Distaflane* 1270, that is 'lane where distaffs were made and sold', from Middle English *distaf*, referring to the stick that holds the bunch of flax or wool in spinning. This was an important item in early times—hence of course the phrase 'the distaff side of the family', since it was usually the women who did the spinning.

Dollis Brook (the upper part of River Brent) Barnet. Marked thus on the Ordnance Survey map of 1877, named from Dollis (Farm) in HENDON, earlier *Dalys* 1563, *(the) Doles* 1574, *Dallys* 1584, *Dollis* 1822, probably 'the portions or shares of land (in the common field)', from Middle English *dole*. It is unlikely that this name is to be connected with DOLLIS HILL which lies to the south, in spite of their identical current spellings.

Dollis Hill Brent. *Daleson* (*sic*) *Hill* 1593, *Dalleys Hill* 1612, *Dalleyes Hill* 1619, *Dolleys Hill* 1819, probably 'hill associated with a family called *Dalley*' (who may have come from *Dawley* in Hillingdon, *see* DAWLEY PARADE & ROAD). There is probably no connection between this name and DOLLIS BROOK which flows just north of here. Dollis Hill House, built in 1823, was once the home of the Earl and Countess of Aberdeen, *see* GLADSTONE PARK.

Dormer's Wells Ealing. Marked as *Dormans Well* on Cary's map of 1786 and as *Dormans Wells* on the Ordnance Survey map of 1822, earlier *Dermodeswell*, *Dermundeswell* 1235, *Dormandeswell* 1571, that is 'spring or stream of a man called Dēormōd or Dēormund', from Old English *wella* and an Old English personal name. There is a small stream here flowing into the River BRENT. It might be noted that the plural form *Wells* is a relatively recent development.

Dorset Square (in Marylebone) Westminster. Laid out *c*.1820 after Thomas Lord moved his first cricket ground to its new site (*see* LORD'S CRICKET GROUND), named from the Duke of *Dorset*, a keen patron of the game in its early years.

Dowgate Hill (off Canon Street) City. Street recorded thus in 1666, earlier *Douegastrete* (*sic*) *c.*1264, named after a watergate and wharf close to where the WALBROOK entered the River Thames, referred to as *Duuegate* 1151, *Douegat* 1244, *Duuegate* 1300, *Dowgate* 1603, that is probably 'gate frequented by pigeons or doves', from Old English *dūfe* and *geat*. An alternative early spelling *Dounegate* 1275, *Down(e)gate* 1603, could represent the Old English genitive case plural *dūfena* 'of the doves'. Dowgate is the name of one of the ancient wards of the City.

Down Barns Farm (at Northolt) Ealing. Marked as *Down Barn* on Cary's map of 1786 and recorded earlier as *Downebarnes* 1535, named from *Ladon* 1202, *la Dune* 1211, *la Doune* 1279, *Down* 1399, that is 'the hill or down', from Old English *dūn* with the French definite article and the later addition of Middle English *barne*. There is only a slight elevation here (152 ft), but traces of the old field system can still be seen on the south-facing slopes.

Downe Bromley. *Dona* 1283, *Dune* 1296, *Doune* 1316, *Downe c.*1762, that is '(place at) the hill or down', from Old English *dūn*. **Down House** (the residence of Charles Darwin from 1842 until his death in 1882) preserves a different spelling of the name (found for instance on the Ordnance Survey map of 1819).

Downham Lewisham. Residential area developed from the 1920s, named after Lord *Downham*, chairman of the London County Council from 1919–20.

Downhills Park (at West Green) Haringey. Named from *Down Hills* 1619, *Downhills* 1877, so called from *le Downe* 1467, 'the down or hill', from Middle English *doun* with the later (tautological) addition of *hill*.

Downing Street (off Whitehall) Westminster. So named by 1660 from the house built here by Sir George *Downing* (1623–84), MP and diplomat, who also developed the street *c.*1680. The well-known No. 10 was acquired by the Crown in 1732, since which date it has been the serving Prime Minister's official residence (whether or not they have chosen to live here!).

Drayton, West, *see* WEST DRAYTON.

Drayton Green Ealing. Marked thus on Cary's map of 1786 and on the Ordnance Survey map of 1822, named from *Drayton* 1387, *Dreyton*

1494, that is 'farmstead at or near a portage or slope for dragging down loads', or 'farmstead where drays or sledges are used', from Old English *dræg* (in one or other of its two related senses) and *tūn*, with the later addition of *grene* 'village green'. The place lies on land enclosed by a large bend of the River BRENT, so the name may refer to the dragging of loads by sledge to and from the river bank or from one bank to another. WEST DRAYTON in Hillingdon is identical in origin, see also next name.

Drayton Park (at Highbury) Islington. Station on a street of the same name which was earlier known as *Highbury Hill Park c.*1850, *see* HIGHBURY; possibly a transferred name from one of the other places called Drayton, or from the surname of some local person or family.

Drury Lane Westminster. Recorded thus in 1598, otherwise *Drewrie Lane* in 1607, named from *Drurye house* 1567, the home of one Richard *Drewrye* 1554. The surname itself is interesting; it derives from Middle English *druerie* 'a love-token or sweetheart'. The lane was earlier called *Oldewiche Lane* 1393, *street called Aldewyche* 1398, that is 'lane or street to *Aldewyche* ('the old trading settlement')', *see* ALDWYCH.

Duck's Hill (near Harefield) Hillingdon. Marked thus on Rocque's map of 1754 and on the Ordnance Survey map of 1822, so named from the local *Duck(e)* family recorded in the 16th-century parish registers.

Ducks Island (near Chipping Barnet) Barnet. Marked thus on the Ordnance Survey map of 1887, district by DOLLIS BROOK and probably self-explanatory, but compare the previous name.

Dudden Hill Brent. *Dodynghill* 1544, *Doddinge Hill* 1549, perhaps 'hill associated with a man called Dodd', from an Old English personal name with medial *-ing-* and *hyll*, *compare* a nearby place called *Doddysforde* 1475, 'Dodd's ford', from Old English *ford*. Alternatively, the names may contain an Old English word **dodd*, **dodding* 'rounded hill'.

Duke of Northumberland's River Hounslow/Richmond. An artificial watercourse constructed to take water from the River CRANE to the corn mill at SYON, so called because the estate here has belonged to the Dukes of Northumberland since the end of the 16th century (SYON PARK is still referred to as *Duke of Northumberland Estate* on modern maps). Another watercourse further to the west with the same name (marked thus on the Ordnance Survey map of 1880) flows from the

River COLNE at LONGFORD to join the River CRANE at North Feltham (*see* FELTHAM). It partly shares its course with LONGFORD RIVER, dividing from it at EAST BEDFONT.

Duke's Meadows (at Chiswick) Hounslow. So called because once owned by the *Dukes* of Devonshire who lived at Chiswick House (*see* CHISWICK).

Dulwich, Dulwich Village Southwark. *Dilwihs* 967 (Anglo-Saxon charter), *Dilwiche* 1127, *Dilewisse* 1210, *Dulwyche* 1555, that is 'marshy meadow where dill grows', from Old English *dile* and *wisc*. The dill plant was used for medicinal purposes from early times. The manor was already divided by the 14th century: **East Dulwich** is *Est Dilewissh* in 1340, **West Dulwich** (now in the borough of LAMBETH) is *West Dilwysh* in 1344. There was a fashionable spa here in the 18th century, marked as *Wells* on the Ordnance Survey map of 1816. **Dulwich College** was founded in the early 17th century. **Dulwich Picture Gallery** was built in 1811–14. Dulwich is pronounced 'Dullidge'.

Duntshill Road (in Earlsfield) Wandsworth. Preserves the old name *Duntshill* still marked on the Ordnance Survey map of 1876, earlier *Duneshull* 1185, *Douneshull* 1413, that is 'hill of the manor called *Done* or *Dune* ('the hill or down')', from Old English *dūn* and *hyll*, *see also* DURNSFORD AVENUE & ROAD which refer to the same lost manor.

Duppas Hill Croydon. Earlier *Doubleshyll* 1437, *Dubbers hyll* c.1530, *Doubers hill* 1543, *Dubbershill* 1548, indicating land owned by a family called *Double* or *Dubber*. The modern spelling has been influenced by the quite distinct surname *Duppa*.

Durants Park (at Enfield Highway) Enfield. Created in 1903 from the estate of the former manor house called *Durrants*, recorded as *Durauntesplace* 1382, *Durantes manor* 1402, so named from the family of Adam *Durant* 1244.

Durnsford Avenue & Road (at Wimbledon Park) Merton. Preserve the old name *Donesford* 1301, *Dunesford* 1535, *Dounesford* 1540, *Dunsford House* 1816, that is 'ford of the manor called *Done* or *Dune* ('the hill or down')', from Old English *dūn* and *ford*, *see also* DUNTSHILL ROAD in Earlsfield which refers to the same lost medieval manor. The ford was over the River WANDLE.

E

Ealing (town and borough). *Gillingas* c.698 (17th-century copy of Anglo-Saxon charter), *Yllinges* c.1170, *Yilling* 1294, *Elyng* 1553, that is '(settlement of) the family or followers of a man called *Gilla', from an Old English personal name and Old English -*ingas*. This is therefore an Anglo-Saxon folk name of ancient type like BARKING and HAVERING. Ealing was sometimes called *Chircheyllinge* (1274) or *Cherchegillyng* (1393) with reference to the 12th-century church of St Mary, to distinguish it from the separate hamlet of **West Ealing** (*Westyilling* 13th century, *Westyellyng* 1408) or **Little Ealing** (*Little Yelling* 1650, *Little Ealing* 1786). **Ealing Common** is marked thus on Cary's map of 1786. **Ealing Studios**, celebrated for the production of comedies and feature films in the 1940s and early 1950s and now owned by the BBC, had their beginnings here in 1904.

Earls Court Kensington & Chelsea. *Earles Court* 1593, *Erls Cort* 1654, *Earls Court* 1822, that is 'the earl's manor house', from Middle English *erl* and *court*. The hamlet grew up around the manor house of the *Earls* of Oxford, lords of the manor of KENSINGTON from the time of Domesday Book until the 16th century (they were superseded in the early 17th century by the Earls of Warwick and Holland). The house itself, which stood on the site of the present Barkston Gardens and Bramham Gardens, was not demolished until 1886. The Earls Court Exhibition Hall was opened in 1937.

Earlsfield Wandsworth. District developed at the end of the 19th century, named from Earlsfield Road which was itself called after a residence near SPENCER PARK known as *Earlsfield House*; land in this area was owned by the *Earls* Spencer, who were lords of the neighbouring manor of WIMBLEDON from the mid-18th and throughout the 19th century. However if the name is in fact older than this, it is perhaps rather to be associated with a family called *Earl(e)* recorded in the parish of WANDSWORTH in 1606. Certainly at an even earlier date this area was part of the ancient manor of *Allfarthing* or *Half Farthing*, for which, *see* ALLFARTHING LANE.

Earl's Sluice (rises near Denmark Hill, flowing into the River Thames at Deptford). Small stream now covered over which joins the *Peck* (for which, *see* PECKHAM RYE), so named from the 1st *Earl* of Gloucester, illegitimate son of Henry I, who was given the manor of PECKHAM by his father.

East Acton Ealing, *see* ACTON.

East Barnet, *see* BARNET, EAST.

East Bedfont Hounslow. *Bedefunt, Bedefunde* 1086 (Domesday Book), *Bedefont* 1198, *Estbedefont* 1235, *Bedfunte* 1279, probably 'spring provided with a drinking vessel', from Old English *byden* or *beden* and **funta*, with *East* to distinguish it from neighbouring West Bedfont in Surrey. The 'spring' may have been a natural one or a well sunk into the gravel. The situation of this place on the old Roman road from London to Silchester is significant: early travellers would have been able to replenish their water supplies here. In medieval times it was also sometimes known as *Chirchebedfounte* (as in 1405), with reference to the 12th-century church of St Mary here.

Eastbury Court & Square (at Barking), **Eastbury Level** Barking & Dagenham. Preserve the old name *Estberi* 1321, *Esbury* 1557, *Eastbury Farm* 1805, *Eastbury House* 1888, 'east manor', from Middle English *est* and *bury*, so called in contrast with *Westbury* 1348, *Westbury Farm* 1805, 'west manor'. *Eastbury Level* and *Westbury Level* are marked on the Ordnance Survey map of 1888, earlier called *Barking Level* on the 1805 map, from *level* in the sense 'a flat stretch of ground'.

Eastcheap City. *Eastceape* c.1100, *Estchepe* 1211, *Estchep* 1213, (street called) *Estchepe* 1246, that is 'the east market', from Old English *ēast* and *cēap*, thus distinguished from *Chepe* or *Westchepe* for which, *see* CHEAPSIDE. The street takes its name from the market, which was from an early date one of the chief meat markets of medieval London.

Eastcote, Eastcote Village (near Ruislip) Hillingdon. *Estcotte* 1248, *Estcote* 1296, *Astcote* 1435, *Eastcot* 1822, that is 'eastern cottage(s)', from Old English *ēast* and *cot*, a hamlet so named from its situation east of RUISLIP and contrasting with another hamlet called *Westcott* in 1780 (no doubt also much older than this).

East Dulwich, Southwark, *see* DULWICH.

East End, The. Term found from the late 19th century to describe the heartland of East London (the area lying *east* of the City), compare the parallel term WEST END.

East End (at Pinner) Harrow. Marked thus on the Ordnance Survey map of 1877, earlier *Esthend* 1453, 'east end of the parish', from Middle English *est* and *ende*, in contrast to *le Westhend* 1448, *West End* 1822.

East End Road (at Finchley) Barnet. Preserves the old name *East End*, now East Finchley (*see* FINCHLEY). Finchley's *Manor House* (built 1723 and now a school) lies on this road and is marked thus on the Ordnance Survey map of 1822.

East Finchley Barnet, *see* FINCHLEY.

East Hall (near Rainham) Havering. Marked thus on the Ordnance Survey map of 1805, earlier *Esthull* (*sic*) 1518, that is 'east manor house' from Middle English *est* and *hall* (the 1518 spelling shows confusion with Middle English *hull* 'hill').

East Ham Newham, *see* HAM, EAST & WEST.

East India Docks Tower Hamlets. Marked thus on the Ordnance Survey map of 1805, although not opened until the following year; they were closed down in 1967. They were named from the *East India Company* (founded 1600), which had already traded with India and China for two centuries and whose ships had been built and repaired in earlier docks (including the *Blackwall Yard* established in 1614 and the old *Brunswick Dock* so named from the ducal house of Brunswick in honour of George III) situated here at BLACKWALL. The famous *Cutty Sark*, built in 1869 and now in permanent dry dock across the river at Greenwich, was one of the large tea clippers that once berthed here. See also WEST INDIA DOCKS.

East Sheen Richmond. *Sceon c.*950, *Shenes c.*1210, *Shene* 1230, *Estshene* 1258, *East Shyne* 1610, that is 'the sheds or shelters', from Old English **scēo* in a plural form **scēon*. East Sheen was thus distinguished from *West Sheen* (the earlier name of RICHMOND) from the 13th century. **East Sheen Common** is marked as *Sheen Common* on the Ordnance Survey map of 1816. **North Sheen** is marked thus on the Ordnance Survey map of 1904 when it was still mainly an area of market gardens lying to the north of the ancient manor of Sheen; it was developed as a residential district from the 1920s.

East Smithfield (near The Tower) Tower Hamlets. Now a small street to

the east of THE TOWER, but once a large open area recorded as
Smethefeld 1140–4, *Estsmethefeld* 1229, *Est Smythefeld* 1272, that is 'the
eastern smooth or level field', from Old English *smēthe* and *feld*, with
Middle English *est* to distinguish it from West Smithfield on the other
side of the City, *see* SMITHFIELD STREET. An annual fair lasting 15 days
was held here during the 13th century.

East Wickham Bexley. *Wikam* 1240, *Wykham* 1254, *Estwycham* 1284, *Est
Wycham* 1292, *East Wickham* c.1762, probably 'homestead associated
with a *vicus*, i.e. an earlier Romano-British settlement', from Old English **wīc-hām*. 'East' to distinguish this place from WEST WICKHAM
which lies some 10 miles south-west and has the same origin: both
names are likely to belong to the earliest stratum of Saxon names (see
Introduction: 'The Anglo-Saxon Period'). Its situation is significant,
lying as it does just north of the old Roman road from London to Dover
(WATLING STREET) and some 3 miles from the probable site of the
Roman town of *Noviomagus* (*see* CRAYFORD).

Eaton Place & Square Westminster. Built in the 1820s on part of the
Grosvenor estate, named from *Eaton* Hall in Cheshire, the country seat
of the Dukes of Westminster, *see* BELGRAVIA and GROSVENOR SQUARE.

Ebury Bridge, Square & Street Westminster. Streets laid out c.1820 on
the site of the ancient manor of *Ebury* which once occupied the west
part of the present City of WESTMINSTER including HYDE PARK. It is
recorded as *Eia* in 1086 (Domesday Book), *Eye* 12th century, *Eyebury*
1323, *Ebery* 1535, that is 'the island of dry land in marsh', from Old
English *ēg*, with the later addition of Middle English *bury* 'manor'.

Eccleston Square Westminster. Built in 1835 on part of the Grosvenor
estate, named after Eccleston in Cheshire where the Dukes of Westminster had an estate, *see* BELGRAVIA and GROSVENOR SQUARE.

Eden Park Bromley. Marked thus on the Ordnance Survey map of 1876,
but simply *Eden* on the earlier map of 1819. The farm and mansion
here, originally part of the Langley Estate (*see* LANGLEY PARK), were so
named from the family of William *Eden*, later the 1st Lord Auckland,
who bought the property in 1807.

Edgware Barnet. *Ægces wer* c.975 (Anglo-Saxon charter), *Eggeswera* 1168,
Eggewere 1294, *Edggeware* 1489, that is 'weir or fishing-enclosure of a
man called Ecgi', from an Old English personal name and Old English
wer. According to the 10th-century charter the weir was located where

Edgware Brook (then called *Stan burnan* 'the stony stream') was crossed by WATLING STREET.

Edgware Bury (near Edgware) Barnet. Marked thus on the Ordnance Survey map of 1822, earlier *Ye Berrey in Edgware* 1657, from Middle English *bury* 'a manor, a manor house'. It gives name to Bury Farm.

Edgware Road Westminster. Station named from the road so called in the 18th century, earlier *Edgware High Waie* 1574, which follows the course of the old WATLING STREET northwards to St Albans via EDGWARE.

Edmonton Enfield. *Adelmetone* 1086 (Domesday Book), *Edelmeton* 1202, *Edelmintone* 1211, *Edmenton* 1369, *Edelmeton alias Edmonton* 1464, that is 'farmstead or estate of a man called Ēadhelm', from an Old English personal name and *tūn*. The modern form seems to derive from medieval spellings (like that from 1211) containing medial *-ing-* 'associated with'. This place gave its name to one of the ancient hundreds of Middlesex. **Lower Edmonton** and **Upper Edmonton** are marked thus on the Ordnance Survey map of 1822.

Eel Brook Common Hammersmith & Fulham. Named from *Hillebrook* 1408, *Hellebrook* 1444, *Helbroke* 1554, *Eelbrook* 1820, that is 'brook by a hill', from Old English *hyll* (here used of only a slight elevation in an otherwise flat terrain) and *brōc*. The later development is the result of folk etymology.

Eel Pie Island (in the River Thames at Twickenham) Richmond. Recorded thus on the Ordnance Survey map of 1876, and referred to as *the Eel-pie island* in Charles Dickens's *Nicholas Nickleby* (1838–9), but earlier called *Gose Eyte* in the 15th century and *the parish ayte* in 1608, that is 'goose or parish islet', from Middle English *eyte* or *ayte*. The later name refers to the popularity of the island for picnics by boating parties in the 19th century, the tavern here being renowned for its *eel pies*, a favourite traditional Cockney dish. In the 18th century, there was also a popular tavern called *Eel Pie House* at ISLINGTON.

Effra, River (rising in Upper Norwood, joins the River Thames just below Nine Elms). This stream, now mostly covered over, is first recorded as *Effra* in 1840, and the name survives in Effra Road, Brixton (which it ran alongside after skirting BROCKWELL PARK, which may preserve an earlier name for the stream). The origin of the name Effra is obscure, unless it is an unusual 19th-century antiquarian revival of an Old English word *efer or *yfer* meaning 'bank, ridge' appearing in the 7th-century bounds of BATTERSEA and WANDSWORTH in the phrase *hēah yfre* 'high bank or ridge' at a point near to where the stream meets the Thames.

Elephant & Castle Southwark. Busy road junction and locality named from an 18th-century coaching inn (replaced in the 19th century and now again rebuilt on a new site) which had a large cast model of an elephant and castle as its sign. The combination of elephant and castle (often with the castle on the elephant's back) is an old heraldic sign, found for instance in the arms of the Cutlers' Company (which dealt in ivory) from 1622, and its use as an inn name is paralleled by a lost tavern called *The Elephant and Castle* in Lincoln recorded from 1733.

Elmers End, Upper Elmers End (near Beckenham) Bromley. Recorded as *Aylmersende* in 1494, *Elmers End* in 1682, and *Aylmers End* in 1769, a manorial name from the family of Richard *Elmer* 1226 and Ralph *Aylmer* 1240, both mentioned in connection with BECKENHAM, with Middle English *ende* 'district or quarter of a village'. Elmers End and Upper Elmers End are differentiated thus on the Ordnance Survey map of 1905, but appear as *Elmours Green* and *Elmours End* respectively on Hasted's map of 1797, as *Elm-end Green* and *Elm-end* on the Ordnance Survey map of 1819, and as *Lower Elm End* and *Upper Elm End* on the 1876 map. The mansion here, built *c.*1710 and demolished *c.*1860, was known as *Elmer Lodge*.

Elm Park (near Hornchurch) Havering. Named from *Elm Farm* 1777, *Elms* 1883; the farm is still recalled in Elms Farm Road.

Elmstead (near Chislehurst) Bromley. Marked as *Elmsted* on the Ordnance Survey map of 1805, earlier recorded as *Elmsted* in 1320, that is 'place where elm trees grow', from Old English *elm* and *stede*. The mansion here is shown as *Emsted Place* (sic) on Bowen's map of *c.*1762. **Elmstead Wood** (also giving name to Elmstead Woods station) is marked thus on the Ordnance Survey map of 1876, earlier *Elmystedis-wood* 14th century, from Middle English *wode*. The valuable timber from the woodland here, which belonged to the Bishop of Rochester, was much used for shipbuilding in early times.

Eltham Greenwich. *Elteham, Alteham* 1086 (Domesday Book), *Helteham* 1203, *Eltham* 1224, possibly 'homestead or river meadow frequented by swans', from Old English *elfitu* with *hām* or *hamm*. Alternatively, perhaps 'homestead or river meadow of a man called *Elta', with an Old English personal name as first element. The mainly 20th-century development of **New Eltham**, marked thus on the Ordnance Survey map of 1905, was formerly called *Pope Street* as on the earlier map of 1805, no doubt 'hamlet associated with a family called Pope'. **Eltham Common** and **Eltham Park** are marked thus on the Ordnance Survey map of 1876. **Eltham Lodge** was built in 1664. **Eltham Palace** has a great hall dating back to the 15th century.

Elthorne Heights & Park (near Greenford and Hanwell) Ealing. Modern names, transferred (but with no apparent historical link) from that of the ancient Middlesex hundred of Elthorne (*Helethorne* in 1086 Domesday Book, 'thorn tree of a man called Ella') within which GREENFORD and HANWELL were situated.

Ely Place (in Clerkenwell) Camden. Marked thus on the mid-16th century 'woodcut map', alternatively *Ely House* 1677. This marks the site of the London residence of the Bishops of Ely from the late 13th century until 1772, when it was demolished (although the late 13th-century chapel survives), *see* SAFFRON HILL and Vine Hill (*under* VINE STREET).

Embankment Westminster. Station named from VICTORIA EMBANKMENT.

Emerson Park (near Hornchurch) Havering. Recorded thus *c.*1895, residential estate named by the developer William Carter after his eldest son *Emerson*.

Enfield (town and borough). *Enefelde* 1086 (Domesday Book), *Einefeld* 1214, *Enfeld* 1293, *Enfild* 1564, that is 'open land of a man called Ēana, or where lambs are reared', from Old English *feld* with an Old English personal name or with Old English *ēan* 'lamb'. The *feld* would have referred to a tract of land cleared of trees within the extensive area of woodland later to become ENFIELD CHASE. **Enfield Town** is at the centre of the original settlement, around the former village green. **Enfield Highway**, marked thus on the Ordnance Survey map of 1822, is a settlement mainly from the 18th century named from *the kings highe way leading toward London* 1610, a reference to the old Roman road called ERMINE STREET (now the A1010). **Enfield Lock** is recorded thus in 1710, earlier *Norhtlok* 1355, *The Locke* 1657, 'the (northern) lock or river barrier (near Enfield)', from Middle English *lok*; it is by the River

LEA. **Enfield Wash** is recorded thus in 1675 and on the Ordnance Survey map of 1822, from Old English *(ge)wæsc* 'a place that floods'; there was probably once a ford here where ERMINE STREET crosses Turkey Brook (*see* TURKEY STREET). The London Borough of Enfield was created in 1965.

Enfield Chase Enfield. *Enefeld Chacee* 1325, *chace of Enefelde* 1373, from Middle English *chace* 'a chase, a tract of ground for breeding and hunting wild animals', *see* ENFIELD. This was first created out of the extensive woodland here in 1136, became Crown property in 1399, and remained a royal hunting preserve until it was subject to enclosure in 1777. It is said that Princess Elizabeth (later Queen Elizabeth I) often hunted here after she was granted the estate of WEST LODGE PARK by her brother Edward VI in 1547.

Epping Forest (part of) Waltham Forest. In medieval times parts of this vast forest, covering the south-west corner of the county of Essex and earlier known also as WALTHAM FOREST, stretched as far south as Leytonstone and Wanstead, *see* FOREST GATE and Wanstead Flats (*under* WANSTEAD). The name *Epping Forest* is on record from 1662; Epping itself (in Essex, some 6 miles north-east of Chingford) is an old folk name, *Eppinges* in 1086 (Domesday Book), probably '(settlement of) the people of the ridge used as a lookout place', from Old English *yppe* and *-ingas*. Throughout the medieval period, and indeed up to the 17th century, the forest was used as a royal hunting ground, and Elizabeth I hunted here, *see* QUEEN ELIZABETH'S HUNTING LODGE.

Erith Bexley. *Earhyth* 677, *Earhith* c.960 (Anglo-Saxon charters), *Erhede* 1086 (Domesday Book), *Erhethe* 1278, that is 'the muddy or gravelly landing place', from Old English *ēar* and *hȳth*. The ancient harbour and settlement developed where prehistoric trackways met the River Thames. Earith in Cambridgeshire is identical in origin, and in fact the current pronunciation of the London name is also 'Earith'.

Ermine Street (name no longer used). Old Roman road which ran north from London (leaving the City at BISHOPSGATE) through STOKE NEW-INGTON and ENFIELD and on via Lincoln to York. This already ancient route was called *Earninga stræt* by the Anglo-Saxons in the 10th century, that is 'Roman road of the *Earningas* (the family or followers of a man named *Earn(a))*', from an Old English personal name with *-inga-* and *stræt* (the same folk gave their name to Arrington in Cambridgeshire through which the road passes). The road is still in use, its course represented by Bishopsgate, Norton Folgate, Shoreditch High Street, Kingsland Road, Stoke Newington Road & High Street, Stamford Hill, High Road (Tottenham), Fore Street (Edmonton), and Hertford Road. Enfield Highway takes its name from its proximity to this road, *see* also Enfield Wash (*under* ENFIELD).

Essex Road Islington. Self-explanatory, the station named from the road which was earlier called *Lower Street* in the 18th and 19th centuries (in contrast with *Upper Street* which is still so called).

Euston, Euston Square Camden. Transferred name from Euston in Suffolk, which was the seat of the 2nd Duke of Grafton, lord of the manor of TOTTENHAM COURT when **Euston Road** (then called *the New Road*) was constructed across this estate in the 18th century. The railway station, opened in 1837, was named from the Square, built in 1827.

F

Fagg's Bridge & Road (at Feltham) Hounslow. Named from the family of George *Fagg* recorded here in 1845; the bridge takes the road across DUKE OF NORTHUMBERLAND'S RIVER.

Fair Cross (near Barking) Barking & Dagenham. Marked thus on the Ordnance Survey map of 1805, earlier *Fairecrouch* 1456, *Fayercrosse* 1609, probably 'beautiful cross' from Middle English *faire* and *cros* (replacing synonymous Middle English *crouch* from Old English *crūc* 'cross'), though the first element could be Middle English *feire* 'a fair'. Perhaps a reference to a wayside crucifix at the early crossroads here.

Fairkytes (in Hornchurch) Havering. The present building (now an Arts Centre) dates from the late 17th century, but the name is on record from as early as 1520; it is no doubt a manorial name from a Middle English surname *Fairkyte* of some local family.

Fairlop Redbridge. Named from a famous oak tree, in what was then Hainault Forest (*see* HAINAULT), called *Fair Lop Tree* in 1738, *Fairlop Oak* on the Ordnance Survey map of 1805, and cut down in 1820. In spite of other colourful traditions about the origins of the name, it means 'lopped tree where fairs took place'; an annual fair was held under the shade of the tree in the 18th century.

Falcon Brook (rising near Balham and flowing into the Thames at Battersea). Small tributary of the River Thames now covered over, named from the 18th-century *Falcon Inn* which stood near the site of Clapham Junction station (*see* CLAPHAM) and which also gave name to Falcon Park & Road at BATTERSEA The inn itself was apparently so called from the crest of the St John family, lords of the manor of BATTERSEA. The stream was earlier called *Hideborne* as in 1085, that is 'stream running through the hide of land', from Old English *hīd* and *burna*, with reference to an area called *Hyde* (that is 'the hide of land', now lost) in CLAPHAM.

Falconwood Bexley. This district was developed in the 1930s as *Falcon-wood Park* on the site of a large wood called *West Wood* on the Ordnance

Survey maps of 1805 and 1876 (earlier *Westwood* 1551). It is said to have been given this name to attract new residents.

Fallow Corner (at Finchley) Barnet. *Follow Corner* 1680, *Fallow Corner* 1710, that is 'land in the corner of a field, or by a road junction, left fallow or uncultivated'.

Farnborough Bromley. *Ferenberga* 1180, *Farnberga, Farinberghe* late 12th century, *Farnberg* 1226, *Farnboro c.*1762, that is 'hill or mound growing with ferns', from Old English *fearn* and *beorg*. An even earlier reference occurs in an Anglo-Saxon charter describing the bounds of BROMLEY in 862 in the phrase *Fearnbiorginga mearc,* that is 'boundary of the people of Farnborough', from Old English *-inga* (genitive case of *-ingas* 'dwellers at') and *mearc* 'mark, boundary'.

Farringdon Islington. Station named from **Farringdon Road** which was constructed in 1845–6, this being a continuation of **Farringdon Street** in the City which was built over the FLEET river in 1737. All preserve the name of Farringdon, one of the ancient wards of the City, which was so called from two of its aldermen in the early 13th century, William and Nicholas *de Farindon*. These two goldsmiths, father- and son-in-law, were among the most prominent citizens of their day; their surname originates from one of the several places called Far(r)ingdon or Farndon in various English counties, all meaning 'fern-covered hill' from Old English *fearn* and *dūn*. The large ward of Farringdon was divided into two, **Farringdon Within** and **Farringdon Without** (that is 'inside and outside the wall') in 1394.

Farthing or Fairdean Downs (near Coulsdon) Croydon. Marked thus on the Ordnance Survey map of 1878, but simply *Farthing Downs* on the 1816 map and earlier recorded as *Ferthyngdoune* 1322, *Ferthingdown* 1549, *Farthing Downs c.*1768, from Old English *fēorthing* 'a fourth part or quarter of an estate', with *dūn* 'hill, down'. It will be noted that the alternative spelling *Fairdean* given on some modern maps is quite unhistorical.

Farthing Street (near Downe) Bromley. Marked thus on the Ordnance Survey map of 1819, earlier recorded as *Ferthyngs* 1332, *Ferthyng* 1366, probably (like the previous name) from Old English *fēorthing* 'fourth part or quarter of an estate', with later *street* in the sense 'street of houses, hamlet'.

Fawns Manor Road (in East Bedfont) Hounslow. Named from the

16th-century Fawns Manor, so called from the family of Alan *Foun* 1317.

Feltham Hounslow. *Feltham* 969 (spurious Anglo-Saxon charter), *Felte-ham* 1086 (Domesday Book), *Feltham* 12th century, *Feltam* 1655, probably 'homestead or enclosure where mullein or a similar plant grows', from Old English *felte* and *hām* or *hamm*. Alternatively, the first element may be Old English *feld* 'open land'. **Felthamhill** is marked as *Feltham Hill* on the Ordnance Survey map of 1822. **Lower Feltham** and **North Feltham** are residential areas mainly developed in the 20th century.

Fenchurch Street City. Recorded as *Fancherchestrate* 1283, 'street of *Fanchurche*' 1337, *Fancherchestret* 1378, *Fanchurche Strete* 1510, that is 'street by the church which stands in fenny or marshy ground', from Old English *fenn* and *cirice*. The stream called *Langborne*, if it existed, is said by Stow (1603) to have risen here, *see* LANGBOURN and LOMBARD STREET. The early spellings with *-a-* (*Fan-*), still found alternatively in Pepys's Diary (1667), represent the usual south-east dialect form (from Old English *fænn*).

Fetter Lane (off Fleet Street) City. *Faytureslane* 1292, *Faitereslane* 1312, *Fewterlane* 1556, *Feterlane* 1568, that is 'lane frequented by impostors or cheats', from Middle English *faitour*. In medieval times the word was especially used of vagrants and beggars who feigned illness.

Figge's Marsh (at Mitcham) Merton. *Fygmershe c.*1530, *Figges Marsh* 1876, named from the family of William *Fige*, recorded in connection with MITCHAM in 1351, with Middle English *mershe*.

Finch Lane (off Cornhill) City. *Finkeslane c.*1235, *Fynkeslane* 1275, *Fyncheslane* 1376, *Fynke lane* 1548, so named from a family called *Fink* who were tenants here from the end of the 12th century.

Finchley Barnet. *Finchelee, Fincheleya c.*1208, *Finchesleg* 1235, *Fincheleye* 1258, *Finchesle* 1291, that is 'woodland clearing frequented by finches', from Old English *finc* and *lēah*. **East Finchley** is marked thus on the Ordnance Survey map of 1904 and was earlier *East End*, so named on the Ordnance Survey maps of 1822 and 1877 and recorded as *Estend* 1558, that is 'the eastern quarter of the parish'; this is preserved in EAST END ROAD. **North Finchley** was developed mainly in the late 19th century.

Finsbury Islington. *Vinisbir* 1231, *Finesbury* 1254, *Fynesbury* 1294, *Fynnesbury* 1535, that is 'manor of a man called Finn', from an Old

Scandinavian personal name and Middle English *bury*. The area was once part of the marshy ground (later drained) north of the City wall that gave name to MOORGATE and MOORFIELDS and on the mid-16th century 'wood-cut map' of London *Fynnesburie Field* is still shown as open ground with horses, archers, and windmills. **Finsbury Circus & Square** were laid out as part of a new residential suburb between 1777 and 1817.

Finsbury Park (near Stroud Green) Haringey/Islington. Marked thus on the Ordnance Survey map of 1904, the park was opened in 1857 and so named because it was designated for the use of the inhabitants of the old parliamentary borough of FINSBURY (though this place itself lies some 3 miles to the south). The site of the park was earlier called *Hornsey Wood* (as on Rocque's map of 1741 and the Ordnance Survey map of 1822).

Fish Street Hill (near the Monument) City. *Fysshstretehyll* 1568, *Fishe-streete Hill* 1633, earlier *Fhistrete* 1318, *Fysshstrete c.*1390, that is 'street where fish was sold', from Middle English *fishe* and *strete*, with the later addition of *hill*. This street was conveniently close to BILLINGSGATE and other places for landing fish close to LONDON BRIDGE.

Fitzrovia Camden/Westminster. Name in use from *c.*1940 for a small compact area south of FITZROY SQUARE towards OXFORD STREET. Clearly a playful coinage (perhaps somewhat modelled on BELGRA-VIA), reputedly that of writers (among them the poet Dylan Thomas) who frequented the *Fitzroy* public house here.

Fitzroy Square & Street (near Tottenham Court Road) Camden. De-veloped from 1793 by Charles *Fitzroy*, created Baron of Southampton in 1780, who had inherited the manor of TOTTENHAM COURT from his grandfather, *see* FITZROVIA.

Flamsteed House (in Greenwich Park) Greenwich. Mansion (now a museum) built by Sir Christopher Wren *c.*1675 for John *Flamsteed*, the first Astronomer Royal at the Royal Observatory at GREENWICH.

Fleet (river, covered over since the 18th century, flowing into the River Thames at Blackfriars). Recorded as *Fleta c.*1012, *Flietam* 1159, *Flete* 1199, 'the inlet or creek', from Old English *flēot*. The name was originally given to the short navigable part of the *Holborn* stream (for which, *see* HOLBORN), but was later applied to its entire course. It gives its name to **Fleet Street** in the City, which is *vicus de Flete c.*1188,

Fletestrete 1272, 'the street leading to the Fleet river' and also to **Fleet Lane** (off Farringdon Street), which is *Fletelane* in 1544.

Foots Cray Bexley. *Crai* 1086 (Domesday Book), *Fotescraei c.*1100, *Fotescraye* 1210, that is 'estate on the River Cray held by a man called Fot', from a Celtic river name (*see* CRAY) with the byname of Godwine *Fot* who held this manor during the reign of Edward the Confessor (1043–66). The nickname *Fot* (from Old English *fōt* 'foot') would probably have been given to someone with a foot of peculiar size or shape.

Forestdale Croydon. A recent name for a 1970s development north-east of SELSDON on earlier farmland and woodland.

Forest Gate Newham. Recorded thus in the late 17th century and marked on the Ordnance Survey map of 1883, named from a former gate in Woodgrange Road (*see* WOODGRANGE PARK) intended to prevent cattle from straying from the forest into the main road. The gate was taken down in 1883. On the Ordnance Survey map of 1805, the area just north of here now called Wanstead Flats (*see* WANSTEAD) is still marked *Epping Lower Forest*.

Forest Hill Lewisham. Recorded thus in 1797 and on the Ordnance Survey map of 1816, area developed from the early 19th century and named from the once extensive tract of woodland in this area called *la Forest de Leuesham* ('the forest of LEWISHAM') in 1292 and *Forest Wood* in 1520, from ME *forest* 'wooded area set aside for hunting'.

Fore Street (near Moorgate) City. Recorded as *le Forstrete* 1330, *le Forestret* 1338, that is 'street in front (of the wall)', from Old English *fore* 'in front of', referring to its course along the outside of the old City wall, *see* LONDON WALL.

Fortis Green Haringey. *Fortessegreene* 1613, *Fortes Greene* 1638, *Forty Green* 1754, *Fortis Green* 1813, from Middle English *grene* 'village green, hamlet' with an uncertain first element, possibly the surname of some local family.

Fortune Green (at West Hampstead) Camden. Recorded thus in 1646, probably a complimentary name for a well-favoured place, with *fortune* in the sense 'luck, success, prosperity'.

Forty Avenue & Lane (at Wembley) Brent. Named from *Forty Farm* (marked thus on the Ordnance Survey map of 1822), earlier

Wembleyfortye 1446, from Old English *forth-ēg* 'higher ground in surrounding marsh', as in next name.

Forty Hill Enfield. *Fortyehill* 1610, *Fortie hill* 1619, *Fortee hill* 1686, named from *Fortey c.*1350, that is 'the island (of higher ground) in marsh', from Old English *forth-ēg* with reference to slightly rising ground above the River LEA marshes. The same feature gives name to **Forty Hall**, marked thus on the Ordnance Survey map of 1887 but (incorrectly) as *Four tree Hall* on that of 1822; this house (now a museum) was built in 1629 for the Lord Mayor of London, Sir Nicholas Rainton.

Foster Lane (off Cheapside) City. *Seint uastes lane* 1271, *Seint Fastes lane* 1321, *Seynt Fastreslane* 1360, *Faster Lane* 1524, 'St Vedast's lane', so named from the church of St Vedast (rebuilt by Wren in 1670–3 on the site of a 12th-century church).

Four Wantz Cottages (at Upminster) Havering. Literally 'four paths or ways', from Middle English *wente*, referring to a crossroads, see next name.

Four Wents (at Chingford) Waltham Forest. Street name recorded as *Four Wantes* or *Fower Wants* in 1641–2, identical in origin with the previous name.

Foxgrove Avenue & Road (at Beckenham) Bromley. Preserve the name of the old manor of *Foxgrove*, recorded as *Foxgrave* 1275, *Foxgrove* 1355, *Fox Grove* 1805, that is 'grove or copse frequented by foxes', from Old English *fox* and *grāf(a)*.

Foxley Wood (near Kenley) Croydon. Marked thus on the Ordnance Survey map of 1816, earlier *Foxele* 1279, *Foxle* 1431, *Great Foxley, Lyttle Foxley* 1552, that is 'wood or clearing frequented by foxes', from Old English *fox* and *lēah*.

Franks Farm (near Upminster) Havering. Marked as *Franks* on the Ordnance Survey map of 1805, earlier *Frankesgrove* 1323, *Frankys* 1418, a manorial name from lands here held by a certain *Frank de Scottelonde* mentioned in 1262; the farmhouse itself dates partly from the 15th century.

Fray's Bridge, Farm & River (near Ickenham) Hillingdon. The bridge and farm are earlier *Frayesbridge* 1624, *Frays Farm* 1880, both named from the family of John *Fray* 1430.

Freezywater Enfield. Recorded as *Freezwater* 1768, *Freezy Water* 1819, originally the name of a pond here, so called from its bleak and exposed situation.

Friary Park (in Friern Barnet) Barnet. Marked thus on the Ordnance Survey map of 1904, but *Friern Park* on that of 1877, earlier *Freren parke* 1507. The modern name has replaced the original *freren* 'of the brothers' found also in the affix of Friern Barnet (*see* BARNET, FRIERN). This is now a public park but was earlier part of the grounds of the manor house known as the *Friary*.

Friday Hill (near Chingford) Waltham Forest. Marked thus on the Ordnance Survey map of 1805, earlier *Friday-hill* 1588, *Fridaies*, *Freydayes Hill* 1589, district and road named from a local family called *Friday*; John *Friday* is recorded as holding a tenement here in 1467, and Thomas *Friday* in 1471–83. In the late 16th century, the original house at Friday Hill became the manor house of CHINGFORD; it was demolished in 1838 and replaced by another mansion in the following year.

Friday Street (off Cannon Street) City. Recorded as *Fridaiestraite* or *Frideistrate* in the 12th century, *Frydaystrate* 1277, either 'street associated with a man called *Frīgedæg* or a family called *Friedai*', from a late Old English personal name or early Middle English surname (from the day of the week), or 'street with a Friday market, perhaps for fish' (it is not very far from QUEENHITHE, *compare also* FISH STREET HILL).

Friern Barnet, see BARNET, FRIERN.

Friern Road (off Lordship Lane) Southwark. Preserves the name of the old manor of *Friern*, marked as *Friern Farm* on the Ordnance Survey map of 1816 and as *Freierne Manor Farm* on Bryant's map of 1823, earlier *Freryn Camerwell alias Frerne* 1544, that is 'the CAMBERWELL manor of the brothers', from Middle English *freren*, with reference to land here granted to Holywell Priory in Shoreditch (*see* HOLYWELL LANE).

Frith Manor House (near Finchley) Barnet. *la Frithe* 1294, *Fryth* 1535, *Frith Manor* 1822, 'the woodland or scrub', from Old English *fyrhth(e)*. This area was once well wooded.

Frog Island (near Rainham) Havering. Marked thus on the Ordnance Survey map of 1888, no doubt so called from the number of frogs frequenting this small marshy promontory where Rainham Creek (*see* RAINHAM) flows into the Thames.

Frognal (in Hampstead) Camden. *ffrognal* 1372, *Frogenhall* 1542, *Frognall* 1795, that is 'nook of land frequented by frogs', from Old English *frogga* (genitive case plural *froggena*) and *halh*. In early times the area was well watered, with a cattle pond fed by a brook.

Frognal House (in Sidcup) Bromley. Marked as *Frognall* on a map of 1769 and as *Frognal* on the Ordnance Survey map of 1805, but the house, rebuilt *c*.1670, has early Tudor origins. Possibly identical with the previous name, although its earlier name seems to have been *Frogpool(e)*, as on Bowen's map *c*.1762.

Fryent Fields & Way (at Kingsbury) Brent. Preserve the old name of *Fryent Farm* (marked thus on the Ordnance Survey map of 1877), earlier *Freryn Court c*.1516, *Friarn Manor* 1593, *Friant* 1754, *Fryern Farm* 1822, that is 'court or manor house of the friars or brethren', from Middle English *frere* (plural *freren*), referring to possession of the manor by the Knights of St John of Jerusalem (as with Friern Barnet). It will be noted that the final *-t* in the modern spelling is quite unhistorical.

Fulham Hammersmith & Fulham. *Fulanham c*.705 (17th-century copy of Anglo-Saxon charter), *Fullanhamme c*.900 (Anglo-Saxon Chronicle), *Fuleham* 1086 (Domesday Book), *Fulham* 1274, that is 'river-bend land of a man called *Fulla', from an Old English personal name (genitive case *-n*) and Old English *hamm*. **Fulham Broadway** station (opened in the 1880s as WALHAM GREEN) takes its present name from the street so called. **Fulham Palace**, manor house of the Bishops of London (lords of the manor of Fulham from the 8th century) and their official residence up to 1973, dates from the 16th century, *see* BISHOP'S PARK. The London Borough of Hammersmith & Fulham was created in 1965.

Fullwell Cross Redbridge. Crossroads named from *Folewell* 1332, *Fulwellhacch* 1456, *Fulwell*, *Fulwellhache* 1530, *Fullwell Hatch* 1883, that is 'foul or dirty spring or stream', from Old English *fúl* and *wella*, with the later addition of Middle English *hache* (Old English *hæcc*) 'hatch gate' (once giving access to Hainault Forest, *see* HAINAULT).

Fulwell Richmond. Recorded thus in 15th-century sources and as *Fulwell Lodge* on the Ordnance Survey map of 1816, probably identical in origin with the previous name. **Fulwell Park** is so named on the Ordnance Survey map of 1904.

Furzedown (east of Tooting) Wandsworth. Marked as *Furze Down* on the

Ordnance Survey map of 1876, that is 'down on which furze or gorse grows', from Middle English *furse*. Local records from the 17th century refer to the cutting of furze (for fuel) by the inhabitants of TOOTING on the common land here.

G

Galley Lane (Farm) (near Arkley) Barnet. The farm, marked *Galleylane Farm* on the Ordnance Survey map of 1887, is named from the lane, earlier *Galowlane* 1475, that is 'lane by which a gallows stands', from Old English *galga*. The lane forms the old county boundary between Hertfordshire and Middlesex.

Gallions Reach Newham. Marked thus on Bowen's map of 1746 and as *Gallion Reache* on a Thames chart of 1588, a stretch of the river so called from Gallions Cottages, earlier *Gallion* 1588, *Gallions* 1609, *c*.1762, a manorial name from the family of John and Richard *Galyan* or *Galyon* mentioned in 14th-century records. **Gallions Point** (*Gallion Nesse* 1588, from Old English *næss* 'headland') is a promontory at the south end of the Reach.

Gallows Corner (near Gidea Park) Havering. A junction on the old Roman road to Colchester (now the A12), so called because it was once the site of a gallows.

Gants Hill Redbridge. Named from the family of Richard *le Gant* 1285; other local names indicating land owned in early times by the same family include *Gantesgrave* 1291, *Gauntes Hethe* 1545, and *Gauntsfeild* 1609, from Old English *grāf(a)* 'grove, copse', *hæth* 'heath', and *feld* 'field'.

Garlick Hill City. *Garlyk hill c*.1510, that is 'hill where garlic was sold', named from *Garleckhithe* 1281, *Garlickhith* 1550, 'landing place for garlic', from Old English *gār-lēac* with *hyll* and *hȳth*. The landing place must have been on the Thames due south of Garlick Hill near QUEENHITHE. The church at the foot of the hill is still known as St James Garlick-hythe.

Garratt Green & Lane (in Earlsfield) Wandsworth. The former is recorded as *Garrat greene* 1609, *Garret Green* 1816, preserving the name of a tenement called *le Garret* 1538, *Ye Garret* 1580, from Old French *garite* 'a watchtower'. There is a mill called *Garret Mill* by the River WANDLE on the Ordnance Survey map of 1816. The old hamlet of *Garratt*, well known in the 18th century for its mock elections to appoint a 'Mayor of Garratt' to protect its rights on the Common, came later to be called SUMMERSTOWN.

Gattons Plantation & Wood (at North Cray) Bexley. Named from the *Gatton(e)* family, mentioned as holding lands here in the early 14th century.

Gerpins Farm (near Rainham) Havering. Marked as *Gerpins* on the Ordnance Survey map of 1805, earlier recorded as *Gerpilesplaces* (*sic*) 1401, *Gerpeviles alias Gerdviles* 1510, a manorial name from the family of John and Laurence *de Jarpe(n)ville* who are mentioned in 13th-century records and who came from Gerponville in France.

Gidea Park Havering. First recorded as *Guydie hall parke* in 1668, named from *la Gidiehall* 1258, *Giddyhalle* 1376, *Gydihall* 1466, *Gidea Hall* 1805, literally 'the foolish or crazy hall', from Middle English *gidi* and *hall*, perhaps alluding to a building of unusual design or construction, but possibly to the eccentric behaviour of those who lived there! The hall, in the mid-16th century the home of Sir Anthony Cooke, a tutor to King Edward VI, was demolished in the 1930s after the residential garden suburb of Gidea Park had been established in its grounds. A print in Essex Record Office shows the departure of Charles I and his mother-in-law, Marie de Medici, Queen Mother of France, from *Gidde Halle* in 1638.

Giltspur Street (near West Smithfield) City. Recorded as *Gyltesporestrete* or *Gyltspurstreate* in the mid-16th century, that is 'street where gilt spurs were made', or perhaps 'street where a particular spurrier had a sign of a gilt spur over his workshop'. Spurs were much in demand in medieval times for use in jousts and tournaments, one venue for which was nearby West Smithfield (*see* SMITHFIELD). An alternative name for this street in the 16th century was *Knyghtryders Strete*, perhaps alluding to knights who rode at these spectacular displays, *compare* KNIGHTRIDER STREET near ST PAUL'S.

Gipsy Hill (near West Norwood) Lambeth. Named, like nearby Gipsy Road, from the gypsies who frequented this once wooded area in the 17th, 18th, and early 19th centuries before it was developed.

Gladstone Park Brent. Named *c.*1901 to commemorate W. E. *Gladstone*, Prime Minister from 1868–74, a frequent visitor of the Earl and

Countess of Aberdeen who lived at Dollis Hill House, *see* DOLLIS HILL.

Globe Town (near Bethnal Green) Tower Hamlets. District named from **Globe Road** recorded thus in 1808 but earlier *Globe Lane* 1708, probably from an inn called *The Globe*. Before that the lane was called *Theven lane* c.1600, *Theeving Lane* 1703, 'lane of the thieves or robbers', from Middle English *theef* (plural *theven*).

Gloucester Road Kensington & Chelsea. Station named from the road so called in 1826 after Maria, Duchess of *Gloucester* who built a house here in 1805. It was earlier *Hog moore lane* 1612, that is 'lane through marshy ground where hogs are kept', a name still used until c.1850.

Goddington (near Orpington) Bromley. Marked thus on the Ordnance Survey map of 1876, recorded earlier as *Godinton* in 1240, a manorial name from the *de Godinton* family who took their name from the hamlet of Godinton near Ashford in Kent.

Godliman Street (off Queen Victoria Street) City. *Godalming Street* in 1746, perhaps so named from a kind of leather originally prepared at Godalming in Surrey and once sold here.

Golden Lane (off Beech Street) City/Islington. *Goldeslane* 1274, *Goldyng lane* c.1290, *Golden lane* 1317, *Goldyngeslane* 1361, probably 'lane of a family called *Golde* or *Golding*'.

Golders Green Barnet. *Golders Greene* 1612, *Goulders Green* 1680, *Goldhurst Green* 1795, probably 'village green or hamlet associated with a family called *Golder* or *God(y)er*', from Middle English *grene*, *see* GOLDERS HILL PARK which may have been named from the same family. An alternative name for Golders Green in the 18th century was *Groles Green* 1754, *Groles or Godders Green* 1790, perhaps a reference to another family with property here.

Golders Hill Park (near Golders Green) Barnet. Named from *Godereshill* c.1406, probably 'hill associated with a family called *God(y)er*', from Middle English *hill*. There is mention of a John *le Godere* and a John *Godyer* in 14th-century records concerning HENDON.

Goldhawk Road Hammersmith & Fulham. The road from which the station takes its name was earlier *Gould Hawk Lane* 1813, so called, like the 15th-century places *Goldehawkes* and *Goldhawkesdych*, from the

Goldhawk family mentioned frequently in local records from the medieval period.

Goodge Street Camden. Recorded thus in 1777, named from Francis and William *Goodge* who owned the site (then known as *Crab Tree Field*) and began developing it *c.*1746.

Goodmayes Redbridge. Recorded thus in 1456 and as *Goodmays* on the Ordnance Survey map of 1805, indicating an estate held by the family of John *Godemay* 1319. It is apparently only coincidence that the stream flowing south near here is called Mayes Brook, *see* MAYES-BROOK PARK which lies about a mile away. The surnames behind both names derive from Middle English *may* 'young lad or girl'.

Gooshays Drive & Gardens (at Harold Hill) Havering. Named from *Goshaye* 1334, *Gosayes* 1378, *Goseyes* *c.*1510, *Gooses* 1805, that is 'enclosures where geese are kept', from Old English *gōs* and *hæg*.

Gordon Hill Enfield. Station named from a house, formerly near here, which belonged to the father of Lord George *Gordon*, the notorious organizer of the anti-Catholic riots of 1778 (also known because he figures in Dickens's novel *Barnaby Rudge*).

Gores Bridge, Goresbrook Park, The Gores (in Dagenham) Barking & Dagenham. Named from *Cory* 1389, *Coryes* *c.*1568, a manorial name indicating one of the two estates in DAGENHAM once held by the family of John *Cory* 1304 and Henry *Coory* 1327. The small brook now called *The Gores* (marked thus on the Ordnance Survey map of 1870 and recorded as *The Gorse* in 1766) flows south into the Thames.

Gosbury Hill (in Hook) Kingston. *Gosborough Hyll* 1537, *Goseburye hill* 1598, probably 'hill where geese are pastured', from Old English *gōs* and *beorg*, with the later addition of 'explanatory' *hill*.

Gospel Oak Camden. District named from an oak tree mentioned in 1761 and shown on Greenwood's map of 1819. The *oak* formerly stood on the HAMPSTEAD–ST PANCRAS parish boundary and the name alludes to the reading of a passage from the *gospel* here during the traditional Rogationtide ceremony of beating the bounds.

Goulds Green Hillingdon. *Gouldes grene* 1592, from Middle English *grene* 'village green'. Named from the family of John *Golde*, mentioned in local documents in 1373.

Gracechurch Street City. *in vico de Graschirche* 1240, *Garscherchestrate*
1284, *Greschirchestrete* 1326, *Graschirchestrete* 1424, *Gracechirche strete
alias Graschirche strete* 1437, that is probably 'street by the church on a
grassy plot', from Old English *græs* and *cirice*. The ancient church
referred to was probably *All Hallows Gracechurch*, which was once
situated on the west side of the street and is recorded as *Gerschereche* in
an 11th-century charter. There was also a church of *St Benet Gracechurch*
on the east side of the street. Alternatively, the name could allude to
the fact that the roof of the church may have been made of turves.
However it certainly long pre-dates the 13th-century evidence for the
important corn market here (later a general market), so that Stow's
reference (1603) to a hay (grass) market as an explanation of the name
appears purely fanciful.

Grahame Park (near Colindale) Barnet. Estate built 1965–75 and named
after Claude *Grahame*-White, the aircraft enthusiast and pioneer who
opened HENDON Aerodrome in 1911 and in the same year started his
aviation company here. The Royal Air Force Museum, established in
1963, is appropriately sited nearby on part of the former Aerodrome.

Grand Union Canal. Name used since 1929 for a system of canals, built
in the early 19th century, linking London with the Midlands. The
eastern branch once called *Regent's Canal* (as on the Ordnance Survey
map of 1822) was opened in 1820 and runs from PADDINGTON Basin
and LITTLE VENICE through REGENT'S PARK (hence the name) to the
River Thames at LIMEHOUSE. The western branches (earlier known as
Paddington Canal and *Grand Junction Canal* as on the 1822 map) run from
Paddington Basin through UXBRIDGE towards Watford with a spur
entering the Thames at BRENTFORD.

Grange Park Enfield. Named from *Old Park Grange* (marked thus on the
Ordnance Survey map of 1887) which was in *Old Park* (also 1887),
earlier *the oulde park* 1658, *Old Bull Park* 1822, from Middle English
grange 'outlying farm where crops are stored'.

Graveney, River (a tributary of the River Wandle, rising at Upper
Norwood). Marked thus on the Ordnance Survey map of 1876, a back-
formation from Tooting Graveney (*see* TOOTING) through which it
flows.

Gray's Inn (in Holborn) Camden. *Grayesin* 1403, *Greys yn* 1413, that is
'residence of the *de Grey* family', from Middle English *inn*. This was

formerly the manor house of *Purtepole* 1203, *Portepole* 1240, *Portpole maner called Grays Inn* 1396, that is 'pool of a man called *Purta', from an Old English personal name and Old English *pōl, see* PORTPOOL LANE. This manor was held by Reginald *de Grey* at the time of his death in 1308. The manor house was already used by a community of lawyers by 1370, and Gray's Inn is one of the four surviving Inns of Court. The Hall of the Inn dates from 1556. **Gray's Inn Road** is *Purtepolestrate* 1234, *Grayes Inne Lane* 1419.

Greater London, see LONDON.

Great Marlborough Street Westminster, *see* MARLBOROUGH STREET, GREAT.

Great North Road, see HIGHGATE and HOLLOWAY for this main route north out of London already established by the 12th century as an alternative to the more ancient ERMINE STREET.

Great Portland Street Westminster, *see* PORTLAND PLACE.

Great Scotland Yard (off Whitehall) Westminster. Recorded as *Scotland Yard* in 1656, earlier referred to as *a parcel of land late of the king of Scotts* in 1440, *Kyng of Scottis ground* in 1462, *le Scotland ground c.*1510. This was the London residence of the Kings of Scotland after the 12th century. In 1829, part of the Scotland Yard precincts became the headquarters of the Metropolitan Police, and when they moved in 1891, the name **New Scotland Yard** was applied to their new premises on VICTORIA EMBANKMENT, and later (in 1967) to their new building in VICTORIA itself.

Great Tomkyns (near Upminster) Havering. The name is recorded as *Tomkyns Wood* 1612, *Tompkins* 1629, a manorial name from a family so called; the present house is from the 16th century.

Great West Road . Main route to the West through BRENTFORD and HOUNSLOW (the A4), opened in 1925 and extended back to HAMMER-SMITH *c.*1950. Of course the ancient major routes to the West are also still in use. The main road corresponding to the Roman road to Silchester, which left the City at NEWGATE, is represented by the course of HOLBORN, OXFORD STREET, GOLDHAWK ROAD, etc. A second old main route to the West (formerly known as 'Akeman Street', *Akemannestræte c.*1000, from an Old English personal name *Acemann and *stræt*) left the City at LUDGATE and followed the line of FLEET STREET, STRAND, etc. before joining up with the first at BRENTFORD.

Greenford Ealing. *Grenan forda* 845 (Anglo-Saxon charter), *Greneforde* 1086 (Domesday Book), *Greneford Magna* 1254, *Muche Greneford* 1572, that is '(place at) the green ford', from Old English *grēne* and *ford*, probably a reference to water plants or other vegetation. The earlier affixes (Latin *magna* 'great' and Middle English *muche* 'large') distinguish it from *Little Greenford (now* PERIVALE). There were probably fords over the river BRENT at both places in early times. **Greenford Bridge** (no doubt on the site of a ford) was earlier called *Styclyndon Brigge* 1343, *Sticleton bridge* 1625, so named from *Stickelyndon* 1294, that is 'the steep hill or down', from Old English *sticol* (dative case *-an*) and *dūn*, a name still preserved in the street name **Stickleton Close**. **Greenford Green**, marked thus on the Ordnance Survey map of 1822, was originally *Grenefeld Grene* 1538 (from Middle English *feld* 'field'), later *Greenford Green alias Greenfield Green* 1558, *Greenford Greene* 1625, from Middle English *grene* 'village green, hamlet'.

Greenhill Harrow. *Grenehulle* 1334, *Grenehill* 1563, *Green Hill, Girnell* 1675, apparently self-explanatory, 'the green hill' from Old English *grēne* and *hyll*. However the name may be manorial in origin, from a family called *de Grenehulle* mentioned in local records from the end of the 13th century, since there is no appreciable hill here.

Greenland Dock (at Rotherhithe) Southwark. Part of Surrey Commercial Docks (*see* SURREY DOCKS) and so named from the whaling ships that once docked here. It was earlier known as *Howland Great Wet Dock* because built (in 1699) on land once belonging to John *Howland*.

Green Park Westminster. So named on Rocque's map of 1746, appropriately enough if rather unimaginatively; it was formerly part of ST JAMES'S PARK.

Greenshaw Wood Sutton. Earlier *Thikgreneshawe* 1512, that is 'dense green copse or wood', from Middle English *grene* and *shawe* with *thicke* 'thick, dense', also giving name to *Greenshaw Farm* on the Ordnance Survey map of 1876.

Green Street (at Upton Park) Newham. This street name preserves the name of the old hamlet of *Grenestrete or Grene Lane* 1527, later *Greenstreet* as on the Ordnance Survey map of 1888, that is 'the green or grassy hamlet', from Middle English *grene* and *strete*. *Green Street House*, marked thus on the 1805 Ordnance Survey map, was a 16th-century mansion popularly known as *Anne Boleyn's Tower* and *Boleyn Castle* because of the tradition that Anne Boleyn occasionally resided here during her courtship by Henry VIII. *Grenestreet Park* (no doubt the grounds of the house) is mentioned in the late 16th century. The house was demolished in 1955, but the immediate area is still known locally as 'The Boleyn' and several nearby roads are named after Henry VIII's wives.

Green Street Green Bromley. Marked thus on Bowen's map of *c*.1762 and as *Greenstreet Green* on the Ordnance Survey map of 1819, earlier *La Grenestrete c*.1290, *Grenstrete* 1292, *Grenestrete* 1293, that is 'the green or grassy hamlet', from Middle English *grene* (adjective) and *strete*, with the later addition of *green* (noun) 'village green'.

Greenwich (town and borough). *Grenewic* 964, *Grenawic* 1013 (Anglo-Saxon Chronicle), *Grenviz* 1086 (Domesday Book), *Grenewic* 1226, that is 'the green trading settlement or harbour', from Old English *grēne* and *wīc*. 'Green' may refer to grass or other vegetation. The place is mentioned in the Anglo-Saxon Chronicle because a Viking army was encamped here for several years in the early 11th century. **Greenwich Park**, open to the public since the 18th century, dates back to the early 15th century. The Royal Naval College (earlier the Royal Naval Hospital) occupies the site of *Greenwich Palace*, which was built in 1426 and was the favourite residence of Henry VIII and Elizabeth I; the oldest of the four present buildings (King Charles's building) dates from the late 17th century. Greenwich is of course known worldwide for its association with the prime meridian, since 1884 accepted as that passing through the Royal Observatory here (founded in 1675 and now part of the National Maritime Museum). Greenwich is pronounced 'Grinidge', 'Grinitch', or 'Grenitch', that is with a short vowel and without sounding the medial -*w*-.

Gresham Street City. Created in 1845 and named after Sir Thomas *Gresham*, the enterprising Elizabethan merchant and financier who founded the first ROYAL EXCHANGE in 1570 (on the site of the present building which was opened in 1844) and Gresham College in 1579. Part of the street was once called *Cateaton Street*, earlier *Cattestrate* 1271, *Cattonlane alias Cattestrete* 1449, that is 'lane or street frequented by cats', from Middle English *catt* (although this may be a reference to prostitution: the word *cat* is evidenced in the slang sense 'prostitute' from 1401).

Grim's Ditch or Grim's Dyke (near Pinner and Stanmore) Harrow. The remains of a massive linear earthwork (probably dating from the 5th century and formerly much more extensive than now), marked *Grimes Dike* on the Ordnance Survey map of 1877 and recorded as *Grimesdich* 1289, *Grymesdich* 1541, that is 'ditch associated with Grīm', from Old English *dīc*. The same name occurs for similar earthworks in other English counties, *Grim* being probably a nickname for the heathen god Woden, to whose activities these earthworks were ascribed by superstitious Saxon settlers! It gives name to Grimsdyke House (built 1872), once the home of W. S. Gilbert.

Grosvenor Square & Street Westminster. Laid out during the 18th century on the estate belonging to the *Grosvenor* family, Dukes of Westminster, *see* BELGRAVIA.

Grove, The (at Carshalton) Sutton. Recorded as *Kersalton grove* in 1409, that is 'the grove or copse at CARSHALTON', from Old English *grāf(a)*.

Grovelands Park (at Southgate) Enfield. Named from Grovelands House, built in 1797 and marked thus on the Ordnance Survey map of 1887, now Grovelands Priory, a psychiatric hospital. Earlier called *Southgate Grove* and probably to be associated with *le Grofe c*.1500, from Old English *grāf(a)* 'a grove or copse'. The park, now a public place, was landscaped by Humphrey Repton in the early 19th century.

Grove Park (at Chiswick) Hounslow. Named from *Chiswick Grove* 1822, earlier *Grava c*.1210, *the Grove* 1412, from Old English *grāf(a)* 'a grove or copse'. The former *Grove House* here survived until 1928.

Grove Park Lewisham. First recorded on the Ordnance Survey map of 1905, self-explanatory, see previous name.

Guildhall Buildings & Yard City. Small streets named from the Guildhall, the centre of civic government for the City of London. The present building, dating back to the 13th century (*Gildhall* 1260) and to 1411, was partly destroyed by the Great Fire of 1666 and was again badly damaged by an air raid in 1940. There was an earlier building on the same site, perhaps the guildhall recorded *c*.1128.

Gunnersbury Hounslow. *Gounyldebury* 1334, *Gunnyldesbury* 1348, *Gonelsbury* 1487, *Gunnersbury* 1593, that is 'manor house of a woman called Gunnhildr', from Middle English *bury* and an Old Scandinavian personal name. There is no documentary support for the local legend that the woman in question was Gunhilda, niece of King Canute, but she was probably of Anglo-Danish stock. **Gunnersbury Park** formerly belonged to the early 19th-century house called *Gunnersbury Park* (marked thus on the Ordnance Survey map of 1876–7, now a museum).

Gutteridge Wood Hillingdon. Marked thus on the Ordnance Survey map of 1880, earlier *Great Headge Wood c.* 1600, *woods called Great Hedge* 1610, *Grutedge Wood* 1754, that is 'wood with a large hedge', from Middle English *grete* and *hegge*. The modern form of the name results from its pronunciation in the local dialect.

Gutter Lane (off Cheapside) City. *Godrun lane c.*1185, *Godrunelane c.*1200, *Gotherlane* 1349, *Gutterlane* 1472, that is 'lane of a woman called Guthrún', from Middle English *lane* and an Old Scandinavian personal name.

Guy's Hospital Southwark. Named after Thomas *Guy* (1644–1724), publisher and benefactor, who built and endowed the original hospital here, opened in 1726.

H

Hackbridge (near Carshalton) Sutton. *Hakebruge c.*1235, *Hakebrygge* 1360, *Hakebregge* 1429, that is 'bridge at the hook-shaped piece of land', from Old English *haca* and *brycg*. The first element probably refers to the area of land between two headstreams of the River WANDLE which merge just upstream from where the bridge (still called **Hack Bridge**) crosses.

Hackney (district and borough). *Hakeneia* 1198, *Hakeneye* 1242, *Hackeneye* 1253, *Hackney* 1535, possibly 'island, or dry ground in marsh, of a man called *Haca', from an Old English personal name (with genitive -*n*) and *ēg*. Alternatively, the first element could be Old English *haca* 'hook-shaped ridge or tongue of land', *compare* previous name and also HACTON. Hackney was still largely rural in character up to the beginning of the 19th century. **Hackney Downs** are referred to as *lands called the Downe* 1550 and were the home of William *atte Doune* 1302, that is '(living) at the down or hill', from Middle English *atte* and *doun*. **Hackney Marsh** is referred to as *Hakenemersshe* in 1397 and was the home of John *de Mersshe* 1307, from Middle English *mershe* 'marsh'. The residential district of **South Hackney** was still mainly farmland on the Ordnance Survey map of 1822.

Hackney Wick Hackney. Marked thus on the Ordnance Survey map of 1822, earlier *la Wike* 1231, *ferm of Wyk* 1299, *Wyke* 1399, that is 'the specialized farm or trading settlement (at HACKNEY)' from Old English *wīc*. Its situation on the River LEA is significant.

Hacton Havering. *Haketon* 1310, *Aketon* 1380, *Hackton* 1805, 'farmstead on a hook-shaped piece of land', from Old English *haca* and *tūn*, referring to a tongue of land formed by the junction of INGREBOURNE RIVER and a small tributary formerly called *Hakelondsbroke* 1318, that is 'hook-land's brook'.

Hadley, Monken Hadley Barnet. *Hadlegh* 1248, *Hadle, Hedle* 1291, *Monken Hadley* 1489, *Munkyn Hadley* 1553, that is 'clearing where heather grows, heath clearing', from Old English *hǣth* and *lēah*. Affix is Middle English *monken* 'of the monks', referring to early possession of the manor by the Benedictine monks of Walden Abbey in Essex. **Hadley Common** is marked thus on the Ordnance Survey map of 1887. **Hadley Green** is also marked on the 1887 map and is referred to in the surname of William *atte Grene* (i.e. '(living) at the green') 1345. It was near here that the decisive Battle of Barnet was fought between Yorkists and Lancastrians in 1471. See also HADLEY WOOD.

Hadley Wood Enfield. Marked thus on the Ordnance Survey map of 1904, named from (MONKEN) HADLEY; this residential district developed on the western edge of ENFIELD CHASE after the Great Northern Railway built a station here in 1884.

Haggerston Hackney. *Hergotestane* 1086 (Domesday Book), *Hergotestune* c.1220, *Hergodeston* c.1225, *Hargarston* 1593, probably 'boundary stone of a man called Hærgod', from an Old English personal name and *stān* (although the spelling from c.1220 may rather indicate a second element *tūn* 'farmstead, settlement').

Hainault Redbridge. *Henehout* 1221, *Hyneholt* 1239, *Hineholt* 1323, *Heynold* 1513, that is 'wood belonging to a religious community', from Old English *hīwan* (genitive plural *hīgna*) and *holt*, referring to its possession in medieval times by the ancient abbey of BARKING. The modern spelling, found only from the 17th century, is due to a fictitious connection with Philippa of Hainault (1314–69), queen to Edward III. The 'wood' itself was once part of WALTHAM or EPPING FOREST, and **Hainault Forest** (called *Henhault Forest* on the Ordnance Survey map of 1805) is what remains of it.

Hale, The (near Edgware) Barnet. Marked thus on the Ordnance Survey map of 1822, and as simply *Hale* on the 1877 map, recorded earlier as *the Hale* 1294, *Hale* 1525, *Netherhale* 1588, that is 'the nook or corner of land', from Old English *halh* (dative case *hale*), with reference to its situation in the far north-west corner of the old parish of HENDON.

Hale End Waltham Forest. Recorded thus in 1636 and on the Ordnance Survey map of 1805, named from *la Hale* 1285, *the Hale* 1517, that is 'the nook or corner of land', from Old English *halh* (dative case *hale*) with the later addition of Middle English *ende* 'district, quarter'. In 1640 it is referred to as *Woodend otherwise Hale(s)end* from its proximity to part of EPPING FOREST.

Halfway Reach (stretch of the River Thames off Thamesmead). Marked thus on the Ordnance Survey map of 1805, so named from *Halfway House* on the same map, earlier *Half Way House* on Bowen's map of *c*.1762. This house was situated on the south bank promontory of CROSS NESS, and like *Half Way Tree* shown on the opposite bank (in DAGENHAM) on Bowen's map (earlier *Middwaye tree* in 1588), was no doubt so called because it marked the *halfway* point for ships sailing up river from Gravesend and Tilbury to the POOL of London.

Haling Park Croydon. So called on the Ordnance Survey map of 1876, named from *Halling(es)* 1200, *Halinge* 1202, *Hal(l)ink* 1229, *Haling* 1251, *Halynke c*.1320. A difficult name, possibly manorial in origin from a family *de Halling* (from Halling in Kent, '*Heall's people'), but perhaps from Old English *hlinc* 'ledge' with an uncertain first element.

Halliwick Hospital & Road (at Colney Hatch) Barnet. Preserve the old name *Halewike* 1227, *Hallewyc* 1235, *Halewyke* 1252, *Hollicke* 1593, from Old English *wīc* 'specialized farm or trading settlement', possibly with Old English *halh* 'nook or corner of land'. The name also survives in a different form in Hollick Wood Avenue.

Hall Place (at Old Bexley) Bexley. Marked thus on Bowen's map of *c*.1762 and on the Ordnance Survey map of 1876, the present mansion (now a library and museum) dates from the 16th century. It replaced an earlier 'hall house', once the dwelling (or workplace) of a family called *ate halle* (thus in 1301), that is '(living) at the hall', from Middle English *atte* and *hall*.

Ham Richmond. *Hama c*.1150, *Hamme* 1154, *Hammes* 1235, *Ham* 1532, from Old English *hamm*, here in the sense 'land in a river bend' (referring to the great loop in the River Thames). **Ham Common** is so called on the Ordnance Survey map of 1816. The magnificent **Ham House** dates from the early 17th century.

Ham, East & West Newham. *Hamme* 958 (Anglo-Saxon charter), *Hame* 1086 (Domesday Book), *Westhamma* 1186, *West Hamm* 1198, *Estham* 1206, *Esthamme* 1219, *Esthammes, Westhammes c*.1250, from Old English *hamm* here used in the sense 'area of dry land bounded by water or marsh' (referring to the situation of East and West Ham between the valleys of the Rivers LEA and RODING and north of the Thames marshes).The distinguishing affixes *east* and *west* show that the original estate was already divided by the late 12th century. Whereas East Ham remained an agricultural village until the late 19th century, West Ham

was relatively populous and industrialized even in medieval times.
West Ham Park is marked thus on the Ordnance Survey map of 1904,
earlier simply *Ham Park* (next to *Ham House*) on that of 1888; this was
once a private estate, in the 18th century the site of an important
botanical garden.

Hamfrith Road (in West Ham) Newham. Preserves the old name *Ham-
me(s)frith* 1285, *Westhamfrith* 1353, that is 'woodland at West Ham',
from Old English *fyrhth(e)* 'sparse woodland, scrub'; the wood here
survived until about 1700.

Hammersmith Hammersmith & Fulham. *Hamersmyth* 1294, *Hamere-
smithe* 1312, *Hamyrsmyth* 1535, *Hammersmith* 1675, that is '(place with) a
hammer smithy or forge', from Old English *hamor* and *smiththe*. Hammersmith was part of the Bishop of London's manor of FULHAM until
1834. **Hammersmith Bridge**, built in 1887, replaced another suspension bridge (the first in London) built some sixty years earlier. **Hammersmith Flyover** was built in 1961 to take traffic on the GREAT WEST
ROAD (A4) out of the town centre. The London Borough of Hammersmith & Fulham was created in 1965.

Hampstead Camden. *Hemstede* 959, *Hamstede* 978 (Anglo-Saxon charters), *Hamestede* 1086 (Domesday Book), *Hampstede* 1258, that is 'the
homestead', from Old English *hām-stede*. It will be noted that the
spelling with intrusive *-p-* first appears in the mid-13th century. **South
Hampstead** was developed from the later 19th century. The older
district of **West Hampstead** was formerly known as *West End*, *see* WEST
END LANE. **Hampstead Heath** is *Hampstede Heth* 1543, from Old English
hæth; it was still a wild tract haunted by wolves in the 13th century.
One of the ponds here is mentioned at this period, as *la ponde in villa de
Hamstede* 1274, from Middle English *ponde*. A medicinal chalybeate
spring discovered on the south-west edge of the heath in the late 17th
century resulted in a fashionable spa known as *Hampstead Wells*, recalled in Well Walk (recorded thus in 1698). North of the Heath is
HAMPSTEAD GARDEN SUBURB.

Hampstead Garden Suburb Barnet. Residential area north of HAMP-
STEAD HEATH developed from 1907 according to the ideas of the well-
known philanthropist Dame Henrietta Barnett.

Hampton Richmond. *Hamntone* 1086 (Domesday Book), *Hantune* c.1130,
Hamton 1202, *Hampton* 1237, that is 'farmstead or estate in a river

bend', from Old English *hamm* and *tūn*, referring to the great bend in the River Thames here. **Hampton Hill** is mainly a 19th-century development, marked thus on the Ordnance Survey map of 1904 but earlier called *New Hampton* as on the map of 1876. *See also* HAMPTON COURT and HAMPTON WICK.

Hampton Court, Hampton Court Palace Richmond. There is record of *Hampton Courte* in 1476, that is 'manor house at HAMPTON' from Middle English *court*, referring to the earlier medieval manor house here which was pulled down by Cardinal Wolsey when he bought the estate in 1514 and started to build his own much grander residence. On Wolsey's fall from favour in 1529, the new *Hampton Court* was then transformed by Henry VIII into the splendid royal palace to which further additions and improvements were made in later centuries (notably by Sir Christopher Wren at the end of the 17th). The district is therefore named from the Palace. **Hampton Court Park** is *The Greate Parke of Hampton* in 1563, *see also* BUSHY PARK. The present **Hampton Court Bridge**, opened in 1933, replaced earlier bridges here, the first built in 1753.

Hampton Wick Richmond. *Wica* 13th century, *Hamptone la Wyke* 1263, *Wīk* 1274, *Hamptonwicke* 1615, that is 'the harbour or trading settlement for HAMPTON', from Old English *wīc*. This hamlet (on the Thames some 4 miles downstream from the main settlement at Hampton itself and therefore much closer to London) no doubt developed as a landing place for goods passing into and out of the manor.

Hanger Hill Ealing. Shown thus on Seller's map of 1710 and on the Ordnance Survey map of 1822, marking the site of a former wood called *le Hangrewode* 1393, *Aungrewode c.*1420, *Hangar wood* 1539, that is 'wood on a steep slope', from Old English *hangra* and *wudu*. It gives name to **Hanger Lane** (now of course mainly known for its 'gyratory system') which was earlier *Hanger Hill Lane* on Rocque's map of 1741–5 and the site of *Hangerlane Farm* marked thus on the Ordnance Survey map of 1876–7.

Hanover Square (near Oxford Circus) Westminster. Laid out *c.*1720 and named from the royal house, the Elector of *Hanover* having come to the throne as George I in 1714.

Hanwell Ealing. *Hanewelle* 959, *Hanawella* 998 (Anglo-Saxon charters), *Hanewelle* 1086 (Domesday Book), *Hanwell* 1402, that is probably 'spring or stream frequented by cocks (of wild birds)', from Old English *hana* and *wella*. The corresponding Old English masculine personal name *Hana* is perhaps less likely in this name, *compare* HANWORTH.

Hanworth Hounslow. *Haneworde* 1086 (Domesday Book), *Haneworth* 1359, *Hanneworth* 1389, *Hanworth* 1428, that is probably 'enclosed settlement of a man called Hana', from Old English *worth* and an Old English personal name, compare previous name. **Hanworth Park** is marked thus on the Ordnance Survey map of 1822 and earlier on Norden's map of 1593; Hanworth Park House was built here *c.*1820. The earlier medieval manor house of Hanworth, destroyed by fire in 1797, was once used by Henry VIII as a hunting lodge.

Happy Valley Croydon. A recent complimentary name for open land near FARTHING DOWNS, usually bestowed on a spot considered particularly pleasant and favourable for picnics and the like (there are several examples of the same name in other parts of England). However nearby **Devilsden Wood**, named from The Devil's Den (*Devils Den* 1810), suggests that the area was once thought to be rather more sinister and dangerous!

Harefield Hillingdon. *Herefelle* (*sic*) 1086 (Domesday Book), *Herrefeld* 1115, *Herefeld* 1206, *Harefeld* 1223, probably 'open land used by an army', from Old English *here* and *feld*. The exact significance of the name is not clear, but it may allude to an encampment by a Viking army during the Danish invasions of the 10th and early 11th centuries. **Harefield Moor** is *Herfeld Moor* 1394, from Old English *mōr* 'marshy ground'; this is low-lying land (now mainly sand and gravel pits) by the River COLNE and gives name to MOORHALL COTTAGES. Nearby **South Harefield** is a 20th-century development.

Hare Street (near Romford) Havering. *Herstrate* 1344, *Hare Street* 1514, *Hare Strett* 1523, literally 'army road', that is 'main road suitable for the passage of an army', from Old English *here-strǣt*. The reference is to the old Roman road from London to Colchester (here called Main Road).

Haringey (borough). The name of this new London borough (created 1965) is taken, with a change in spelling that is more historically accurate, from the district called HARRINGAY, *see also* HORNSEY for discussion of the origin of the name.

Harlesden Brent. *Herulvestune* 1086 (Domesday Book), *Herleston* 1195, *Harleston* 1365, *Harlesden* 1606, that is 'farmstead or estate of a man called Heoruwulf or Herewulf', from an Old English personal name and Old English *tūn*. It will be noted that the current spelling -*den*, found from 1606, is unhistorical, likewise the spelling -*don* which is sometimes found in early records (e.g. *Herlesdon* in 1291). It appears as *Holsdon Green* on the Ordnance Survey map of 1822.

Harley Street (in Marylebone) Westminster. Particularly famed for its doctors since the mid-19th century, previously a residential street laid out in the early 18th century, named after Edward *Harley*, 2nd Earl of Oxford, who possessed the manor of MARYLEBONE until his death in 1741. His extensive collection of books and manuscripts were bought from his heiress, the Duchess of Portland, for the British Museum.

Harlington Hillingdon. *Hygereding tun* 831 (Anglo-Saxon charter), *Herdintone* 1086 (Domesday Book), *Hardlyngton* 1475, *Harlyngton* 1521, that is 'farmstead or estate associated with a man called Hygerēd', from an Old English personal name with Old English medial -*ing*- and *tūn*.

Harmondsworth Hillingdon. *Hermondesyeord* (*sic*) 781 (14th-century copy of Anglo-Saxon charter), *Hermodesworde* 1086 (Domesday Book), *Heremodesworth* 1222, *Hermondesworth* 1316, *Harmesworth* 1485, that is 'enclosed settlement of a man called Heremund or Heremōd', from an Old English personal name and Old English *worth*. The 1485 spelling represents the old local pronunciation of the name.

Harold Court, Harold Hill & Harold Park Havering. All named from nearby HAROLD WOOD. A farm called *Haroldshill Farm* is marked on the Ordnance Survey map of 1883.

Harold Wood Havering. *Horalds Wood* c.1237, *Haroldeswoode* c.1272, *Horoldswode* 1281, *Hareldyswode* 1490, that is 'wood belonging to Harold', from Old English *wudu*. The reference is to Earl Harold, King of England for some ten months in 1066 until his defeat by William the Conqueror at Hastings. At the time of his death, Harold held the manor of HAVERING-ATTE-BOWER.

Harringay (near Hornsey) Haringey. District which takes its name from *Harringay House* (built in 1792 and marked *Harringhay House* on the Ordnance Survey map of 1822). The owner artificially revived an old alternative spelling of the name HORNSEY, which then became the name of the district and later (in a more historically accurate form) the name for the London borough in which Hornsey lies, *see* HARINGEY. **Harringay Stadium** station is named after the former stadium for greyhound racing here, opened in 1927 and closed in 1987.

Harrow (borough), **Harrow on the Hill**. *Gumeninga hergae* 767, *Hearge* 825, *Hergas* 832 (all Anglo-Saxon charters), *Herges* 1086 (Domesday Book), *Herwes* 1234, *Harwes c.* 1250, *Harwe* 1278, *Harowe* 1369, that is 'the heathen shrine(s) or temple(s)', from Old English *hearg* (with alternating singular and plural forms in early records). The fuller name **Harrow on the Hill** is first found at the end of the 14th century, as *Harowe atte Hille* 1398, *Harowe on the Hill* 1426, from Middle English *hill*. The prominent hill here (408 ft), now crowned by the church of St Mary partly dating back to the 11th century, was clearly an important site of pagan worship before the conversion of the Anglo-Saxons to Christianity from the early 7th century onwards. The earliest record of the name seems to mean 'heathen temple of a tribe called the *Gumeningas*' (of whom nothing more is known; their name too is obscure in origin). The prestigious **Harrow School** was founded here in 1572 by a local yeoman farmer, John Lyon, whose family is recorded in the neighbourhood from the 13th century. The residential district of **South Harrow** was developed from the late 19th century, **North** and **West Harrow** not until the 20th.

Harrow Green (at Leytonstone) Waltham Forest. Now named from an inn recorded as *Le Harrow* in 1651 (referring to the agricultural implement). It was earlier called *Sols Green* 1716, *Sauls Green* 1723, *Salts Green* 1805, from the surname *Sole* or *Saul* and Middle English *grene* 'village green'.

Harrow Lodge (at Hornchurch) Havering. Marked thus on the Ordnance Survey map of 1883, earlier *Harrow Farm* on maps of 1777 and 1805. Probably a transferred name from HARROW rather than an independent formation.

Harrow Weald Harrow. *Weldewode* 1282, *Welde* 1294, *Harewewelde* 1388, *Harrow Weelde* 1553, that is 'the forest or woodland at HARROW', from Old English *weald, see* WEALDSTONE. The old farmhouse here dates from *c.*1500.

Hart Street (off Mark Lane) City. Recorded as *Herthstrete* 1348, *Hertstrete* 1405, 'street where hearths or hearthstones were made and sold', from Middle English *herth* (Old English *heorth*) 'floor on which a fire is made'.

Harwood Hall (near Upminster) Havering. Marked as *Herwood* on a map of 1777 and on the Ordnance Survey map of 1805, but with its present spelling on the map of 1883, possibly 'stony wood' from Old English **hær* and *wudu*; the hall itself dates from the late 18th century.

Hatcham Park Road (at New Cross Gate) Lewisham. Preserves the name of the old manor of *Hatcham*, marked thus on the Ordnance Survey map of 1816 and recorded earlier as *Hacheham* 1086 (Domesday Book), *Hachesham* 1234, *Hechesham* 1247, that is 'homestead or enclosure of a man called Hæcci', from Old English *hām* or *hamm* and an Old English personal name. The district once occupied by this manor is now NEW CROSS GATE.

Hatch End Harrow. Recorded as *le Hacchehend* 1448, *Hacheend* 1475, that is 'parish district near the hatch gate', from Middle English *hache* and *ende*. The reference is to a gateway giving access to Pinner Park (a deer park in medieval times, *see* PINNER), which lies to the south.

Hatton Hounslow. *Hatone* 1086 (Domesday Book), *Hattone* 1211, *Hatton* 1293, that is 'farmstead or estate on the heath', from Old English *hæth* and *tūn*. The same heathy tract west of River CRANE gave name at a later date to HEATHROW. **Hatton Cross** refers to a crossroads here.

Hatton Garden (in Clerkenwell) Camden. Street called *Hatton streete* in 1665, it takes its name from the mansion known as *Hatton House* built *c.*1576 for Elizabeth I's Chancellor, Sir Christopher *Hatton*.

Haven Green Ealing. Marked thus on the Ordnance Survey map of 1876–7, so named from *Ealing(s) Haven* shown on Rocque's and Cary's maps of 1741–5 and 1786. Perhaps from *haven* in the sense 'a place of shelter or retreat, a refuge, an asylum', although its exact significance is not apparent, *see* EALING.

Havering (borough). Modern borough (formed 1965) named from HAVERING-ATTE-BOWER. In medieval times the Royal Liberty of Havering, created by a charter of Edward IV in 1465, covered much the same area, containing as it did the parishes of HORNCHURCH and ROMFORD as well as Havering-atte-Bower itself.

Havering-atte-Bower Havering. *Haueringas* 1086 (Domesday Book), *Haveringes* 1166, *Hauering atte Bower* 1272, *Haverynge atte Bure* 1305, that is '(settlement of) the family or followers of a man called *Hæfer', from an Old English personal name and *-ingas*. This is therefore an ancient folk name of the same type as BARKING and EALING. The affix, found from the 13th century, means 'at the bower or royal residence', from Middle English *atte* and *bour* (Old English *būr*), and refers to the former royal palace which once dominated the hilltop here close to the present village green. It was used by English kings and queens from the 11th century but had fallen into decay by the 17th century, although some of its stones and a coat of arms were incorporated into the mansion known as BOWER HOUSE, which of course also preserves its name. **Havering Park** is named thus on the Ordnance Survey map of 1805 and gives name to Park Farm; in fact a medieval *park* (i.e. 'tract of land for hunting') is recorded here as *parcus de Haveringes* in 1170.

Haverstock Hill Camden. Marked thus on Rocque's map of 1795 and on the Ordnance Survey map of 1822, but first recorded in 1741. The origin of the name is obscure, but it is perhaps manorial, from some landowning family from Stock near Chelmsford in Essex, which was called *Haverstocke* in the 17th century.

Hawk Wood, The (at Chingford) Waltham Forest. Marked as *Hawkwood* on the Ordnance Survey map of 1883, named from *Chyngeforde(s)halke* 1323, *Chyngford Hauke* 1501, that is 'the nook or corner of Chingford', from Middle English *halke*. The wood lies along the northern parish boundary of CHINGFORD.

Hawley's Corner Bromley. Marked thus on the Ordnance Survey map of 1871 and recorded as *Horley's Corner* in 1881, a hamlet situated at the south-west *corner* of the parish of CUDHAM and of the ancient hundred of RUXLEY, no doubt so called from the surname *Hawley* or *Horley* of some local family.

Haydon Hall Park (at Eastcote) Hillingdon. Named from *Haydon Hall* (marked thus on Greenwood's map of 1819), earlier *Heydons* 1611, so called from the family of John *Heydon* mentioned in local records in 1382. The original hall was built *c.*1630 and is now demolished. The present Haydon Lodge was built *c.*1880.

Haydons Road (South Wimbledon) Merton. Station named from the road, known as *Haydon's Road c.*1910 but earlier *Heydon Lane* 1860, so called after farmer George *Heydon* who managed a large farm to the west of the present road from the 1760s.

Hayes Bromley. *Hesa* 1177, *Hese* 1254, *Heys* 1610, from Old English *hæs(e)* 'land overgrown with brushwood', see also next name. **Hayes Common** is marked thus on the Ordnance Survey map of 1819. *Hayes Place*, a mansion pulled down in 1934, was built for William Pitt who died there in 1778. **Hayesford Park Drive** preserves the old name *Hayesford* marked thus on Bowen's map of *c*.1762, *Hayes Ford* in 1819, so called from a former *ford* here across the RAVENSBOURNE RIVER.

Hayes, Hayes Town Hillingdon. *linga hæse* 793, *Hæse* 831 (Anglo-Saxon charters), *Hesa* 1086 (Domesday Book), *Hese* 1232, *Hayes alias Hese* 1648, identical in origin with the previous name. The early prefix *linga* has not been explained. **Hayes End** is *Heese ende* 1571, *Heys End* 1675, from Middle English *ende* 'district of a village'; it lies at the extreme north-west end of the parish.

Hayes Lane (at Kenley) Croydon. Named from *Hays Farm* (marked thus on the Ordnance Survey map of 1816) or *Hays House* (on the 1878 map), from Old English *hæs(e)* 'land overgrown with brushwood' like the previous names.

Haymarket (near Piccadilly) Westminster. Marked *Hay Market* on the mid-16th century 'wood-cut map' of London. This street was once a lane where a market for hay and straw was held until 1830.

Haynes Park Havering. To be associated with a family called *Haynes* mentioned in local records from the 15th century.

Hay's Wharf (near London Bridge) Southwark. Named from Alexander *Hay* who first built a wharf here in 1651.

Hazelwood (near Downe) Bromley. Hamlet named from a wood nearby still called Hazel Wood, which is marked thus on the Ordnance Survey map of 1876 and recorded earlier as the surname of Geoffrey *Hasilwode* of CUDHAM in 1458, self-explanatory, 'hazel wood' from Old English *hæsel* and *wudu*.

Headstone Harrow. *Hegeton* 1348, *Heggestone* 1367, *Heggeton* 1398, *Hedston* 1754, probably 'farmstead enclosed by a hedge', from Old English *hecg* and *tūn*. The unhistorical spellings with *He(a)d-* do not make their appearance until the late 17th century. The original name no doubt refers to **Headstone Manor** (on Headstone Lane which gives name to the station), a moated manor house partly dating from the 14th century and referred to on the Ordnance Survey map of 1822 as *Headstone Farm*; it is now the Harrow Museum and Heritage Centre.

Heath Park (near Romford) Havering. So named from the former heathland here, still also recalled in nearby SQUIRRELS HEATH.

Heathrow Hillingdon. Marked on the Ordnance Survey map of 1822 as *Heath Row*, earlier *La Hetherewe* c.1410, *Hitherowe* 1547, that is 'the row of houses on or near the heath', from Middle English *hethe* and *rewe*. The reference is to the tract of heathland west of the River CRANE that gave name at an earlier date to HATTON. The old settlement was swept away when **Heathrow Airport** was built, opened in 1946.

Hendon Barnet. *Hendun* 959, *Heandun* c.975 (Anglo-Saxon charters), *Handone* 1086 (Domesday Book), *Hendon* 1199, that is '(place at) the high hill', from Old English *hēah* (dative case *hēan*) and *dūn*. The church of St Mary around which the original settlement developed stands on a prominent hill, reaching 280 ft and visible for many miles from the west and south-west. Hendon Aerodrome, opened here in 1911, was famous for its annual air displays in the 1920s and 1930s, *see* GRAHAME PARK. **West Hendon** was mainly developed from the end of the 19th century.

Herne Hill Southwark/Lambeth. So called in 1789, also *Hern Hill* on the Ordnance Survey map of 1816, probably named from a field called *le Herne* c.1495, that is 'the angle or corner of land' from Old English *hyrne*, with the later addition of *hill*. Alternatively, it may take its name from the family called *Herne* mentioned in connection with nearby DULWICH from the 17th century (although their surname almost certainly derives from the same, or a similar, early place name).

Heron Quays Tower Hamlets. Station named from Heron Quay, part of WEST INDIA DOCKS.

Heston Hounslow. *Hestone* c.1125, *Hestune* c.1130, *Heyston* c.1495, *Hesson* 1635, that is 'farmstead or estate among the brushwood', from Old English **hǣs* and *tūn*.

Hewitts (near Chelsfield) Bromley. Marked thus on a map of 1799 and on the Ordnance Survey map of 1876, earlier *Hewette* 1268, *la Hewette* 1305, that is 'place where trees have been hewed or cut down, a woodland clearing', from Old English *hīewet*.

Higham Hill (near Walthamstow) Waltham Forest. Marked thus on the Ordnance Survey map of 1822, earlier *Heighamhill* 1501, so named from *Hecham* 1086 (Domesday Book), *Heyham* 1264, *Heghham* 1307,

Higham 1368, that is 'high (or chief) homestead or enclosure', from Old English *hēah* and *hām* or *hamm*, with the later addition of *hill*. Nearby **Highams Park**, also marked as *Higham Hill* on the Ordnance Survey map of 1822 but as *Highams* on that of 1883, is named from the same ancient manorial estate. The park itself was once part of the grounds of *Higham(s) House*, built 1768; the area known as Highams Park takes its name from the railway station so called, opened in 1873.

High Barnet, *see* BARNET, CHIPPING & HIGH.

Highbury Islington. *Heybury c.*1375, *Heyghbury* 1407, *Highbury* 1535, that is 'high manor', from Middle English *heghe* and *bury*, so called because it stands on higher ground than both BARNSBURY and CANONBURY. Earlier the manor was called *Neweton Barrewe* (as in 1274) or *Newenton Barwe* (1294), indicating that it was once part of the neighbouring parish of STOKE NEWINGTON, the addition being manorial from a family called *de Barewe* here in the 13th century.

High Elms (near Downe) Bromley. Marked thus on a map of 1769 and as *High-elms Farm* on the Ordnance Survey map of 1819, self-explanatory. The later mansion here, built in 1842, was destroyed by fire in 1967.

Highgate Haringey. *Le Heighgate* 1354, *Heghegate* 1377, *Heygate* 1391, *Highgate* 1440, that is 'the high toll gate', from Middle English *heghe* and *gate*. The reference is to a toll gate set up here in early times on the Great North Road by the Bishop of London, then lord of the manor of HORNSEY. At 426 ft, this is one of the highest spots in the old county of Middlesex; **Highgate Hill** is recorded as *Highegate Hill* in 1565. **Highgate Cemetery**, established in the early 19th century, is well known as the resting place of many famous people, including the philosopher Karl Marx (1833), the poet Christina Rossetti (1894), and the novelist Mrs Henry Wood (1887). **Highgate Wood** was once also part of the Bishop of London's estate, *see* BISHOPSWOOD ROAD.

High Timber Street (near Queenhithe) City. Referred to as 'road into *la Tymberhethe*' 1272, *Tymberhuthe-strete* 1297, *Timber Hithe* or *Timber street* 1603, street named from the former riverside wharf recorded as *Tymberhethe c.*1210, that is 'landing place for timber', from Old English *timber* and *hȳth*.

Highwood Hill (near Mill Hill) Barnet. *Highwodhyll* 1543, *Hyewoodhill* 1568, named from *alto bosco* (Latin) 1321, *Highwode*, *Hiwode* 1523, self-explanatory, 'the high wood' from Middle English *heghe* and *wode* with the later addition of *hill*. The elevation here is 443 ft.

Hill End (at Harefield) Hillingdon. Marked as *Hillend* on the Ordnance Survey map of 1880, that is 'district (of the village) by the hill', from Middle English *ende*. The hill referred to is called ONE TREE HILL (268 ft).

Hillingdon (town and borough). *Hildendune* c.1080, *Hillendone* 1086 (Domesday Book), *Hillindon* 1248, *Hillingdon* 1291, that is 'hill of a man called Hilda', from an Old English personal name (genitive case *-n*) and Old English *dūn*. **Hillingdon Court** and **Hillingdon Heath** are marked thus on the Ordnance Survey map of 1880. The residential district of **North Hillingdon** is a 20th-century development. The London Borough of Hillingdon was created in 1965.

Hillside Bexley. Recent name for residential area near BELVEDERE.

Hither Green Lewisham. Marked thus on the Ordnance Survey map of 1805, earlier spelt *Hether* or *Heather Green* in 18th-century parish registers and *Hether* or *Hither Green* on 18th century maps, but no doubt from *hither* meaning 'nearer to LEWISHAM' in view of a neighbouring *Further Green* recorded from the early 19th century (and giving name to Further Green Road). In medieval times this area was known as *Rumbergh* 1241, that is probably 'the wide hill or barrow', from Old English *rūm* and *beorg* (preserved in ROMBOROUGH GARDENS & WAY).

Hockenden, Upper Hockenden (near Ruxley) Bromley. *Hokindenne* 1240, *Hokynden* 1258, *Hokyn(g)denn* 1278, *Hockendon* c.1762, probably 'woodland pasture (for swine) associated with a man called Hōc', from an Old English personal name with Old English medial *-ing-* and *denn*.

Hoe Street (in Walthamstow) Waltham Forest. Recorded thus in 1697 and on the Ordnance Survey map of 1805, from Old English *hōh* 'ridge'.

Hogsmill River (flowing from Ewell into the River Thames at Kingston). So named in 1638 from Hogs Mill (in KINGSTON) which is *Hoggs Myll* 1535, from a local family called *Hogg*. The earlier name of the river was *Lurtebourne* 1439, that is 'dirty or muddy stream', from Old English **lort(e)* and *burna*. The main source of the river is at Ewell in Surrey, the name of which means 'river-spring', from Old English *ǣwell*.

Holborn Camden. *Holeburne* 1086 (Domesday Book), *Holeburn* 1191, *Howeborne* 1551, *Holbourne* 1567, that is '(place by) the hollow stream, or stream in a hollow', from Old English *hol* (as adjective or noun) and *burna*. The stream itself which gave name to the place, the *Holborn*, is referred to as *Holeburne* in an Anglo-Saxon charter of 959; the 'hollow' can still be seen in part along the course of the present Farringdon Road (*see* FARRINGDON). This was originally the name of the upper part of the stream known later as the FLEET river. The street now known as **(High) Holborn** is referred to as *Holeburnstreete* in 1249. **Holborn Circus** dates from 1872. **Holborn Viaduct**, bridging the valley of the *Holborn* or FLEET, was opened by Queen Victoria in 1869. The pronunciation of Holborn is 'Holeburn' or 'Hoeburn' (with or without sounding the *-l-*).

Holcombe Hill, Holecombe Dale (near Mill Hill) Barnet. Named from *Hocumfeild* 1574, *Hocome Hill* 1686, probably 'deep or hollow valley', from Old English *hol* and *cumb*.

Holders Hill (near Hendon) Barnet. *Oldershyll* 1584, *Holders Hill* 1750, that is 'hill associated with a family called *Holder*'; one Roger *le Holdere* is mentioned in local records in 1294.

Holland Park Kensington & Chelsea. Marked thus on the Ordnance Survey map of 1876, named from **Holland House**, earlier *The Earle of Hollands House* 1658, *Holland House* 1664, once home of the Earls of *Holland*. This Jacobean mansion (built *c*.1606 and still partly preserved) was inherited by the wife of Henry Rich, 1st Earl of Holland, in 1621.

Holloway, Lower & Upper Islington. *Le Holeweye in Iseldon* 1307, *Holway* 1473, *Holowey* 1543, *Hollowaye* 1554, that is 'the hollow road, the road in a hollow', from Old English *hol* and *weg*. The road referred to, a section of the Great North Road crossing relatively low-lying land between HIGHGATE and ISLINGTON, is still called **Holloway Road**. The hamlets of **Lower & Upper Holloway** on its route (marked thus on the Ordnance Survey map of 1822) are distinguished by the 16th century; they are recorded as *Holway the lower* and *Holway the upper* on Norden's map of 1593. **Holloway Prison** was opened here in 1852 and rebuilt in 1970; it has been the country's main prison exclusively for women since 1902 (among its inmates in the years after 1906 were Mrs Pankhurst and other suffragettes). Holloway's most famous resident (at 'The Laurels, Brickfield Terrace') was probably the fictitious Mr Charles Pooter, hero of G. and W. Grossmith's *The Diary of a Nobody* (1892)!

Holly Lodge Estate (at Highgate) Haringey. Garden suburb created in the 1920s, named after a former mansion called *Holly Lodge* built *c*.1830.

Holwood Bromley. Marked thus on the Ordnance Survey map of 1819, earlier recorded as *Holwod* 1484, *Holewoode Hill* 1601, that is 'wood in a hollow', from Old English *hol* and *wudu*. The present **Holwood House** was built in 1827; in its grounds is 'Wilberforce Oak' where William Pitt the Younger (who owned the earlier house here) and William Wilberforce are said to have discussed the abolition of the slave trade. Also in the grounds is 'Caesar's Camp', see under KESTON.

Holywell Lane (in Shoreditch) Hackney. Recorded as *Haliwellelane* 1382 and preserving the name of the Augustinian priory of Holywell, which is *Haliwelle* 12th century, *Halywell* 1426, *Holywell* 1510, that is 'the holy spring', from Old English *hālig* and *wella*. The priory was founded here in 1152–8 and owned a great deal of land in SHOREDITCH until it was dissolved in 1539. Indeed Shoreditch High Street was called *Haliwelle-strete* in medieval times. The well here is mentioned as *Fons Sacer* (Latin for 'holy well') in William FitzStephen's account of London in 1174, as one of three wells named as popular gathering places for young people, *see* CLERKENWELL and ST CLEMENT DANES.

Homerton Hackney. *Humburton* 1343, *Homberton* 1355, *Hummerton* 1581, *Hommerton* 1822, that is 'farmstead or estate of a woman called Hūn-burh', from an Old English personal name and Old English *tūn*. Other early names referring to female ownership or occupation include GUNNERSBURY, GUTTER LANE, and LEATHER LANE.

Honey Lane (off Cheapside) City. Preserves the old name of *Hunilane* c.1200, *Honylane* 1275, *Honilane* 1279, that is 'lane where honey was produced and sold' (and no doubt where beekeepers lived), from Middle English *huni* and *lane*. This was one of several specialized market streets near to the main City market of *Cheap* (for which, *see* CHEAP-SIDE). The present alley lies some 150 ft east of the medieval lane.

Honor Oak, Honor Oak Park Southwark. Originally referring to an oak tree situated on ONE TREE HILL marking the boundary between CAM-BERWELL (in Surrey) and LEWISHAM (in Kent), called *the Oke of Honor* in 1609 and giving name to *Oak of Honour Wood* 1763, reputed to be so called because Queen Elizabeth I dined under it in 1602 on one of her visits to Lewisham, from Middle English *hon(o)ur* 'renown, high rank, dignity'. The name has retained the early English spelling *honor*, widely used alongside *honour* until the mid-17th century. The original oak was struck by lightning c.1884 but another was planted in its place.

Hook Kingston. *Hoke* 1227, *La Hoke* 1235, *Houke* 1312, *Hook* 1680, that is 'the hook-shaped spur of land', from Old English *hōc*, with the French definite article in the 1235 form. The name could also describe the shape of the parish, which is elongated north–south with a curved tip at its northern end.

Hornchurch Havering. *Monasterium Cornutum* (a Latinized form of the name) 1222, *Hornechurch* 1233, *Hornedechirche* 1291, *Hornedecherche* 1311, that is 'church with horn-like gables', from Old English *horn* (noun) or *hornede* (adjective) and *cirice*. The figure of the bull's head with horns now affixed to the east end of the church here is probably no older than the late 18th century in date. The name must refer to a much more ancient architectural feature, probably to gables notable for their width and size. **South Hornchurch** is a relatively recent development on what was formerly open farmland and market gardens.

Hornfair Park (in Charlton) Greenwich. Named from the notorious 'Horn Fair' held at CHARLTON (originally on the village green) from early times up to 1872, *see* CUCKOLD'S POINT. It is to be noted that the old manor of *Horne* (*see* HORN PARK) lay just to the south of Charlton; it is perhaps a possibility that the idea for the fair arose in the first place from a fanciful association of the topographical name *Horne* with the horns of a cuckold!

Horniman Museum (at Forest Hill) Lewisham. Founded in 1901 by the tea merchant Frederick J. *Horniman* whose anthropological and musical collections are housed here.

Horn Park (near Eltham) Greenwich. Marked thus on Bowen's map of *c.*1762 and on the Ordnance Survey map of 1805, an old manor recorded as *Horne* 1242, *park of Horne* 1481, from Old English *horn* 'projecting horn-shaped piece of land'.

Hornsey Haringey. *Haringeie* 1201, *Harengheye* 1232, *Haringesheye* 1243, *Harynsey* 1401, *Haringsaye alias Harnesey* 1557, *Haringay alias Hornesey* *c.*1580, probably 'enclosure of a man called *Hæring', from Old English *hæg* and an Old English personal name. Alternatively, 'enclosure in or by the grey wood', if the first element is rather an Old English word *hāring* (a derivative of Old English *hār* 'grey, hoar'). Hornsey is a regular development of *Haringesheye*, but the alternative old form of the name, *Haringeie* or *Haringay* without medial -*es*-, was adopted in the 19th century as the name of a district within Hornsey and eventually

for the London borough created in 1965 in which it lies, *see* HARINGEY
and HARRINGAY. **Hornsey Vale** is a self-explanatory modern name for a
relatively low-lying area mainly developed in the late 19th century.

Horns Green (near Cudham) Bromley. Marked thus on maps of 1821
and 1871, to be associated with the family of John *de Horne* 1292,
whose name derives from Old English *horn* 'a horn-shaped feature, a
projecting piece of land'.

Horseferry Road Westminster. Named from the old horse ferry across
the River Thames belonging to the Archbishops of Canterbury and
linking Lambeth Palace (*see* LAMBETH) with WESTMINSTER, recorded as
le Horsefery in 1536. The ferry closed down when WESTMINSTER BRIDGE
was built in 1750, although the first LAMBETH BRIDGE only appeared
in 1862.

Horse Guards Parade (near Whitehall) Westminster. Sited on the tilt-
yard of *Whitehall Palace* (*see* WHITEHALL), the setting for spectacular
tournaments and exercises in the 16th century, but now chiefly famous for the annual ceremony of 'Trooping the Colour' on the monarch's official birthday in early June. The present **Horse Guards**
buildings, dating from 1750–8, replaced a much smaller 17th-century
guardhouse originally built opposite the *Palace*.

Horselydown Lane (at Bermondsey) Southwark. Preserves the old name
Horseidune c.1175, *Horseyedoune* 1255, *Horsadown* c.1450, *Horslydown*
c.1580, that is 'hill at the dry ground in marsh where horses are kept',
from Old English *hors* and *ēg* with *dūn*, the final element referring to
relatively higher ground in low-lying marshland by the River Thames.
The medial *-l-* is unhistorical, first appearing in the 16th century.

Horsenden Hill & Wood Ealing. *Horsendun* 1203, *Horsindune* 1262, *Hor-
sindon* 1302, *Horsington Hill* 1819, *Horsington Wood* 1822, that is 'hill of a
man called Horsa', from an Old English personal name (genitive case
-n) and Old English *dūn*, with the later addition of (explanatory) *hill* and
wood. The hill here reaches an elevation of 277 ft.

Hosier Lane (off Smithfield Street) City. *Hosiereslane* 1328, *Hosierelane*
1333, 'lane of the hosiers', from Middle English *hosiere* 'maker or seller
of hose (i.e. stockings, leggings, and socks)'.

Houndsditch City. Street named from *Hondesdich* 1275, *Hundesdich* 1502,
possibly 'ditch frequented by (wild or stray) dogs', from Old English

hund and *dīc*, although the first element may alternatively be an Old English personal name *Hund (*see* HOUNSLOW). The ditch, originally describing part of the moat that once bounded the City wall, had been filled in and built upon by the end of the 16th century. A petition in 1927 by a group of local businessmen to have the name changed, no doubt because of its seemingly unpleasant connotations, was fortunately unsuccessful!

Hounslow (town and borough). *Honeslaw* (*sic*) 1086 (Domesday Book), *Hundeslawe* 1217, *Hundeslowe* 1275, *Houndeslowe* 1341, that is 'mound or tumulus of the hound, or of a man called *Hund', from Old English *hlāw* with Old English *hund* or with the same word used as a personal name. This was the meeting place of the Domesday hundred of ISLE-WORTH; the old hundreds were often named from some conspicuous feature, such as a burial mound, at the site of the assembly. **Hounslow Heath** is *Houndesloweheth* in 1382, from Old English *hǣth*; the first civil airport in the country was opened here in 1919. The three Underground stations here, **Hounslow Central, East & West**, although opened in the 1880s were first named thus in 1925. The London Borough of Hounslow was created in 1965.

Howbury Lane (in Slade Green) Bexley. Preserves the name of the old manor of *Howbury* (marked thus on the Ordnance Survey map of 1876), earlier *Hov* 1086 (Domesday Book), *Litelhou* 1242–3, *Littleho* 1254, *Hobury* 1379, so called from Old English *hōh* 'heel of land, projecting hill-spur' with the later addition of Middle English *litel* 'little' and *bury* 'manor'. The moated grange here, now a ruin, dates back to the 17th century, although the moat itself was probably built in the 12th century around an earlier building.

Hoxton Hackney. *Hochestone* 1086 (Domesday Book), *Hocston* 1221, *Hoxtone* 1254, *Hoggeston* 1352, that is 'farmstead or estate of a man called *Hōc', from an Old English personal name and Old English *tūn*. In the 19th century, Hoxton was particularly renowned for its music halls, among them the *Britannia Theatre* (opened 1841) and *McDonald's Music Hall* (opened 1864).

Huggin Hill (off Upper Thames Street) City. Earlier *Hoggenelane* 1330, *Hoggenlane* 1375, *Huggen lane* 1603, 'lane where hogs were kept', from Middle English *hogge* 'pig'.

Hundred Acre Bridge (at Mitcham) Merton. No doubt so named from some local field once called *Hundred Acres*, a common field name which could have either a literal meaning (i.e. 'a large field approximately 100 acres in area') or an ironic application (i.e. 'a very small field').

Hungerford Bridge (crossing the Thames at Charing Cross). This railway bridge (incorporating a footbridge), built in 1864, replaced Brunel's *Hungerford Suspension Bridge* (a footbridge only) opened in 1845. The first bridge was built to serve the former *Hungerford Market*, demolished in 1860 to make way for Charing Cross Station (*see* CHARING CROSS). All are named from a house near Charing Cross known as *Hungerford Inne* in 1472 (from Middle English *inn* 'residence'), so called from one Sir Robert *Hungerford* who owned it and whose successor Sir Edward *Hungerford* set up the market in 1682.

Hurlingham House & Park Hammersmith & Fulham. Named from *Hurlingham* 1626, earlier *Hurlyngholefeld* 1489, *Hurlynghamfyld* 1550, and with other variant spellings such as *Furnynghamfeld* 1550 and *Furlingham feld* 1573. These relatively late and inconsistent forms, showing interchange of the initial consonant between *H-* and *F-*, leave the origin uncertain. Hurlingham House, home of the Hurlingham Club, was built in 1760.

Hurst Road, School & Springs, Hurstwood Avenue Bexley. Preserve the name of the old hamlet of *Hurst*, recorded thus from 1690 and marked on the Ordnance Survey map of 1805, from Old English *hyrst* 'wooded hill'. It is called *Hurst Mount* on Bowen's map of *c.*1762.

Hyde, The (at Hendon) Barnet. Recorded thus on the Ordnance Survey map of 1822, earlier *la Hyde* 1281, *Hepeworthe Hyde* 1315, *Hide* 1675, 'the hide of land', from Old English *hīd*, the 14th-century form alluding to a family called *Heppeworthe* recorded as holding land in HENDON in 1285. A hide was an amount of land considered sufficient for the support of one free family and its dependants, usually about 120 acres.

Hyde Park Westminster. Recorded as *Hide Park* in 1543, thus named from a part of the ancient manor of *Ebury* (*see* EBURY SQUARE) called *Hida* 1204, *la Hyde* 1257, that is 'the hide of land', from Old English *hīd*. An estate assessed at one hide was usually about 120 acres (see previous name), but this area may have been extended when Hyde became a sub-manor of *Ebury* in the 13th century. The present Park was created by Henry VIII as a royal hunting ground after he took over the estate in 1536, not being opened to the public until the 17th century. **Hyde Park Corner**, recorded as *Hyde Parke Corner* in 1553, refers to the south-east *corner* of the Park at the road junction where Park Lane meets PICCADILLY. There was once a toll gate here marking the entrance to WESTMINSTER from the west. Constitution Arch which now stands here was erected in 1828.

I

Ickenham Hillingdon. *Ticheham* 1086 (Domesday Book), *Tikeham* 1176, *Tikenham* 1203, *Ikeham* 1203, *Ikenham* 1236, that is 'homestead or village of a man called Tic(c)a', from an Old English personal name (genitive case *-n*) and *hām*. Initial *T-* was lost during the 13th and 14th centuries due to confusion with the preposition *at* (i.e. '*at Tickenham*' became '*at Ickenham*').

Ilford Redbridge. *Ilefort* 1086 (Domesday Book), *Yleford* 1171, *Hileford* 1234, *Hyleford* 1300, 'ford over the river called *Hyle*', from Old English *ford* and a Celtic river name meaning 'trickling stream'. *Hyle* was an early name for the River RODING below Ongar. This Ilford (on the east bank of the river) was distinguished from LITTLE ILFORD (on the west bank) as *Great Ilford* (thus on the Ordnance Survey map of 1883), earlier *Illeford Magna* 1254, *Michill Ilford* c.1462, with the Latin affix *magna* 'large' and Old English *micel* 'great'.

Ingrebourne River (flowing into the Thames at Rainham Creek). Marked as *Ingerburn River* on the Ordnance Survey map of 1805, but recorded much earlier as *Ingceburne* in 1062, from Old English *burna* 'stream' with an uncertain first element, possibly the Old English masculine personal name *Inga*, thus 'Inga's stream'. Its upper course is known as WEALD BROOK.

Inwood Park Hounslow. From Middle English *inwode* 'wood near the main homestead or residence of an estate'.

Ironmonger Lane (off Cheapside) City. *Ysmongerelane* c.1190, *Ismongers Lane* 1227, *Irmongerlane* 1422, *Ironmongerlane* 1485, that is 'lane of the ironmongers', from Middle English *ismongere* or *ire(n)mongere* and *lane*.

Isabella Plantation (in Richmond Park) Richmond. Marked thus on the Ordnance Survey map of 1876 and dating from 1823, but referred to as *Isabell Slade* in 1771, from Middle English *slade* 'valley'; the first part of the name seems to be an allusion to some unidentified lady called *Isabell* or *Isabella* (pet forms of *Elizabeth*).

Island Gardens Tower Hamlets. These riverside gardens near the southern end of the ISLE OF DOGS, with fine views across to Greenwich, were opened in 1895.

Isle of Dogs Tower Hamlets. First mentioned in connection with ships docking at *the Isle of Dogs* in 1520, later marked on a Thames chart of 1588 as *Ile of Dogges* and on Norden's map of 1593 as *Isle of doges ferm*, other references being *The Ile of Dogs* c.1641, *Isle of Doggs* 1769, *Poplar Marshes or Isle of Dogs* 1799. The origin of the name has been the subject of much speculation, and various unlikely explanations have been (and still are) offered, ranging from that suggesting that it refers to dead dogs floating down the Thames and being washed up on its left bank, to those claiming that the name is a corruption of 'Isle of docks', 'Isle of doggers (i.e. fishing boats)', or even 'Isle of ducks'! But there seems to be no reason whatsoever why the name should not be taken more literally. The interpretation based on the legend (apparently originating in 1720 with John Strype's enlarged version of Stow's *Survey*) that the royal hunting dogs were kennelled here when the king resided at GREENWICH is not implausible but has never been supported by any evidence. It is therefore more convincing to suppose that the name is even more straightforwardly descriptive: this marshy peninsula (hence 'isle') may well have been frequented by (wild or stray) dogs. However, taking into account the reference to dogs as well as the structure and phrasing of the name (*Isle of Dogs* rather than *Dogs' Isle*), it is difficult to avoid the impression that the name is intended to be a little facetious, even derogatory. Other names with this particular formation (Isle of Ely, Grain, Man, Purbeck, Sheppey, Thanet, Wight, etc.) seem to have an older place name as final element, and their appeal is somewhat elegant, almost poetic. In this sense, Isle of Dogs jars a little, its elegant phrasing somehow mismatched with its literal content. Indeed the unusual nature of the name raises the interesting possibility that the farm (or peninsula) was originally named by way of whimsical allusion to the Spanish island of Canary, etymologically also 'isle of dogs', *see* CANARY WHARF. What nicer irony than to give this cold flat marshy peninsular the same name as that hot rocky exotic island (well known for its wines, which were shipped to England from at least as early as the 16th century)! At an earlier date the settlement (farm or house) here, dating from the late 12th century, was known as *Pomfret* or *Pountfret* (so called because it was the estate of William of *Pontefract* or *Pomfret*). Also in medieval times, the district as a whole was known as *marsh of Steben-hithe* 1365, *Stepheneth mershe* 1432, that is 'Stepney marsh'; it lies south-east of STEPNEY and south of POPLAR.

Isleworth, Old Isleworth Hounslow. *Gislheresuuyrth* 677 (later copy of Anglo-Saxon charter), *Gistelesworde* 1086 (Domesday Book), *Istleworth* 1231, *Thystelworth* (*sic*) 1477, *Isellworth* 1576, that is 'enclosed settle-ment of a man called Gīslhere', from Old English *worth* and an Old English personal name. **Isleworth Ait** is an island in the Thames, the word *ait* being from Middle English *eyte* or *ayte* 'a small island, an islet'. The current pronunciation of the name is 'Izelworth'.

Islington (town and borough). *Gislandune* c.1000 (Anglo-Saxon charter), *Iseldone, Isendone* 1086 (Domesday Book), *Isledon* 1320, *Islyngton* 1464, that is 'hill of a man called *Gīsla', from an Old English personal name (genitive case -*n*) and Old English *dūn*. It will be noted that the modern spelling with medial -*ing*- (developing from -*an*-, -*en*-) and final -*ton* (replacing historical -*don*) dates only from the 15th century.

J

Jack Straw's Castle (in Hampstead) Camden. Old coaching inn at the edge of Hampstead Heath (*see* HAMPSTEAD), now rebuilt, named after *Jack Straw*, leader of a band of rebels in the Peasants' Revolt of 1381.

Jack Wood (near Shooters Hill) Greenwich. Probably from the word *jack* in the sense 'smaller in size' (that is, relative to OXLEAS WOOD).

Jacob Street (in Bermondsey) Southwark. Recalls the district once known as *Jacob's Island*, an infamous slum in the mid-19th century and the site of Bill Sykes's death in Charles Dickens's *Oliver Twist* (1837–8).

Jamaica Road (in Bermondsey) Southwark. So named from the *Jamaica Tavern* which once stood near the old *Cherry Garden*, *see* CHERRY GARDEN PIER.

Jewry Street (near Aldgate) City. Earlier called *la Porejewerie* 1366, *the poor Jurie* 1603, that is 'the poor Jewish district', no doubt to distinguish it from OLD JEWRY which must have been considered more prosperous.

Jubilee Park (at Edmonton) Enfield. Opened in 1939, so named to commemorate the Silver Jubilee of King George V and Queen Mary in 1935.

K

Kelsey Park (in Beckenham) Bromley. Marked thus on the Ordnance Survey map of 1876, named from an estate called *Kelsies* 1479, this being a manorial name from the family of William *Kelshulle* who was granted land in BECKENHAM in 1408.

Kemnal Manor (in Chislehurst) Bromley. *Kemeshol, Kemehal* 1240, *Kemenhole* 1301, *Kymenhole* 1387, *Kenmale* 1480, that is 'hollow or valley of a man called Cȳma', from an Old English personal name and Old English *hol*.

Kenley Croydon. *Kenele* 1255, *Kenelee* 14th century, *Kenle* 1403, *Kenley* 1548, that is 'woodland clearing of a man called Cēna', from an Old English personal name and Old English *lēah*. **Kenley Common** is marked thus on Rocque's map of 1765; the aerodrome here was extensively used during both World Wars.

Kennington Lambeth. *Chenintune* 1086 (Domesday Book), *Kenintone* 1229, *Kenyngton* 1263, that is 'farmstead or estate associated with a man called Cēna', from an Old English personal name with Old English medial connective *-ing-* and *tūn*. The Black Prince (1330–76) had a residence here, hence the street name Black Prince Road. **Kennington Park** was formerly *Kennington Common*, to the south of which a gallows stood in the 18th century.

Kensal Green Brent. *Kynsale Grene* 1550, *Kensoll grene* 1557, *Kensell Grene* 1658, named from *Kingisholte* 1253, *Kyngesholt* 1367, that is 'the king's wood or thicket', from Old English *cyning* and *holt* with the later addition of Middle English *grene* 'village green'. It is not known to which king the name refers. **Kensal Rise** is a residential area named from the rising ground to the north of Kensal Green. Also named from Kensal Green is KENSAL TOWN, an early 19th-century development to the south-east.

Kensal Town Kensington & Chelsea/Westminster. Marked as *Kensal New Town* on the Ordnance Survey map of 1876, a residential area near

KENSAL GREEN from which it takes its name. It developed in the 1840s with the arrival of the railway in this part of CHELSEA.

Kensington (borough with Chelsea). *Chenesitun* 1086 (Domesday Book), *Kinsentona* early 12th century, *Kensintone* 1221, *Kensington* 1235, that is 'farmstead or estate associated with a man called Cynesige', from an Old English personal name with Old English medial connective *-ing-* and *tūn*. **Kensington Gardens**, marked thus on the Ordnance Survey map of 1822, were originally the grounds belonging to *Nottingham House* (later Kensington Palace). **Kensington Palace** was so called from the early 18th century; the former Jacobean mansion (called *The Park House* 1664 and later *Nottingham House* from the 2nd Earl of *Nottingham* who lived here) was completely reconstructed for William III and Queen Mary when they bought it in 1690. **Kensington Square** was called simply *The Square* in 1690 soon after it was laid out, then later *Kings Square*. The title of 'Royal' was conferred on the old metropolitan borough of Kensington in 1901 to commemorate the birth (in 1819) and childhood of Queen Victoria at Kensington Palace and has been retained in the name of the Royal Borough of Kensington & CHELSEA created in 1965. The residential districts of **North, South, & West Kensington** were mainly developed from the 19th century.

Kensington Gore Westminster. Street in KENSINGTON preserving the name of an estate called *Gara c.*1130, *Kyngesgore* 1270, *the Gore* 1646, *the Kings Gore* 1657, and still marked as simply *Gore* on the Ordnance Survey map of 1822, that is 'the wedge-shaped or triangular plot of ground', from Old English *gāra*. It refers to the triangle of land extending east from Queen's Gate to the junction of Brompton Road and KNIGHTSBRIDGE. It is not known to which king the earlier forms refer.

Kent House Bromley. Station named from a house (demolished in 1957) which is marked *Kent House* on the Ordnance Survey map of 1816 and which is recorded as *Kent Hous* in the 14th century. It was so called from its situation near the county boundary between Kent and Surrey, being the first house in Kent on the route out of London.

Kentish Town Camden. *Kentisston* 1208, *Kantistun c.*1220, *Le Kentishton* 1294, *Kentisshtown* 1488, probably 'estate held by a family called *(le) Kentish*', from Middle English *toun*. The meaning of the surname is 'man of Kent'.

Kenton Harrow. *Keninton* 1232, *Kenygton* 1307, *Kenyngton next Harogh*

1368, *Kenton alias Kynyton* 1548, that is 'farmstead or estate associated with a man called Cēna', from an Old English personal name with Old English medial *-ing-* and *tūn*. This name is thus identical in origin with KENNINGTON. It gives name to **Kenton Brook**.

Ken Wood, Kenwood (on Hampstead Heath) Camden. *Canewood* 1530, *Cane Wood* c.1570, *Caen Wood* 1640, *Ken Wood* 1741, possibly 'wood of the canons', from Middle English *canoun* and *wode*. In 1530 it belonged to the Prior of Holy Trinity, ALDGATE, a house of Augustinian canons. The form *Caen Wood*, frequent in the 17th century, also still found on the Ordnance Survey map of 1822 and surviving in the spelling of **Caen Wood Towers Farm**, is due to influence from the French place name. **Kenwood House** (now in the care of English Heritage) dates back to the 17th century.

Keston Bromley. *Cysse stanes gemæro* 973 (Anglo-Saxon charter), *Chestan* 1086 (Domesday Book), *Kestan* 1205, that is 'boundary stone of a man called *Cyssi', from an Old English personal name and Old English *stān*. The first spelling (from a description of the bounds of BROMLEY) contains Old English *gemǣre* 'boundary'. An even earlier reference (in another Bromley charter dated 862) is the phrase *Cystaninga mearc*, that is 'boundary of the people of Keston', from Old English *-inga* (genitive case of *-ingas* 'dwellers at') and *mearc* 'mark, boundary'; this last word is preserved in **Keston Mark**, shown thus on the Ordnance Survey map of 1819 (it stands on the boundary between the parishes of Keston and Bromley). **Keston Common** is also marked thus on the 1819 map; the mill here dates from 1716. Also on the Common is 'Caesar's Well' (a spring, the source of the River RAVENSBOURNE) and nearby (in the grounds of Holwood House, *see* HOLWOOD) 'Caesar's Camp' (an Iron Age earthwork from *c*.200 BC), both linked with Julius Caesar through the local tradition that he encamped here with his army (a nice story no doubt invented by early antiquarians).

Kevingtown (near St Mary Cray) Bromley. *Keuington* 1610, *Kevington* 1690, *Kevingtowne* c.1762, probably 'farmstead or estate associated with a man called *Cyfa', from an Old English personal name with Old English medial connective *-ing-* and *tūn*. The name appears twice, as both *Kevington* and *Kevingtown*, on the Ordnance Survey map of 1876, and the farm here is still called Kevington Farm.

Kew Richmond. *Cayho* 1327, *Kayho* 1330, *Keyhow* 1439, *Kewe* 1535, probably 'key-shaped spur of land', from Old English *cǣg* and *hōh*.

Alternatively, 'spur of land with a quay', if the first element is rather Middle English *key* 'a quay or landing place'. The present **Kew Bridge**, opened in 1903, replaced early bridges here, the first one built in 1758; Kew Railway Bridge dates from 1864–9. **Kew Gardens** (the Royal Botanic Gardens), marked as *Royal Gardens* on the Ordnance Survey map of 1876, date back to the 18th century; they were earlier part of the original Richmond Park (*see* RICHMOND). **Kew Palace**, up to *c.*1730 called the *Dutch House*, was built in 1631 over the vaults of an earlier Tudor mansion.

Kidbrooke Greenwich. *Chitebroc c.*1100, *Ketebroc* 1202, *Ketebrok* 1240, that is 'brook frequented by kites', from Old English *cȳta* and *hrōc*. The small stream which gives its name to the place is still called **Kid Brook**. On the Ordnance Survey map of 1805 the two small hamlets here are distinguished as *Lower Kidbrook* and *Upper Kidbrook*.

Kidney Wood (in Richmond Park) Richmond. So called from its shape.

Kilburn Brent. *Cuneburna c.*1130, *Kyneburna c.*1170, *Keleburne* 1181, *Kylleburne* 1229, possibly 'stream of a man called *Cylla*', from Old English *burna* and a personal name, but some early spellings show characteristic interchange of *n* and *l*, or suggest 'cows' stream', from Old English *cū* (genitive plural *cūna*, *cȳna*). **Kilburn Park**, a residential area developed *c.*1860, is marked thus on the Ordnance Survey map of 1876, but **West Kilburn** (in Westminster) is a relatively recent name. There was a small priory at Kilburn in medieval times, founded *c.*1130 on a site later occupied by an inn.

King Edward Street City. So named in 1843 in memory of King Edward VI who founded Christ's Hospital for orphans in 1553 nearby. The street was originally known as *Styngkynglane* 1228, *Stinkendelane* 1285, *Stinking Lane* 1603, a self-explanatory reference to the many butchers' slaughterhouses here up to the end of the 17th century.

King Edward VII Memorial Park (in Shadwell) Tower Hamlets. Park commemorating King Edward VII (1901–10), opened by George V in 1922.

King George V Dock Newham. Completed in 1921 and named after the reigning monarch. It was smaller than its neighbours the ROYAL ALBERT and ROYAL VICTORIA DOCKS, but was once the berth of P & O liners including (in 1939) the *Mauretania*. It was closed in 1981.

King George V Memorial Gardens (at Canons Park) Harrow. Gardens commemorating King George V (1910–36), one of several parks and open spaces in Greater London named from this monarch.

King's Bridge (at Longford) Hillingdon. Marked thus on the Ordnance Survey map of 1816–22, one of the bridges on the site of 'the long ford' that gave name to LONGFORD. *King* is probably a surname, *see* KINGSEND.

Kingsbury Brent. *Cyngesbyrig* 1003–4, *Kynges byrig* c.1046 (Anglo-Saxon charters), *Chingesberie* 1086 (Domesday Book), *Kingesbir* 1199, that is 'the king's manor', from Old English *cyning* and *burh* (dative case *byrig*). It was apparently a royal possession in Anglo-Saxon times, but the English kings probably lost their interest in the manor long before the Conquest. The old centre of the settlement (around St Andrew's Church in Old Church Lane) is still marked *Kingsbury* on the Ordnance Survey map of 1822. The later hamlet of **Kingsbury Green** (a mile or so to the north) is also marked thus on the same map and is earlier *Kingsbury grene* 1574, from Middle English *grene*.

King's Cross Camden. 'The king's crossroads', district so called from a stone statue of King George IV (reigned 1820–30) which stood between 1830 and 1845 at the junction of Euston Road with Gray's Inn Road and Pentonville Road. The name was transferred to the railway station (marked on the Ordnance Survey map of 1876) when it was opened in 1852. The earlier name of the district was *Battlebridge*, *see* BATTLE BRIDGE ROAD.

Kingsend (at Ruislip) Hillingdon. Recorded as *Kings End* in 1550 and as *Great & Little Kings End* on the Ordnance Survey map of 1822, from Middle English *ende* 'district of a parish', possibly named from the *Kyng* family found in local records from the late 13th century, but alternatively because land here was held by King's College, Cambridge in the 16th century.

Kingsland (near Dalston) Hackney. *Kyngeslond* 1395, *Kings land* 1822, that is 'estate held by the king', from Old English *cyning* and *land*. It was probably a part of Hackney belonging to the Crown when the manor was held by the Bishop of London.

King's Road (in Chelsea) Kensington & Chelsea. Famous posing and shopping street earlier referred to as *The King's High Way from Chelsea to London* in 1620, and as *The King's Private Road* in 1717. It was constructed as a royal route between WHITEHALL and HAMPTON COURT and first became a public road in 1830.

Kingston upon Thames (town and borough). *Cyninges tun* 838 (Anglo-Saxon charter), *Chingestune* 1086 (Domesday Book), *Kingeston* 1164, *Kyngeston super Tamisiam* 1321, *Kingestowne upon Thames* 1589, that is 'the king's manor or estate', from Old English *cyning* and *tūn*. It belonged to the king in Saxon times and at the time of Domesday Book and is in fact the oldest Royal Borough in England. Edward the Elder was crowned here in 899, as were all his successors down to Ethelred II in 982. The affix (upon Thames) distinguishes it from other places called Kingston, of which there are examples in several English counties. However this Kingston is the earliest recorded of any of them and became a major market centre in medieval times. The present **Kingston Bridge**, opened in 1828, is on the site of earlier bridges, the first recorded from the early 13th century. Up to 1750 this was the first crossing of the River Thames upstream from LONDON BRIDGE, thus bestowing on Kingston an undoubted strategic importance. **Kingston Vale**, marked thus on the Ordnance Survey map of 1876, was alternatively known as *Kingston Bottom*, the reference being to the valley of BEVERLEY BROOK. This spot was once the haunt of highwaymen, *see* ROBIN HOOD GATE.

King Street (off Cheapside) City. Laid out as a continuation of QUEEN STREET after the Great Fire of 1666, named after Charles II.

Kingsway (in Holborn) Camden. A modern thoroughfare opened in 1905 by King Edward VII (1901–10) after whom it is named.

Kings Wood (near Sanderstead) Croydon. Marked thus on the Ordnance Survey map of 1816, earlier *Kinges Woodes* 1595, so named from the family of William *Kyng* 1332.

King William Street City. Built in 1829 as an approach road to the 'new' LONDON BRIDGE, named after William IV who opened it in 1831.

Kneller Gardens & Hall (at Whitton) Richmond. Named from the court portrait painter Sir Godfrey *Kneller* (1649–1743) who lived at Kneller Hall (built in 1709–11) which is marked thus on the Ordnance Survey map of 1876 (since 1857 it has been occupied by the Royal Military School of Music).

Knighton Wood (at Woodford) Redbridge. Recorded thus *c*.1640, prob-
ably to be associated with a place in nearby CHINGFORD called
Knyghton 16th century, 'estate belonging to the Knights (of St John of
Jerusalem)', from Middle English *knight* and *toun*.

Knightrider Street (near St Paul's) City. *Knyghtridestrete* 1322, *Knyghtri-
derestrete* 1349, that is 'street of the mounted knights', possibly an
allusion to knights who rode at jousts or tournaments or simply to
knights (the word *ridere* meant 'knight' besides 'mounted warrior,
horseman' during the Middle English period, so that the meanings of
the two words overlapped), compare the alternative early name for
GILTSPUR STREET.

Knightsbridge Westminster. *Cnihtebricge c*.1050, *Knichtebrig* 1235,
Cnichtebrugge 13th century, *Knyghtesbrugg* 1364, that is 'bridge of the
young men or retainers', from Old English *cniht* (genitive case plural *-a*)
and *brycg*. The bridge was where one of the old roads to the west
crossed the WESTBOURNE stream. The allusion may simply be to a
place where *cnihtas* congregated: bridges and wells seem always to
have been favourite gathering places for young people, *see also* CLER-
KENWELL. However there is possibly a more specific reference to the
important *cnihtengild* ('guild of *cnihtas*') in 11th-century London and to
the limits of its jurisdiction (certainly Knightsbridge was one of the
limits of the commercial jurisdiction of the City in the 12th century).

Knights Hill (in West Norwood) Lambeth. Recorded as *Knyghtes Hill* in
1545 and giving name to *Knights Hill Common* on the Ordnance Survey
map of 1816, so called from the family of Thomas *Knyght* 1545.

L

Ladbroke Grove Kensington & Chelsea. Named from a family called *Ladbrooke*; Richard *Ladbrooke* owned land here in 1624, and the family sold it for building purposes in 1845 after which date the area was developed.

Ladderstile Gate (Richmond Park) Richmond. This name of a gate near the southern corner of Richmond Park (*see* RICHMOND) is said to recall the means of gaining access used by John Lewis, leader of a campaign against the Crown in the early 18th century to win a public right of way through the park.

Ladywell Lewisham. Marked as simply *Well* on the Ordnance Survey map of 1816, but appearing as *Ladywell* in 1793 and on the map of 1876, with reference to a holy spring dedicated to the Blessed Virgin, first recorded in 1592 and also giving name to **Ladywell Fields** adjoining St Mary's Church. The spring was near to the west bank of the River RAVENSBOURNE on the site of the present-day **Ladywell Bridge**.

Lambeth (town and borough). *Lambehitha* 1062, *Lamhytha* 1089, *Lambhythe* c.1150, *Lambeth* 1255, 'landing place for lambs', that is a harbour to or from which they were shipped, from Old English *lamb* and *hȳth*. **South Lambeth**, marked thus on the Ordnance Survey map of 1822, is already recorded as *Sutlamehethe* in 1241, *Suthlambheythe* in 1263, thus differentiated from *North Lamhuth* 1309, *North Lambhethe* 1315. In medieval times there was an area of marshland here referred to as *Lambythemersh* 1377, *Lambeth Marshe* 1597, drained in the 18th century but giving name to the street called LOWER MARSH at Waterloo. **Lambeth Bridge**, dating from 1932, replaced an earlier bridge built in 1862. Before the bridges, there was a horse ferry across the Thames here, belonging to the Archbishop of Canterbury, which gives name to HORSEFERRY ROAD. **Lambeth Palace**, official residence of the Archbishops of Canterbury (lords of the manor of Lambeth since 1197), was rebuilt in 1834 but partly dates from the 13th to 15th centuries. **Lambeth Walk**, famous for giving its name to the Cockney dance and song first performed in 1937, had a thriving market by the early 19th century and was earlier (*c*.1695) the site of a spa known as *Lambeth Wells*. The name Lambeth is pronounced as it is spelt, an interesting reminder that in Old English the *b* in the word *lamb* was not a silent letter.

Lambeth Hill (off Victoria Street) City. Originally *Lamberdeshul* or *Lambardeshull* in 1283, *Lamberdeshill* 1306, *Lambart* or *Lambard Hill* 1603, that is 'hill of a man called Lambert', from Middle English *hull* or *hill*. A certain *Lambertus wodemangere* ('Lambert the wood merchant') was a tenant near here *c*.1200. The change from *Lamberd* to *Lambeth* is due to folk etymology, *see* LAMBETH.

Lammas Park Ealing. Named from a field called *Lammas* 1839, a reference to meadow land once used for grazing cattle after Lammas (1 August). The word itself is from Old English *hlāf-mæsse*, that is 'loaf mass or festival', this being the harvest thanksgiving held on that day.

Lamorbey (near Sidcup) Bexley. Recorded as *Lamborbey c*.1762, *Lamienby* or *Lamberby* 1778, *Lamb Abbey* (*sic*) 1805, *Lamorbey* 1876, a manorial name for an estate and house (originally built in the early 16th century) belonging to the family of Thomas *Lamendby alias Sparrowe* 1513.

Lampton Hounslow. *Lamptonfeld* 1376, *Lampton* 1426, *Lambton* 1611, that is 'farmstead or estate where lambs are reared', from Old English *lamb* and *tūn* (with *feld* 'open land' in the earliest spelling). Its situation just south of OSTERLEY (also a name related to sheep farming) is interesting.

Lancaster Gate Westminster. One of the gates into Kensington Gardens (*see* KENSINGTON), leading into **Lancaster Walk** which crosses the Gardens to the ALBERT MEMORIAL, perhaps so called in honour of Queen Victoria who was also Duchess of *Lancaster*. The street called Lancaster Gate, named from the gate itself, was built in 1865–6.

Langbourn City. An ancient ward of the City, originally *Langebord* 12th century, *Longebrod* 1252, that is 'the long table(s)', from Old English *lang* and *bord*, perhaps with reference to market stalls. This was later changed to *Langb(o)urn*, according to Ekwall the result of confusion in the early name of LOMBARD STREET, originally *Langebordstrete* ('street leading to *Langebord*') but becoming *Langburnestrete* 1285, *Langbournestrete* 1312. Although these forms clearly suggest 'street by the long stream', from Old English *lang* and *burna*, the existence of such a stream has been doubted. However Stow (1603), calling it *Langborne water*, describes it as having once flowed west along Lombard Street from where it rose in FENCHURCH STREET, but states that even in his day it had long been covered over.

Langley Park (near Beckenham) Bromley. Marked thus on the Ordnance Survey map of 1819 and recorded as *Langley c*.1762, often taken to be a manorial name from the family called *de Langele(y)* recorded here from the late 13th century (e.g. *de Langele(y)* 1278). However the name is possibly to be identified with *langan leage* in an Anglo-Saxon charter dated 862 describing the bounds of BROMLEY, that is 'the long wood or woodland clearing', from Old English *lang* and *lēah*: commentators have found difficulty with the identification, but it should be noted that the 'long *lēah*' may well have covered an extensive area. The family name *de Langele(y)* would then be derived from the place, and not vice versa. The mansion here was burnt down in 1913, but **Langley Court** (now a medical research laboratory) was built in 1886 on the site of *Langley Farm* (marked thus on the Ordnance Survey map of 1876). **Park Langley** is a mainly 1930s residential development.

Langthorne Hospital & Road (in Leyton), *see* STRATFORD.

Langtons (in Hornchurch) Havering. The present building (now a registry office) dates in part from the 18th century, but the name is much older, appearing as *Langedune* (the home of Thomas *de Langedun*) in the 13th century, later as *Langtonsland* in 1514 and *Langton* in 1777, so originally 'the long hill or down' from Old English *lang* and *dūn*.

Larks Wood, Larkswood Park (at Chingford) Waltham Forest. *Larkewood* 1545, *Larks Hill Wood* 1805, like *Larkys* 1515 and *Larks Farm* 1883 named from the family of Thomas *Laverk* 1319 (a surname derived from Old English *lāwerce* 'a lark'). Larks (Hall) farmhouse (now a public house) dates from the 16th century.

Latimer Road Kensington & Chelsea. Station named from a road running through land once owned by Edward *Latymer c*.1600; he bequeathed the land to support a school he had established.

Lauderdale House (in Highgate) Haringey. Mansion (now an arts centre) named after the 2nd Earl of *Lauderdale* who *c*.1645 completely rebuilt the originally 16th-century house after it had been inherited by his wife.

Launder's Lane (in Rainham) Havering. Named from *Launder's Barn* (marked thus on the Ordnance Survey map of 1883), earlier *les Laundres* 1365, *Lawnders* 1559, a manorial name from the family of John *Launder* 1503.

Laurence Pountney Hill & Lane (off Cannon Street) City. The lane is 'St Laurence's lane' in 1248, *Seint Laurencelane* 1320, *Poultney lane* 1603, named from the church of *St Laurence Pountney* which was burnt down in the Great Fire of 1666 and not rebuilt. The church itself was called after Sir John *de Poulteney*, four times Lord Mayor in the 1330s, who lived nearby.

Lavender Hill (in Battersea) Wandsworth. Named from the *lavender* cultivated in the market gardens which once lay to the north of this road in *Battersea Fields*, *see* BATTERSEA.

Layham's Farm & Road (in West Wickham) Bromley. The farm is marked as *Leyhams Farm* on the Ordnance Survey map of 1819, so named from *Leyham* 1289, probably 'the fallow or unploughed enclosure', from Old English **læge* and *hamm*.

Laystall Street (at Clerkenwell) Camden, *see* MOUNT PLEASANT.

Lea (or Lee), River (rising in Bedfordshire, flows south to join the Thames at Canning Town). This important river, once the boundary between the counties of Middlesex and Essex, has an ancient name of Celtic origin. It is recorded from the 9th century, although its name is much older. Spellings from the Anglo-Saxon period include *Lig(e)an* in 880 and *Lygan* in 895 (both with Old English *-n* inflection), and in the early medieval period it is usually *Luye* or *Leye*. It seems to be derived from a Celtic root **lug-* meaning 'bright or light' which was also the base of a name for a deity, so the meaning may be 'bright river' or 'river dedicated to the god Lugus'. It gives name to LEYTON.

Lea Bridge Hackney. Marked thus on the Ordnance Survey map of 1822 along with *Lea Bridge Farm* nearby (in Leyton). The River LEA is crossed here by Lea Bridge Road, referred to as *Lea Bridge Turnpike* in 1777. The present bridge is on the site of earlier bridges; an 18th-century wooden bridge was replaced by an iron bridge in 1820.

Leadenhall Street City. *Leaden Hall Street* 1605, named from *La Ledenehalle* 1296, *le Ledenhalle* 1322, that is 'the hall or large house with a lead roof', from Old English *lēaden* (adjective) and *hall*. The mansion was acquired by the City authorities in 1411 and a market subsequently built here, but destroyed in the Great Fire of 1666. The present buildings of **Leadenhall Market** date from 1881.

Leamouth (near Blackwall) Tower Hamlets. *Leemouthe* on a Thames chart of 1588, an area by EAST INDIA DOCKS developed in the 19th century at the *mouth* of the River LEA.

Leather Lane (in Clerkenwell) Camden. Recorded as *Le Vrunelane* 1233, *Leueronelane* 1306, *Liveronelane* 1331, *Lither alias Liver Lane* 1604, probably 'lane of a woman called Lēofrūn', from an Old English personal name and *lane*.

Leaves Green (near Biggin Hill) Bromley. Marked thus on the Ordnance Survey map of 1819, earlier *Lese Green* 1500, *Leves Green* c.1762, so named from a family called *Leigh* recorded at ADDINGTON from 1447, from Middle English *grene* 'village green'.

Lee, River, *see* LEA.

Lee Lewisham. *Lee* 1086 (Domesday Book), *Le* c.1100, *Legh* 1262, *la Lee* 1278, that is '(place at) the wood or woodland clearing', from Old English *lēah* (dative case *lēa*). This is a common English place name, variously spelt Lee or Leigh according to the Old English forms from which the names are derived. **Lee Green** is marked thus on Bowen's map of c.1762 and on the Ordnance Survey map of 1876, from Middle English *grene* 'village green, hamlet'.

Leg of Mutton Pond (in Richmond Park) Richmond. So called from its shape. There are other ponds with this name in BUSHY PARK and on Hampstead Heath (*see* HAMPSTEAD).

Leicester Square Westminster. Marked thus on a map of 1708, but earlier known as *Leicester Fields* 1682 because they adjoined *Leicester House*. This mansion was built in 1631–5 by Robert Sidney, 2nd Earl of *Leicester* who had earlier acquired the land here. It was demolished in 1792; **Leicester Place**, laid out in the 1790s, occupies part of the site of the house and its gardens. Leicester Square itself (still also called **Leicester Fields** on some modern maps) was laid out c.1675.

Leigham Court Road (in Streatham) Lambeth. Preserves the name of the old manor of *Leygham* 1165, *Legham* 1259, *Leyham* 1291, *Leighams Courte* 1541, probably 'the fallow or unploughed enclosure', from Old

English *lǣge and *hamm*, with the later addition of Middle English *court* 'manor house'.

Lessness Heath Bexley. Marked as *Leesing Heath* (*sic*) on Bowen's map of *c*.1762 and as *Lesness Heath* on the Ordnance Survey map of 1805, named from *Leosne* mid-11th century, *Lesneis, Loisnes* 1086 (Domesday Book), *Hlosnes* late-11th century, *Lesnes* 1194. This is a difficult name which has been explained, not very convincingly in view of the earliest spellings, as 'headland with pasture or meadowland on it', from Old English *lǣs* and *nǣss*. A possible alternative suggestion is that it might be from an Old English word *hlēosn* 'burial mound' or 'shelter'. In any case it was the name of one of the medieval hundreds of Kent, the meetings of which were held here on the heath. **Lesnes Abbey Woods**, marked *Abbey Wood* on the Ordnance Survey maps of 1805 and 1888 (hence also the name of the residential district of ABBEY WOOD), are so called from **Lesnes Abbey**, the remains of which are still to be found here on the north side of the surviving woodland. This Augustinian abbey was founded in 1178 and survived until it was suppressed by Wolsey in 1525.

Levehurst Way (at Stockwell) Lambeth. Preserves the name of the old manor of *Leferst* 1219, *Lefhirst* 1286, *Levehirst* 1453, *Levehurste* 1544, that is 'wooded hill of a man called Lēofa', from an Old English personal name and Old English *hyrst*.

Lewisham (town and borough). *Lievesham* 918 (Anglo-Saxon charter), *Levesham* 1086 (Domesday Book), *Leueseham* 1203, *Leusham c*.1762, that is 'homestead or village of a man called *Lēofsa*', from an Old English personal name and Old English *hām*. An even earlier reference occurs in an Anglo-Saxon charter of 862 describing the bounds of BROMLEY in the phrase *Liofshema mearc*, that is 'boundary of the people of Lewisham', from Old English *hǣme* 'dwellers' and *mearc* 'mark, boundary'. The Riverdale Centre here takes its name from the early 19th-century *Riverdale Mill*, one of several mills once situated along the River RAVENSBOURNE.

Leyton Waltham Forest. *Lugetune c*.1050, *Leintune* 1086 (Domesday Book), *Luiton* 1201, *Leyton* 1226, that is 'farmstead or estate on the River LEA', from Old English *tūn*. This name is thus identical in origin with Luton in Bedfordshire. From the 16th to 19th centuries it was often known as *Low Layton* or *Low Leyton* (as on the Ordnance Survey maps of 1805 and 1883) because part of the parish is on low-lying land by the

Lea. Essex Hall, a late 15th-century timber-framed house, survives on the site of the original manor house.

Leytonstone Waltham Forest. *Leyton atte Stone* 1370, *Leyton Stone* 1426, *Leghton Stone* 1449, *Layton Stone* 1805, that is 'part of LEYTON at the stone', from Middle English *atte* 'at the' and *stone*, referring to the 'High Stone', reputed to be on the site of a Roman milestone. Leyton-stone High Road (now also the name of a railway station) follows the course of the old Roman road from London to Epping Forest and Waltham, *see also* WALLWOOD ROAD.

Lillyputts (near Hornchurch) Havering. Marked as *Lily-Put* on a map of 1777, and as *Lilyput* on the Ordnance Survey map of 1805. This is probably a fanciful literary name, the allusion being to the imaginary country of *Lilliput* peopled by pygmies in Jonathan Swift's *Gulliver's Travels* (1726). The same name occurs as Lilliput near Poole in Dorset.

Limehouse Tower Hamlets. Recorded as *le Lymhostes* 1367, *Les Lymehostes near London* 1387, *Lymost* 1496, *Lymehouse* 1547, that is 'the lime oasts or kilns', from Old English *līm* and *āst*. In a local deed of 1380 Peter atte Hacche, *limeburner*, was granted a cottage and garden here. Lime, obtained from chalk or limestone by heating it in the kilns, was an important product in early times, being used for bleaching, preparing hides for leather tanning, making mortar and fertilizing soil; supplies of stone for the limeburning here came from Kent (probably from Cliffe or from the place called Chalk near Gravesend, *Cealca c.*975, from Old English *cealc* 'chalk'). Later, in the 18th and 19th centuries, the main industry in Limehouse was shipbuilding. **Limehouse Cut**, a navigational channel from the River LEA to Limehouse Basin, is marked thus on the Ordnance Survey map of 1822. **Limehouse Reach**, a stretch of the River Thames, is also so named on the 1822 map and is earlier *Limehowse Reche* in 1536.

Lime Street City. *Limstrate c.*1180, *Lymstrate* 1258, that is 'street where lime was burnt and sold', from Old English *līm* and *strǣt*. For the importance of lime in medieval times for building and in other trades, *see* LIMEHOUSE. This street gives name to one of the ancient wards of the City.

Lincoln Island (at Wanstead) Redbridge. An island in the River RODING marked thus on the Ordnance Survey map of 1883, perhaps a trans-ferred name, or so called from some local person or family.

Lincoln's Inn (in Holborn) Camden. *Lincolnesynne* 1399, *Lyncolnes Inne* 1488, originally the name of a house, occupied by the Society of the Inn, which had once belonged to a certain Thomas *de Lincoln*, from Middle English *inn* 'residence'. The name was transferred when *c.*1422 the lawyers moved to new premises (on their present site) which happened to be near the former house of Henry de Lacy, Earl of *Lincoln*, by tradition a patron of the Society, thus confirming the use of the name. Lincoln's Inn is one of the four surviving Inns of Court. **Lincoln's Inn Fields**, recorded as *Lincolnes Inne Feildes* 1598 and now London's largest square, consisted originally of two fields called *Cuppefeld* 1529 and *Pursefeld* 1527 (both probably so named from their shape).

Lisson Green & Grove (in Marylebone) Westminster. Lisson Green appears as *Lylleston Grene* 1547, *Lising Green* 1610. Lisson Grove is first on record in the late 18th century. Both preserve the name of the ancient manor of *Lilestone* 1086 (Domesday Book), *Lilleston* 1198, *Lylleston* 13th century, that is 'farmstead or estate of a man called Lill', from an Old English personal name and Old English *tūn*.

Little Britain City. *Lyttell Bretton* 1602, *Little Brittain* 1673, earlier *Brettonestrete* 1329, *Britten Strete* 1547, named from one Robert *le Bretoun* who in 1274 inherited a number of tenements and houses here in the parish of St Botolph without Aldersgate. Although the Middle English surname means 'the Breton', the transformation of *Brettonestrete* to *Lyttell Bretton* in the early 17th century would suggest that the name was falsely understood as indicating a foreign enclave inhabited by people from Brittany.

Little Britain (at Cowley) Hillingdon. Marked thus on Greenwood's map of 1819, probably a transferred name from the City street (see previous name) or a whimsical nickname for a tiny settlement. The same name also occurs as a street name in Dorchester, Dorset.

Little Ealing, *see* EALING.

Little Grove (in East Barnet) Barnet. Recorded thus in 1680, earlier called *Danegrove* 1556 from the family of Richard *ate Den* 1291 (that is 'at the valley'), from Old English *denu* 'valley' and *grāf(a)* 'grove, copse'.

Little Heath Redbridge. *Lytel Ylleford heth* 1369, *Litelheth* 1456, self-explanatory, 'little heath (near ILFORD)', from Middle English *litel* and *hethe*.

Little Ilford Newham. This ancient parish west of the River RODING is *Yleford parua* 1272, *Lilford c.*1462, *Little Ilford* 1805, thus distinguished from ILFORD itself (formerly *Great Ilford*) by the Latin affix *parva* 'small' and Middle English *litel* 'little' (the 15th-century spelling suggesting a colloquial pronunciation at that date).

Little Roke Croydon, *see* ROKE.

Little Stanmore, *see* STANMORE and WHITCHURCH.

Little Venice (near Warwick Avenue) Westminster. Name used from the 1950s for this pleasant spot on the GRAND UNION CANAL, but already thought somewhat to resemble Venice by the 19th-century poets Lord Byron and Robert Browning.

Little Woodcote Sutton, *see* WOODCOTE.

Liverpool Street City. Named after Lord *Liverpool*, Prime Minister from 1812 to 1827.

Lloyd Park Croydon. Originally farmland, made a public park in 1927 after the death of Mr Frank *Lloyd* who had owned the *Coombe House* estate here (*see under* COOMBE FARM) since 1892.

Lloyd Park (in Walthamstow) Waltham Forest. Named after Edward *Lloyd*, whose family presented the estate, consisting of WATER HOUSE and its grounds, to the local council in 1898. The estate was earlier known as *The Winns* (as on the Ordnance Survey map of 1883) from the family of John *Wynne* 1498, a name surviving in nearby Winns Avenue & Terrace, and before that as *Crykylwoods* or *Capps* from the families of Robert *de Crikelwode* 1319 and William *Cappe* 1394.

Locksbottom (near Farnborough) Bromley. Marked as *Locks Bottom* on a map of 1769 and on the Ordnance Survey map of 1819, 'valley associated with a family called *Lock*', from Old English *botm*; a family of this name was here in 1776.

Lombard Street City. *Lumbardstret* 1318, *Lumbardestrete* 1321, named from the *Lombard* merchants from Northern Italy who established banking and moneylending here in the late 13th century. The street was earlier referred to as 'the street running to *Longebrod*' 1252, or as *Langburnestrate* 1285, *see* LANGBOURN.

London. An ancient name for the capital city that has until very recently eluded any really convincing etymological explanation. It is found in various sources from as early as the 2nd century. It is recorded in classical sources as *Londinium* *c.*115 (Tacitus), *Londinion* *c.*150 (Ptolemy), *Londinio* and *Lundinio* in the 4th century (Antonine Itinerary), and *Lundinium* in the late 4th century (Ammianus Marcellinus). It is inscribed *Londini* on an early 2nd-century jug in the Museum of London, and appears with the same spelling in a letter found at *Vindolanda* (Chesterholm) dating from *c.*105. For a time in the 4th century, London was alternatively known as *Augusta* in official circles (as a kind of honorific Latin title), but this attempt (if it was that) to substitute a Roman name for the native one was not successful and the name was not remembered in post-Imperial times. Spellings from the Anglo-Saxon period include *Londinæ* 672–4 (13th-century copy of Anglo-Saxon charter), *Lundonia* *c.*730 (Bede's Ecclesiastical History), *Lundenne* and *Lundenceaster* *c.*890 (Old English translation of Bede), *Lundenburg* *c.*900 and *Lundene* 962 (Anglo-Saxon Chronicle), with the expected additions of Old English *ceaster* 'Roman city' and *burh* 'fortified town'. In an Anglo-Saxon charter dated 743–5 there is mention of *lundentunes hyth*, that is 'London-town's landing place', from Old English *tūn* and *hȳth*. This is almost certainly a reference to the important 7th- to 9th-century Saxon trading settlement of *Lundenwic* which lay to the west of the City and which is recorded from the 680s (*see* ALDWYCH and Introduction: 'The Anglo-Saxon Period'). Typical medieval spellings are *Lundin*, *Lunden*, *Londen*, as well as *London*.

Thus the earliest spellings point to a Romano-British form *Londinium* which developed to *Lundinium* from the 4th century. There have been many attempts to explain the name. The earliest, charming but completely fanciful, was that of the 12th-century chronicler Geoffrey of Monmouth in his *History of the Kings of Britain*, in which he claims that London was named after the legendary King Lud who was said to have rebuilt the city (*see also* LUDGATE HILL). A much later explanation, first advanced in 1899 and for a long time the standard view, was that it is a Celtic name meaning 'place belonging to a man called *Londinos*, from a supposed Celtic personal name meaning 'the wild or bold one' with a derivational suffix indicating habitation, but this etymology is now rejected by Celtic scholars. More recently (1998) a plausible case has been made by Professor Richard Coates that *Londinium* may be derived from two pre-Celtic (Old European) roots with added Celtic suffixes describing a settlement or location on the lower course or estuary of the Thames (below its lowest fordable point at WESTMINSTER, *see* WATLING STREET), with a meaning something like 'place at the navigable or unfordable river' (for the complex philology involved, see article cited in Select Bibliography).

Of course until relatively recent times the name London referred only to the City of London, with even WESTMINSTER remaining a separate entity. But when the County of London was created in 1888, the name often came to be rather loosely used for this much larger area, which was also sometimes referred to as *Greater London* from about this date. However in 1965, **Greater London** was newly defined as a much enlarged area. The old London County Council, with jurisdiction over some 117 square miles, was replaced by the Greater London Council (since abolished), with jurisdiction over 610 square miles and with its newly created London Boroughs (as mapped and listed at the beginning of this book).

London Bridge Southwark. This is on the site of various early bridges. It is likely that the Romans built the first bridge here in about AD 100, probably a timber structure linking the City with the point where two Roman roads met on the south bank of the river, and with an alignment thought to have been some 100 metres downstream from the present bridge. At an even earlier date, just upstream from here, the prehistoric (possibly Bronze Age) structure recently revealed at VAUXHALL may have been part of a bridge or system of raised tracks across the river. In Saxon times the first probable reference to a bridge at or near where London Bridge now stands is *c.*1000, and 11th-century records report the repair and renewal of various wooden structures. These were replaced *c.*1176–1209 by the first stone bridge, built with twenty arches and surmounted by houses and shops. This bridge or its predecessors gave name to the wards of the City known as **Bridge Within** and **Bridge Without** (the former in the City itself, the latter once comprising the borough of SOUTHWARK). The present bridge dates from 1972, having replaced a bridge built in 1831 (this was sold and reconstructed in Lake Havasu City, Arizona). The well-known nursery rhyme 'London Bridge is falling down' dates from the 17th century, and is sometimes claimed to refer to an actual event in 1014 in which, according to Snorri Sturleson's early 13th-century saga, King Ethelred and the Norseman Olaf pulled down the bridge to disrupt the Danish Vikings who occupied the city.

London City Airport Newham. Opened in 1987 with its runway situated on the old quay between the KING GEORGE V DOCK and the ROYAL ALBERT DOCK (both closed to shipping in 1981).

London Fields Hackney. *London Field* 1540, *London Felde* 1547, an area of ground once used for the grazing of sheep, probably so called because it was on the *London* side of HACKNEY parish.

London Stone (in Cannon Street) City. A mason-shaped, round-topped, limestone block, mentioned in records from the 12th century onwards, originally standing on the south side of CANNON STREET, now preserved in the wall of No. 111 on the north side. It is possibly a Roman milestone, or is perhaps to be associated with the large Roman building dating from *c.*80–100, possibly the Provincial Governor's Palace, which excavations have revealed once stood on the site of Cannon Street station.

London Wall City. Street named from the City *wall* built by the Romans *c.*200, referred to as 'the highway near London Wall' in 1388 and as *London Walle* in 1547, from Old English *wall.* The street follows closely the line of the northern stretch of the original wall. In the 14th century, part of the street was called *Babeloyne*, clearly a name transferred from the city of Babylon: perhaps the noise here invited comparison with the Tower of Babel!

Lonesome (north of Mitcham Common) Merton. Named from *Lonesome Chemical Works* marked thus on the Ordnance Survey map of 1876.

Long Acre Westminster. Street named from a narrow strip of ground recorded as *pasture called Longeacre* in 1547 and as *The Long Acurs, the baksyde of Charing Cross* in 1556, from Old English *æcer* 'plot of cultivated or arable land'. In medieval times this plot of land, like COVENT GARDEN, belonged to the monks of Westminster Abbey (*see* WESTMINSTER).

Longford (near Harmondsworth) Hillingdon. *Longeforde* 1294, *Langeforde* 1327, *le Longeforth* 1430, 'the long ford', from Old English *lang* and *ford.* The ford was no doubt so named because it crossed two branches of the River COLNE here, later replaced by two bridges, KING'S BRIDGE and MOOR BRIDGE. Like the latter, **Longfordmoor** takes its name from the *moor* 'marshy ground' by the river.

Longford River Hillingdon/Hounslow/Richmond. Named from LONGFORD, where this artificial watercourse, constructed in the 17th century to supply the lakes at HAMPTON COURT with water from the River COLNE, begins; it divides from the westerly DUKE OF NORTHUMBERLAND'S RIVER, with which it partly shares its course, at EAST BEDFONT.

It is called *Queen's or Cardinal's River* on the Ordnance Survey map of 1880, probably alluding to Henrietta Maria, wife of Charles I, and to Cardinal Wolsey, builder of the palace at Hampton Court.

Longlands (near Sidcup) Bromley. Marked thus on the Ordnance Survey map of 1876, earlier *Long Lands* on the 1805 map, though a hamlet here is referred to as early as 1635, 'the long strips of arable land' (i.e. in the common fields), from Middle English *long* and *land*.

Long Lane (near West Smithfield) City. Recorded as *Long Lane* in 1530, *Longlane* in 1532, self-explanatory.

Lord's Cricket Ground (in St John's Wood) Westminster. Famous headquarters of English cricket owned by the MCC (MARYLEBONE Cricket Club), named after Thomas *Lord* who first opened a cricket ground just south-east of here (in DORSET SQUARE) in 1787, later removed to this site in 1816.

Lordship Lane (at Tottenham) Haringey. Marked thus on the Ordnance Survey map of 1822 and also so called in 1600; it refers to a lane running through land once belonging to the lord of the manor (perhaps that of BRUCE CASTLE which is on this road), see next name.

Lordship Lane (at Dulwich) Southwark. Named from *the litle Lordshipp* 1609, from Middle English *lordship* 'a manor or estate', probably with reference to the old manor of *Friern*, *see* FRIERN ROAD. Lordship Lane formed the boundary between this manor and DULWICH.

Lothbury City. Street named from an ancient manor (later a City ward) recorded as *Lodebure c.*1190, *Lothebiri* 1232, *Lothebery c.*1234, *Lothebury* 1349, that is 'manor of a man called *Hlotha', from Old English *burh* (dative case *byrig*) and an Old English personal name.

Loughborough Junction, Loughborough Park & Road (near Brixton) Lambeth. Preserve the name of *Loughborough House* (marked on the Ordnance Survey map of 1816), so called because it was the residence of Henry Hastings, created Lord *Loughborough* in 1643. The area was developed as a residential district after the house had been pulled down in 1854. The medieval manor on this site was known as *Wyk*, a name preserved in nearby WYCK GARDENS. Loughborough Junction is so named from the number of lines that converged here with the coming of the railways in the 1860s.

Love Lane (off Wood Street) City. Recorded as *Lovelane* in 1336, just one of the four lanes so called that existed in the City in medieval times, possibly a reference to prostitutes but perhaps with the more innocent connotation of 'lane where lovers walked' (the same name is found in many other towns and cities).

Lower Clapton Hackney, *see* CLAPTON.

Lower Edmonton Enfield, *see* EDMONTON.

Lower Feltham Hounslow, *see* FELTHAM.

Lower Holloway Islington, *see* HOLLOWAY.

Lower Marsh (at Waterloo) Lambeth. Street so called from the former marshland here known as *Lambethe Marshe*, *see* LAMBETH.

Lower Place (near Harlesden) Brent. District named from a large house (probably on the site of the manor house of *East Twyford*, for which *see* TWYFORD ABBEY), marked thus on Rocque's map of 1754 and on the Ordnance Survey map of 1822. Self-explanatory, from *place* 'residence, large house' with reference to its low-lying situation on marshy ground in the flood plain of the River BRENT.

Lower Sydenham Lewisham, *see* SYDENHAM.

Loxford Redbridge. Recorded thus in 1319 and on the Ordnance Survey map of 1805, 'ford of a man called Locc', from an Old English personal name and *ford*. On the Ordnance Survey map of 1888, *Loxford Hall* is marked on the stream called *Loxford Water* (earlier *Loxford brooke* c.1580), a small tributary of the River RODING; the original ford was no doubt on this stream.

Ludgate Hill City. Street name recorded thus in 1548, earlier *Lutgate-strate* c.1195, *Ludgatstrete* 1359, named from *Ludgate* c.1170, *Luthgate* 1190, *Lutgate* 1312, that is 'the back gate or postern', from Old English *ludgeat*. This western gateway into the City, originally built by the Romans c.200, was demolished in 1760. It may be referred to as one of the 'west gates' in 857, *see* NEWGATE STREET. The name has been associated with a legendary King Lud, said by early writers (beginning with the 12th-century chronicler Geoffrey of Monmouth in his *History of the Kings of Britain*) to have rebuilt the City of London, but of course the story (though charming) is pure myth (*see* LONDON).

Lusted Hall Farm (near Biggin Hill) Bromley. *Lovestedesdoune* 1402, *Lovested* 1545, *Lofested* 1552, *Lustead Farm* 1819, probably 'pasture or homestead of a man called Lufa', from Old English *stede* and an Old English personal name. However it is possible that the first element is the Old English word *lufu* 'love', in which case the name might be a complimentary one for a pleasant or fertile place, or refer to a 'morning gift' or dowry, or even be an allusion to a secluded spot considered suitable for courtship and lovemaking!

Luxted (near Downe) Bromley. *Luckestethel* 1317, *Lostede* 1348, *Luxsted* 1778, possibly 'site with an enclosure', from Old English **lūce* and *stede* (alternating with a synonymous Old English **stethel* in the earliest form).

Lyonsdown (in East Barnet) Barnet. Marked *Lions Down* on the Ordnance Survey map of 1822 and recorded as *Lyondownes* or *Lionsdownes* in the 16th and 17th century, so called from the family of John *Lyount* 1421, with Middle English *doun* 'hill, down'. The residential estate so named developed on what had earlier been meadowland after the coming of the railway in the mid-19th century.

M

Mad Bess Wood (near Ruislip) Hillingdon. So named from one area of the present woodland, referred to as *Mad Bess* in the 18th century. The reason for the name is not known, but conceivably it could have been called after someone nicknamed 'Mad Bess'. It gives name also to Mad Bess Stream and Bess Ride on the edges of the wood. The name given on the Ordnance Survey map of 1822, *Claytons Wood*, is apparently an error (it belongs to a different wood south of here in HAYES).

Mad Bridge (near Longford) Hillingdon. Marked thus on the Ordnance Survey map of 1816–22, earlier *Madebryggeford* c.1380, *Mad bridg* 1686, that is 'bridge by the meadow', from Old English *mǣd* and *brycg*.

Maida Hill & Vale Westminster. *Maida Hill* is marked thus on Mogg's map of 1817, *Maida Vale* is mentioned in 1868. The district is called simply *Maida* on the Ordnance Survey map of 1822. The name is from the Battle of *Maida* in southern Italy, the site of a British victory against the French in 1806.

Maitland Park (near Chalk Farm) Camden. Residential estate named after Ebenezer *Maitland*, the treasurer of an orphanage established here in the mid-19th century.

Malden Manor, Old Malden Kingston. *Meldone* 1086 (Domesday Book), *Meldon* 1206, *Maldon* 1225, *Maulden* 1602, that is 'hill with a cross or crucifix', from Old English *mǣl* and *dūn*, thus identical in origin with Maldon in Essex. **New Malden**, originally part of the manor of KINGSTON and a mainly 19th-century development after the coming of the railway, is marked thus on the Ordnance Survey map of 1876. On the same map the district of **Malden Green** is shown as *Maldengreen*.

Malden Rushett (near Chessington) Kingston. Marked as *Lower Malden* on the Ordnance Survey map of 1876 (no doubt to distinguish it from OLD & NEW MALDEN) but otherwise combined with the name of nearby RUSHETT FARM. Malden itself lies some 3 miles to the north-east, but this manor may have possessed some rights in the 'rush bed' at Rushett.

Mall, The Westminster. Created *c.*1660 in ST JAMES'S PARK by Charles II
to replace PALL MALL as an alley for the game of *pallemaille*. By the time
the game started to become less popular in the early 18th century, The
Mall had become a fashionable promenade for the well-to-do (this
development providing the derivation of the word *mall* 'a public walk'
in later English).

Manor House (near Stoke Newington) Hackney. Station opened in
1932, named from the *Manor House* public house which up to 1931 was
known as the *Manor Tavern* (built *c.*1820). The actual manor house of
STOKE NEWINGTON was formerly situated about a mile south of here
near the old church, but most of the area of the parish north of Church
Street once belonged to the manorial demesne.

Manor Park (near Plashet) Newham. Marked thus on the Ordnance
Survey map of 1904, named from the *Manor House* (built in the 1820s)
still shown here on the earlier map of 1883; the station of this name
was opened in 1872. The district covers the ancient parish of LITTLE
ILFORD.

Mansfield Hill & Park (at Chingford) Waltham Forest. Named from
Manfield 1533, *Maunfeld* 1538, that is 'the common field, the field held
in common', from Old English *(ge)mǽne* and *feld*. It will be noted that
the medial *-s-* is unhistorical, perhaps influenced by Mansfield in
Nottinghamshire or by the title of Jane Austen's novel.

Mansion House City. Official residence of the Lord Mayor of London
during his year of office, from the word *mansion* in the sense 'large and
stately house'. The building was completed in 1752. The station
named from it was opened in 1871.

Mapesbury Road (in Brondesbury) Brent. Preserves the name of the old
manor of *Mapesberi c.*1250, *Mapesbury* 1254, *Mapesbery* 1322, that is
'manor of a man called *Map*', from Middle English *bury*. Walter *Map*, a
prebendary of ST PAUL'S, is mentioned *c.*1180 in connection with
WILLESDEN. *Mapesbury House* is marked on the Ordnance Survey map
of 1876–7, earlier shown as simply *Mapes* on the map of 1822.

Marble Arch Westminster. Triumphal arch built in Italian marble,
designed by John Nash to commemorate Nelson's victories and originally erected in 1827 as the gateway to BUCKINGHAM PALACE. It was
moved to its present position at the north-east corner of HYDE PARK in
1851, where since 1908 it has been islanded by traffic. Nearby, by way

of historical contrast, are SPEAKER'S CORNER and the gallows site of
Tyburn Tree (for which, *see* TYBURN WAY).

Marble Hill (Park) (at Twickenham) Richmond. Recorded as *Marble Hill*
in 1650 and as *(Little) Marble Hill* in 1816, but earlier *Mardelhylle* in 1350.
The spelling since the 17th century is clearly the result of folk etymology; the original meaning is unclear, but it may have been 'hill at
the woodland clearing frequented by martens', from Old English
mearth 'a marten' (a once common animal resembling a weasel) and
lēah, with the addition of *hyll*. The present **Marble Hill House** (now
owned by English Heritage) is a delightful Palladian villa built 1724–9.

Mardyke Farm (near South Hornchurch) Havering. Marked thus on the
Ordnance Survey map of 1805, named from *Markediche c.*1270, *Markediche* 1367, *Mardiche* 1589, that is 'boundary ditch', from Old English
mearc and *dīc*; this was the earlier name of nearby BEAM RIVER.

Mare Street Hackney. *Merestret* 1443, *Meerstreete* 1593, *Mayre street* 1605,
Marestreete 1621, that is 'street of houses or hamlet on the boundary',
from Middle English *mere* and *strete*. Mare Street is now the main
street of HACKNEY, but was originally a small hamlet at the extreme
south of the parish where the road meets the border with BETHNAL
GREEN.

Margaret or Tripcock Ness (near Plumstead) Greenwich. A promon-
tory on the River Thames, called *Magott Nesse* on a river chart of 1588,
from the feminine personal name *Maggot*, a pet-form derivative of
Margaret, or from the corresponding Middle English surname, with
Old English *næss* 'headland'. The alternative name is from *Tripcotts* and
Tripcott Reache, thus in 1588, also giving name to *Tripcock Trees* on the
Ordnance Survey map of 1805 (apparently a line of trees by the river),
probably from a surname *Tripcott*.

Markfield Road (at South Tottenham) Haringey. Preserves the old name
Merkefeld 1502, *Markfield House* 1877, that is 'field on a boundary', from
Old English *mearc* and *feld*, with reference to its situation on the
boundary of both the parish of TOTTENHAM and the hundred of
EDMONTON.

Mark Lane (near The Tower) City. Recorded as *Marthe lane c.*1200,
Martelane 1276, *Martlane* 1466, *Markelane* 1481. The change to *Mark* is
relatively late, the early spellings suggesting derivation either from
the woman's personal name Martha (Old French *Marthe*) or from Old

English *mearth* 'marten' (a small weasel-like animal much valued in early times for its fur, which was perhaps sold in this lane).

Marks Gate (north of Chadwell Heath) Barking & Dagenham. Recorded thus in 1777 and on the Ordnance Survey map of 1883, named from *Merkes* 1368, *Markys* c.1480, *Markes* 1594, *Marks* 1805, a manorial name indicating the estate of the family of Simon *de Merk* 1330. The moated site of the manor house, Mark's Hall (called *Marks House* in 1663), can still be seen. The 'gate' refers to an entrance into Hainault Forest (*see* HAINAULT) which once extended north from here, and the surname *de Merk* is from Old English *mearc* 'boundary', here alluding to the edge of the forest.

Marlborough Street, Great (in Soho) Westminster. Marked *Marlborough Street* on a map of c.1710, named after John Churchill, 1st Duke of *Marlborough*, whose celebrated victory at Blenheim was in 1704. **Marlborough House** in PALL MALL is also named after the Duke, or rather the Duchess for whom it was built in 1709.

Marling Park (near Hampton) Richmond. Residential district mainly developed in the later 20th century on earlier farmland once given over to nurseries. *Marling Park* (marked thus on the Ordnance Survey map of 1904) was so named in 1890 by a Major W. B. *Marling* who had bought the estate here.

Maryland (near Stratford) Newham. Named from **Maryland Point**, first recorded in the late 17th century and marked thus on the Ordnance Survey map of 1805, a name transferred from Maryland in the USA. The first houses in this hamlet are said to have been built by a Stratford merchant who had made his fortune there when it was still a colony.

Marylebone Westminster. *Maryburne* 1453, *Marybourne* 1492, *Marybon* 1542, *Marylebone* 1626, that is '(place by) St Mary's stream', from Old English *burna* and with reference to the dedication of the church built in the 15th century. It is to be noted that the medial *-le-* is intrusive and dates only from the 17th century. It was probably introduced on the analogy of other names like St Mary-le-Bow (for which, *see* BOW LANE) where it has a loose connective sense. This *-le-* is usually sounded now in current pronunciations of the name, 'Marrylebon' or 'Marlibon'. The earlier name of the settlement was *Tiburne* 1086 (Domesday Book), *Teyborne* 1312, *Tyborne* 1490, so called from the original name of the stream here, the *Tyburn*, first recorded as *Teoburnan*, 'the boundary stream' from Old English **tēo* and *burna*, in an Anglo-Saxon charter of 959 (it formed the boundary between the manors of EBURY and WESTMINSTER), *see* TYBURN WAY. The stream in question rose at HAMPSTEAD and flowed into the Thames near the present Vauxhall Bridge (*see* VAUXHALL).

Maryon Park, Maryon Wilson Park (in Charlton) Greenwich. Adjacent parks named after the *Maryon Wilson* family who owned the manor of Charlton House (*see* CHARLTON) until 1925.

Masons Hill Bromley. Recorded thus in 1729 and on the Ordnance Survey map of 1819, otherwise marked as *Gravill or Masons Hill* on Bowen's map of *c*.1762, no doubt from some local family called *Mason* who formerly held land here. There were once gravel pits near to where Bromley South station now stands.

Maswell Park Hounslow. Named from *Massewelle* 1485, *Maswell* 1498, that is 'spring or stream of a man called **Mæssa*', from Old English *wella* and an Old English personal name.

Maudsley Hospital (on Denmark Hill) Southwark. Opened in 1916 and named after its founder, Dr Henry *Maudsley*.

Mawney (near Collier Row) Havering. Originally *Mawneys*, a manorial name from the family of Sir Walter *de Manny* who is mentioned in 14th-century records.

Mayesbrook Park Barking & Dagenham. Named from **Mayes Brook**, a small tributary of the River RODING, marked as *Great Mays Brook* on the Ordnance Survey map of 1805 and recorded earlier in field names like *Maybroke meade* 1587 and *Eastmaybrokes* 1609, so called from the family of Robert *le May* 1285 and Richard *le May* 1314. The name GOODMAYES just a mile north of here seems not to be related, although the medieval surname *Godemay*, like *May*, derives from Middle English *may* 'young lad or girl'.

Mayfair Westminster. District named from the 'May Fair' once held here. This area was still largely open land until the late 17th century, and the great annual fair held here on the 1st of May and lasting for 15 days is on record from 1686, surviving until it was suppressed (having become notorious for its riotous and lewd behaviour) in the mid-18th century. The fair was held in a field called *Greate Brooke feilde* (1650) beside the River *Tyburn* (for which, *see* BROOK STREET, MARYLEBONE, and TYBURN WAY), now the site of CURZON STREET and SHEPHERD MARKET.

Maylands (near Harold Hill) Havering. Marked thus on the Ordnance Survey map of 1883, earlier *Maylond* 1524, *Mavlande* 1568, *Mayland* 1777, from Middle English *land* 'cultivated land, estate', possibly with *may* 'hawthorn'.

Maypole (near Chelsfield) Bromley. Marked thus on the Ordnance Survey map of 1871, no doubt alluding to a site where May festivities took place in earlier times. Of the many maypoles there must once have been, few have given rise to names, although there is another place called Maypole near Old Bexley (*see* BEXLEY) and there are several Maypole street names in the Greater London area. From the 16th to 18th centuries there was even a maypole standing on the green outside the church of St Mary in the STRAND!

Maze Hill Greenwich. Station named from street running along the east side of Greenwich Park (*see* GREENWICH), marked as *Mays Hill* on Rocque's map of 1745 and as *Maze* or *Maize Hill* on Bacon's map of 1888, recorded earlier as *Mays Hill* 1694, *Mayeshile* 1717, probably named from Sir Algernon *May* who lived near here until 1693.

Mecklenburgh Square (in Bloomsbury) Camden. Laid out *c.*1800 and so named in honour of Queen Charlotte, formerly Princess of *Mecklenburg*-Strelitz, George III's consort.

Merton (town and borough). *Mertone* 949 (Anglo-Saxon charter), *Meretone* 1086 (Domesday Book), *Meritone* 12th century, *Mirton alias Marten* 1679, that is 'farmstead or estate by the pool', from Old English *mere* and *tūn*. The 'pool' was no doubt in or by the River WANDLE which flows through Merton; *Merton Mill* is marked on the river on the Ordnance Survey map of 1816. The original settlement would have been near to where the old Roman road from London to Chichester crossed the river, thus providing a convenient watering place and overnight halt for early travellers. The identification of Merton with a place called *Merantun*, where according to the Anglo-Saxon Chronicle, King Cynewulf of Wessex met his death in 786, is exceedingly doubtful; the naming of the recently built Merantun Way in the town is therefore simply meretricious and deceptive. In medieval times there was a large Augustinian priory here, founded in 1114 and demolished by Henry VIII in 1538, the stones being used for the building of his palace at Nonsuch, *see* WORCESTER PARK; there is only a distant echo of its existence in the name Merton Abbey (marked thus on the Ordnance Survey map of 1816) for an area near ABBEY RECREATION GROUND & ROAD where the priory once stood. **South Merton** is on record as early as 1324. **Merton Park** was developed as a garden suburb on what had been agricultural land by John Innes, a successful City businessman, at the end of the 19th century (he is also commemorated in the name of John Innes Park here). The London Borough of Merton was created in 1965.

Middlesex Street City. Earlier called *Hog Lane* and PETTICOAT LANE (still surviving as the name of the famous market here), it was renamed thus *c.*1830. It was so called because the old lane formed the boundary between the City and the ancient county of Middlesex (that is '(territory of) the Middle Saxons', originally a tribal name from Old English *middel* and *Seaxe*).

Milbourne House (in Barnes) Richmond. Referred to as *Melbornes* 1443, *Mylborns* 1498, so named from the family of William *Milbourne* 1415. The mainly 16th-century house, home of the novelist Henry Fielding in 1750–2, may incorporate parts of the 15th-century building.

Mile End Tower Hamlets. *La Mile ende* 1288, *le Milende* 1307, *Mylesende* 1395, *the Miles ende* 1603, that is 'the hamlet a mile away', from Middle English *mile* and *ende*. This hamlet on the old London–Colchester road was so named because it was about 1 mile from ALDGATE. It became known as *Mile End Old Town c.*1691 when the name *Mile End New Town* was given to another hamlet further west, adjoining SPITALFIELDS. The road itself, here **Mile End Road** (marked thus on the Ordnance Survey map of 1822), was earlier referred to as *Oldestrete* 1383. In medieval times the open land here was much used for recreation and gatherings; it was here during the Peasants' Revolt of 1381 that the men of Essex met Richard II and successfully demanded the abolition of feudal serfdom.

Milk Street City. *Melecstrate c.*1140, *Milkestrete c.*1160, *Melcstrate* 1212, *Milkstret* 1260, that is 'street where milk was sold', from Old English *meoluc* and *strǣt*. This was one of several specialized market streets near the main City market of *Cheap* (for which, *see* CHEAPSIDE).

Milkwood Road (near Herne Hill) Lambeth. Named from *Mylkewell* *woodde* 1540, thus preserving the name of the old manor of *Milkewelle* 1291, *Milkwelle* 1305, *Milkewell* 1615, that is 'spring or stream with milk-coloured (probably chalky) water', from Old English *meoluc* and *wella*, with the later addition of Middle English *wode*.

Millbank Westminster. Riverside road named from *land called the Mill Bank* 1546, referring to former mills (the last of them demolished *c.*1736), situated along the Thames and belonging to Westminster Abbey (*see* WESTMINSTER).

Millfields, North & South Hackney. *Mellefeld iuxta* ('next to') *Mellelane* 1443, *lee* ('the') *Northmyllefeld*, *Southmyllefeld* 1547, self-explanatory, 'field by the mill', from Middle English *mille* and *feld*, with a later division into *north* and *south* (the two are separated by Lea Bridge Road). The reference is no doubt to an early watermill on the River LEA; *Mellelane* ('mill lane') is probably to be identified with the present Millfields Road.

Mill Hill Barnet. *Myllehill* 1547, *Milhill, Mylhyll* 1563, self-explanatory, 'hill with a windmill' from Middle English *mille* and *hill*. The ground rises here to 389 ft. There is still an open space near St Mary's Abbey called The Mill Field (recorded thus in 1754) and the old mill house also survives.

Mill Hill Road (in Barnes) Richmond. Named from *Milhyll* 1443, *compare* previous name. The former windmill here is also referred to in the field name *Windmillfeild* 1664. Mill Lodge just north of here is marked thus on the Ordnance Survey map of 1876.

Mill Meads (near Stratford) Newham. Marked thus on the Ordnance Survey map of 1876 together with *Three Mills* from which the meadows are named. The three mills (also giving their name to THREE MILL LANE and THREE MILLS WALL RIVER) belonged to the former abbey of *Stratford Langthorne* (*see* STRATFORD) and are recorded as early as the 16th century; the name of ABBEY MILLS pumping station nearby still preserves this association. This was an industrial area at a very early date; in the Domesday Book of 1086, no less than eight mills are recorded on the tributary streams of the River LEA in this part of Stratford.

Millwall Tower Hamlets. This district on the ISLE OF DOGS, marked thus on the Ordnance Survey map of 1876, is so called from a stretch of river wall (earlier *Marsh Wall* 1754) on which several mills stood in the

17th and 18th centuries. These were replaced by shipyards in the 19th century, among them the one from which Brunel's *Great Eastern*, at the time Britain's largest ship, was launched in 1859. The **Millwall Dock**, built in 1864–8, was closed in 1980.

Milton Street (near Barbican) City. Originally *Grubbestrete* in the early 13th century, *Grobstrat c.*1240, *Grubbestrate* 1281, possibly 'street infested by caterpillars and worms', from Middle English *grubbe*, but more likely 'street named from a family called *Grubbe*' (a nickname from the same word, on record in London from the 13th century). In the 17th century 'Grub Street' became a byword for mean or needy authors, or literary hacks, because, as Dr Johnson later puts it, the street was 'much inhabited by writers of small histories, dictionaries, and temporary poems'. No doubt for this reason the residents had the name changed to *Milton Street* in 1830, this being an allusion to the illustrious poet John *Milton* (by no means a hack) who had once lived nearby.

Mincing Lane City. *Mengenelane* 12th century, *Menechinelane* 1274, *Mynchenelane* 1360, *Minnchinge Lane* 1568, that is 'lane of the nuns', from Old English *myncen* (genitive case plural *myncena*) and *lane*. A small community of nuns may already have existed here by the 12th century, or nuns may have owned property here.

Minories City. Street (earlier *Minorie Street* 1624) named from a former nunnery, the abbey of the Franciscan nuns or *Minoresses* of St Clare established on the east side of the present street in 1294 (hence nearby ST CLARE STREET) and dissolved in 1538. The abbey (or the street) is recorded as *The Minoresses without Alegate* (that is 'outside ALDGATE') 1341, *Le Myneris* 1548, *le Menoryse* 1554, *the Mynorisse* 1568, from Middle English *menouresse* 'a nun of the second order of St Francis, known as Poor Clares'.

Mitcham Merton. *Michelham* 1086 (Domesday Book), *Micheleham* 1176, *Michham* 1178, *Micheham* 1202, that is 'the large homestead or village', from Old English *micel* and *hām*, perhaps by contrast with CLAPHAM and STREATHAM (which contain the same second element). The name dates back to an early phase of Anglo-Saxon colonization, even though pre-Conquest spellings sometimes cited (*Micham* 727, 933) are from forged charters. Indeed the age of the settlement is suggested by the discovery of a large Anglo-Saxon pagan cemetery here, which excavation has shown dates from the period 450–600. **Mitcham Common** is marked thus on the Ordnance Survey map of 1819 (also showing the windmill here, built in 1806 and taken down in 1905, which gives name to Windmill Road).

Mitchley Hill & Wood Croydon. The latter is recorded as *Mitcherley Wood* in 1843, possibly (if the name is an old one) 'large wood or clearing', from Old English *micel* and *lēah.*

Moat Mount (near Highwood Hill) Barnet. Recorded thus in 1754 and as *Moatmount* on the Ordnance Survey map of 1877, named from a house which was still surrounded by a moat in 1799.

Monken Hadley Barnet, *see* HADLEY.

Monkfrith Close & Way (at East Barnet) Barnet. Preserve the old name *Monke(n)frith*, for which, *see* OAK HILL PARK.

Monkham's Avenue, Drive & Lane (at Woodford Green) Redbridge. Street names preserving the old name *Munckombe* 1630, *Monkham* 1805, *Monkhams* 1843, earlier *Monekenebukhurst* 1286, *Monnekenhyll alias Monk-hyll* 1547, that is '(part of) Buckhurst belonging to the monks' and 'hill of the monks', from Middle English *monk* (plural *-en*) and *hill*, with reference to its early possession by the monks of *Stratford Langthorne* Abbey (*see* STRATFORD). Thus, *Munckombe* and *Monkham* represent simply an alteration of the first part of the original names. Buckhurst Hill (*Bocherst* 1135, 'wooded hill growing with beeches', from Old English *bōc* and *hyrst*) lies in Essex just to the north of WOODFORD.

Monks Orchard (near Shirley) Croydon. Named from *Monks Orchard Farm & Wood* on the Ordnance Survey map of 1819 and to be compared with *Monksmead* 1661, all indicating lands once owned here by a family called *Monk* who came originally from ADDINGTON. The name *Monks Orchard* was given to a mansion built in 1854 and later to the district.

Monkwell Square (near Barbican) City. From a family called *de Mukewell* who gave their name to *Mukewellestrate* in the late 12th century, *Mukewellstrete c.*1200, which was later altered through folk etymology or prudishness to *Munkeswell streete* 1603. The place itself (from which the surname is derived) is *Mukewell* in 1206, that is 'spring, stream, or well of a man called Muc(c)a', from an Old English personal name and Old English *wella*: it may have been somewhere in this vicinity.

Monoux Grove (in Walthamstow) Waltham Forest. On the site of the house called *Moones* or *Mones* in the 16th century, and *Moons* on the

Ordnance Survey map of 1805, so named from Sir George *Monoux*, Lord Mayor of London in 1514, who lived here.

Monument Street City. Named from the **Monument**, the 202-ft high column designed by Sir Christopher Wren and constructed 1671–7 to commemorate the Great Fire of 1666 which started in PUDDING LANE and which rapidly destroyed much of the old City of London within the walls.

Moor Bridge (at Longford) Hillingdon. Marked thus on the Ordnance Survey map of 1816–22, earlier *Moor Bridg* 1720, named from the *moor* or marshy ground by the River COLNE to which nearby Moor Lane (*le Morlane* 1337) in HARMONDSWORTH also refers, *see* Longfordmoor (*under* LONGFORD).

Moorfields City. Marked as *Moor Field* on the mid-16th century 'wood-cut' map of London, that is 'field in the moor or marshland', originally referring to the marshy ground north of the City wall which also gives name to MOORGATE and MOOR LANE. The 'moor' was drained in 1527 and the field is shown on the mid-16th century map as an open space used for cloth-drying and other pursuits.

Moorgate City. Marked as *Moor Gate* on the mid-16th century map, that is 'gate to the moor or marshland', thus named from a postern gate in the City wall built in 1415. The 'moor' or marshy ground (Old English *mōr*) north of the City wall is referred to as *thæne mor with-uten Crepelesgate* (that is 'the moor outside CRIPPLEGATE') in an 11th-century document, and as *La More* in 1265. It also gives name to nearby MOORFIELDS and MOOR LANE.

Moor Hall (near Rainham) Havering. Marked thus on the Ordnance Survey map of 1805, earlier *Morehall* 1333, that is 'manor house on the moor or marshy ground', from Middle English *more* and *hall*.

Moorhall Cottages, Dell & Road (at Harefield) Hillingdon. Named from a farm marked as *Moor Hall* on the Ordnance Survey map of 1822, earlier *More Halle* 1301, *Morhalle* 1339, identical in origin with the previous name, with reference to Harefield Moor (*see* HAREFIELD). Moorhall Dell contains the word *dell* 'hollow' (probably a disused gravel or sand pit).

Moor Lane City. Recorded as *le Morstrate* 1310, *le Morelane* 1332, *Morelane or Morestrete* 1502, named from the 'moor' or marshy ground that once lay north of the City wall, *see* MOORFIELDS and MOORGATE.

Morden Merton. *Mordune* 969 (spurious Anglo-Saxon charter), *Mordone* 1086 (Domesday Book), *Moreden* 1204, *Moorden* 1440, that is 'hill in marshy ground', from Old English *mōr* and *dūn*, referring to its situation on slightly elevated land between the valleys of BEVERLEY BROOK and the River WANDLE. It will be noted that the spelling -*den* (for the more historical -*don*) occurs from quite an early date. **Morden Hall**, a 17th-century house rebuilt *c*.1840, is marked thus on the Ordnance Survey map of 1876; Morden Hall Park, its former deer park, is now owned by the National Trust. **Morden Park**, formerly the private park for a Georgian mansion built here in 1770, is marked *Mordon Park* on the Ordnance Survey map of 1819.

Mornington Crescent Camden. Named from the Earl of *Mornington*, related by marriage to the Fitzroy family who owned the estate, *see* FITZROY SQUARE.

Mortlake Richmond. *Mortelage* 1086 (Domesday Book), *Murtelac* 1135, *Mortelak* 1227, *Mourtlake* 1465, probably 'small stream in which young salmon are found', from Old English *lacu* and an Old English word **mort* 'a young salmon or similar fish'. The name no doubt refers to some small stream now lost (perhaps an arm of BEVERLEY BROOK) which once flowed into the Thames where the original settlement grew up, the site of a fishery before 1066 mentioned in Domesday Book.

Moselle, The (river) Haringey. This stream, which joins the River LEA at TOTTENHAM, is first recorded as *The Moselle* in 1600. The spelling of its name may have been influenced by the famous River Moselle in France and Germany, but it is in fact a late back-formation from MUSWELL HILL through which area it flows!

Mossford Green (at Barkingside) Redbridge. Marked thus on the Ordnance Survey map of 1883, but *Mossfoot Green* on earlier maps of 1777 and 1805, so possibly 'mossy foot (of a hill)', from Old English *mos* and *fōt*, with *grene* 'village green'.

Moss Hall at Finchley) Barnet. Marked thus on the Ordnance Survey map of 1822 and also so called in a document of 1696, named from the family of John *Mosse* 1474.

Motspur Park Kingston. Originally *Furse Farm* 1623, *Motes Firs Ferm* 1627, later *Motts Spur Farm* 1823, *Mosper Farm* 1876, that is 'farm among the furze or gorse belonging to a family called *Mot*', from Middle English *furse* and a local surname found in 14th-century records.

Alternative spellings current in the 18th and 19th centuries like *Nutcars Farm* on the Ordnance Survey map of 1819 are also corruptions of the original form.

Mottingham Bromley. *Modingahammes gemæro* 973, *Modingeham* 1044 (Anglo-Saxon charters), *Modingham* 1206, *Motingham* 1610, that is 'homestead or enclosure of the family or followers of a man called *Mōda*', from an Old English personal name with *-inga-* (genitive case of *-ingas*) and *hām* or *hamm*. The first spelling (from a description of the Anglo-Saxon bounds of BROMLEY) contains the Old English word *gemære* 'boundary'. An even earlier reference occurs in another Anglo-Saxon charter describing the bounds of Bromley in 862 in the phrase *Modinga hema mearce*, that is 'boundary of the people of Mottingham', from Old English *hæme* 'dwellers' and *mearc* 'mark, boundary'.

Mount Pleasant (at Harefield) Hillingdon. This district alongside PARK WOOD (earlier *Harefield Park* on the Ordnance Survey map of 1822) was developed from the early 19th century as an industrial area on the newly built Grand Union Canal with lime kilns, copper mills, and iron works. Thus, this outwardly 'complimentary' name has almost certainly an ironical application here (no doubt with reference to spoil heaps and the like). There are several other examples of the name Mount Pleasant in the London area, and some of these too may be ironic in origin. This is certainly the case with **Mount Pleasant** in CLERKENWELL, a street that also gives name to the Post Office sorting depot on it. Once just a country track leading to the FLEET river, it is so named in 1732 from the heap of cinders and other refuse dumped on the river bank (hence also nearby **Laystall Street** from the word *laystall* 'a place where refuse was laid').

Mudchute (on Isle of Dogs) Tower Hamlets. So named from the dumping of mud pumped out of Millwall Dock (*see* MILLWALL) from 1875 onwards, the second element being *chute* or *shoot* 'place where debris is "shot" or "tipped"'.

Muswell Hill Haringey. *Mussell Hill* 1631, *Muscle Hill* 1746, named from *Mosewella* c.1155, *Mosewelle* c.1200, *Muswell* 1535, that is 'the mossy or boggy spring', from Old English *mēos* 'moss', also 'bog, marsh', and *wella*, with the addition of *hill* from the 17th century. The reference is to an ancient spring or well here on land bestowed on the Augustinian priory of St Mary at CLERKENWELL by the Bishop of London in the 12th century. The hill itself (rising to over 300 ft) was earlier *Pinnesknol* 1288,

Pinnesnoll Hill alias Muswell Hill 1610, that is 'Pinn's knoll or hill' from Old English *cnoll* and a personal name or surname (or Old English *pinn* 'pointed hill' as in PINNER).

Mutton Brook (a tributary of the River Brent at Hendon) Barnet. Marked thus on Greenwood's map of 1819, earlier *Mordins Brooke* 1574, 'brook associated with a family called *Mordin*'. This family appears in local records as *de Mordon* or *de Morden* from the 14th century and had a tenement in HENDON called *Mordyns* or *Mordins* in 1574. The modern name is no doubt a corruption of the 16th-century form.

N

Nash (near Keston) Bromley. Marked as *Upper Nash* and *Nash Farm* on the Ordnance Survey map of 1819. The name means '(place at) the ash tree', from Middle English *ashe* with initial *N-* from Middle English *atten* 'at the', *compare* NOAK HILL for a similar formation.

Neasden Brent. *Neosdune c.*1000 (Anglo-Saxon charter), *Nisedon* 1194, *Nesdone* 1254, *Nesedon* 1320, that is 'the nose-shaped hill', from Old English **neosu* and *dūn*, referring to the marked hill here. The spelling *Neasdune* 939 sometimes cited is from a spurious charter. As with its neighbour WILLESDEN, spellings with *-den* replacing the historical *-don* are relatively recent (from the 18th century).

Neckinger, Neckinger Street (in Bermondsey) Southwark. Two streets, the former marked as *Neckinger Road* on Rocque's map of 1746, named from an old stream called *Neckinger* in 1682, earlier *Neckercher* or *Devills Neckercher* 1570–9. The name alludes to the 'Devil's neckerchief', once a popular term for the hangman's noose, probably with reference to the great loop the stream made in its course through BER-MONDSEY (it rose near ST GEORGE'S CIRCUS, flowing first east and then north-west to join the Thames at ST SAVIOUR'S DOCK). An alternative explanation that the name refers to a gallows for pirates, once situated on a wharf where the stream enters the Thames, is probably only a legend. The spot where the Neckinger stream was crossed by the old road to Canterbury (*see* OLD KENT ROAD) was known as *the wateryng of Seint Thomas* in Chaucer's time, from Middle English *watering* 'watering place'; his pilgrims in the *Canterbury Tales* (*c.*1387) water their horses here on their way to visit the shrine of St Thomas at Canterbury.

Nelson Column (in Trafalgar Square) Westminster. Monument erected 1839–43 to commemorate Lord *Nelson*'s victory at Trafalgar in 1805, *see* TRAFALGAR SQUARE. **Nelson Dock** in ROTHERHITHE, a dry dock built in the 18th century, was so named *c.*1820 after the same man.

New Addington Croydon, *see* ADDINGTON.

New Barnet, *see* BARNET.

New Beckenham Bromley, *see* BECKENHAM.

Newbury Park (near Ilford) Redbridge. Named from *Newbury* 1348, *Newberry* 16th century, *Newbury* 1805, *Great Newbury* 1883, that is 'the new manor or manor house', from Middle English *newe* and *bury*.

New Change (off Cannon Street) City. Built just to the east of the medieval street called *Old Change* which was destroyed by bombing in 1941. The old street, known as 'Old Change' by 1294 and recorded as *Chaunge* 1297, *le Eldechaunge* 1316, *the Olde Chaunge* 1555, was probably so named from the exchange of old coins for new undertaken by the goldsmiths and moneyers of the vicinity, in a building dedicated to that purpose, up to *c*.1250.

New Charlton Greenwich, *see* CHARLTON.

New Cross Lewisham. Recorded as *New Crosse* in 1675, probably so called from the *crossroads* on the Kent–Surrey county boundary where the old east–west road from Dartford to London (here New Cross Road) is joined by the road from LEWISHAM and the south. The road junction may have been 'new' at quite an early date, since the locality is also referred to in the 15th century as *New Cross Heath*. The name almost certainly precedes the old coaching inn once situated here called the *Golden Cross* from which it is sometimes said to be derived.

New Cross Gate Lewisham. Named from the toll gate set up on the NEW CROSS turnpike road in 1718; the OLD KENT ROAD from the City meets the road from WESTMINSTER here. The district is marked *Hatcham* on the Ordnance Survey map of 1816, *see* HATCHAM PARK ROAD.

New Eltham Greenwich, *see* ELTHAM.

Newgate Street City. Recorded thus in 1617, earlier referred to as *vicus regius versus Newgate* (that is 'king's highway leading to *Newgate*') 1275. The gate known as *Newgate*, originally built by the Romans *c*.200, was the main entrance into the City from the west: indeed it is first referred to by the Saxons as *Uuestgetum* in 857 (that is 'the west gates', the plural form possibly alluding to a double gateway here or to Newgate and LUDGATE together). It no doubt acquired its later name ('the new gate') after it had been rebuilt at some time in either the late Saxon or early Norman period. The gate was demolished in 1767. The notorious *Newgate Prison*, once situated on this street and also pulled down in 1767, stood on a site occupied by a prison since the 12th century.

Newham (borough). A recent name artificially created in 1965 for the 'new' London borough comprising East and West Ham (*see* HAM).

Newington Southwark. *Neuton* c.1200, *Niwentone* 13th century, *Newenton* 1258, *Neuwyngton* 1325, that is 'the new farmstead or estate', from Old English *nīwe* (oblique case *nīwan*) and *tūn*. **Newington Butts** is recorded thus from 1558 and recalls the site of the old archery *butts* here. **Newington Causeway**, on the line of STANE STREET, the Roman road from Chichester and the south, is *the Cawsey* 1609, from Middle English *caucie* 'a raised way across marshy ground'.

Newington Green (near Canonbury) Islington. Marked thus on the Ordnance Survey map of 1822 and recorded as *Newyngtongrene* in 1480, 'the village green near STOKE NEWINGTON', from Middle English *grene*. It is said that this area was favoured by Henry VIII for hunting and that he installed his mistresses in a house to the south of the Green.

Newlands (near Edgware) Barnet. Marked thus on the Ordnance Survey map of 1877, earlier *Newlandes close* 1535, that is 'newly cleared land, land newly brought into cultivation', from Old English *nīwe* and *land*.

Newlands (at Nunhead) Southwark. Victorian estate developed at the end of the 19th century, but the name is no doubt older, see previous name.

New Malden Kingston, *see* MALDEN MANOR.

New River. An artificial channel or watercourse constructed by Sir John Myddelton in 1609–13 to bring water into London from springs near Amwell in Hertfordshire. There are still large reservoirs at New River Head near FINSBURY where the channel terminated. It is marked *New River* on the Ordnance Survey map of 1822 and is recorded earlier as *the newe River* in 1625 and *the New Rivulet* in 1646. It gives name to **New River Sports Centre** in WOOD GREEN.

New Southgate Enfield, *see* SOUTHGATE.

Newyears Green (near Ruislip) Hillingdon. So called on Rocque's map of 1754 and appearing as *New Years Green* on the Ordnance Survey map of 1822. Possibly a reference to festivities once held here on New

Year's Day, but perhaps more likely to be from the surname of some local family (the area is referred to as *Newes* in 1699, which suggests a manorial name).

Nicholas Lane (off Cannon Street) City. *S. Nicholas Lane* 1259, *Seint Nicholaslane* 1381, so named from the church of *St Nicholas Acons* (probably derived from an early benefactor called *Haakon*), an 11th-century foundation but destroyed in the Great Fire of 1666.

Nine Elms (near Battersea) Wandsworth. Marked thus on the Ordnance Survey map of 1822, named from *ix elmes farme* 1646, no doubt a literal reference to a prominent clump or row of these trees, *compare* SEVEN SISTERS. The New COVENT GARDEN Market, opened in 1974, is sited here.

Noak Hill Havering. Recorded with this spelling in 1490, then as *Nookhill* 1523, *Noke Hill* 1570, and *Nook Hill* on the Ordnance Survey map of 1805. The name means '(place at) the oak tree', from Middle English *oke* with initial *N-* from Middle English *atten* 'at the'. This was no doubt the home of Richard *ate Noke*, that is '(living) at the oak tree', recorded in a local document *c.*1290.

Noble Street (off London Wall) City. *Noble streete* in 1603, so named from the family of Thomas *le Noble* 1322.

Noel Park (near Wood Green) Haringey. Residential estate laid out from 1883, so named after Ernest *Noel* MP, the chairman of the company that built it.

Norbiton Kingston. *Norberton* 1205, *Norbeton* 1272, *Norbiton* 1531, that is 'the northern grange or outlying farm', from Old English *north* and *bere-tūn*, so called in relation to SURBITON; both were granges of the royal manor of KINGSTON. **Norbiton Common**, marked thus on the Ordnance Survey map of 1876, was enclosed in 1808.

Norbury Croydon. *Northbury* 1359, *Norbury* 1422, that is 'northern manor house', from Middle English *north* and *bury*, referring to its situation in the north of CROYDON parish. **Norbury Park**, marked thus on the Ordnance Survey map of 1876, was formerly the grounds of Norbury Hall (built 1802).

Norland Place, Road & Square (near Holland Park) Kensington & Chelsea. This area, developed in the mid-19th century, preserves the old name *Northlandes* 1428, *Norlandesgate* 1438, *Norlands* 1607, *Norland*

Hall 1822, that is 'the north open lands' of KENSINGTON parish, from Middle English *north* and *land*.

Normand Park (at Fulham) Hammersmith & Fulham. Named from *Noemansland* 1492, that is 'no man's land, a piece of land in disputed ownership', from Old English *nān-mann* and *land*. The 17th-century *Normand House* which once occupied this site was demolished *c.*1950.

Norman Park Bromley. Commemorates the local *Norman* family, one of whom, James *Norman*, had a large residence on Bromley Common (*see* BROMLEY) called *The Rookery* (built in the early 18th century and shown on the Ordnance Survey map of 1876), which gives name to Rookery Lake & Lane.

Normanshire Drive (in Chingford Hatch) Waltham Forest. Preserves the old name *Normanshire (Farm)* (marked thus on the Ordnance Survey maps of 1805 and 1883), which is probably identical with the earlier *Normansland* 1519, perhaps an altered form of *No mans land*, that is 'land in disputed ownership' (*see* NORMAND PARK), with the later substitution of *shire* in the sense 'estate'.

North Acton Ealing, *see* ACTON.

North Cheam Sutton, *see* CHEAM.

North Cray Bexley. *Craie* 1086 (Domesday Book), *Northcraei c.*1100, *Northcray* 1254, that is 'northern estate on the River Cray', from a Celtic river name (*see* CRAY) with Old English *north* to distinguish this from the other manors named from the river.

North End Bexley. Marked thus on Bowen's map of *c.*1762 and on the Ordnance Survey map of 1805, 'north district or hamlet (of CRAY-FORD)', from Middle English *ende*.

North End (at Hampstead) Camden. So marked on Rocque's map of 1741–5 and on the Ordnance Survey map of 1822, 'the northern district (of HAMPSTEAD)', thus distinguished from the hamlet of *West End*, for which, *see* WEST END LANE.

North End Road (near Barons Court) Hammersmith & Fulham. Named from the old hamlet of *Northend* 1459, *North End* 1822, 'northern district (in the parish of FULHAM)', from Middle English *north* and *ende*.

North Feltham Hounslow, *see* FELTHAM.

Northfields Ealing. A residential district name preserving the old field names *Northfeld* 1455, *le Nether* and *le Over Northefeld* 1459, that is 'the lower and upper north fields', from Middle English *feld*.

North Finchley Barnet, *see* FINCHLEY.

North Harrow, *see* HARROW.

North Hillingdon, *see* HILLINGDON.

North Hyde Hounslow. *Northyde* 1243, *la Northhide* 1274, *Northhide* 1710, that is 'the northern hide of land', from Old English *north* and *hīd*, a hide being an amount of land considered sufficient for the support of one free family and its dependants, usually about 120 acres. The hamlet lay at the north end of the parish of HESTON.

North Kensington, *see* KENSINGTON.

North Ockendon Havering. *Wokendune c.*1070, *Wochenduna* 1086 (Domesday Book), *Wokindon* 1230, *North Wokyndon* 1397, that is 'hill of a man called *Wocca', from an Old English personal name (genitive case *-n*) and *dūn*. Spellings showing the loss of initial *W-* appear as early as the 12th century. South Ockendon (*South Wokyndon* 1291, *Southwokyngton* 1407) is still in the county of Essex. *See also* CRANHAM which was alternatively known as 'Bishop's Ockendon' in early times.

Northolt Ealing. *Northhealum* 960 (Anglo-Saxon charter), *Northala* 1086 (Domesday Book), *Northale* 1214, *Northalle* 1235, *Northall alias Northolt* 1631, that is 'northern nook(s) of land', from Old English *north* and *h(e)alh* (with dative case plural *-um* in the 10th century form). 'North' distinguishes this place from neighbouring SOUTHALL which contains the same word in spite of the contrasting modern spellings; indeed it will be noted that the final *-t* in Northolt (first appearing in the 17th century and no doubt influenced by the word *holt* 'wood, thicket') is quite unhistorical. **Northolt Aerodrome** was opened here in 1915.

North Sheen Richmond, *see under* EAST SHEEN.

Northumberland Avenue (near Charing Cross) Westminster. Constructed in 1875 on the site of the demolished *Northumberland House*, the town house of the Dukes of *Northumberland* built in the early 17th century.

Northumberland Heath Bexley. Recorded as *Northumberlond Hethe* 1529, named from an earlier place called *Northumbre* 1292 which is possibly '(land) north of a stream called *Humbre*', from an ancient pre-Celtic river name of uncertain origin and meaning which also occurs elsewhere in England (as in the River Humber in Yorkshire), with Middle English *north*, and later with *land* 'tract of land, estate' and *hethe* 'heath'. The small stream referred to flows into the River Darent.

Northumberland Park (near Tottenham) Haringey. Station named from a street and estate laid out in the 1850s. The nearby district is referred to as *Park* on the Ordnance Survey maps of 1877 and 1904, and an earlier reference is the field name *Parkefeld* 1502 (there was in fact a hunting park in this vicinity in the 16th century). The first part of the later name derives from the Dukes of *Northumberland* into which family a Tottenham resident, Hugh Smithson, married in the 18th century, eventually becoming Duke himself. Of course the Tottenham Hotspur Football Club, who play at nearby WHITE HART LANE, get their name through the same aristocratic connection, *Hotspur* being originally the nickname for Sir Henry Percy (1364–1403), eldest son of the 1st Earl of Northumberland, whose fiery character figures in Shakespeare's *Richard II* and *1 Henry IV*.

North Wembley Brent, *see* WEMBLEY.

Northwick Park (near Harrow) Brent. Named from the *Northwick* family, lords of the manor of HARROW at the end of the 18th century.

Northwood Hillingdon. *Northwode* 1435, *Norwoode* 1565, *North Wood* 1880, self-explanatory, 'the northern wood', from Middle English *north* and *wode*. Originally woodland lying to the north of RUISLIP and later a farming area, the present town developed after the construction of the railway *c*.1880. The higher ground at **Northwood Hills** (a mainly 1930s development) is the site of *Northwood Farm* on the Ordnance Survey map of 1880 (now New Farm).

North Woolwich Newham. This area, first incorporated into the new borough of Newham in 1965, lies across the River Thames from WOOLWICH itself in what was for some 900 years a small detached part of the county of Kent. The name *North Woolwich*, first used for a station in 1847, is marked thus on the Ordnance Survey map of 1888.

Norton Folgate (near Spitalfields) Tower Hamlets. *Nortune c*.1110, *Nortonfolyot* 1433, *Norton Folyet* 1456, *Norton Folgate otherwise Norton Folyott* 1568, 'north farmstead or estate', from Old English *north* and *tūn*, with manorial affix from the *Foliot* family. Now surviving only as a street name, this was once a manor just north of the City boundary belonging to ST PAUL'S. The reference may be to Gilbert *Foliot*, Bishop of London 1163–87 or to Richard *Foliot*, a canon of St Paul's in 1241.

Norwood, South & Upper Croydon, **Norwood, West** Lambeth. *Norwude* 1176, *Northewode* 1272, (wood called) *Norwood* early 16th century, *Northwode* 1543, that is 'the north wood', from Old English *north* and *wudu*. This referred to a large tract of woodland to the north of CROYDON, part of which still remained in the early 19th century. It is said that the Archbishops of Canterbury, lords of the manor of Croydon, hunted here in early times. *Upper Norwood*, *Lower Norwood*, and *South Norwood* are marked thus on the Ordnance Survey map of 1876; on the 1904 map, *Lower Norwood* has been replaced by *West Norwood*. **Norwood New Town** is an area of Upper Norwood developed during the 20th century.

Norwood Green Ealing. So called in 1724, named from *Northuuda* 832 (Anglo-Saxon charter), *Northwude* 1235, *Norwode* 1453, that is 'the northern wood', from Old English *north* and *wudu* with the later addition of *grene* 'village green'. Perhaps so named in relation to the ancient parish of HESTON.

Notting Hill Kensington & Chelsea. Recorded as *Knottynghull* 1356, *Notynghyll* 1550, *Noding Hill* 1680, *Notting Hill* 1876–7. In the same vicinity were *Knottyngwode* 1376, *Nuttyng Woode* 1550, *Knottyngesbernys* 1462, *Notingbarns* 1519. These are perhaps best interpreted as 'the hill, wood, and barns at *Knottyng*', in which *Knottyng* might be an old hill name formed from Old English *cnotta* 'knot, lump', or an old place name meaning '*Cnotta*'s place, estate associated with a man called *Cnotta*', from an Old English personal name and *-ing*, with the later addition of Middle English *hull* or *hill*, *wode* and *bern*. Alternatively, the first element could be a Middle English surname *Knottyng* indicating lands held here by a family from Knotting in Bedfordshire ('hill people', or '*Cnotta*'s people', from the element or personal name cited above with *-ingas*). *Notting Barn* is still marked on the Ordnance Survey map of 1876–7 and is recalled in Notting Barn Road in North KENSINGTON. Notting Hill is now of course particularly well known for its Caribbean carnival, held on August Bank Holiday every year since 1966.

Notting Hill Gate Kensington & Chelsea. Named from a turnpike gate at NOTTING HILL which formerly stood on the main Oxford road (now

Bayswater Road) near the site of the present Underground station. The district was once known as *Kensington Gravel Pits* (marked thus on the Ordnance Survey map of 1822), earlier *the Gravilpits* 1654, *Kinsington grauill Pittes* 1675.

Nower Hill (at Pinner) Harrow. Recorded thus in 1733 and on the Ordnance Survey map of 1877, earlier *atte Nore* 1282, *Nowre* 1548, that is '(place) at the elongated flat-topped hill', from Old English *ōra* with initial *N-* from Middle English *atten* 'at the'. This name refers to the same feature as gives name to PINNER itself. There is a steep hillside here.

Nunhead Southwark. Recorded as *Nunhead* 1680, *None Head* c.1745, *Nonehead Hill* 1789, *Nun Head* 1816, said to take its name from a 17th-century inn here called *The Nuns Head*. According to local legend (colourful but without factual basis), the inn itself was so named because a Mother Superior was beheaded here for opposing Henry VIII's dissolution of the monasteries. **Nunhead Cemetery**, consecrated in 1840, is marked thus on the Ordnance Survey map of 1876.

O

Oak Hill Park (at East Barnet) Barnet. Marked as *Oakhill Park* on the Ordnance Survey map of 1887, named from *Oak Hill* 1822, earlier called *le Monkefrith* 1273, *Monkynfrythe* 1536, *Oak hill heretofore called Moncken Frieth or Monkham Frieth* 1790, that is 'woodland of the monks', from Old English *fyrhth(e)* and Middle English *monken* 'of the monks'. The reference is to the monks of St Alban's Abbey who once owned the manor of East Barnet (*see* BARNET). The old name is preserved in the local street names MONKFRITH CLOSE & WAY.

Oakington Brent, *see* TOKYNGTON.

Oakleigh Park Barnet. A modern district name dating only from the late 19th century, probably suggested by the much older name of OAK HILL PARK nearby.

Oaks Park, The (near Carshalton Beeches) Sutton. Marked thus on the Ordnance Survey map of 1876, named from the mansion called *The Oaks* on the same map (shown as simply *Oaks* on the earlier map of 1819). Now demolished, the house belonged to the Earls of Derby in the 18th century (hence the names given to the famous horse races at Epsom, 'the Derby' and 'the Oaks').

Oakwood Enfield. Self-explanatory, named from *Oak Farm* (marked thus on the Ordnance Survey map of 1822), later *Oak Lodge* (on that of 1887).

Oat Lane (off Noble Street) City. *Oatelane* in 1603, no doubt 'lane where oats were sold'. One Nigel *le Avener* ('the oatmonger') is mentioned in this district in 1319.

Ockendon, *see* NORTH OCKENDON.

Old Bailey City. This street is recorded as *Old Baily* 1444, *tholde Baylye* 1549, earlier simply 'highway called *la Ballie*' 1287, 'street called *Le Bayl*' 1290, and is named from *Bali* c.1166, *le Bail* 1298, *le Baille* 1311, this referring to an 'outwork or defensive rampart on the outside of the City wall', from Middle English *baille*. The famous building also so called, the seat of the Central Criminal Court, was built in 1774; an earlier building is referred to as *le Justice Hall in le Olde Bailie* 1555.

Old Bexley, *see* BEXLEY.

Old Brentford Hounslow, *see* BRENTFORD.

Old Broad Street City, *see* BROAD STREET, OLD & NEW.

Oldchurch (in Romford) Havering. First recorded as *Oldechirchehawe* 1451, that is 'enclosure (Old English *haga*) near the old church', referring to a former church here at the original medieval settlement site of ROMFORD (the town was later moved to higher ground to avoid the frequent flooding of the River Rom). The name is preserved in Oldchurch Bridge, Park & Road.

Old Coulsdon Croydon, *see* COULSDON.

Old Ford Tower Hamlets. *Eldeford* 1268, *le Eldeforde* 14th century, *Oldeforde* 1313, *Aldeforde* 1381, 'the old ford', from Old English *(e)ald* and *ford*. This was an early crossing of the River LEA which apparently went out of use in favour of the ford downstream which gave name to STRATFORD or of the bridge which gave name to BOW.

Old Isleworth Hounslow, *see* ISLEWORTH.

Old Jewry City. This street is recorded as *la Oldeiuwerie* 1328, *Juwerielane* 1348, *the Olde Jury* 1553, that is 'district formerly occupied by Jews', from Middle English *juerie*. The street lies within a large area frequented by Jews in the medieval City during the 12th and 13th centuries until they were persecuted during the reign of Henry III and expelled by Edward I in 1290. There was another Jewish quarter in medieval times near ALDGATE, *see* JEWRY STREET.

Old Kent Road Southwark. Follows close to the line of the old road into Kent (*see* TABARD STREET, earlier *Kentstret* or *Kentisshestrete*), which meets STANE STREET (the Roman road from Chichester) at SOUTHWARK. The spot where Chaucer's pilgrims watered their horses, *the wateryng of Seint Thomas*, was on this old road out to Canterbury, *see* NECKINGER.

Old Malden Kingston, *see* MALDEN MANOR.

Old Oak Common (near North Acton) Ealing. Marked thus on the Ordnance Survey map of 1822, earlier *common called Old Oake* 1650, this being probably a corruption of *Eldeholt* 1380, *Oldeholte* c.1415, that is 'the old wood or thicket', from Old English *(e)ald* and *holt*.

Old Seacoal Lane (off Ludgate Hill) City. *Sacolelane* 1253, *Secolelane* 1279, that is 'lane where seacoal was sold', from Middle English *secole* (so called because it was transported by sea from Newcastle). It may well have been landed here from the FLEET river which once flowed by the west end of the present lane.

Old Street Islington. Recorded as *Ealdestrate* c.1200, *Eldestrete* 1275, *le Oldestrete* 1373, self-explanatory, 'the old street or paved road', from Old English *(e)ald* and *strǣt*. This was an important ancient route out of the City, described as 'old' even at the end of the 12th century.

Olympia Hammersmith & Fulham. An arbitrary name, given to the exhibition hall (used at first for shows and circuses) built in the 1880s and enlarged forty years later, transferred from the famous place in the Peloponnese where the Olympic games were first held.

One Tree Hill (at Honor Oak) Southwark. Apparently a reference to the notable oak tree that gave its name to HONOR OAK. The hill reaches 300 ft and was used as a beacon site during the Napoleonic Wars, see next name.

One Tree Hill Recreation Ground (at Alperton) Brent. Self-explanatory, no doubt simply descriptive, see previous name. There is another One Tree Hill at HILL END in Harefield.

Orpington Bromley. *Orpedingtun* 1032, *Orpinton* 1086 (Domesday Book), *Orpington* 1226, *Arpington* c.1762, that is 'farmstead or estate associated with a man called *Orped'*, from an Old English personal name with Old English medial connective *-ing-* and *tūn*. The personal name *Orped* is from Old English *orped* 'active, bold, valiant'.

Osidge Barnet. *Huzeheog* (sic) c.1195, *Osehegh* 1317, *Osehegge* 1376, *Ousage* 1551, that is 'hedge of a man called Ōsa', from an Old English personal name and Old English *hecg*.

Osterley Hounslow. *Osterle, Ostrele* 1274, *Osterlegh* 1299, *Oysterle* 1302, that is 'woodland clearing with a sheepfold', from Old English *eowestre* and *lēah*. **Osterley Park** is *Osterly Park* on the Ordnance Survey map of 1822, earlier referred to as *Osterley Parke House* in 1576. The present elegantly neoclassical 18th-century villa (now owned by the National Trust) was extensively remodelled for the Child family by Robert

Adam from the earlier 16th-century Tudor mansion. It might be noted that the name LAMPTON just south of here also refers to sheep farming in early times.

Outwich Street (off Houndsditch) City. Named from a family called *de Ottewich* or *de Oteswyche* who are on record in this area during the 13th to 15th centuries and who also gave their name to the parish and church of *St Martin Outwich* (demolished in 1874). The place called *Ote(s)wich* may have been near here: it is from Old English *wīc* 'specialized farm or building' with the Norman personal name *Ote*.

Oval, The (at Kennington) Lambeth. Famous cricket ground (headquarters of the Surrey County Club) so called from its elliptical shape (which is already clearly shown on the Ordnance Survey map of 1822). There was originally a market garden here, but it was first used for cricket in 1845.

Oxford Street Westminster. Referred to as *The Road to Oxford* in 1682 and as *Oxford Road* in 1720, but alternatively known as *Oxford Street* by 1718. This was an ancient route to the West, described as *thære wide here stræt* ('the wide military road or highway', from Old English *here-stræt* 'army road') in an Anglo-Saxon charter dated 959, and as *via regia qui ducit de London versus Tyborne* ('king's road leading from *London* towards *Tyborne*') in the 13th century (it crossed the River *Tyburn*, for which, *see* MARYLEBONE). However, its present name seems to have been confirmed by the strange coincidence that land to the north of the street was acquired and developed by the 2nd Earl of *Oxford* in 1713. At its junction with REGENT STREET, it gives name to **Oxford Circus**, which was in fact originally called *Regent Circus* (with the word *circus* used in the sense 'circular open space at a street junction').

Oxgate Gardens & Lane (at Dollis Hill) Brent. Named from *Oxgate Farm* which is marked thus on the Ordnance Survey map of 1822, earlier *Oxegate c.*1250, that is 'gate used for oxen', from Old English *oxa* and *geat*. It may originally have referred to a gate preventing cattle from straying on to nearby WATLING STREET (now the A5). The lane from the farm to the main road is clearly shown on the 1822 map; the 16th–17th century farmhouse still survives.

Oxleas Wood (near Shooters Hill) Greenwich. Marked thus on the Ordnance Survey map of 1876, 'wood by the meadow land for oxen', from Middle English *oxe* and *lese*; the wood lies next to Oxleas Meadows.

P

Paddenswick Road (at Ravenscourt Park) Hammersmith & Fulham. Preserves the old name *Paddingswick* which dates back to the 13th century, *see* RAVENSCOURT PARK.

Paddington Westminster. *Paddingtone* 998, *Padington* c.1050, *Padintune* 1222, *Padyngton* 1294, that is 'farmstead or estate associated with a man called Padda', from an Old English personal name with Old English medial connective *-ing-* and *tūn*. The earliest settlement was probably in the vicinity of what is now **Paddington Green** (recorded thus from the 18th century). **Paddington Station** was opened in 1838.

Padnall Corner Redbridge. *Padnalles corner* 1609, *Padnal Corner* 1805, named from *Padenhale* 1303, *Patenhale* 1369, *Padnale* 1456, that is 'nook of land belonging to a man called Pad(d)a', from an Old English personal name and *halh* with the later addition of the nearly synonymous word *corner*, referring to its situation on the boundary of the parish of ILFORD.

Page Green (at South Tottenham) Haringey. Marked thus on the Ordnance Survey map of 1877, earlier *Pagisgrene* 1467, 'village green associated with a family called *Page*'; this family occurs in local records from the 16th century.

Paine's Bridge & Brook (near Harold Park) Havering. The bridge, where this tributary of INGREBOURNE RIVER (marked *Paines Brook* on the Ordnance Survey map of 1883) is crossed by the old Roman road to Colchester, is recorded as *Paynes Brydge* in 1568, so called from the family of Margaret *Paynes* 1320.

Pale Well, Palewell Common & Fields (at East Sheen) Richmond. *Palewell Common* is recorded thus in 1802, so named from a field called *the Pale* 1560, from Middle English *pale* 'land enclosed by a fence'.

Pall Mall Westminster. Street name recorded as *Pall Mall Walk* 1650, *Pall Mall* 1658, *Pell Mell* 1659, so called from the game of *pallemaille* or *pall-mall* first played here in the 17th century. Introduced into England from Italy and France, the game was played down a long alley and consisted of driving a ball with a mallet through an iron ring. Samuel Pepys in his Diary (1661) describes the Duke of York playing the game here, and Charles II created a new alley in ST JAMES'S PARK parallel to this one (*see* THE MALL). An earlier name for Pall Mall was *Spittelstrete* 1222, from Middle English *spitel* 'hospital', because it led to St James's Hospital (*see* ST JAMES'S).

Palmers Green Enfield. Recorded as *Palmers grene* 1608, 'village green associated with a family called *Palmer*' (mentioned in local records from the 14th century), from Middle English *grene*. The long street called Green Lanes (*sic*) which runs through here is also referred to in the 17th century, as *Green Lane End* in 1662.

Pancras Lane (off Queen Street) City. *St Pancresse Lane* 1548, so named from the church of St Pancras which was destroyed in the Great Fire of 1666. An earlier name of the lane was *Nedlerslane* 1401, that is 'lane where needlers (makers or sellers of needles) lived', from Middle English *nedlere*.

Panyer Alley (near St Paul's) City. *ye Panyer Ale* 1442, *Paniar Alley* 1603, so named from an early tavern called *the Panyer* ('the basket') in PATERNOSTER ROW.

Paris Garden Southwark. Preserves the name of the old riverside manor of *Paris Garden*, recorded as *Parysgardeyn* 1453, *Parrisgarden* *c.*1570, probably from a family called *de Paris* who once owned the estate. Earlier names for the manor are *Wideflete* 1113, *Wythyflete* 1318, or *Wylos* 1464, *Pares garden otherwise Wylys* c.1470, that is 'willow inlet or creek', from Old English *wīthig* 'withy, willow' and *flēot* (no doubt referring to some inlet along the Thames bank here), or 'the willows', from Old English *welig*. In the 16th and 17th centuries *Paris Garden* was well known as a place of entertainment.

Park Farm (at Chessington) Kingston. Marked thus on the Ordnance Survey map of 1876, no doubt with reference to the earlier *Chesinton Parke* 1537, *see* CHESSINGTON.

Park Langley Bromley, *see* LANGLEY PARK.

Park Royal Brent. District named from the *Royal Agricultural Show Ground* marked thus on the Ordnance Survey map of 1904 as is *Park Royal* station. The attempt by the Royal Agricultural Society to establish a permanent showground here was unsuccessful, and instead the area became industrialized.

Park Wood (at Harefield) Hillingdon. Marked thus on the Ordnance Survey map of 1880, so named because it was originally part of *Harefield Park*. This is shown thus on the map of 1822, earlier appearing as *Harvill Park* in 1680 and in the surname of Robert *atte* ('at the') *Parke* in 1388, from Middle English *parke* in the sense 'an enclosed tract of land set apart for hunting', see next name.

Park Wood (at Ruislip) Hillingdon. Marked thus on the Ordnance Survey map of 1880, earlier *Ruislip Park* on that of 1822. There is mention of a *park* (that is in the medieval sense, see previous name) at RUISLIP in the 13th century and even as early as Domesday Book (1086).

Parliament Hill (on Hampstead Heath) Camden. Marked thus on the Ordnance Survey map of 1904, and recorded from *c*.1875, the hill reaches 319 ft. The precise origin of the name is unknown, but according to tradition it was here that the associates of Guy Fawkes and his fellow conspirators awaited the expected blowing up of Parliament in 1605, hence also its alternative 19th-century name *Traitors' Hill*.

Parsloes Park Barking & Dagenham. Named from *Passelewesmede* 1390, *Passhlewes* 1456, *Parslowes* 1609, *Parsloes* 1634, a manorial name indicating the estate (earlier the *mede* or meadow) of the family of Hugh *Passelewe* 1250. The surname is from an Old French phrase meaning 'cross the water', probably referring originally to a merchant or traveller.

Parsons Green Hammersmith & Fulham. *Personesgrene* 1391, *Personagegrene* 1457, *Personnesgrene* 1534, that is 'village green where the parson lives, or by the parsonage', from Middle English *persone* (alternating with *personage*) and *grene*. This hamlet developed around the parsonage of FULHAM which stood to the west of the Green and was demolished in 1882. There was still a large pond on the Green until the late 19th century, and annual fairs were held here until the 1820s.

Parson's Pightle (at Old Coulsdon) Croydon. From a Middle English word *pightel* 'a small enclosure'. It is marked as *The Rectory* on the Ordnance Survey map of 1878.

Paternoster Row City. *Paternosterowe* 1334, *Paternostererowe* 1374, earlier *Paternosterstrete* 1307, *Paternosterlane* 1321, that is 'street, lane, or row of houses occupied by paternosterers or makers of rosaries', from Middle English *paternostrer* (derived from Latin *pater noster* 'our Father', the first words of the Lord's Prayer) with *strete*, *lane*, and *rowe*. This gives name to **Paternoster Square** also within the precincts of ST PAUL'S.

Pates Manor Drive (in East Bedfont) Hounslow. Named from the 16th century Pates Manor, so called from the family of John *Pate* 1404.

Peckham Southwark. *Pecheham* 1086 (Domesday Book), *Pecham* 1178, *Peckham* 1241, *Pekkham* 1361, that is 'homestead by a peak or hill', from Old English **pēac* and *hām*, probably referring to the hill now known as TELEGRAPH HILL. The same name is found as East & West Peckham in Kent.

Peckham Rye Southwark. Recorded thus in 1512, and as *Peckham Rithe* in 1520, *Peckham Ry* in 1589, from Old English *rīth* 'a small stream', *see* PECKHAM. The watercourse referred to is now covered over and was once known as the *Peck*, a back-formation from the place name. **Peckham Rye Common** is marked thus on the Ordnance Survey map of 1816. **Peckham Rye Park** was opened in 1894 on the site of *Homestall Farm* (named from the dialect word *homestall* 'a farmyard').

Pembroke Lodge (in Richmond Park) Richmond. Marked thus on the Ordnance Survey map of 1876, so named from the Countess of *Pembroke* who lived here from 1780 to 1830. The much smaller original house here was known as *The Molecatcher's* in the early 18th century (no doubt indicating the occupation of the tenant).

Penge Bromley. *Penceat* 1067, *Pange* 1204, *Penge* 1206, *Pengewode* 1472, that is 'wood's end, top of the wood', from Celtic **penn* 'head, end' and **cēd* 'wood', with the later addition of Middle English *wode* 'wood' in the 15th-century spelling (the Cornish place names Penquite and Pencoose and the Welsh Pencoed are exact parallels). This interesting name may suggest the survival of a native British population to the south of London after the Anglo-Saxon settlement. Penge was originally a woodland swine pasture for the manor of BATTERSEA; indeed it remained a detached hamlet of Battersea parish (which lies some 5 miles north-west) until 1888, when it was transferred from Surrey to Kent.

Pen Ponds (in Richmond Park) Richmond. Marked thus on the Ordnance Survey map of 1876, so called with reference to the nearby *pens* or folds for deer. The ponds lie in the middle of the area marked 'Deer Park' on modern maps.

Pentonville Islington. Marked thus on the Ordnance Survey map of 1822, named after Henry *Penton*, MP for Winchester, who owned land here which he began to develop for building *c*.1773. The suburb gave name to **Pentonville Prison**, built as a 'model prison' in 1840–2.

Perivale Ealing. *Pyryvale* 1508, *Peryvale* 1524, *Pyryvale otherwise Lyttle Greneford* 1566, *Perryvale* 1637, that is 'pear-tree valley', from Middle English *perie* and *vale*, earlier called *Little Greenford* to distinguish it from GREENFORD itself (earlier *Great Greenford*). *Little Greenford* is recorded as *Greneforde* 1086 (Domesday Book), *Little Greneford* 1386.

Perry Hill, Perry Rise & Vale Lewisham. *Perry Hill* is marked thus on the Ordnance Survey map of 1816, along with *Perry Stow* (*sic*) at the junction of the roads now called Perry Rise and Perry Vale. *Perry Stow* is an error for *Perry Slow* or *Slough* (thus in 18th-century records). The locality is recorded earlier as *Perystrete* 1474, *Perry Street c*.1762, and in 1320 there is mention of a Gerard *atte Pirie*. All take their names from Middle English *perie* 'pear tree', with Middle English *strete* 'street of houses, hamlet', *atte* 'at the', *hill*, and *slough* 'mire, muddy place'.

Perry Street (in Chislehurst) Bromley. *Perrystreet* 1442, *Piry Streete* 1525, *Peristrete* 1527, from Middle English *perie* 'pear tree' and *strete* 'street of houses, hamlet', see previous names.

Peter Pan's Pool Lewisham. Now named from the famous character (his statue graces the pool) in the children's story by J. M. Barrie, but once the mill pond for the *Lower Mill* on the River RAVENSBOURNE at SOUTHEND where cutlery was made in the 18th century and where corn was still ground in the early 1900s.

Petersham Richmond. *Patricesham* 1086 (Domesday Book), *Pytrichesham* 1255, *Petrichesham* 1266, *Petrisham* 1416, that is 'river-bend land of a man called *Peohtrīc*', from Old English *hamm* and an Old English personal name. It lies within the same loop of the River Thames as nearby HAM. Earlier spellings sometimes cited for this name like *Piterichesham* 727 and 933 are from spurious charters forged by monks at a later date. The church here, mainly 17th century but with a 13th-century chancel, is dedicated to St Peter, a result no doubt of the association of the first part of the place name with the more familiar personal name. **Petersham House** dates from the late 17th century.

Petticoat Lane & Square City. The lane (now officially MIDDLESEX STREET) is recorded as *Peticote Lane* in 1602, *Petticotelane* in 1618, no doubt because makers or sellers of ladies' petticoats lived here. The well-known street market has its origins in the 18th century. An even earlier name for the lane was *Hog Lane* 1534, suggesting that at one time it was just a country track along which hogs were driven to and from pasture.

Petts Wood Bromley. Mainly 1930s residential area named from woodland still known as Petts Wood (marked thus on the Ordnance Survey map of 1876), from a shipbuilding family called *Pett* recorded as having a lease of oak woods in CHISLEHURST in 1577.

Petty France (near Victoria) Westminster. Street recorded as *Petefraunce* in 1494, *Pety Fraunce* in 1518, that is 'little France', possibly so called because it was once a district lived in by French merchants.

Phillimore Gardens, Place & Road (in Kensington) Kensington & Chelsea. Area developed from the late 18th century by William *Phillimore* whose family owned land here.

Philpot Lane (off Fenchurch Street) City. Recorded thus from 1480, so named from Sir John *Philpot*, a wealthy grocer and Lord Mayor of London in 1378–9.

Phipps Bridge (Road) Merton. *Pypesbrige* 1535, *Pippebridge* 1548, *Phips Bridge c.*1745, probably 'bridge associated with a family called *Pipp*' (also recorded in other local names like *Pyppis Meade* and *Pypis Grove* in the 16th century). The bridge was over the River WANDLE.

Picardy Manorway, Road & Street (at Belvedere) Bexley. Preserve the name of the hamlet called *Picardy* marked on the Ordnance Survey maps of 1805 and 1888. A transferred name from Picardy in Northern France, another low-lying area like this one which borders ERITH Marshes by the River Thames.

Piccadilly Westminster. This strange-looking street name has rather a bizarre origin. It seems that the name first appears as *Pickadilly Hall* in 1623, otherwise *Pickadel Hall* in 1636, as a (no doubt humorous) nickname for a house belonging to one Robert Baker, a successful tailor who had made his fortune from the sale of *piccadills* or *piccadillies*, a term used for various kinds of collars, highly fashionable at the time, for both men and women. The name of the hall was then transferred to the district (as in *Pickadillie* 1627, *Pickadilla* 1633) and to the street (as in *Piccadilly Street* 1673, *Pickadilly* 1682). **Piccadilly Circus** was created in 1819 at the junction with REGENT STREET which was then being built (for the word *circus*, *see* Oxford Circus, *under* OXFORD STREET).

Pickett's Lock (near Lower Edmonton) Enfield. Marked thus on the Ordnance Survey map of 1877, that is 'lock (on the River LEA) associated with the *Picot* or *Pickett* family'. *Picketts feild* 1669 somewhere nearby is also named from this family, who take their surname from one *Picot de Marisco* ('of the marsh') recorded locally in the 13th century.

Pickhurst Green & Lane Bromley. *Pickhurst* and *Pickhurst Green* are marked thus on the Ordnance Survey map of 1819, recorded earlier as *Pikehurst* 1289, *Pykherst* 1292, *Pikeherst* 1327, that is 'wooded hill with a point or peak', from Old English *pīc* and *hyrst*.

Pield Heath Hillingdon. Marked thus on the Ordnance Survey map of 1880, earlier *Peeld Heath* 1592, *Peelde Heath* 1670, *Peal Heath* 1747, that is 'the bare heathland', from early Modern English *pealed* 'bare of vegetation'.

Pimlico Westminster. This district south of VICTORIA is first recorded as *Pimlico* in 1626, and appears as *Pimplico* in 1630 and *Pimlico* on Rocque's map of 1747. The name was almost certainly copied from that of the well-known alehouse in HOXTON referred to as *Pimlyco* or *Pimlico* in 1609. This inn (famous for its *Pimlico* ale and apparently called after its publican, Ben *Pimlico* or *Pemlico*, who is mentioned as early as 1598), was particularly well-known among theatrical folk, no doubt because of the two early theatres established near here (*see* CURTAIN ROAD). An indication of its fame is the number of references to the Hoxton *Pimlico* in the early 17th-century plays of Dekker, Jonson, and others. Its existence is still recalled in the small street called **Pimlico Walk** in Hoxton. The origin of the name Pimlico (both as surname and place name) has long been held to be obscure. But recently the case has been convincingly argued that it is a transferred name from the *Pamlico* (or *Pamticough*) Indians of North America who lived along the banks of the Pamlico river, near to the abortive Roanoke settlements of Sir Walter Ralegh's Virginia founded in 1585–7. The lack of success of these early colonists must have been hot news during the late 1580s, and indeed some of them returned to England with Drake in 1586. The exotic Indian name *Pamlico* or *Pemlico* may well have become attached to one of their number as a kind of nickname. But whatever the circumstances of its transference, Pimlico is almost certainly the first native American place name to have been introduced into England!

Pimlico Wood (near Aperfield) Bromley. Marked thus on the Ordnance Survey map of 1871 beside a house or farm called *Pimlico*, no doubt so named from the 17th-century inn at HOXTON or the district in WESTMINSTER, see previous name. Other instances of the same name in the London area are *Pimlico House* in Hadley Green (*see* HADLEY) and a field called *Pimlico* in SOUTHALL in 1821.

Pimp Hall Park (at Chingford) Waltham Forest. Named from *Pimps Hall* (marked thus on the Ordnance Survey map of 1805), earlier *Pympis* 1543 or *Pympes manor* 1568, so called from Elizabeth *Pympe* who married the lord of the manor in the mid-16th century. The house was demolished in 1989, although the dovecote survives.

Pinkwell Lane & Park (at Harlington) Hillingdon. Named from *Pinkwell* 1754, 1816, probably 'minnow stream' from Old English **pinc* and *wella*, referring to a small tributary flowing into the River CRANE at CRANFORD. The upper part of the stream is now called Frogs Ditch (giving name to Frogs Ditch Farm).

Pinn, River (rises near Pinner and flows into River Colne at Cowley). A late back-formation from the name PINNER; it was earlier called simply *le Broke* 1446 ('the brook' from Middle English *broke*) or *Pinner Brook* 1825.

Pinner Harrow. *Pinnora* 1232, *Pinnore* 1248, *Pinnere* 1332, *Pynnor* 1483, that is 'peg-shaped or pointed flat-topped hill', from Old English *pinn* and *ōra*, referring to the elongated ridge in Pinner Park, to the south of which is NOWER HILL which is derived from the same word. **Pinner Green** is so called on the Ordnance Survey map of 1822, as is **Pinner Park** which is also referred to as earlier as *park of Pynnore* 1348; it was originally a medieval deer *park* belonging to the Archbishops of Canterbury who were lords of the manor of HARROW in medieval times. **Pinnerwood Park** is named from **Pinner Wood**, marked thus on the Ordnance Survey map of 1822.

Pitshanger Park Ealing. Named from the house called *Pitch-hanger* on the Ordnance Survey map of 1822, earlier *Putleshangre* 1222, *Pittleshangre* 1294, *Pytteshangre* 1493, that is 'wooded slope of the mousehawk, or of a man called Pyttel', from Old English *pyttel*, or the same word used as a personal name, with Old English *hangra*. The earlier farmhouse, rebuilt *c*.1800 by the architect John Soane and known as Pitshanger Manor, is now a museum housing the Martinware Pottery Collection.

Plaistow Bromley. *la Pleystowe* 1278, *Playstowe* 1467, *Plaistow c*.1762, that is 'place where people gather for play or sport', from Old English *pleg-stōw*. The next name has the same origin.

Plaistow Newham. *Playstowe* 1414, *Plastow* 16th century, *Plaistow* 1805, identical in origin with the previous name. The current local pronunciation is 'Plasstow', as already indicated by the 16th-century spelling.

Plashet Newham. Recorded as *Placet* 1578, *Plashett* 1805, but referred to earlier in the surname of John *atte Plass(c)het* 1327–32, from either Old French *plaissiet* 'enclosure made with interlaced fencing' or Old French *plaschiet* 'marshy pool', with Middle English *atte* 'at the' in the earliest form.

Plumridge Farm & Hill (near Botany Bay) Enfield. Both marked thus on the Ordnance Survey map of 1887, but the latter is *Plumridge Hill* in 1658, self-explanatory, 'ridge where plum trees grow'.

Plumstead Greenwich. *Plumstede* 961–71 (Anglo-Saxon charter), *Plume-stede* 1086 (Domesday Book), *Plumsted* 1206, that is 'place where plum trees grow', from Old English *plūme* and *stede*. Plumstead in Norfolk is identical in origin. **Plumstead Common** and **Plumstead Marshes** are marked as *Plumsted Common* and *Marshes* on the Ordnance Survey map of 1805.

Pole Hill (at Chingford) Waltham Forest. Recorded thus *c*.1840 and on the Ordnance Survey map of 1904, but as *Pale Hill* on the earlier map of 1883. This preserves the name of the old manor of Chingford St Pauls, called *Poules fee* in 1498, that is 'Paul's estate (in CHINGFORD)' because it once belonged to the Dean and Chapter of ST PAUL's in London. The Pole Hill obelisk was erected in 1824 to mark the direction of true north from Greenwich (although the meridian was later shifted 19 ft to the east).

Ponders End Enfield. Marked thus on the Ordnance Survey map of 1822, earlier *Ponders ende* 1593, that is 'end or quarter of the parish associated with the *Ponder* family' from Middle English *ende*. A certain

John *Ponder* of ENFIELD is mentioned in a document of 1373; the surname may well mean 'keeper of, or dweller by, a fish-pond or mill-pond'. The place is situated in the south-east corner of Enfield parish near to the River LEA, and there is still a working corn mill here on the site of a much earlier medieval mill.

Pool (of London), The (a reach of the River Thames below London Bridge divided into the Lower Pool and the Upper Pool). Referred to as *la Pole in aqua Tamisie juxta Turrim London* ('the pool in the River Thames beside the Tower of London') in 1258 and as *Pool* on the Ordnance Survey map of 1822, from Old English *pōl* 'a pool or creek, a deep in a river'. Up to the end of the 19th century, this stretch of the Thames was crowded with shipping of all kinds.

Pool River (flows north to join the River Ravensbourne near Rushey Green). Marked thus on the Ordnance Survey map of 1876, from *pōl* 'pool or stream'.

Poplar Tower Hamlets. *Popler* 1327, *Popeler* 1340, *Le Popler* 1351, *Poplar* 1486, that is '(place at) the poplar tree', from Middle English *popler*. The name is interesting because the word *popler* (from Old French *poplier*) is not otherwise recorded in English until 1356, even though the species known as the 'black poplar' is probably native to Britain.

Portland Place, Great Portland Street Westminster. Streets developed in the 18th century and named after the 2nd Duke of *Portland* who possessed an estate here in MARYLEBONE through his marriage in 1734.

Portman Square (near Marble Arch) Westminster. Laid out *c*.1764 by Henry William *Portman*. The Portman Estate in MARYLEBONE, originally purchased by Sir William Portman, Lord Chief Justice of England, in 1553, was developed during the 18th century, this accounting for several street names in this area named from the family's West Country estates.

Portobello Road Kensington & Chelsea. Shown on the Ordnance Survey map of 1822 as a lane leading to *Porto Bello House*, later *Porto Bello Farm* (on that of 1876). This was so named from the city of Puerto Bello on the Caribbean in Panama, the site of a British victory under Admiral Vernon in 1739. The road is now of course the venue for the renowned antique market, which dates back to *c*.1875 when gypsies gathered here to sell their wares.

Portpool Lane (in Clerkenwell) Camden. Preserves the name of the old manor of *Purtepole*, *see* GRAY'S INN.

Portsoken Street (off Minories) City. Named from one of the ancient wards of the City, recorded as *Portesokne* 1224, *Portsoken ward without the walls* 1603, *Portsoken-Ward* 1660, from Middle English *portsoken* 'district outside a city over which jurisdiction is extended' (from Old English *port* 'town' and *sōcn* 'jurisdiction'). This large ward lay on the outside of the eastern wall of the City.

Poultry City. *Poletria* 1298, (street of) *Puletrie* 1315, *Pulterye* 1422, *le Pultrye* 1547, from Middle English *pultrie* in the sense 'market where domestic fowls are sold, poultry market'. The name for the specialized market here, at the east end of *Cheap* (for which, *see* CHEAPSIDE), was transferred to the street at an early date. Appropriately enough, there was a tavern here called the *Rede Cok* ('Red Cock') in 1423.

Poverest (near St Mary Cray) Bromley. Marked thus on the Ordnance Survey map of 1904, earlier *Poverish* on the maps of 1819 and 1876, a manorial name from the family of Margaret *de Pouery* 1327, the final *-t* being a modern addition.

Pratt's Bottom (near Chelsfield) Bromley. Recorded as *Sprat(t)s Bottom* in 1791, 1799, and 1819, but in its present form in 1779, 1801, and 1821, probably 'valley associated with a family called Pratt', from Old English *botm*. A family named *Prat*, recorded in this area from the 14th century, also gave name to nearby **Pratt's Grove** (noted from 1871), but clearly the early spellings show confusion with a different surname. The surname Pratt (found as early as the 12th century) is derived from an Old English noun *prætt* 'a trick' or its corresponding adjective meaning 'tricky, cunning'.

Preston (near Harrow) Brent. Recorded as *Preston* from 1194, that is 'farmstead or estate of the priests', from Old English *prēost* and *tūn*, a common English place name found in several counties. As early as in the Domesday Book of 1086 there is mention of a priest holding land in the parish of HARROW (in which this manor lay). **Preston Road** station was opened in 1908.

Priests Bridge (at East Sheen) Richmond. *Prestbrig* 1479, *Prists Bridge* 1525, that is 'the bridge used by the priest or priests', from Middle English *prest* and *brigge*. The bridge is a crossing of BEVERLEY BROOK and the name probably alludes to the route taken by priests travelling

to MORTLAKE from WIMBLEDON, where the parish church was
situated until at least the mid-14th century (in early times the manor
of Mortlake, held by the Archbishop of Canterbury, included
Wimbledon).

Primrose Hill (near Chalk Farm) Camden. Marked thus on the Ordnance Survey map of 1822, earlier *Prymrose Hill* 1586, self-explanatory,
'hill where primroses grow'. In the 16th century the hill, which
reaches 206 ft, was still meadowland.

Prince's Street (near Bank) City. Laid out, along with KING STREET and
QUEEN STREET, after the Great Fire of 1666 and during the reign of
Charles II.

Priors Farm (at South Ruislip) Hillingdon. Marked as *Pryor Farm* on
Greenwood's map of 1819 and as *Priors Field* on Rocque's map of 1754,
earlier *Priores feilde* 1565, alluding to land once belonging to the small
medieval priory of RUISLIP, a cell of the Abbey of Bec in Normandy.

Pudding Lane (off Lower Thames Street) City. *Puddynglane* 1360,
Podynglane 1452, *Puddinglane* 1506, that is 'lane used for the disposal of
offal', from Middle English *pudding* 'bowels, entrails, guts'. The meaning is confirmed by the fact that in 1402 the butchers of the meat
market at EASTCHEAP were given the lane so that their offal could be
carted down to the Thames to be loaded into dung barges. There was a
watergate on the river here called *Rederesgate* 1108–48, 1275, that is
'cattle gate', from Old English *hrȳther* and *geat*, and in fact an earlier
(and then alternative) name for Pudding Lane was *Redereslane* 1301,
Retheresgateslane 1323, *Retherlane alias Puddynglane* 1373. No doubt cattle
were landed here at an early date for the Eastcheap market, probably
from ROTHERHITHE ('cattle harbour') on the opposite bank.

Puddle Dock (near Blackfriars) City. Street named from a former small
inlet on the north bank of the Thames referred to as *Puddle wharf* in
Stow's *Survey of London* (1603), from Middle English *puddel* 'a small dirty
pool', no doubt a derogatory name for the original wharf.

Purley Croydon. *Pirlee* 1200, *Pirile* 1201, *Purle* 1220, *Pyrelegh* 1332, that is
'wood or clearing where pear trees grow', from Old English *pyrige* and
lēah. **Purley Downs**, marked thus on the Ordnance Survey map of 1876,
are earlier *Pyrlesdon* 1255, that is 'hill or down near Purley', from
Middle English *doun*. **Purley Oaks** (station) is marked on the Ordnance
Survey map of 1905.

Putney Wandsworth. *Putelei* (*sic*) 1086 (Domesday Book), *Puttenhuthe* 1279, *Putneth* 1474, *Putney alias Puttenheath* 1639, that is 'landing place of the hawk, or of a man called Putta', from Old English *hȳth* with an Old English noun **putta* or the personal name derived from this word, in either case with genitive *-n*. There is mention of a fishery here in early times, and in fact a small fishing industry survived until the early 19th century. **Putney Bridge**, built in 1886 and famous as the starting point of the University Boat Race, replaced an earlier wooden structure built in 1729 (which in turn replaced a ferry). **Putney Heath** is recorded as *Putneth heth* 1524, *Putnehethe* 1552, from Old English *hǣth*. **Putney Vale**, like nearby Kingston Vale (*see* KINGSTON) referring to the valley of BEVERLEY BROOK, is marked thus on the Ordnance Survey map of 1904.

Pymmes Brook (a tributary of the River Lea) Enfield. Marked thus on the Ordnance Survey map of 1877, earlier called *Medeseye c.*1200, that is 'meadow marsh-stream', from Old English *mǣd* and **sǣge*. Like **Pymmes Park** at Edmonton, also shown on the 1877 map, the present name derives from the *Pymme* family, mentioned in local records from the early 14th century.

Pyrgo Park Havering. *Pergore park* 1544, *Pergo Park* 1805, named from *Purgore* 1490, *Pirgoe alias Pirgore* 1559, probably 'triangular plot of ground where pear trees grow', from Old English *pyrige* and *gāra*.

Q

Quaggy River (a small tributary of the River Ravensbourne, rising on Bromley Common). Recorded in 1883 as *The Quaggy*, so called from the adjective *quaggy* 'boggy' (related to *quagmire*). It was notorious for causing floods near Lee Green (*see* LEE) in the early 19th century. There is mention of *lands called the Quaggs* in a LEWISHAM document of 1809, from the corresponding noun *quag* 'wet boggy ground'.

Queen Elizabeth's Hunting Lodge (at Chingford) Waltham Forest. A 16th-century building (now a museum) referred to as *the great lodg* in 1588 and as *Q. Eliz. Lodge* on the Ordnance Survey Map of 1805. Built in 1543 for Henry VIII, it was used by Queen Elizabeth I as a grandstand from which to view the hunting on her visits to EPPING FOREST.

Queen Elizabeth's Walk (in Stoke Newington) Hackney. Recorded thus in 1734, said to commemorate the visits of Elizabeth I to the local manor in the period before she came to the throne.

Queenhithe City. A small street running down to the Thames, recorded as *Quenehith* 1547 and named from an ancient harbour on the river here, *Quenhyth* in 1151–2, 'the queen's landing place', from Old English *cwēn* and *hȳth*, with reference to Queen Matilda, wife of Henry I (1100–35), in whose possession it was in the early 12th century. In medieval times successive queens continued to have the right to gather tolls here, and it remained the most important dock in London until the 15th century. It gave name to one of the City wards. The natural inlet which formed the harbour is still visible. A much earlier reference to Queenhithe is in an Anglo-Saxon charter dated 898 where it is called *Ætheredes hyd*, that is 'Æthelred's harbour', probably an allusion to King Alfred's son-in-law, the *Ealdormann* (or underking) of Mercia, *see* ALDERMANBURY. The identification is confirmed by the mention in a late 12th-century document of *Ripa Reginae quae appellatur* ('river bank of the queen which is called') *Atheres hythe*.

Queen's Bridge (at Isleworth) Hounslow. Marked as *Queens Bridge* on the Ordnance Survey map of 1816, earlier *Quenebryg* 1450, 'the queen's bridge', from Old English *cwēn* and *brycg*; the queen referred to is unidentified, but may be Isabella, wife of Edward II (1307–27).

Queensbury Harrow. An invented modern name (the winning entry in a newspaper competition) bestowed on the Metropolitan Line railway station, opened in 1934, to contrast with KINGSBURY (itself an ancient name), the next station to the south; it was later transferred to the suburb.

Queen's Park (near Kensal Green) Brent. Name of the residential district developed from 1875, as well as of the park just to the north opened in 1887, both so called in honour of Queen Victoria.

Queen's Road (at Peckham) Southwark. Originally known as *Deptford Lane* (*see* DEPTFORD), renamed in 1866 in honour of Queen Victoria; the station so named was opened here in the same year.

Queenstown Road (at Battersea) Wandsworth. Station named from the road so called, which leads to Chelsea Bridge (*see* CHELSEA) after first crossing Prince of Wales Drive at Queen's Circus (a roundabout), referring to Queen Victoria.

Queen Street (off Cheapside) City. Laid out, along with its continuation KING STREET, after the Great Fire of 1666, and named after Charles II's queen, Catherine of Braganza.

Queensway (in Bayswater) Westminster. Earlier known as *Queens Road*, named in honour of Queen Victoria soon after she came to the throne in 1837 because it was said that as a Princess she rode along it to Kensington Palace (*see* KENSINGTON) when it was still a country lane.

Queen's Wood (near Highgate) Haringey. Earlier called *Bottom Wood* as on the Ordnance Survey map of 1877, but renamed in honour of Queen Victoria when it became a public open space in 1898.

Queen Victoria Street City. A new street cut through the City in 1867–71, named after the reigning monarch.

R

Rainham Havering. *Renaham*, *Reneham*, *Raineham* 1086 (Domesday Book), *Renham* 1205, *Reinham* 1234, possibly 'homestead or village of a man called *Regna', from an Old English personal name and *hām*. Alternatively, this name may be identical in origin with Rainham in Kent on the opposite side of the Thames, recorded as *Roegingaham* in 811, probably 'homestead of the *Roegingas*' (an Old English tribal name of uncertain meaning, but possibly 'the ruling or powerful people'). **Rainham Creek**, *Rainam Creeke* in 1588 and *Rainham Creek Mouth* on the Ordnance Survey map of 1805, was earlier called *Raynam flete* 1547, from Old English *flēot* 'estuary, inlet'; it refers to the lower course of the INGREBOURNE RIVER, where there was a small trading port (*Rainham Wharf*) in earlier times while the river was still navigable. **Rainham Hall** dates from the early 18th century. **Rainham Lodge** is marked thus on the Ordnance Survey map of 1805. **Rainham Marshes**, *Rainam Marshe* in 1588 and *Rainham Marsh* on the Ordnance Survey map of 1805, are earlier simply *le merssh* 1487, from Old English *mersc*.

Rammey Marsh Enfield. Marked thus on the Ordnance Survey map of 1887, named from *Ramhey* 1538, *Rammey* 1610, probably 'island (of dry ground in marsh) where rams are pastured', from Old English *ramm* and *ēg*. It lies on low ground by the River LEA.

Ramsden (near Orpington) Bromley. Marked thus on the Ordnance Survey maps of 1871 and 1876, origin uncertain without earlier spellings but possibly from Old English *denn* 'woodland pasture' like nearby HOCKENDEN and TUBBENDEN.

Ranelagh Gardens Kensington & Chelsea. Formerly the fashionable and much frequented pleasure gardens laid out in the 18th century on an estate of the Earl of *Ranelagh*, now part of the grounds of the Chelsea Hospital (*see* CHELSEA). The celebrated centrepiece of the gardens, a huge rococo rotunda built in 1741, was demolished in 1805. There was a Ranelagh Club at BARN ELMS from 1884–1939 named after the Chelsea gardens and still recalled in the local street name **Ranelagh Avenue**.

Raphael Park (near Gidea Park) Havering. Named after Sir Herbert *Raphael*, a Liberal MP, who presented it to the town of ROMFORD in 1904.

Ratcliff Tower Hamlets. Recorded as *la Rede clive* 1294, *Radeclyve* 1305, *Radclif* 1422, *Ratclyffe* 1524, that is 'the red bank or cliff', from Old English *rēad* and *clif*, no doubt so called from the reddish brown colour of the soil here at what was a natural landing place on the north bank of the River Thames (*see* STEPNEY). In the late medieval period ships were fitted out and repaired at Ratcliff, and Tudor voyagers set sail from here, notably Sir Martin Frobisher *c.*1575 in search of the North-west Passage.

Ravenor Park (at Greenford) Ealing. Named from the local family of Symon *Ravener* who is mentioned in a parish register of 1591 and whose ancestors are alluded to in the GREENFORD field name *Ravyners Land* 1461.

Ravensbourne River (rising in Keston, flows north to enter the River Thames at Deptford). *Randesbourne* 1360, *Rendesburne* 1372, *Randysborne* 1516, *Ravensburn* 1575, probably 'boundary stream', from Old English *rand*, **rend* and *burna*. The later spelling is thus due to folk etymology. In its 10-mile course, the Ravensbourne forms the boundary between several sets of parishes. The river gives name to **Ravensbourne** station (near BECKENHAM).

Ravensbury Park (near Morden) Merton. Recorded thus on the Ordnance Survey map of 1876, named from *Ravesbury c.*1220, *Rasebery* 1377, *Ravenesbury* 1473, *Ravisbury alias Ravensbury c.*1580, that is 'manor of a man called Ralf', from Middle English *bury* and a Norman-French personal name (from Old German *Radulf*). The substitution of *Raven-* for the original first element from the 15th century is probably due to folk etymology.

Ravenscourt Park Hammersmith & Fulham. Named from *Ravenscourt formerly known by the name of Paddingswick* 1765, *Raven's Court* (a house) 1819. The older name (surviving in PADDENSWICK ROAD) was earlier *Palyngewyk* 1270, *Paleswyk* 1294, *Pallyngwyk* 1307, *Paddyngeswyke* 1553, that is 'specialized farm or trading settlement associated with a man called Pælli', from an Old English personal name with Old English medial connective -*ing*- and *wīc*. The name of the manor house here (destroyed in the Second World War) was changed to *Ravenscourt c.*1747 when it was purchased by Thomas Corbett, Secretary to the Admiralty, who had a *raven* in his coat of arms (the surname *Corbett* being in fact derived from Old French *corbet* 'a raven').

Rayners Lane Harrow. An old lane from PINNER to ROXETH, now also a station (opened 1906) and district, according to local tradition said to take its name from an old shepherd called *Rayner* who lived in a solitary cottage along the lane at the end of the 19th century.

Raynes Park Merton. Marked thus on the Ordnance Survey map of 1905, originally the name of a station opened in 1871. The name commemorates one Edward *Rayne* (1778–1847) who formerly owned land here developed by the London & South Western Railway Company in the mid-19th century.

Rectory Park (near Northolt) Ealing. Named from the Rectory at Northolt, marked as *The Vicarage* on the Ordnance Survey map of 1880.

Rectory Road (at Stoke Newington) Hackney. Station named from the road leading to the Rectory of STOKE NEWINGTON.

Redbridge Redbridge. This district as well as the London borough of which it is part (created in 1965) are named from the old *Red Bridge* which stood where Eastern Avenue (the A12) now crosses the River RODING at Wanstead. The bridge (demolished in 1922) is marked *Red Bridge* on maps of 1746 and 1805, and the name is no doubt self-explanatory. It was earlier called *Hocklee's Bridge* in 1650, from the *de Hockelegh* family who owned an estate here in the 14th century.

Redlees Park (at Isleworth) Hounslow. Public park opened in 1932, named from a house called *Redlees* recorded thus in the late 19th century.

Redriff Road (in Rotherhithe), *see* ROTHERHITHE.

Reedham (in Purley) Croydon. Named from the *Reedham Orphanage* (marked *Reedham Asylum* on the Ordnance Survey map of 1878) founded in 1856 by the Revd Andrew *Reed* and demolished in 1980.

Regent's Park Westminster/Camden. Marked thus on the Ordnance Survey map of 1822, earlier *The Regents Park* 1817, named in honour of the Prince *Regent*, afterwards King George IV (reigned 1820–30). Its area corresponds roughly with the earlier *park of Maryborne* 1558, *Marybone Park* 1574, named from MARYLEBONE. *Regent's Canal* (now part of the GRAND UNION CANAL), opened in 1820 and shown on the 1822 map, was also so called after the Prince *Regent*, as was REGENT STREET. London Zoo was established in the north corner of the Park in 1828.

Regent Street Westminster. Constructed *c*.1820 and named after the Prince *Regent*. It was designed as a kind of royal drive to link up the Regent's Palace at ST JAMES'S with REGENT'S PARK (named from the same man some three years earlier).

Richmond (town and borough). *West Shene* 1258, *Shene otherwise called Richemount* 1502, *West Shene nowe called Rychemond* 1515, *Richmond alias Shene c*.1522, *Richmount* 1577, a name transferred from Richmond in North Yorkshire (meaning 'strong hill', from Old French *riche* and *mont*), when Henry VII rebuilt the old royal palace at (West) Sheen after its destruction by fire in 1499 and renamed the even grander building after his Yorkshire earldom. The old name survives in EAST SHEEN. The Palace had fallen into decay by the 18th century and only the Gateway and the restored Wardrobe buildings survive, but it is recalled in the local street names Old Palace Place, Terrace & Yard. **Richmond Bridge**, the oldest surviving crossing of the River Thames, was opened in 1777. **Richmond Green**, recorded as *the Greene* in 1492 and *le grene de Richemount* in 1548, was used in medieval times for jousting tournaments and other spectacles; the street by the Green called Maids of Honour Row takes its name from the terrace of houses built *c*.1725 by Frederick George, Prince of Wales, for the maids of honour attending on his wife Princess Caroline. **Richmond Hill** is marked thus on the Ordnance Survey map of 1876 and in 1650 there is reference to *Richmond hill common*; the top of the hill was the site of the famous *Star and Garter* inn, *see* STAR & GARTER HOME. **Richmond Park** is recorded as *le Newe Parc de Shene* 1463, *park called Richmond Park* 1541 (both referring to the older park north of Richmond, now Old Deer Park and Kew Gardens (*see* KEW)), and as *The New Park of Richmond alias Richmond Great Park* 1649 (referring to the present park created 1635–7 by Charles I to provide a convenient hunting ground). The new London Borough of Richmond was created in 1965.

Riddlesdown Croydon. *Redelsdon* 1277, *Ridelesdoune* 1331, *Riddels Downe* 1670, *Riddles Downs* 1765, named from *Redele* 1338, *Ridle* 1422, *Riddeley* 1461, that is 'cleared woodland', from Old English *(ge)ryd(d)* and *lēah* with the later addition of Middle English *doun* 'down'.

Ridgeway, The (at Mill Hill) Barnet. An old route running south-east to north-west on the highest ground in the district, referred to in the field name *Ridgwaie feld* 1574, from Old English *hrycg-weg* 'road along a ridge'. There were originally eight inns along this road, of which three remain.

Ripple Road, Rippleside Barking & Dagenham. Named from *Ripple* 1271, *Rypill* 1536, *Reple* 1557, 'the strip of land' from Old English **rippel*, referring to the narrow stretch of higher ground north of the Thames marshes along which the road runs. Rippleside is *Rypleside* 1609, *Ripple Side* 1805, from Middle English *side* 'land alongside'.

Risebridge (near Romford) Havering. *Risebregge* 13th century, *Rysebrigge* 1315, *Rysebrugge* 1323, *Risebridge* 1448, that is 'causeway made with brushwood', from Old English *hrīs* and *brycg*, probably with reference to the crossing of a once marshy area through which flow two small streams into the River BEAM. This place gives its name to nearby **Rise Park**.

Riverhill (near Tolworth) Kingston. Named from *Riverhill House* marked thus on the Ordnance Survey map of 1876, so called from its situation by HOGSMILL RIVER.

Robin Hood Gate Richmond. This gate at the south-east corner of Richmond Park (*see* RICHMOND) is marked thus on the Ordnance Survey map of 1816 and is shown as *Robin Hoods Gate* on Cary's map of 1785. It is to be associated with *Robynhood Walke c.*1530, *Robynhodes walke* 1548, which must have led to the Gate, from Middle English *walke* 'path through a wood', and of course they take their name from the legendary hero and outlaw. There was until recently also a farm just south of the Gate called *Robin Hood Farm* (thus on the Ordnance Survey map of 1816, *Robinhoods Farm* on Cary's map of 1785), and the lane which led to the farm is still called Robin Hood Lane (in Kingston Vale), this now linking up with Robin Hood Way and Robin Hood Road (crossing Wimbledon Common, *see* WIMBLEDON). The original allusion to Robin Hood may have been simply to commemorate him as a popular figure (the outlaw's legend was particularly strong in the 16th century), but it is perhaps more likely that the reference is to the presence of highwaymen on this stretch of the road between KINGSTON and WANDSWORTH as it crosses what would have been in earlier times a remote and wooded tract. Certainly by the 18th century this area (now Kingston Vale, *see* KINGSTON) was notorious as the haunt of footpads and highwaymen.

Roding, River (flowing into River Thames as Barking Creek at CREEK-MOUTH). Recorded as *Rodon* 1576, *Roding* 1586, a late back-formation from Roding in Essex (earlier *Rodinges*, that is '(settlement of) the family or followers of a man called *Hrōth(a)', from an Old English personal name and *-ingas*). The original name of the river, at least lower downstream, was *Hyle* (recorded from the 10th century), hence ILFORD, 'ford over the river *Hyle*'.

Roe Green, Roe Green Park (at Kingsbury) Brent. *Wrogrene* 1574, *Wroe Greene* 1632, *Rowe Green* 1680, named from (a field called) *le Wroo* 1422, from Middle English *wro* 'a nook or corner of land, a secluded spot' with the later addition of *grene* 'village green'. This is a rare instance of the word *wro* in the south of England, since it derives from a Scandinavian word *vrá* introduced by the Vikings.

Roehampton Wandsworth. *Rokehampton* 1350, *Rowhampton* 1553, *Rokehampton alias Roughampton* 1639, earlier *Est Hampton* 1318 or simply *Hampton* 1332, from Old English *hām-tūn* 'home farm or settlement', with affixes *est* 'east' and later *roke* 'rook' to distinguish this place from HAMPTON in Richmond. The full form of the affix *Roke-* indicating 'frequented by rooks' survives until the mid-17th century.

Roke, Little (at Kenley) Croydon. Marked thus on the Ordnance Survey map of 1816 along with *Roke Farm* (formerly *Great Roke*), named from *le Roke* 1550, *Roke* 1552, that is '(place) at the oak tree', from Middle English *atter* 'at the' and *oke*, the initial *R-* resulting from the misdivision of the phrase *atter oke* as *atte roke*. The name is recorded earlier in the surname of Adam *atte Roke* (that is 'living at the oak tree') 1367 and in the field names *le Rokegrofe* and *le Rokelond* 1431, with Middle English *grove* 'copse' and *land* 'arable strip'.

Romborough Gardens & Way (at Hither Green) Lewisham. Preserve the name of the medieval manor of *Rumbergh*, *see* HITHER GREEN.

Romford Havering. *Romfort* 1177, *Rumford* 1199, *Romford* 1306, *Roumford* 1399, that is 'the wide or spacious ford', from Old English *rūm* and *ford*. The river name **Rom** (used to describe the middle stretch of the BEAM RIVER) is a late back-formation from the place name. The ford must have been where the old Roman road to Colchester crossed the Beam River.

Rood Lane (off Fenchurch Street) City. Recorded thus in 1557, from a *rood* or holy cross once set up in the churchyard of St Margaret Pattens while the church was being rebuilt, but destroyed in 1538.

Rose Alley (near Bankside) Southwark. Named from the *Rose* Theatre, the first of the BANKSIDE playhouses, built 1586–7 on the site of an old house known by the sign of the Rose, and demolished *c.*1606.

Rosehill Sutton. Suburb named from *Rosehill Farm* which is so called on the Ordnance Survey map of 1876 (changed to *Rosehill House* on the 1905 map).

Roselane Gate (near Chadwell Heath) Barking & Dagenham. Recorded thus in 1777 and on the Ordnance Survey map of 1883, named from *Roselane* 1609, a lane running through an estate called *Roses* 1456 which had belonged to the family of Richard *Rose* 1392. The 'gate', like that at nearby MARKS GATE, was at an entrance into Hainault Forest (*see* HAINAULT) which lay to the north.

Rosslyn Hill (in Hampstead) Camden. So named from *Rosslyn House*, a former mansion built here by the Earl of *Rosslyn* in 1793. It was formerly known as *Red Lion Hill*, from an inn called the *Red Lion* demolished in 1868.

Rotherhithe Southwark. *Rederheia c.*1105, *Retherhith* 1127, *Rotherhuthe* 1238, *Rutherheth* 1255, *Rotherhith alias Redderiffe* 1621, 'landing place for cattle', that is a harbour to or from which they were shipped, from Old English *hrȳther* and *hȳth*. Cattle were no doubt transported across river from here to *Rederesgate* ('cattle gate') just east of London Bridge on their way to the meat market at EASTCHEAP, *see* PUDDING LANE. The alternative 17th-century spelling *Redderiffe* represents the old local pronunciation of the name, contrasting with the current written form with its more conservative spelling and still preserved in the local street name **Redriff Road**. The **Rotherhithe Tunnel** under the Thames, linking Rotherhithe with SHADWELL, was opened in 1908.

Rotten Row (in Hyde Park) Westminster. Recorded thus in 1781, but the origin is uncertain. It seems extremely unlikely that it is a corruption, as has been suggested, of *Route du Roi* (referring to its use by William III to cross HYDE PARK when riding to ST JAMES'S from his new Palace at KENSINGTON). Such a forced corruption, even if current in 18th-century colloquial speech, would hardly have become the official name. A more mundane explanation, that *rotten* referred to the extremely soft, loose soil along this *row* ('row of trees, tree-lined road') designed for horses and carriages, is after all much more likely. Even so, the application of this name to such a prestigious location may have been somewhat mischievous or jocular, since it occurs as a derogatory street name, in the form Ratton or Rotten Row, in several towns elsewhere in England (e.g. in Lewes and in medieval Grimsby, Norwich, and Nottingham), where it has the sense 'rat-infested row (of houses)', from Middle English *ratoun* 'a rat'! There is another example of Rotten Row, also a horse-riding path and no doubt named from this one, on Hampstead Heath (*see* HAMPSTEAD).

Round House Farm Havering. So called because of its distinctive oval shape, the Round House was built *c*.1792 for William Sheldon, a prosperous London merchant. In the 19th century it was nicknamed 'The Tea Canister' because of its unusually deep eaves which give the roof the appearance of a lid.

Roundshaw (near South Beddington) Sutton. Residential district built 1965–7 on part of the old CROYDON airport site, the name itself meaning 'round wood or copse' from the word *shaw*.

Roundwood Park (in Harlesden) Brent. Now a public open space but part of the estate of *Roundwood House* which is marked on the Ordnance Survey map of 1876–7. An earlier name for this area is *Hunger Hill* 1416, usually a derogatory nickname for infertile ground.

Rowdown Wood (near New Addington) Croydon. Named from *la Rughedune* 1263, *Rowedoune* 1279, that is 'the rough hill', from Old English *rūh* and *dūn*.

Rowley Green Barnet. Recorded thus in 1668, named from *Roweleye* 1287, *Rouley* 1386, 'the rough woodland clearing', from Old English *rūh* and *lēah* with the later addition of *grene* 'village green'.

Roxborough Avenue, Park & Road Harrow. Preserve the old name *Rokisborw* 1334, *Rokesbergh* 1446, *Roxbourgh* 1462, that is 'hill or barrow of a man called *Hrōc', from an Old English personal name and Old English *beorg*. The same man seems to have given his name to nearby ROXETH.

Roxeth Harrow. *Hroces seathum* 845 (Anglo-Saxon charter), *Roxhe* 1235, *Roxeth* 1280, *Roxhethe* 1282, that is 'the pit(s) or hollow(s) of a man called *Hrōc', from an Old English personal name (*see also* ROXBOR-OUGH) and *sēath*, probably referring to the depression in which are springs giving rise to the River CRANE. In the earliest form the name is in the dative case plural (-*um*).

Royal Albert Dock Newham. Marked thus on the Ordnance Survey map of 1888, opened in 1880 and named after Prince *Albert*, Queen Victoria's consort (died 1861); the docks were closed to shipping in 1981.

Royal Albert Hall, *see* ALBERT HALL & MEMORIAL.

Royal Exchange (between Cornhill and Threadneedle Street) City. The first *Royal Exchange*, thus named by Queen Elizabeth I when she opened it in 1570, was founded by Sir Thomas Gresham, *see* GRESHAM STREET. It was replaced by a larger building opened in 1669, but this was destroyed by fire in 1838. The present Royal Exchange was opened by Queen Victoria in 1844.

Royal Mint Street (near the Tower) Tower Hamlets. Renamed thus in 1850, from the *Royal Mint* which was moved here from the Tower of London itself in 1810. In medieval times the street was called *Hache-strate* or *Heggestrete* (probably from Old English *hæcc* 'a hatch gate', perhaps referring to the Tower Postern), and later, from the 17th century, *Rosemary Lane* (from the plant).

Royal Naval Yard (in Deptford) Lewisham. This former dockyard, earlier known as *Kings Dock Yard* as on the Ordnance Survey map of 1822, was established in 1513 for the construction and servicing of Henry VIII's navy.

Royal Oak (near Bayswater) Westminster. Station and district named in the 1870s from an old inn (now demolished) so called.

Royal Victoria Dock Newham. Marked *Victoria Dock* on the Ordnance Survey map of 1888, opened by Prince Albert in 1855 and named in honour of Queen *Victoria*; the docks were closed in 1981.

Ruckholt Manor & Road (at Leyton) Waltham Forest. Named from *Rocholt* 1200, *Rokeholt* 1247, *Rukholde* 1488, *Rockholts* 1805, that is 'wood frequented by rooks', from Old English *hrōc* and *holt*.

Ruislip Hillingdon. *Rislepe* 1086 (Domesday Book), *Ruslep* 1227, *Risselepe* 1241, *Ruysshlep* 1341, probably 'leaping place (across the river) where rushes grow', from Old English **rysc* and *hlȳp*. The name refers to a crossing of the River PINN. **Ruislip Common** is marked thus on the Ordnance Survey map of 1904. There was a small priory at Ruislip in medieval times, *see* PRIORS FARM; the 16th-century Manor Farmhouse is on the site of the Prior's house, and the 13th-century Great Barn survives nearby. The old manor is referred to in **Ruislip Manor**, the name of a station (opened 1912) and residential district which, like neighbouring **South** and **West Ruislip** and **Ruislip Gardens**, is a 20th-century development. **Ruislip Lido** is marked *Reservoir* on the Ordnance Survey map of 1822; it was created in 1811 as a feeder for the Grand Junction Canal. The local pronunciation of Ruislip is either 'Rizelip' or 'Ryeslip'.

Rushett Farm & Lane (near Chessington) Kingston. The former is marked as *Rushet Farm* on the Ordnance Survey map of 1819, earlier *Russhet* 1548, that is 'place growing with rushes', from Old English **ryscett*. HOGSMILL RIVER rises near here, *see also* MALDEN RUSHETT.

Rushey Green (at Catford) Lewisham. Marked thus on the Ordnance Survey map of 1816, earlier *Rishotetes Grene* (sic) 1500, *Rushet Green* 1544, *Rushy Green* 17th century, *Rush Green* c.1762. The first spellings are to be associated with land called *Russchete* and *Russheteslond* c.1320, from Old English **ryscett* 'a rush bed, a place growing with rushes', to which Middle English *grene* 'village green' was later added. This locality not far from the River RAVENSBOURNE is low-lying and would have been marshy in early times. There was a mansion here called *Rushy Green Place* in the early 16th century.

Rush Green Havering. Marked thus on a map of 1777 and on the Ordnance Survey map of 1805, earlier recorded as *Rush Greene* in 1651, self-explanatory, 'village green where rushes grow'.

Rushmore Hill (near Pratt's Bottom) Bromley. Marked as *Rushmoor Hill* on the Ordnance Survey map of 1876, earlier *Richmore Hill* on the map of 1819 and on Bowen's map of c.1762, possibly 'marshy ground where rushes grow', from Middle English *rishe*, *rushe* and *more*, although the second element may originally have been *mere* 'pool'.

Ruskin Park (near Denmark Hill) Lambeth. Commemorates the Victorian writer and critic John *Ruskin* (1819–1900) who for 30 years (1842–72) lived in an imposing house on DENMARK HILL now demolished.

Russell Hill (at Purley) Croydon. Recorded thus on the Ordnance Survey map of 1876, probably named from the *Russell* family mentioned in local documents from 1541.

Russell Square (in Bloomsbury) Camden. So named in 1800 when the Square was first laid out, from the family name *Russell* of the Dukes of Bedford, the ground landlords, *see* BEDFORD SQUARE.

Ruxley, Upper Ruxley Bromley. *Rochelei* 1086 (Domesday Book), *Roche(s)lea* 1175, *Rokeli* 1199, *Rokeslega* 1211, possibly 'wood or clearing frequented by rooks', from Old English *hrōc* and *lēah*. Alternatively, the first element may be an Old English personal name *Hrōc(a)*.

S

Sadler's Wells Islington. Named from one Thomas *Sadler* who had a 'Musick House' here *c.*1683 and discovered a mineral spring in its garden. A new theatre replaced the earlier building in 1765, and the present theatre was built in 1927-31.

Saffron Hill (in Clerkenwell) Camden. Street name on record from 1602, named from a garden, part of the grounds of the Bishops of Ely (*see* ELY PLACE), where the saffron crocus was once grown. The orange-yellow extract was highly valued in medieval and later times as a dye and for flavouring food, but was not widely cultivated in England until the 16th century.

St Bartholomew's Hospital City. The oldest hospital in London, founded at West Smithfield (*see* SMITHFIELD) in 1123 as an Augustin-ian priory and hospital dedicated to St Bartholomew, now familiarly known as 'Bart's'. It gave name to the massive fair held here from the 12th century, the subject of Ben Jonson's satirical play *Bartholomew Fair* (1614); the fair was not suppressed until 1855, soon after which date it was replaced by Smithfield meat market.

St Botolph Row & Street (near Aldgate) City, *see* BOTOLPH LANE.

St Chad's Park Barking & Dagenham. A nice example of a saint's name resulting from folk etymology, *see* CHADWELL HEATH. The first ele-ment of the name Chadwell (originally Old English *ceald* 'cold') has been reinterpreted as the name of the saint, to whom the church here is also dedicated: the famous St Chad referred to was the first Bishop of Lichfield, where he died in 672.

St Clare Street City. Recalls the medieval nunnery of *St Clare*, dissolved in 1538, for which *see* MINORIES.

St Clement Danes Westminster. The present late 17th-century church was designed by Sir Christopher Wren, but it incorporates the tower of a much older church dating from the beginning of the 11th century or earlier. There are references to *parochia Sancti Clementis ecclesie*

Dacorum ('parish of St Clement's church of the Danes') from the early 12th century, to *Denscheman parosch* ('parish of the Danish people') in 1261, to *parochia Sancti Clementis le Daneys extra Lond'* ('parish of St Clement 'the Danish' outside London') in 1274, and to *Seynt Clement Danes* in 1500. The early spellings suggest that by the year 1100 there was a strong Danish community here by the Thames, *see also* STRAND, part of which was known as *vicus Dacorum* or *Densemanestret* ('street of the Danes or Danish people') in the early 13th century. Such a community, perhaps going back to a settlement of Viking merchants and craftsmen that may have been established just outside the City during the reign of the Danish King Cnut (1016–35), would be ideally placed here for trade by river or road. There is a legend found in early sources (reported for instance by Stow in 1603) concerning the burial here of King Harold I ('Harefoot'), illegitimate son of Cnut after whom he reigned 1035–40, and other Danes. This story fits the other evidence, whether or not the building of a church preceded or followed these burials. It should be noted that *Danes* in the present name is not a plural form but from Old French *daneis*, Middle English *daneys* 'Danish' (as in the 1274 form), often also used as a surname in medieval times (*le/la Daneys* 'the Dane'), and that *Dacorum* in the earliest spelling is the genitive plural of Latin *Dacus* 'a Dacian' (commonly though erroneously used of Danes from the 12th century onwards). The early dedication to St Clement, considered to be the patron saint of sailors, is an appropriate one. Also named from the church is **St Clement's Lane**, marked thus on a map of 1677, near to which was 'St Clement's Well'. This is referred to as *Fons Sancti Clementis* in William Fitz-Stephen's account of London in 1174, where it is named as one of three wells that were popular gathering places for young people, *see* CLERKENWELL and HOLYWELL LANE. The reference in the traditional nursery rhyme 'Oranges and Lemons' to 'the bells of St Clement's' may be to this church or to another with the same dedication near EASTCHEAP, *see* CLEMENT'S LANE.

St Dunstan's Hill & Lane (near Great Tower Street) City. The lane is recorded as *Donstoneslane* 1329, *Seint Dunstoneslone* 1363, the hill is first mentioned on a map of *c*.1570. Both are named from the old church of St Dunstan (destroyed in the Second World War except for the tower and part of the nave).

St George in the East Tower Hamlets. Parish name established in 1727 for the hamlet of WAPPING; the church itself, built 1714–29, was badly damaged during the Blitz.

St George's Circus (near Elephant & Castle) Southwark. Named from *St George's Fields*, a large open space until the end of the 18th century, so called from the nearby church of St George the Martyr (which dates from the 14th century).

St Giles in the Fields Camden. *Hospitali Sancti Egidii extra Londonium* ('hospital of St Giles outside London') *c.*1120, *paroch' Hospital' de Sancto Egidio* ('the parish of the hospital of St Giles') 1274, *Seintgilespitel* 1374, *Seynt Gyles in the Field* 1563, *St Giles in the Feildes* 1615. The parish was named from the dedication of the hospital (Middle English *spitel*) and church here to St Giles (Latin *Egidius*). The village was originally isolated in the *fields* to the west of (the City of) London. It gives name to **St Giles Circus**.

St Helier Sutton. Residential district built 1928–36 as a garden suburb to rehouse people from inner London, named in honour of Lady *St Helier*, a London County Council alderman who worked tirelessly to relieve poverty until her death in 1931.

St James's, St James's Palace & Park Westminster. All named from the medieval Hospital dedicated to *St James* (once a leper hospital for young women), which was founded in the 12th century and stood on the site now occupied by St James's Palace. It is recorded as *Hospital' Leprosis puellis de Sancti Jacobi* ('hospital of St James for leprous young women') in 1204, and as *Hospital of St James by Charyng* in 1386. The Palace was built by Henry VIII after acquiring the site of the Hospital in 1531. St James's Park, the oldest of the royal parks, was created at the same date out of what had earlier been marshy swine pastures; it is recorded as *Seynt James Newe Parke* in 1555.

St James's Park (at Walthamstow) Waltham Forest. Named (like **St James Street** and the parish of *St James's* marked thus on the Ordnance Survey map of 1877) from the dedication of the church here.

St Johns Lewisham. Station and residential district named from the dedication of the church here in St John's Vale off Lewisham Way.

St John's Wood Westminster. Recorded as *Seynt Johns Woode* in 1524, earlier as *Boscum Prioris Sancti Johannis* ('wood of the Priory of St John') in a Latin document of 1294. The name refers to the Knights Hospitallers of *St John*, who came into possession of the woodland here at the end of the 13th century. The area remained wooded throughout the medieval period, and was still essentially rural until development began in the early 19th century.

St Katharine's Dock Tower Hamlets. The 19th-century dock was built 1825–7 and was opened in 1828, the work of Thomas Telford; it was closed in 1968 and is partly now a marina. The name however is much older, found as *Katerines Dokke* 1422, *Saint Katerines Wharf* 1446, *St Catrins Docke* 1594, from Middle English *dok* and *wharfe*. This dock or wharf belonged to the former Hospital of St Katharine (now the Royal Foundation of St Katharine) founded in 1148 as a hospital for the poor by Queen Matilda, wife of King Stephen. In medieval times the hospital became a royal peculiar with its own jurisdiction and it developed its own trades and industries.

St Luke's (near Finsbury) Islington. District named from St Luke's Church in OLD STREET, built 1727–33.

St Margarets (near Twickenham) Richmond/Hounslow. Residential district developed from the mid-19th century (formerly part of *Twickenham Park* marked thus on the Ordnance Survey map of 1816), named from the mansion here, earlier itself called *Twickenham Park* but given the name *St Margarets* c.1820 by its then owner the Marquis of Ailsa (also commemorated in the local street names Ailsa Avenue & Road). The name *St Margarets* was first transferred to a new mansion built in 1852 (destroyed by bombing in 1940) before it was applied to the district and station (opened 1872).

St Martin in the Fields (in Trafalgar Square) Westminster. The present church was rebuilt in 1722–4 but the site is an old one. There was already a church here with its own parish by the 12th century, recorded as *ecclesia Sancti Martini* in 1254, *St Marteyn in lez Feildes* in 1493, and alternatively described as *St Martin by les Mewes* in 1406, so called because the church originally stood in the *fields* adjoining the royal *mews* or falconry, *see* TRAFALGAR SQUARE.

St Martin's le Grand (near St Paul's) City. 'the street of St Martin le Grand' 1265, *Seint Martynslane* 1414, *S. Martins lane* 1603, named from the former collegiate church of *St Martin le Grand*, founded in the mid-11th century when it is recorded as *Sancte Martines mynster*.

St Mary at Hill (off Eastcheap) City. *venella* ('lane') *Sancte marie de la Hulle*

1275, *seint mary hill lane* 1521, street named from the church of St Mary at Hill (founded in the 12th century), from Middle English *hull* 'hill'.

St Mary Axe (off Leadenhall Street) City. *strata Sancte Marie atte Ax* 1275, *Sainte Marie Strate* 1260, street named from the former church of *St Mary Axe* (founded in the 12th century) which was closed in 1560. The strange dedication derives from its claim to have possessed one of the three axes used by Attila the Hun to behead the 11,000 virgins said to have accompanied St Ursula on a mission to convert the heathen.

St Mary Cray Bromley. *Sudcrai* 1086 (Domesday Book), *Creye sancte Marie* 1257, *Seynte Mary Crey* 1270, that is 'estate on the River Cray with a church dedicated to St Mary', *see* CRAY. In the Domesday Book form, Old English *sūth* 'south' indicates its position relative to the other manors named from the river. St Mary's Church here dates from the 13th century.

St Marylebone Westminster, *see* MARYLEBONE.

St Mary Overie, *see* SOUTHWARK.

St Pancras Camden. *Sanctum Pancratium* 1086 (Domesday Book), *ecclesia Sancti Pancratii* c.1183, *Parochia Sancti Pancratii* 1291, *St Pancras in the Fields* 1531, *Pankeridge alias St Pancras* 1588, 'place with a church dedicated to St Pancras (Latin *Pancratius*)'. The church (Latin *ecclesia*) gave name to the parish (Latin *parochia*) and the old village. St Pancras Old Church, though restored c.1848, dates partly from the 14th century but the discovery here of a Saxon altar from c.600 indicates a much earlier church on the site. **St Pancras Station** dates from the 1860s; together with the splendidly Gothic *Midland Grand Hotel*, it was built on a site once occupied by the slums of *Agar Town* (a notorious shanty town developed in the 1830s by one William *Agar*), *see* AGAR GROVE & PLACE.

St Paul's City. District named from **St Paul's Cathedral**, the present building designed by Sir Christopher Wren and built 1675–1710. There have been no less than four earlier cathedrals on the site, all dedicated to St Paul, the earliest founded in 604 by Ethelbert, King of Kent. A second Saxon cathedral, referred to as 'church of *Paulesbyri*' (from *burh* 'fortified place') in 704–9, *Ecclesia Sancti Pauli Apostoli* in Bede's History (c.730) and *Sancte Paules Kirke* c.950, was destroyed by fire in 962. A third was burnt down in 1087. This was in turn replaced by the large stone cathedral built in the 11th to 13th century (later known as 'Old St Pauls'), which had fallen into decay by c.1650 and which was finally destroyed in the Great Fire of 1666.

St Paul's Cray Bromley. *Craie* 1086 (Domesday Book), *Craye Paulin* 1258, *Paulinescreye* 1270, *Paulscray* 1610, that is 'estate on the river Cray with a church dedicated to St Paulinus', *see* CRAY. The old church here, closed in 1977, is now a day centre for the elderly.

St Saviour's Dock (on the Thames east of London Bridge) Southwark. Marked thus on Rocque's map of 1746, earlier known as *Savory's Dock* 1682, *Savory Dock* 1720, so called from the dedication of the medieval abbey at BERMONDSEY to *St Saviour*. The stream called NECKINGER flowed into the River Thames here.

St Swithin's Lane (off Cannon Street) City. *vicus* ('street') *Sancti Swithuni* 1270, *venella* ('lane') *Sancti Swithuni* 1279, *Seint Swithoneslane* 1411, named from the church of St Swithin which was bombed in the Second World War.

St Thomas's Hospital (near Waterloo) Lambeth. The present building dates from 1871 but the original hospital was founded on a different site in SOUTHWARK in the 12th century, probably as part of the former Priory of *St Mary Overee* (*see* Southwark Cathedral, *under* SOUTHWARK). Its name was at first the *Hospital of St Thomas the Martyr* (with reference to St Thomas Becket, Archbishop of Caterbury 1162–70, canonized 1172), but at the Reformation, in 1551, this was changed to the *Hospital of St Thomas the Apostle*.

Salmon's Brook (stream rising near Hadley Wood and flowing into River Lea at Edmonton). Marked thus on Rocque's map of 1754, probably named from the family of John *Salemon* of EDMONTON mentioned in 1274.

Sanctuary, Broad & Little Westminster. *The Seyntwary c.*1440, *The Sanctuary* 1519, *Brode Sentwarye* 1581. The two streets so called occupy an area once within the precinct of Westminster Abbey (*see* WESTMINSTER) where in medieval times refugees and even criminals could take refuge and have immunity from arrest.

Sanderstead Croydon. *Sondenstede c.*880 (Anglo-Saxon charter), *Sandestede* 1086 (Domesday book), *Sanderstede* 1221, *Saundrestede* 1276, that is 'sandy homestead' (referring to sandy ground), from Old English *sand* and *hǽm-styde*. Sanderstead remained a small rural village until the 1930s.

Sands End Hammersmith & Fulham. Marked thus on the Ordnance

Survey map of 1876 but earlier *atte Sonde* 1408, *Sand end* 1655, *Sandy End* 1816, that is 'district (of the parish of FULHAM) with sandy soil', from Middle English *sand* and *ende*. The first spelling means '(place) at the sand', from Middle English *atte* 'at the'. It lies by the River Thames near the small inlet called Chelsea Creek (*see* CHELSEA).

Savile Row (near Piccadilly) Westminster. Street now famous for its gentlemen's tailors, first laid out in 1733 and marked as *Savill Row* on Rocque's map of 1746. It is named after Lady Dorothy *Savile*, wife of the 3rd Earl of Burlington, *see* BURLINGTON ARCADE & GARDENS.

Savoy Hill, Place & Street (off Strand) Westminster. All named from the old manor of *Le Sauveye* 1324, *Savoie* 1348, *Savoy* 1476, an estate originally held by Peter, Count of *Savoy* (now part of south-east France), uncle to Henry III, who was granted land here by the STRAND in 1246. The splendid mansion here, known as *Savoy Palace*, existed by the 13th century and had its heyday in the 14th as the residence of John of Gaunt, Duke of Lancaster, until it was partly burnt down. After being rebuilt and serving intermittently as a hospital, the site of the Palace was cleared in the early 18th century and is now covered by the Savoy Hotel and Theatre and various streets in the vicinity.

Scadbury Park Bromley. Marked thus on the Ordnance Survey map of 1876, earlier *Scadhebir* 1254, *Scathebury* 1292, *Scadbery* 1300, *Scadbury* c.1762, that is '(disused) fortification used by robbers or thieves', from Old English *scatha* and *burh* (dative case *byrig*). The name is no doubt older than the former medieval moated manor house here. This was replaced by a Tudor mansion pulled down in 1752 and later by an 18th-century house damaged by fire in 1976.

Scotland Yard, New Westminster, *see* GREAT SCOTLAND YARD.

Scratch Wood (near Edgware Bury) Barnet. Marked thus as a piece of woodland on the Ordnance Survey map of 1822, perhaps originally so called because it was considered haunted or ill-favoured, since *Scratch* is an old dialect word for 'the Devil'. It gives name to the Scratchwood Service Area on the M1 motorway.

Seacoal Lane City. So named from OLD SEACOAL LANE.

Seething Lane (near The Tower) City. Recorded as *Shyvethenestrat* 1257, *Sivethenestrate* 1281, *Sivethenelane* 1305, *Seythin Lane* 1556, that is 'street or lane full of chaff or bran', from an Old English **sifethen* (a derivative of Old English *sifetha* literally 'siftings', related to the words *sieve* and *sift*). This was probably where corn was threshed and winnowed ready for market.

Seething Wells (near Surbiton) Kingston. Named from a spring near the River Thames called *Seething-Well* in 1719, from the word *seething* 'bubbling or foaming (as if boiling)'. The spring was considered therapeutic and was much visited in the 1700s and early 1800s. More mundanely, since 1852 this has been the site of a large Water Works, noted for its Romanesque towers.

Selhurst Croydon. *Selherst* 1229, *Selhurst alias Selherst* 1540, probably 'wooded hill where sallow willows grow', from Old English *sealh* and *hyrst*. Woodland called *Sellhurst Wood* is shown near *Sellhurst* on the Ordnance Survey map of 1819.

Selsdon Croydon. *Selesdune* c.880 (Anglo-Saxon charter), *Selysdon* 1247, *Sellesdon* 1286, probably 'hill of a man called *Sele or *Seli', from Old English *dūn* and an Old English personal name. Alternatively, the first element could be Old English *sele* 'a dwelling, a hall' or Old English **sele* 'a sallow copse'. **Selsdon Park**, originally a Tudor mansion but much rebuilt and enlarged and now a hotel, is marked thus on the Ordnance Survey map of 1876.

Serpentine, The Westminster. Lake in HYDE PARK marked *Serpentine* on the Ordnance Survey map of 1876 and *Serpentine River* on the earlier map of 1822 and on Rocque's map of 1746. It was created in the 1730s by the damming of the Westbourne Brook (*see* WESTBOURNE), and is so called from its elongated and sinuous (somewhat snakelike) shape.

Seven Dials (near Covent Garden) Camden. Recorded as *les Seven Dials* in 1707, a reference to the dial-like appearance of this road junction described by Evelyn in his Diary of 1694 as a place 'where seaven streetes make a starr from a Doric Pillar placed in the middle of a circular Area'. The actual pillar or column was taken down in 1773 and now stands on Monument Hill at Weybridge in Surrey.

Seven Kings Redbridge. *Sevekyngg, Sevekyngges* 1285, *Sevyn Kynges* 1456, possibly an ancient folk name, '(settlement of) the family or followers of a man called *Seofoca', from an Old English personal name and *-ingas*. Other names of the same early type include BARKING and EALING. It would seem that the reinterpretation of the name already apparent in the 15th-century spelling has led to the local tradition, no doubt fanciful, that this was the meeting place of seven Saxon kings! **Seven Kings Water** (a small stream) is marked thus on the Ordnance Survey map of 1883, earlier *le vij Kinges Wateringes* 1609, from *watering* 'a ditch, a stream'.

Seven Sisters Haringey. A whimsical nickname for seven elm trees which stood near PAGE GREEN where the Seven Sisters Road (made 1831–3) joins the old ERMINE STREET. According to local legend, the trees were planted outside a tavern by seven sisters when departing to go on their separate ways. They are marked as *7 Sesters* on Rocque's map of 1754, and as *Seven Sisters* on the Ordnance Survey map of 1805. Remarkably enough, the same name is found with a totally different application in East Sussex, where it refers to the seven heights in the chalk cliffs west of Eastbourne.

Severndroog Castle (near Shooters Hill) Greenwich. Marked thus on the Ordnance Survey map of 1805, a triangular folly built in 1784 by Lady James and named from the fortress of *Severndroog* on the Malabar coast captured by her husband Sir William James in 1755. It gives its name to Castle Wood.

Shacklewell Hackney. *Shekelwell* 1491, *Shakylwell* 1509, *Shakkelwell* 1530, *Shakelwell* 1532, probably 'spring where animals could be tethered or shackled', from Old English *sceacol* and *wella*.

Shadwell Tower Hamlets. *Schadewelle* 1222, *Shadewell* 1223, *Scaldewell* 1314, *Shaldewell* 1316, that is 'the shallow spring or stream', from Old English **sceald* and *wella*. The place was only thinly populated until the 17th century, when the riverside hamlet became industrialized. **Shadwell Dock Stairs** are named from *Shadwell Dock*, marked thus on the Ordnance Survey map of 1822.

Shaftesbury Avenue Westminster. Laid out *c*.1880 and named after the 7th Earl of *Shaftesbury*, the well-known philanthropist and reformer.

Sheen, East & North Richmond, *see* EAST SHEEN.

Shepherd Market (in Mayfair) Westminster. Marked thus on Rocque's map of 1746, named from Edward *Shepherd*, an architect and builder who established a produce market here in 1735 on part of the site of the notorious 'May Fair' (for which, *see* MAYFAIR).

Shepherd's Bush Hammersmith & Fulham. Marked thus on the Ordnance Survey map of 1822, earlier *Sheppards Bush Green* 1635, *Shepperds*

Bush 1675, *Shepards Bush* 1710, apparently self-explanatory, although the reference could be either to a family called *Shepherd* or to actual shepherds (there is a term *shepherd's bush* denoting a bush from which a shepherd could watch his flock, and there were still farms in this area until the late 19th century).

Sherborne Lane (near Cannon Street) City. Originally *Shitteborwelane* 1273, *Schiteburuelane* 1305, *Shiteburghlane* 1321, this then being first changed to *Shitebournelane* c.1350 and finally to *Shirborne lane* 1540. This change of name is perhaps not surprising (and is certainly in part euphemistic), since the original name is apparently from Middle English **shite-burgh* (Old English **scite-burh*), a jocular term for a privy (no doubt roughly equivalent to 'shithouse'). Names exactly identical to this are found in 13th-century Oxford and ROMFORD.

Shernhall Street (in Walthamstow) Waltham Forest. Recorded thus in 1697 and giving name to *Shern Hall* 1849, but in fact originally *Shernwell Street* 1560, that is 'street along the dirty stream' from Old English *scearn* 'dirt, dung' and *wella*.

Sherrick Green Road (at Willesden) Brent. Preserves the name of the old hamlet of *Sherrick Green* (marked thus on the Ordnance Survey map of 1822), earlier *Sirewic* 1226, *Scyrewyk* 1306, *Shirick Green* 1754, probably from Old English *scīr* in the sense 'district, estate' and *wīc* 'specialized farm or building, trading settlement'.

Shirley Croydon. *Shirleye* 1314, *Shyrley* 1461, *Sherlegh* 1498, probably 'bright woodland clearing', from Old English *scīr* (adjective) and *lēah*. Alternatively, if the first element is rather the Old English noun *scīr*, possibly 'shire clearing' with reference to its situation near the county boundary between Surrey and Kent. **Upper Shirley** is marked thus on the Ordnance Survey map of 1876. **Shirley Oaks** is a residential development dating mainly from the 1970s.

Shoe Lane (off Fleet Street) City. Recorded as *Sholane* 1279, *Scholane* 1285, but even earlier as *Solande* c.1200, *Sholand* 1272, *Scholaunde* 1283, indicating that this is from an interesting Old English term *scōhland*, literally 'shoe land', that is 'land given to a monastic community to provide it with shoes'. This was originally an estate held by the canons of ST PAUL'S.

Shooters Hill Greenwich. Marked thus on Bowen's map of c.1762, earlier *Shitereshell* 1226, *Schetershull* 1240, *Shetereshelde* 1292, *Shetersselde*

1374, that is 'hill or hill-slope of the shooter or archer', from Old English *scēotere, *scȳtere and hyll 'hill', alternating in the early forms with helde 'slope'. The reference may be to hunting, since the conspicuous hill here (reaching 432 ft) was once densely wooded, but alternatively the name may allude to early highwaymen on the main road from Dover to London (WATLING STREET) which crosses the hill.

Shoot Up Hill (at West Hampstead) Camden. Shottuppe Hill 1566, Shoteuphill 1584, Shotuphill 1589, that is 'hill that shoots up', aptly descriptive of the sharp straight rise in the A5 (the old WATLING STREET) here. The hill was once the site of a windmill, still shown on the Ordnance Survey map of 1822.

Shoreditch Hackney. Soredich c.1148, Schoresdich 1221, Schoredich 1236, Shordich 1457, that is 'ditch by a steep bank or slope', from Old English *scora and dīc. Not surprisingly, the precise topographical features originally referred to are no longer evident.

Shortlands Bromley. Marked thus on the Ordnance Survey map of 1876, no doubt with reference to the 18th-century Shortlands House (now a school), but originally a field name meaning 'the short strips of arable land' (i.e. in the common fields), from Middle English short and land.

Shoulder of Mutton Green (at Welling) Bexley. Marked thus on a map of 1769 and on the Ordnance Survey map of 1805, so called from its triangular shape.

Shroffold Road (near Southend) Lewisham. Preserves the name of the old manor of Shroffold, marked Shrofield on the Ordnance Survey map of 1805 and earlier recorded as Shrafholt 1240, Shrofholt 1344, Schroffold 1489, that is 'thicket with a cave or hovel', from Old English scræf and holt.

Shrublands (near Shirley) Croydon. Residential development dating from c.1958 on what was once part of the wooded SPRING PARK.

Sidcup Bexley. Cetecopp 1254, Setecoppe 1301, Sedecoppe 1332, Sidycope 1407, that is probably 'seat-shaped or flat-topped hill', from Old English *set-copp. **Sidcup Place** (now Council offices) is a mansion partly dating from 1743.

Sidmouth Wood (in Richmond Park) Richmond. Planted in 1823 and named after Viscount Sidmouth, formerly Henry Addington, Prime Minister 1801–4.

Silk Stream Barnet. Feeding the reservoir known as WELSH HARP, this is an old river name recorded as *sulh* in 957 and 972–8 (both Anglo-Saxon charters describing the bounds of HENDON), then as *water called Solke or Selke* in the 13th century, from Old English *sulh* 'a narrow gully'.

Silver Street (at Upper Edmonton) Enfield. Station named from the street so called which is recorded thus *c*.1630 and which possibly alludes to silversmiths living here at that date or in earlier times.

Silvertown Newham. Marked thus on the Ordnance Survey map of 1888, named after a firm of manufacturers, S. W. Silver & Co., whose factories producing rubber goods were first built here in the 1850s. *See* CANNING TOWN for a similar name.

Single Street (near Cudham) Bromley. Marked thus on the Ordnance Survey map of 1871, perhaps from Old English **sengel* 'burnt clearing', referring to woodland cleared by burning, with the later addition of *street* 'street of houses, hamlet'.

Sipson (near Harmondsworth) Hillingdon. *Sibwineston* early 13th century, *Sybbeston* c.1310, *Sibston* 1391, *Sipson* 1638, that is 'farmstead or estate of a man called Sibwine', from an Old English personal name and Old English *tūn*.

Slade Green Bexley. Recorded thus in 1561 and on the Ordnance Survey map of 1905 (but *Slads Green* on the earlier map of 1805), from Middle English *slade* 'valley, low-lying marshy land' with *grene* 'village green'.

Sloane Square & Street Kensington & Chelsea. Named from Sir Hans *Sloane*, the great physician whose accumulations of art and books formed the nucleus of the collections in the British Museum (which was founded in 1753). He purchased the manor of CHELSEA from the Cheyne family in 1712. Before it was developed, the earlier name for this area was *Great Bloody Field*, so called from nearby places called *Bloody Bridge* 1719 (a bridge over Westbourne Brook, *see* WESTBOURNE GREEN) and *Bloody Gate* 1590 (perhaps the scene of a battle or feud in early times).

Smallberry Green (at Isleworth) Hounslow. Recorded as *Smalleboro Grene* 1547, *Smallbury Green* 1816, named from *Smalborow* 1436, that is 'the narrow mound or tumulus' (perhaps with reference to a long barrow), from Old English *smæl* and *beorg*, with the later addition of *grene* 'village green'.

Smitham, Smithambottom (in Coulsdon) Croydon. *Smetheden* 1331, *Smithdenbottom* 1536, *Smythedean* 1548, *Smythden Bottom* 1588, *Smitham Bottom* 1816, that is 'smooth valley', from Old English *smēthe* and *denu*, with the later addition of *botm* 'valley bottom'.

Smithfield Street, West Smithfield City. Named from *Smethefelda* c.1145, *Smethefeld* 1197, that is 'the smooth or level field', from Old English *smēthe* and *feld*. This flat open space just outside the City was already being used as a market for horses and other livestock in the 12th century, as vividly described by William FitzStephen in his account of London in 1174: the famous meat market here was opened in 1868. *West* Smithfield is so called to distinguish it from EAST SMITH-FIELD on the other side of the City near the TOWER.

Smith Square, Great Smith Street Westminster. The street is recorded as *Smith Street* in 1708, named after Sir James *Smith* who owned the land on which it was built. Smith Square was laid out in the 1720s on land sold for development by his son Henry *Smith*.

Snaresbrook Redbridge. Recorded thus in 1599 and on the OS map of 1805, from Middle English *broke* 'brook' with an uncertain first element, possibly a surname or Middle English *snare* 'a snare or trap for catching wild animals and birds'. The small stream here flowed into the River RODING; there is still a piece of water at Snaresbrook known as Eagle Pond (named from the *Eagle Inn*, earlier the *Spread Eagle* coaching inn), which was earlier *Snares pond* on Rocque's map of 1746. On this same map the brook itself is marked as *Sayesbrook*, perhaps an alternative name and clearly to be associated with a tenement called *Sayes* 1383 and with the 19th-century field names *Great & Little Seas*: these would all seem to derive from a different Middle English surname *Say* (recorded in nearby Essex parishes from the 13th century).

Snow Hill (near West Smithfield) City. *Snore Hylle* 13th century, *Snowrehille* 1507, *Snourehilstrete* 1544, *Snore hill* 1598, from an Old English word **snōr* 'road that curves across a gradient' and *hyll*. The short road still so named is indeed a relatively steep and winding one, although it is not on the same line as the medieval one.

Soho Westminster. Recorded as *So Ho* 1632, *So Howe* 1634, *Sohoe* 1636, *Soe Hoe feildes* 1684. Named, remarkably enough, from a hunting cry (compare *tally-ho*), from the early association of this area with hunting before the open fields were built upon. There are records of hunting taking place here as early as 1562. Legend has it that this same call was used as a rallying cry by the Duke of Monmouth's supporters in the 1685 Rising, which may be the origin of another instance of the name Soho in Somerset: in fact the Duke's mansion, *Monmouth House* (built for him in the early 1690s, demolished in 1773), stood in Soho Square.

Somerset House (in Strand) Westminster. Marked thus on Norden's map of 1593, so named from the former Renaissance palace built here by the Lord Protector *Somerset* in the reign of Edward VI (1547–53). It was earlier called *Somerset Place* in 1555, and later *Denmark House alias Somerset House alias Stronde House* in 1672, the alternative names referring to its situation in the STRAND and to the fact that James I had given the house to his Queen, Anne of *Denmark*, in 1603. The old house was demolished and replaced by the present imposing building *c*.1775.

Somers Town Camden. Marked thus on Greenwood's map of 1819, earlier *Sommers Town* 1795, so named because this was an urban development (begun *c*.1786) on the estate of Lord *Somers* (the family held lands here from at least as early as 1697).

South Acton Ealing, *see* ACTON.

Southall Ealing. *Suhaull* 1198, *Sudhale* 1204, *Suthale* 1274, *Southalle* 1345, *Southolt* 1710, that is 'southern nook(s) of land', from Old English *sūth* and *halh*, thus distinguished from NORTHOLT which contains the same final element. The manor house at Southall dates partly from the 16th century or earlier and the weekly livestock market here has the oldest horse auctions in London, going back at least 300 years. **Southall Green** is marked thus on the Ordnance Survey map of 1822.

Southampton Buildings, Place & Row (in Holborn) Camden. Named from Thomas Wriothesley, 4th Earl of *Southampton*, *see* Bloomsbury Square, *under* BLOOMSBURY.

South Barnet, *see* BARNET, EAST.

South Beddington Sutton, *see* BEDDINGTON.

Southborough Bromley. Marked thus on the Ordnance Survey map of 1819, earlier *South Barrow* on Bowen's map of *c*.1762, *South Borow* or *Borough* on Hasted's maps of 1783 and 1797, probably 'south mound or hill', from Old English *sūth* and *beorg*; it lies to the south of BICKLEY.

Southborough (near Surbiton) Kingston. Residential district mainly developed from the late 19th century, so called from Southborough House (built 1808), which is marked as *Southborough Park* on the Ordnance Survey map of 1876. This apparently takes its name from nearby *Barrow Farm* on the earlier map of 1819, which represents the medieval manor of *la Bergh* 1241, *Berwe* 1263, *le Berowe* 1439, that is 'the mound or hill', from Old English *beorg*, *see also* BERRYLANDS which is named from the same manor.

South Bromley Tower Hamlets, *see* BROMLEY.

Southbury Enfield. Preserves a medieval name recorded in the old field name *Southberyfeld* 1420, *Southburyfeld* 1610, *Southbury Field c*.1800, that is probably '(field in) the southern part of the manor', from Middle English *bury*.

South Chingford Waltham Forest, *see* CHINGFORD.

South Croydon, *see* CROYDON.

Southend Lewisham. Marked thus on the Ordnance Survey map of 1805, earlier *the South End of Lewysham* in 1516 and *South end* on Bowen's map of *c*.1762, that is 'southern district or hamlet (of LEWISHAM)', from Middle English *ende*. This was a small rural village until the early 20th century, with its two watermills (the *Lower and Upper Mills*, the mill pond of the former surviving as PETER PAN'S POOL).

Southfields Wandsworth. *Suthfeld* 1247, *Southefeld gate* 1582, *South Field* 1816, 'the south arable common field (of WANDSWORTH)', from Old English *sūth* and *feld*. The corresponding *North Field* (shown adjacent to *South Field* on the Ordnance Survey map of 1816) was earlier *Nortfeld* 1247 and has been revived in the street name Northfields.

Southgate Enfield. *Suthgate* 1370, *Southgate* 1372, *le South gate* 1608, self-explanatory, 'the southern gate', from Old English *sūth* and *geat*. This hamlet developed in woodland by the south entrance to ENFIELD CHASE. **New Southgate**, marked thus on the Ordnance Survey map of 1904, developed in the late 19th century with the coming of the Great Northern Railway.

South Hackney, *see* HACKNEY.

South Hall (in Rainham) Havering. Marked thus on the Ordnance Survey map of 1805, earlier *Southhalle* 1338, *Southall* 1498, that is 'south manor house', from Middle English *southe* and *hall*.

South Hampstead Camden, *see* HAMPSTEAD.

South Harefield Hillingdon, *see* HAREFIELD.

South Harrow, *see* HARROW.

South Hornchurch Havering, *see* HORNCHURCH.

South Lambeth, *see* LAMBETH.

South Norwood Croydon, *see* NORWOOD.

South Quay Tower Hamlets. Station named from the southern quay of WEST INDIA DOCKS.

South Ruislip Hillingdon, *see* RUISLIP.

South Street (near Biggin Hill) Bromley. Marked thus on Bowen's map of *c.*1762 and on the Ordnance Survey map of 1819, 'south street of houses, south hamlet', from its situation south of BIGGIN HILL on the road to Westerham.

South Teddington Richmond, *see* TEDDINGTON.

South Tottenham Haringey, *see* TOTTENHAM.

Southwark (town and borough). *Sudwerca* 1086 (Domesday Book), *Suthgeweorke c.*1100, *Suthewerk* 1259, *Suthewark* 1298, that is 'southern defensive work or fort', from Old English *sūth* and *(ge)weorc*, referring to its situation at the southern end of London Bridge and to the south of the City. It is recorded earlier as *Suthriganaweorc* in the 10th century, that is 'fort of the men of Surrey'. The borough of Southwark once comprised a City ward known as *Bridge Without* (that is outside the City wall), created in 1550 and abolished in 1978, *see* THE BOROUGH and LONDON BRIDGE. The local pronunciation of Southwark is 'Sutherk' with a short vowel and with the *w* unsounded, in spite of its conservative spelling. **Southwark Bridge**, opened in 1921, replaced an earlier cast-iron bridge built in 1819. **Southwark Cathedral**, the Cathedral Church of St Saviour and St Mary Overie, is much restored but preserves parts of the earlier 12th- and 13th-century church on the site. Its original name was *St Mary Overee or Overeye* (recorded thus from 1353), that is 'St Mary over the river', from Old English *ēa*, but in 1539 at the Reformation the priory here was supressed and the church became *St Saviour's*, first becoming a Cathedral in 1897. **Southwark Park** was opened in 1869. Southwark was once renowned for its September fair, held here from the 15th century, the last in 1761. The London Borough of Southwark was created in 1965.

South Wimbledon Merton, *see* WIMBLEDON.

South Woodford Redbridge, *see* WOODFORD.

Spa Fields Islington. Recorded thus *c.*1820, named from *The Spaw* 1695, *London Spaw* 1746, that is 'the London spa' which was situated in the middle of the present open space. The chalybeate spring discovered here in 1684 was considered to have medicinal properties and the fashionable spa that developed had its heyday in the 18th century. It also gives name to nearby **Spa Green Estate** built in the late 1940s.

Spaniards Road (in Hampstead) Camden. Leads across Hampstead Heath (*see* HAMPSTEAD) to the 16th-century Spaniards Inn, traditionally said to have been named after two Spanish brothers who once owned it and who killed one another in a duel.

Spankers Hill Wood (in Richmond Park) Richmond. Named from *Spanker Hill* 1843, origin uncertain, but perhaps from the dialect word *spanker* 'something exceptional or striking', also used of 'a horse that travels quickly and smartly, a fast-moving horse'.

Speaker's Corner (at Marble Arch) Westminster. Famous spot at the north-east corner of HYDE PARK near MARBLE ARCH where any would-be public orator may stand and speak on any subject, thus as it were symbolizing everyone's right to free speech in this country. The legal right of assembly was first recognized here in 1872 after a large gathering some years before (protesting about changes in the Sunday trading laws) had been declared illegal.

Spencer Park Wandsworth. So named from land here once owned by the Earls *Spencer*, *see* EARLSFIELD.

Spitalfields Tower Hamlets. *Spittellond* 1399, *Spyttlefeildes* 1561, *Spittle Fields alias Lolsworth Fields c.*1580, *Spittell Feild* 1588, that is 'land belonging to the hospital or religious house', from Middle English *spitel* with *land* and *feld*, referring to property owned by the priory of St Mary Spital founded in 1197 and recorded as *Seintmariespitel in Shordich* 1394 (the site of the priory was in SHOREDITCH parish). The alternative name *Lolsworth* for the fields is earlier *Lollesworthe* 1278, 'enclosure of a man called *Loll', from an Old English personal name and *worth*. Spitalfields was famous for its fruit and vegetable market, established in 1682 but moved to a new site near TEMPLE MILLS in 1991, and in the 18th century it became a flourishing centre for silk-weaving as a result of the settlement of Huguenot refugees here.

Springfield Park (at Upper Clapton) Hackney. A recent self-explanatory name, no doubt like nearby Spring Hill and Spring Lane referring to a spring near the bank of the River LEA.

Spring Grove (at Isleworth) Hounslow. District developed after c.1850 named from a house so called, marked as *Springrove* on the Ordnance Survey map of 1816 and as *Spring Grove House* on Greenwood's map of 1819, occupying the site of an earlier house built 1645, no doubt self-explanatory, 'grove with a spring'. The present house (now part of Hounslow Borough College) was built 1892–4.

Spring Park (near Shirley) Croydon/Bromley. Marked thus on the Ordnance Survey map of 1819 but recorded earlier as *Spring Parke* in 1632, so called from the spring line along the wooded slope; indeed the River BECK rises here. The original wooded estate lay across the Surrey/Kent county boundary (which follows the river), hence the open ground still called Spring Park in WEST WICKHAM. The residential area was mainly developed from the 1930s but the early-18th-century Spring Park Lodge survives. Spring Park was earlier called *Cole Harbour* on Rocque's map of 1765, also *Cold Harbor* in 1819 and *Cold Harbour or Spring Park* in 1820, that is 'cold shelter' from Old English *cald* and *herebeorg*, probably a derogatory name for a cheerless dwelling.

Squirrels Heath Havering. Recorded with this spelling in the 16th century and on the Ordnance Survey map of 1805, so called because land here belonged to the *Squirrel* family whose ancestors appear in local documents from the 13th century as Geoffrey *Scurell* and John *Esquirell*. *Squirrels Farm* is also marked on the 1805 Ordnance Survey map.

Staining Lane (off Gresham Street) City. *Staninge lane* 1181–6, *Stannyngelane* 1273, to be associated with a nearby place called *Stæningahaga* 1053–65. These ancient names mean 'the lane and the messuage of the *Stæningas*' (that is 'the people from Staines' in Middlesex, now Surrey), from Old English *lane* and *haga*.

Stamford Bridge Hammersmith & Fulham. *Samfordesbregge* 1444, *Sampfordbregge* 1449, *Stamfordbregge* 1456, named from *Sandford* 1236, *Saunford* 1340, 'the sandy ford', from Old English *sand* and *ford* with the later addition of *brycg*. The original ford here (over COUNTERS CREEK) was superseded by a bridge carrying the main road from CHELSEA to FULHAM (the present KING'S ROAD).

Stamford Brook Hounslow. Marked thus on the Ordnance Survey map of 1876–7, district called after a small stream (now covered in) flowing into the River Thames just east of CHISWICK, recorded as *Stamford Brooke* in 1650 and named from *Staunford* 1274, that is 'stony ford' from Old English *stān* and *ford*. The original ford was probably where the old main road to the west crossed the stream.

Stamford Hill Hackney. *Saundfordhull* 1294, *Sampfordehill* 1410, *Samfordhell* 1433, *Stamford Hill* 1675, named from *Sanford* 1255, 'the sandy ford', from Old English *sand* and *ford* with the later addition of *hyll* 'hill'. The development here from *Sand-* to *Stam-* is the same as that for STAMFORD BRIDGE. The original ford was probably situated where the road called Stamford Hill crossed the small stream shown on the Ordnance Survey map of 1822 flowing east into the River LEA. The place was still a tiny hamlet in the middle of the 18th century.

Stane Street (name no longer used). Old Roman road which ran south from LONDON BRIDGE to Chichester in Sussex. This already ancient route was called *Stanstrete* in the 13th century, that is 'stone street', from Old English *stān* and *stræt*. Its course is represented by Borough High Street (*see* BOROUGH), Newington Causeway (*see* NEWINGTON), and further south, Kennington Park Road and Clapham Road.

Stanmore Harrow. *Stanmere* 1086 (Domesday Book), *Stanmere magna* 1235, *Greate Stanmare* 1392, *Much Stanmer* c.1580, that is 'stony pool', from Old English *stān* and *mere*, referring to one of the pools which still exist here where there are outcrops of gravel on the clay soil. The spelling *Stanmere* 793 sometimes cited is from a spurious charter. The second element has been confused with, and eventually replaced by, Old English *mōr* 'moor, marshy ground' but spellings in *-more* first appear in the 16th century. The place is still marked *Great Stanmore* on the Ordnance Survey map of 1904, the various affixes (Latin *magna*, Middle English *great* and *muche*) distinguishing it from **Little Stanmore** nearby, which is *Stanmera* 1086 (Domesday Book), *Stanmere parva* 1291, *Little Stanmore* 1599, *see also* WHITCHURCH GARDENS & LANE. **Stanmore Marsh** is marked thus on the Ordnance Survey map of 1822.

Staple Inn (in Holborn) Camden. *le Stapledhalle* 1333, *Stapelhyne in*

Holbourne 1436, *Staple Inne* c.1440, that is 'the hall or residence built with pillars', from Middle English **stapled* and *inn* (earlier *hall*). This was one of the 'Inns of Chancery' from 1378 until the 19th century, its present Hall dating from 1580.

Staples Corner Brent. This busy junction of the A5 with the North Circular was named from the nearby *Staples* bedding factory.

Star & Garter Home (at Richmond Hill) Richmond. Built c.1924 as a home for disabled soldiers, its name recalling the famous *Star and Garter* inn which stood on this site until it was destroyed by fire in 1870. The inn was so called c.1740 from the Earl of Dysart (of Ham House, *see* HAM) who was a member of the Noble Order of the Garter, *see* Richmond Hill, *under* RICHMOND.

Starveall Bridge (near Yiewsley) Hillingdon. Marked thus on the Ordnance Survey map of 1880, a crossing of the Grand Union Canal named from nearby *Starveall Farm* on the same map (altered to *Starvhall Farm* on the later map of 1904). This was a derogatory name for infertile or unproductive land.

Stepney Tower Hamlets. *Stybbanhythe* c.1000 (Anglo-Saxon charter), *Stibenhede* 1086 (Domesday Book), *Stibbeneie alias Stebenuthe* 1274, *Stebenheth alias Stepney* 1466, probably 'landing place of a man called **Stybba*', from an Old English personal name (genitive case -*n*) and Old English *hȳth*. Alternatively, the first element could be an Old English word **stybba* 'a stump, a pile', referring to the construction of the landing place, the original site of which was probably at RATCLIFF. In any case the name clearly indicates commercial activity along this stretch of the Thames as early as the late Anglo-Saxon period. Stepney is the only place in this area to be named in the great Domesday survey of 1086: at that date the manor of *Stibenhede* was the chief Middlesex estate of the Bishop of London. **Stepney Green** is named thus in 1692 and was the home of John *atte Grene* 1367, 'John (living) at the village green', from Middle English *grene*.

Steyne, The (at Acton) Ealing. So named in 1780 and marked thus on the Ordnance Survey map of 1876–7, from Old English **stæne* 'stony place'.

Stickleton Close (at Greenford) Ealing, *see* GREENFORD.

Stockwell Lambeth. *Stokewell* 1197, *Stocwelle* 1225, *Stokwell* 1247,

Stockewell 1294, that is 'spring or stream by a tree stump', from Old English *stocc* and *wella*. Stockwell was still a small rural village until the early 19th century.

Stoke Newington Hackney. *Neutone* 1086 (Domesday Book), *Neweton* 1197, *Newetoon Stoken* 1274, *Stokene Neuton* 1294, *Stokenewington* 1535, that is 'the new farmstead or settlement', from Old English *nīwe* (dative case *nīwan*) and *tūn*, with affix from Old English *stoccen* 'by the tree stumps' or 'made of logs'. The affix first appears in the 13th century and distinguishes this place from *Newenton Barwe*, the earlier name for the manor of HIGHBURY. It gives name to NEWINGTON GREEN.

Stonebridge Brent. Recorded as *Stone Bridge* on the Ordnance Survey map of 1822 and as *Stonebridge Farm* on that of 1876, named from *The Stone Bridge* 1741–5, a bridge taking the Harrow Road over the River BRENT. **Stonebridge Park** is a residential area developed from the 1870s.

Stonecot Hill (near North Cheam) Sutton. Marked as *Stone Cot Hill* on the Ordnance Survey map of 1819, named from *Stonecorte* 1373, *Stonecourt* 1449, *Stonecot House* 1876, that is 'stone-built manor house', from Middle English *stone* and *court* with the later addition of *hill*.

Stone Grove (near Edgware) Barnet. Marked thus on Greenwood's map of 1819 and the Ordnance Survey map of 1877, no doubt originally referring to woodland around the 10–mile stone (marking the distance from MARBLE ARCH) on WATLING STREET (here actually now also called Stonegrove).

Stoop Bridge (in Ilford) Redbridge. To be associated with *le Stulpe* 1609, *the Stoup* 1794, from the Essex dialect word *stoop* 'a short post fixed in the earth as a boundary mark'.

Strand Westminster. An old name, virtually unchanged in 900 years, recorded as *Stronde* in 1185, *la Stranda* in 1220, (street called) *la Straunde* in 1246, from Old English *strand* 'bank, shore'. Originally of course it described the Thames bank itself, at a time before embankment when the river was much wider than it is now, later referring to the important road along the bank linking the two cities of LONDON and WESTMINSTER. An earlier name (in the 13th century) for part of its course was *vicus Dacorum* or *Densemanestret* ('street of the Danes'), indicating a strong Danish community at that date around the church of ST CLEMENT DANES. During the 16th to 18th centuries, a maypole stood in the Strand, erected on the green outside the church of St Mary le Strand, *see* MAYPOLE.

Strand on the Green Hounslow. Recorded as *la Strond* 1269, *Stronde* 1353, *Strand Green* 1593, *Strand on Green* 1795, *Strand Green* 1822, from Old English *strand* 'bank or shore' with the later addition of *grene* 'village green'. The hamlet lies on the north bank of the River Thames. It is interesting to note that the street running along the waterfront is also itself called *Strand on the Green*.

Stratford Newham. *Strætforda* 1067, *Stratforde* c.1075, *Stretford* 1290, *Stratford* 1316, that is 'ford on a Roman road', from Old English *stræt* and *ford*, referring to the crossing of the various branches of the River LEA by the old Roman road from London (ALDGATE) to Colchester. In medieval times this place (in Essex) was given various affixes to distinguish it from Stratford-at-Bow (now BOW) on the other side of the river (then Middlesex): *Estratford* 1291 ('east'), *Stratforde Hamme* 1312 ('in the parish of West Ham'), *Abbei Stratford* 1389 and *Stretford Langthorn* 1366 (from the manor having once been in the possession of the former abbey of *Stratford Langthorne*). This abbey, one of the richest Cistercian houses in England, was founded here in 1135, flourishing for several centuries until it was dissolved in 1538. The affix *Langthorne* derives from land here called *on thone langan thorn* 'at the tall thorn tree' in a charter of 958, from Old English *lang* and *thorn*; this only survives in the names of Langthorne Road and Hospital in LEYTON. **Stratford Marsh**, marked on the Ordnance Survey map of 1876, is a low-lying area between channels of the River LEA. **Stratford New Town** is also named thus on the 1876 map; its southern part was built by the Eastern Counties Railway in the mid-19th century to house workers at its large locomotive and rolling stock works here, and was at first called *Hudson Town* after George Hudson, the so-called 'Railway King' who was then chairman of the company.

Stratford Bridge Hillingdon. So named in 1589, like the previous name originally 'ford on a Roman road' from Old English *stræt* and *ford*. Here the old main road from Bath into London (now the A4020) crosses the little River PINN.

Strawberry Hill (at Twickenham) Richmond. Marked thus on the Ordnance Survey map of 1816, a name given to the villa bought in 1748 by Horace Walpole, 4th Earl of Oxford, but already found in local field names like *Strawberry Hill Close* 1691. Strawberries were cultivated in this area by the Thames for the London markets from the 16th century onwards. The villa was originally built by the Earl of Bradford's coachman in 1698 and was known (perhaps somewhat derogatively) as *Chopped Straw Hall*. This house, transformed into a Gothic mansion by Walpole and later much enlarged, is now the Roman Catholic St Mary's College of Higher Education. A somewhat similar name, **Strawberry House** in BARNES (up to 1939 known as *Barnes Rectory*, of mainly 18th-century date), was perhaps influenced by this one. There is also a **Strawberry Lodge** at HACKBRIDGE.

Streatham Lambeth. *Estreham* (*sic*) 1086 (Domesday Book), *Stratham* 1175, *Stretham* 1225, *Streetham* 1422, that is 'homestead or village on a Roman road', from Old English *strǣt* and *hām*. Pre-Conquest spellings sometimes cited (*Stretham* 727, 933) are from forged charters. The Roman road referred to ran from London to Brighton, and its course from Streatham to CROYDON is closely followed by the A23 (Streatham High Road). **Streatham Common** is marked thus on the Ordnance Survey map of 1816; there was a fashionable spa near here during the 18th century, based on a medicinal spring discovered in 1659 and still marked *Wells* on the 1816 map. **Streatham Hill** is marked thus on the Ordnance Survey map of 1876; the area developed rapidly after the opening of the railway station here in 1856. **Streatham Park** was formerly the estate of the Thrale family, brewers from SOUTHWARK who built a Georgian mansion here in 1840 known as *Streatham Place* (demolished in 1863); their name survives in the street name Thrale Road. **Streatham Vale** was earlier *Lower Streatham*, as on the 1876 map; this area is referred to as *Suthstretham*, that is 'south Streatham', in 1244. Streatham is pronounced 'Strettem' (with a short vowel); in spite of the current spelling (first found in 1510) this has probably been the local pronunciation since medieval times.

Stroud Green (near Woodside) Croydon. *Strodegrene* 1483, *Stroud Green* 1749, named from *la Strode* 1279, *le Strod* 1296, which is Old English *strōd* 'marshy land overgrown with brushwood', with the later addition of Middle English *grene* 'village green'.

Stroud Green Haringey. *Strowde Grene* 1546, *Strodegrene* 1562, named from *Strode* 1407. Identical in origin with the previous name.

Stumpshill Wood, Stumps Hill Lane (near Beckenham) Bromley/ Lewisham. Preserve the old name *Stumeleshull* 1226, *Stomeshull* 1313,

Stombleshelle 1327, *Stumpes Hill* 1609, that is 'hill of the tree stump', from Old English **stumbel* and *hyll*.

Sudbrook Park (near Petersham) Richmond. Marked thus on the Ordnance Survey map of 1876, named from *Suthbrok* 1211, *Sudbrooke* 1550, that is 'the south brook', from Old English *sūth* and *brōc*, referring to a small stream here. The mansion of this name, rebuilt in the early 18th century, is now the home of Richmond Golf Club. **Sudbrook Lodge** dates from the late 17th century.

Sudbury Brent. *Suthbery* 1282, *Sudbery* 1294, *Sudbury* 1382, *Southbery* 1398, from Middle English *bury* in the sense 'manor house', with *s(o)uth* 'south' to distinguish it from a lost place called *Northburie* in the 16th century. Sudbury lies to the south of HARROW, so *Northburie* may refer to the manor house of Harrow itself. **Sudbury Hill** refers to the high ground north of Sudbury; *Sudburyhill House* is marked on the Ordnance Survey map of 1877.

Suffield Hatch & Road (near Chingford Hatch) Waltham Forest. Preserve the old name *Suthfeld* 1269, 'the south field' from Old English *sūth* and *feld*. Suffield Hatch is *Suffeild Hatch Grove* 1641, from Old English *hæcc* 'a hatch gate' as in Chingford Hatch (*see* CHINGFORD).

Suffolk Lane (off Upper Thames Street) City. *Suffolke Lane* in 1581, named from William de la Pole, created Duke of *Suffolk* in 1448, who had a house here.

Summerstown (near Upper Tooting) Wandsworth. First noted as *Summers Town* on Bryant's map of 1823, probably to be associated with the family of *Sumner* or *Summer* who are recorded locally from the 17th century, with *town* in the sense 'newly developed residential area'. This district was earlier known as *Garratt*, *see* GARRATT GREEN & LANE.

Sundridge Bromley. *Sundresse* 1210–12, *Sundrish* 1295, *Sundressh* 1301, *Sundresh* 1421, *Sunderidge* 1805, that is 'the separate or detached ploughed land' (probably indicating arable detached from the main estate), from Old English *sundor* and *ersc*. Sundridge in Kent (near Sevenoaks) has the same origin. **Sundridge Park** is marked on the Ordnance Survey map of 1876; the mansion here dates from the early 19th century.

Surbiton Kingston. *Suberton* 1179, *Surbeton* 1263, *Surpeton* 1486, *Surbiton* 1597, that is 'the southern grange or outlying farm', from Old English *sūth* and *bere-tūn*, so called in relation to NORBITON; both were granges of the royal manor of KINGSTON.

Surrey Docks Southwark. Station named from Surrey Commercial Docks, marked thus on the Ordnance Survey map of 1876 and closed in 1970, *see also* GREENLAND DOCK. The ancient county of Surrey, to which several of the boroughs in the south-west of the Greater London area historically belong (including SOUTHWARK), is recorded as *Suthrige* 722, *Sudrie* 1086 (Domesday Book), that is 'southerly district' (relative to Middlesex), from Old English *sūther* and **gē*.

Sutton (town and borough). *Sudtone* 1086 (Domesday Book), *Suttone* 1164, *Suthtona* 1174, that is 'the south farmstead or estate', from Old English *sūth* and *tūn*, probably so called in relation to MITCHAM and MORDEN. Pre-Conquest spellings sometimes cited like *Suthtone* 727 are from forged charters. **Sutton Common** is marked thus on the 1876 Ordnance Survey map. **Sutton New Town** developed on agricultural land from *c.*1850. The London Borough of Sutton was created in 1965.

Sutton Court Road (at Chiswick) Hounslow. Preserves the name of the old manor of *Sutton Court* (house demolished in 1896) marked thus on the Ordnance Survey map of 1876–7 and recorded from 1597, so named from *Suthtona* 1181, *Suttone* 1222, that is 'the south farm or estate', from Old English *sūth* and *tūn* with reference to ACTON which lies to the north. In the 15th century it is called *Sutton alias Bewregarde*, that is 'fine view' from Old French *beau* and *regard*.

Swakeleys (at Ickenham) Hillingdon. The name of an old manor recorded as *Swaleclyves maner* 1466, *Swalcliff* 1486, *Swacliff alias Swakeley* 1593, *Swakeleys* 1593, that is 'estate held by the *Swaleclyve* family'. Robert *de Swalclyve* (who may have come from Swalcliffe in Oxfordshire, Swalecliffe in Kent or Swallowcliffe in Wiltshire, all meaning 'swallow cliff') held the manor here in 1327. The present mansion was built *c.*1630, probably on the site of the earlier manor house.

Swan Lane (off Upper Thames Street) City. Named from a medieval tavern called *the Olde Swan*, but it was earlier known as *Ebbegate c.*1190, 1421, *Ebgate lane* 1603, referring to a watergate on the Thames, from Middle English *ebb* 'ebb, low tide' and *gate*.

Swiss Cottage Camden. District named from an inn, called *The Swiss Tavern* when it was first built in 1803–4, later renamed *Swiss Cottage* (because built in the style of a Swiss chalet). The original inn was on the site of a tollgate keeper's cottage.

Sydenham, Lower & Upper Lewisham. *Chipeham* 1206, *Shippenham* 1315, *Sipeham* 14th century, *Sypenham* 1560, *Sidenham* 1690, *Sidnum* c.1762, probably 'homestead or enclosure of a man called *Cippa', from an Old English personal name (genitive case -*n*) and Old English *hām* or *hamm*. The early change of *Ch-* to *S-* is probably due to Norman influence, whereas that of medial -*p*- to -*d*- seems to be a relatively late development (dating from the 17th century). The two areas of Lower and Upper Sydenham are thus differentiated on the Ordnance Survey map of 1876. **Sydenham Hill**, another area developed from the early 19th century, is also shown on the 1876 map. **Sydenham Wells Park** recalls the once fashionable spa established here in the 17th century after the discovery of medicinal springs.

Syon House, Syon Lane & Park (at Isleworth) Hounslow. Syon House is on the site of the former monastery of the Holy Saviour and St Brigid, founded at TWICKENHAM by Henry V in 1415 but moved here in 1431, to the name of which *de Syon* (that is 'of Zion') was added, apparently with reference to the hill of Zion in Jerusalem on which David built the Temple. The monastery is referred to as *Syon* in 1428, and after being annexed by Henry VIII in 1534, the monastery and estate were given to Edward Seymour, Duke of Somerset, who built the first house here (referred to as *Istelworth Syon*, that is 'Syon near ISLEWORTH', in 1564). Much improved and enlarged since, Syon house has been the home of the Percys, Dukes of Northumberland, since 1594, *see* DUKE OF NORTHUMBERLAND'S RIVER.

Tabard Street Southwark. Renamed thus in 1877 from its proximity to the site of the former *Tabard* inn (now Talbot Yard), the hostelry where Chaucer's pilgrims met in his *Canterbury Tales* (*c.*1387). Its earlier name was *Kentstret c.*1330, *Kentisshestrete* 1482, that is 'street leading to and from Kent', *see* OLD KENT ROAD.

Teddington Richmond. *Tudintun* 969 (spurious Anglo-Saxon charter), *Tudingtune c.*1000, *Tudington* 1274, *Tedinton* 1294, that is 'farmstead or estate associated with a man called Tuda', from an Old English personal name with Old English medial connective *-ing-* and *tūn*. **Teddington Lock & Weir** (at the highest point upstream of the tidal River Thames) are marked thus on the Ordnance Survey map of 1876; the suspension footbridge below the weir was built in 1888. **South Teddington** was developed from the end of the 19th century.

Telegraph Hill (near Chessington) Kingston. Marked thus on the Ordnance Survey map of 1878 and named from the *Telegraph* shown on the 1816 map; this is the highest spot in the borough at 248 ft. There is another Telegraph Hill near Hampstead Heath (*see* HAMPSTEAD), *see also* next name. These hills were all sites for telegraph stations, used from the end of the 18th century to convey information of impending danger or notable victory (such as Wellington's victory at Waterloo in 1815).

Telegraph Hill Park (near New Cross) Lewisham. Named from *Telegraph Hill* on the Ordnance Survey map of 1876, marked as simply *Telegraph* on that of 1816, *see* previous name. This is probably the hill (reaching 154 ft) referred to in the ancient name of PECKHAM.

Temple, The City. Recorded in 12th-century Latin documents as *Novum Templum* (that is 'the New Temple'), so called because it was a house belonging to the religious Order of Knights Templars, 'new' because it had moved to this site by the Thames *c.*1160 from an original location ('the Old Temple') in HOLBORN. The Templars' church, **Temple Church**, dating back to the 12th and 13th centuries, still survives. The

Order was founded in 1118 to protect pilgrims journeying to the Holy
Land, but became discredited in the 14th century and lost its possessions, including this one (*see* TEMPLE FORTUNE and TEMPLE MILLS for
other properties held by the Templars in medieval times). The premises were leased *c*.1348 to a body of lawyers, who eventually divided
themselves into the societies of the **Inner Temple** (so called in 1440)
and the **Middle Temple** (thus in 1404), these occupying the eastern
and western sides respectively of the original site. Nearby **Temple Bar**,
marking the western limits of the City, is mentioned as *barram Novi
Templi* in 1294 and as *la Temple Barre* in 1405, from Middle English *barre*
'a barrier or gate'. By the mid-14th century the arched gateway here
had a prison on top, and from *c*.1680–1745, after being rebuilt by
Wren, was much used to display the heads of traitors.

Temple Fortune (near Golders Green) Barnet. So named on Rocque's
map of 1754 and on the Ordnance Survey map of 1877. *Temple* is a
reference to the Knights Templars, who held land here or elsewhere in
the parish of HENDON in 1243. *Fortune* may be a complimentary
nickname for a well-favoured or fertile piece of land, with *fortune* in
the sense 'luck, success, prosperity'.

Temple Mills (near Leyton) Waltham Forest. Marked thus on the
Ordnance Survey map of 1876, earlier *Tempylmylle* 1461, *Temple Mill*
1805, so called because the watermill or mills here on the River LEA
belonged to the Knights Templars in medieval times (from the 13th
century). In 1897 the name Temple Mills was adopted for the wagon
department of the Great Eastern Railway.

Thames, River. London's great river has an ancient name of Celtic or
pre-Celtic (Old European) origin. It is recorded as *Tamesis* as early as 51
BC (in the writings of Julius Caesar), and other references include
Tamesa in 115, *Temis* in 683, and *Temes* in 843. The etymology and even
the root from which it is derived are uncertain. It may come from a
Celtic root **tam-* probably meaning 'dark' or rather a pre-Celtic (Old
European) root **tā-* meaning 'melt, flow turbidly' referring to muddy
waters. Other English river names, including the Tame in Yorkshire
and Warwickshire, the Team in Durham, and the Thame in Oxfordshire, may well have the same derivation, whatever that is.

Thamesmead Bexley/Greenwich. New town developed from 1967 on
low-lying land by the River Thames, once part of ERITH and PLUM-
STEAD Marshes.

Thames Street, Lower & Upper City. Recorded as *la rue de Thamise* c.1208 (in a French document), *vicus super Ripam Tamis* 1222 (in a Latin source), *Tamisestrete* 1275, *Temestret* 1308, that is 'street on the bank of the Thames'. This street, the longest in the City and now divided into *Lower* and *Upper* at LONDON BRIDGE, follows the line of the old Roman riverside wall on the south side of the City.

Thornton Heath Croydon. Marked thus on the Ordnance Survey map of 1819, earlier *Thorneton hethe* 1511, that is 'heath by the thorn-tree farmstead', from Old English *thorn*, *tūn* and *hǣth*. The road crossing the heath from CROYDON to STREATHAM was notorious for its highwaymen during the 17th and 18th centuries; indeed the legendary Dick Turpin, hanged at York in 1739, is said to have lived and practised his trade near here.

Threadneedle Street City. First recorded as *Three needle Street* 1598, later as *Thred-needle-street* 1616, *Thridneedle Street* 1656, *Threed Needle Street* 1666. Possibly named from the *three needles* which appear in the arms of the Needlemakers' Company (if the 1598 spelling is reliable), but perhaps more likely so called from the *thread and needle* in the arms of the Merchant Taylors' Company; this guild is much older than its first charter of 1327, and in fact the Merchant Taylors' Hall has stood on its present site in this street since the 14th century.

Three Mill Lane, Three Mills Wall River Newham, *see* MILL MEADS.

Thrift, Great & Little (in Petts Wood) Bromley. Recorded as *the Frythe* 1387, from Old English *fyrhth(e)* 'woodland', often 'sparse woodland or scrub'. The development of *frith* to *thrift* is common in the south-east dialects, see also next name.

Thrift Wood (near Croham Hurst) Croydon. *Frith Wood* 1843, from Old English *fyrhth(e)* 'sparse woodland' as in the previous name.

Throgmorton Street City. Recorded as *Throkmorton* or *Throgmorton Street* in Stow's *Survey of London* (1598), named after Sir Nicholas *Throckmorton* (1515–71), ambassador to France and Scotland during the reign of Queen Elizabeth I. The family surname comes from Throckmorton in Worcestershire.

Tokyngton Brent. *Tokinton* 1194, *Toketon* 1235, *Tokyngton* 1508, *Okington* 1594, that is 'farmstead or estate associated with a man called *Toca', from an Old English personal name with Old English medial *-ing-* and *tūn*. The alternative form *Oakington* with loss of initial *T-* as in the 1594 spelling is found on the Ordnance Survey map of 1822 and was still in use until *c.*1950.

Tollington Park, Road & Way (at Highbury) Islington. Preserve the name of the old manor of *Tollington*, earlier *Tollandune c.*1000 (Anglo-Saxon charter), *Tolentone* 1086 (Domesday Book), *Tolindon* 1274, 'hill of a man called *Tolla*', from an Old English personal name (genitive case *-n*) and Old English *dūn*. Remains of the old moated manor house to the north of Tollington Road survived until the mid-19th century.

Tolworth Kingston. *Taleorde* 1086 (Domesday Book), *Talewurtha* 12th century, *Talworth* 1352, *Tolworth* 1601, that is 'enclosed settlement of a man called *Tala*', from Old English *worth* and an Old English personal name. It still appears as *Talworth* as late as the Ordnance Survey maps of 1819 and 1876. The tall office block known as Tolworth Tower was built in the early 1960s.

Tooley Street (in Bermondsey) Southwark. Remarkably enough, a corruption of *St Olaves Street* 1598, later *St Tooley's Street* 1606, *Towles Street* 1608, *St Tulies Streete c.*1665, *St Olaves alias Tooly Street* 1682, so called from the former church of *St Olave* (demolished in 1928, its site now occupied by HAY'S WHARF). In popular speech the final *-t* of the word *Saint* became attached to the personal name, as in the word *tawdry* which is derived from *St Audrey*.

Tooting Bec & Graveney, Upper Tooting Wandsworth. *Totinge* 727 (spurious Anglo-Saxon charter), *Totinges* 1086 (Domesday Book), *Totinge de Bek* 1255, *Thoting Gravenel* 1272, *Totingraveney* 1316, *Totingbek* 1333, possibly '(settlement of) the family or followers of a man called Tōta', from an Old English personal name and *-ingas*. Alternatively 'people of the lookout place', if the first element is rather the Old English word *tōt*. This is in any case an Anglo-Saxon folk name of early type. The estate was divided into two manors from the time of Domesday Book, hence the distinguishing affixes. **Tooting Bec** (also called *Upper Tooting* as on the Ordnance Survey map of 1816) was held by the Benedictine Abbey of St Mary of *Bech* (Bec-Hellouin in Normandy) from 1086. **Tooting Graveney** (also *Lower Tooting* as on the Ordnance Survey map of 1876) was held by the *de Gravenel* or *de Graveney* family (probably from Graveney in Kent) from the early 13th century; this manor gives its name to the River GRAVENEY. **Tooting Bec Common** is marked thus on the Ordnance Survey map of 1876, but both this and the adjacent **Tooting**

Graveney Common are referred to in the 17th century. **Tooting Broadway** station is named from the street so called.

Topsfield Parade & Road (at Crouch End) Haringey. Preserve the old name of the manor of *Toppesfeldes* 1375, *Toppesfeld* 1467, *Toppesfeld Hall* 1483, so called from the family of Thomas *de Toppesfeld* 1343 who originally came from Toppesfield near Halstead in Essex. The late 18th-century house called *Topsfield Hall*, built to replace the earlier hall, was demolished in 1895.

Tothill Street (near St James's Park) Westminster. Recorded as *Tothull street* in 1372, *Totehilstrete* 1480, so named because it was the street leading to a place called *Tothulle* or *Tothill* in the late 12th century, *Touthull* in 1256, that is 'the lookout hill or mound', from Old English **tōt-hyll*.

Tottenham Haringey. *Toteham* 1086 (Domesday Book), *Totenham* 1189, *Tottenham* 1254, *Totnam* 1515, that is 'homestead or village of a man called Totta', from an Old English personal name (genitive case -*n*) and Old English *hām*. **Tottenham Hale** (marked thus on Rocque's map of 1754) was earlier *le Hale* 1502, *the Hale* 1547, that is 'the nook or corner of land' from Old English *halh* (dative case *hale*), and is referred to in the surname of Richard *atte Hale* 1274 ('at the nook'). The Hale is still the name of a street here. **South Tottenham** was developed from the end of the 19th century.

Tottenham Court Road Camden. Earlier *Tottenham Court Row* 1708, so called because it led from ST GILES to the ancient manor of *Tottenham Court*, recorded as *Thottanheale c.*1000 (Anglo-Saxon charter), *Totteneheale c.*1050, *Totenhale* 1184, *Totenhalecourt* 1487, that is 'nook of land of a man called Totta', from an Old English personal name (genitive case -*n*) and Old English *halh*. The original manor house (still existing in the 18th century) was situated near to the present-day EUSTON. Although this name contains the same Old English personal name as TOTTEN-HAM, it will be noted that the origins of the two names are quite different; it is only in relatively recent times that the old spelling *Totenhale* has been influenced by the name Tottenham, as in *Tottenham Court* on Rocque's map of 1741–5.

Totteridge Barnet. *Taderege* 12th century, *Taterige* 1230, *Tatterigg* 1251, *Tatteridge alias Totteridge* 1608, 'ridge of a man called Tāta', from an Old English personal name and Old English *hrycg*, referring to a ridge of

high ground here rising to some 400 ft. **Totteridge Green** is marked
thus on the Ordnance Survey map of 1822, likewise **Totteridge Park**
which is recorded as *Tattridge Park c.*1570.

Tower, The Tower Hamlets. First on record as *thone tur* 'the tower' in the
Anglo-Saxon Chronicle under the year 1097, from Middle English *tur*
(one of the first French loanwords to enter the English language). The
name of the central nucleus of the fortress, the original stone tower or
keep probably completed in the reign of William Rufus (1087–1101)
and later known as the *White Tower* after it was whitewashed in 1240,
was thus transferred to the whole stronghold. This was considerably
strengthened and added to by successive monarchs until Edward I
(1327–77) completed the great *Outer Wall* which incorporated the
Traitors' Gate. The Tower has been called the most perfect medieval
fortress in Britain, and in its long and turbulent history has served
both as royal palace and prison, as a place of splendid revelry, pa-
geantry and celebration but also of torture and execution. It gives
name to one of the ancient wards of the City. **Tower Bridge**, for almost
a century the only bridge over the Thames below LONDON BRIDGE,
was opened in 1894.

Tower Hamlets (borough). Recorded thus in 1636 and marked on Rocque's map of 1769 and on the Ordnance Survey map of 1904. The
name was first used in the 16th and 17th centuries to indicate a large
area of East London from which the Lieutenant of the TOWER had a
right to exact guard duty and muster a militia. Later it described a civil
and jurisdictional district, consisting of 21 hamlets in 1720, the same
area covered by the parliamentary borough of *Tower Hamlets* established in 1832. The name was then not used after 1918 until revived
for the new London borough created in 1965.

Tower Hill Tower Hamlets. *Tourhulle* 1343, *le Tourhill* 1348, *Toerhil* 1550,
from Old English *hyll.* From the 14th to the mid-18th century this was a
place of public execution, where those considered traitors (often
having been imprisoned in the TOWER) were beheaded (the last in
1747), and even in the later 18th century it was still the site of a
gallows where criminals were hanged. **Great Tower Street**, also named
from the Tower, is recorded even earlier, as *la Tourstrate* 1287.

Tower Royal (off Cannon Street) City. Street named from a large
medieval mansion that once stood here (until it was burnt down in the
Great Fire of 1666), referred to as *la Ryoll* in 1265, later *la Ryole* in 1304,

le Riall alias le toure in le Rioll 1529, so named from La Réole, a town near Bordeaux, from which wine was imported. It was no doubt so called because it was occupied by wine merchants.

Trafalgar Square Westminster. Famous meeting place constructed 1829–41, the name commemorating the Battle of *Trafalgar* (off the Spanish coast) in 1805 in which Lord Nelson was victorious but lost his life, *see* NELSON COLUMN. The Square covers the site of the *King's Mews*, recorded as *les Muwes* 1294, *The Muwes* 1405, originally the royal falconry where the medieval kings kept their hawks for hunting, later the royal stables during the reign of Elizabeth I (hence the word *mews* in the sense 'stable yard or courtyard', originally the plural form of Middle English *mue* or *mew* 'a cage for hawks').

Trent Park Enfield. Marked thus on the Ordnance Survey map of 1822, a transferred name from *Trento* in Northern Italy. The estate here, created out of ENFIELD CHASE in 1776, was leased by George III to his favourite doctor Sir Richard Jebb, who chose this name because it was at Trento (in the Tirol) that the king's brother, the Duke of Gloucester, had recently been saved from a serious illness.

Trig Lane (off Upper Thames Street) City. *Tryggeslane* 1422, *Trigg lane* 1603, so named from a family of fishmongers called *Trigge* recorded as living here by the Thames in the 14th and 15th centuries.

Trinity Place & Square (near Tower Hill) City. So named after *Trinity House*, situated in the square since 1796, the headquarters of the ancient Guild granted a charter by Henry VIII in 1514 with duties to safeguard navigation in territorial waters.

Tubbenden Lane (near Farnborough) Bromley. Preserves the old name *Tubbenden* (marked thus on the Ordnance Survey map of 1876), earlier *Tubindenn* 1240, *Tubbingden* 1309, that is 'woodland pasture (for swine) associated with a man called *Tubba', from an Old English personal name with Old English medial connective *-ing-* and *denn*.

Tufnell Park Islington. Area mainly developed in the 19th century and so named to commemorate William *Tufnell*, lord of the manor of BARNSBURY in 1753.

Tulse Hill Lambeth. Recorded thus in 1823 and named from the *Tulse* family, mentioned in local documents from 1656, who had an estate here. The area was mainly developed from the 1820s, more rapidly with the coming of the railway in 1869.

Turkey Street Enfield. Station named from the street which is recorded as *Tokestrete* 1441, *Tuckhey strete* 1610, *Tuckey street* c.1615, *Turkey street* 1805, probably 'street of houses (i.e. hamlet) associated with a family called *Toke(y)*', from Middle English *strete*. It gives name to **Turkey Brook** (a small tributary of the River LEA). It should be noted that the modern form of the name, *Turkey*, not in use before the 19th century, is no doubt due to folk etymology.

Turnagain Lane (off Farringdon Street) City. *Wendageyneslane* 1293, *Wendeagayneslane* 1349, *Turneageyne lane* 1415, *Windeagaine lane alias Turnagaine lane* 1603, that is 'turn back lane', a name for a blind alley or cul-de-sac from Middle English *wende* 'to turn' (replaced by *turne*) and *ageines* 'against, back'. In medieval times the lane ended at FLEET river.

Turnham Green Hounslow. *Turnhamgrene* 1396, named from *Turneham* c.1232, *Turnham* 1294, that is 'homestead or enclosure at a river bend', from Old English **trun, *turn* and either Old English *hām* or *hamm*, with the later addition of *grene* 'village green'. The first element (literally 'something that turns, hence a rounded or circular feature') probably refers to the great loop in the River Thames near CHISWICK.

Turnmill Street (near Farringdon) Islington. *Trilmullestrete* 1374, *Tryllemylstrete* 1474, *Turnmelstrete* 1567, named from a former mill called *Trillemille* 1294, probably 'mill that turns, mill with a wheel', from Middle English *mille* with the verb *trille* 'to turn' or a corresponding noun meaning 'that which turns, a mill wheel'. In either case the first element has been eventually replaced by the synonymous word *turn*. The mill also gave name to a stretch of the River HOLBORN or FLEET, referred to as *Trynmylbroke* 1422, *Turnemyll Broke* 1502, from Middle English *broke* 'brook'.

Turnpike Lane (at Hornsey) Haringey. Station named from the lane which is referred to as *Turnpike Road* in 1813, so called from the *turnpike* or toll gate at the road junction here (marked *T. Pike* on the Ordnance Survey map of 1822). Turnpikes were to be found on many roads leading into London until they were removed in the mid-19th century.

Turpington Lane (in Southborough) Bromley. Preserves the old name *Turpington* found as *Tropyndenn* 1313, that is 'woodland pasture (for swine) associated with a man called **Troppa*', from an Old English personal name with Old English medial connective *-ing-* and *denn*. The lane itself was earlier known as *Slough Lane*, so named from *Slough Farm*, from Old English *slōh* 'muddy place, marsh'.

Twickenham Richmond. *Tuicanhom* 704, *Tuiccanham* 948 (Anglo-Saxon charters), *Twykenham* 1279, *Twicknem* 1651, probably 'river-bend land of a man called *Twicca', from an Old English personal name (genitive case -*n*) and Old English *hamm*. Alternatively, the first element may be an Old English word *twicce 'river fork' (with reference to the situation of Twickenham on a tongue of land between the River CRANE and the River Thames). **Twickenham Bridge** was opened in 1933. **Twickenham Rugby Football Ground**, the headquarters of the Rugby Football Union, was opened here in 1907; at first it was nicknamed *Billy Williams's Cabbage Patch* after the purchasor of the site!

Twyford Abbey (near Hanger Lane) Ealing. Built in the early 19th century and marked thus on the Ordnance Survey map of 1876–7, named from the ancient parish of Twyford recorded as *Tueverde* 1086 (Domesday Book), *Twiferde* 1183, *Twiford* 1199, that is 'double ford', from Old English *twī-fyrde. There were still two fords near here over the River BRENT until recent times.

Tyburn Way Westminster. Preserves the ancient river name *Tyburn*, also the earlier name for MARYLEBONE where the name is discussed. Here, on a road-island by MARBLE ARCH, is the site of *Tyburn Tree*, the notorious place of execution last used as a gallows in 1783. The nearby Hyde Park Estate, developed in the early 19th century, was formerly known as *Tyburnia* (a coinage of the same kind as BELGRAVIA and FITZROVIA).

Tylers Common (near Harold Wood) Havering. Marked thus on the Ordnance Survey map of 1805, named from *Tigelhyrste* 1062, *Tyelerst* 1270, *Tilherst* 1400, *Tylehurst* 1484, that is 'wooded hill where tiles are made', from Old English *tigel* and *hyrst*. The wood also gave name to the house called *Tyler's* 1768, *Tylers Hall* 1805. The area was known for its brickmaking and tilemaking; *Brick House* is marked just south of Tylers Common on the 1805 Ordnance Survey map. Tilehurst in Berkshire is a name identical in origin.

U

Underhill Barnet. Recorded thus on the Ordnance Survey map of 1887, self-explanatory, 'place beneath the hill'.

Uphall (near Ilford) Redbridge. Marked as *Up Hall* on the Ordnance Survey map of 1805, earlier *Uphall* 1539, probably 'upper or higher manor house', from Middle English *up(p)* and *hall*.

Upminster Havering. *Upmynstre* 1062, *Upmunstra* 1086 (Domesday Book), *Uppeministr* 1216, *Upmenstre* 1247, that is 'higher minster', from Old English *upp* and *mynster* 'minster or large church'. The first element refers to the slightly rising ground above INGREBOURNE RIVER. **Upminster Bridge**, originally referring to a crossing of the river by the road to Hornchurch, is marked on the Ordnance Survey map of 1805. **Upminster Hall**, also shown thus on the 1805 map, dates from the 15th and 16th centuries and was once the hunting lodge of the Abbot of Waltham Abbey. Nearby **Upminster Tithe Barn** also dates from the 15th century, and was probably used by the monks of Waltham. **Upminster Windmill**, a smock mill, was built in 1803.

Upney (near Barking) Barking & Dagenham. Recorded thus in 1456 and 1539 and on the Ordnance Survey map of 1805, '(land) upon the island', from Old English *uppan* and *ēg*. The second element suggests an area of dry ground amid low-lying marshland.

Upper Clapton Hackney, *see* CLAPTON.

Upper Edmonton Enfield, *see* EDMONTON.

Upper Elmers End Bromley, *see* ELMERS END.

Upper Holloway Islington, *see* HOLLOWAY.

Upper Norwood Croydon, *see* NORWOOD.

Upper Ruxley Bromley, *see* RUXLEY.

Upper Shirley Croydon, *see* SHIRLEY.

Upper Sydenham Lewisham, *see* SYDENHAM.

Upper Tooting Wandsworth, *see* TOOTING.

Upper Walthamstow Waltham Forest, *see* WALTHAMSTOW.

Upton (in Bexleyheath) Bexley. Marked thus on the Ordnance Survey map of 1805, earlier *Vpton* in 1292 and 1332, that is 'higher farmstead or estate', from Old English *upp* and *tūn*.

Upton, **Upton Park** Newham. *Hupinton* 1203, *Hopton* 1290, *Upton* 1485, identical in origin with the previous name. There is a slight rise here in an otherwise low-lying area of marshy ground.

Uxbridge Hillingdon. *Wixebrug, Oxebruge* c.1145, *Uxebrigge* 1200, *Woxe-bruge* 1219, *Wyxebrigge* 1220, that is 'bridge of the tribe called the *Wixan*', from Old English *brycg*, referring to an early crossing place over the River COLNE. The ancient Anglo-Saxon tribe called the *Wixan*, first mentioned in records as early as the 7th century, settled here and in other parts of Middlesex, including UXENDON. For the loss of initial *W-* in this and the following name, *compare* NORTH OCKENDON and YIEWSLEY. **Uxbridge Moor** is marked thus on the Ordnance Survey map of 1880, *moor* referring to marshy ground between the River COLNE and FRAY'S RIVER.

Uxendon Crescent & Hill (at Preston) Brent. Preserve the name of the old manor of *Uxendon*, recorded as *Woxindon* 1257, *Woxendon* 1282, *Oxindon* 1298, *Uxendon* 1593, that is 'hill of the tribe called the *Wixan*', from Old English *dūn* and the Old English tribal name also found in UXBRIDGE. The former farm here is shown as *Oxendon Farm* on the Ordnance Survey map of 1822, and as *Uxendon Farm* on the later maps of 1877 and 1904.

V

Valence House & Park (in Becontree) Barking & Dagenham. Named from *Valans* 1456, *Vallance* 1566, *Valence* 1594, a manorial name indicating the estate of the family of Aymer *de Valence*, Earl of Pembroke, who inherited the manor in 1309 (the surname is from one of the places called Valence in France). The present house is mainly 17th century but occupies a medieval moated site.

Valentines Park (near Ilford) Redbridge. Named from *Valentines*, recorded thus in 1665 and on the Ordnance Survey map of 1805, indicating land once held by a family called *Valentine*; the large house here (now the council offices for the borough of REDBRIDGE) dates from 1696.

Vale of Health (by Hampstead Heath) Camden. A once marshy and malarial valley bottom given this enticing complimentary name by developers in the early 19th century.

Vanbrugh Fields, Hill & Park (near Maze Hill) Greenwich. Named from Vanbrugh Castle, a castellated mansion built on MAZE HILL by Sir John *Vanbrugh* in 1719. The building was sometimes formerly known as 'The Bastille' from a fancied resemblance to its prototype in Paris.

Vauxhall Lambeth. *Faukeshale* 1279, *Faukeshalle* 1292, *Fauxhall* c.1600, *Vaux-Hall* 1719, that is 'hall or manor house held by a man called Falkes', from Middle English *hall* and an Old French personal name. The reference is to the infamous baron *Falkes* de Breauté, a supporter of King John who was granted the manor in 1233. **Vauxhall Bridge**, opened in 1906, replaced an earlier bridge (the first iron bridge across the Thames) built in 1816. **Vauxhall Park** was opened in 1890. Vauxhall was the site of the famous *Vauxhall Gardens*, opened c.1655 and known as *New Spring Gardens* until 1785; closed in 1840–1, they had their heyday in the 18th and early 19th century and are recalled in New Spring Gardens Walk near Vauxhall Bridge. Vauxhall is pronounced 'Voxhall'.

Victoria Westminster. District centred on **Victoria Station**, opened in 1860 and like nearby **Victoria Street** (constructed *c*.1850) named after Queen *Victoria*.

Victoria Embankment Westminster. Riverside road between WEST-MINSTER and BLACKFRIARS, constructed when the Thames was embanked in 1864–70 and so named in honour of Queen *Victoria*. It gives name to EMBANKMENT station. In earlier times of course, the road along part of this stretch of the river bank was the STRAND, hence its name.

Victoria Park Hackney/Tower Hamlets. Marked thus on the Ordnance Survey map of 1876. It was created as a public park on land formerly known as *The Bishop's Wood* or *Bonner's Fields* (*see* BONNER HALL BRIDGE), and was opened in 1845, its name celebrating the reigning Queen.

Vine Street (near Aldgate) City. Named thus in 1746, referring to a 'Vine Yard' mentioned in 1720. The street occupies part of what was once the city ditch (*see* HOUNDSDITCH) which was let out for various uses in the 16th century. There is another Vine Street near PICCADILLY, also perhaps the site of an early vineyard. **Vine Hill** in Clerkenwell may mark the site of a vineyard belonging to the Bishops of Ely, *see* ELY PLACE.

Vintry City. An ancient ward of the City, named from *Vinetria* 1244, *la Vinetrie* 1345, *le Vynetrie* 1410, *the Vyntre* 1550, that is 'the wine store', from Middle English *viniterie*, referring to the large wharf on the Thames where wine was unloaded, stored and sold by the vintners or wine merchants in early times. The present Vintners' Hall (on Upper Thames Street), dating from the 17th century, is within the ward, as is also the small street called **Vintners Place** which leads down to the river.

W

Waddington (near Old Coulsdon) Croydon. *Whatindone* 727, *Hwætedune* c.880 (Anglo-Saxon charters), *Watendone* 1086 (Domesday Book), *Whatendon* 1306, *Whadington* 1558, that is 'hill used for growing wheat', from Old English *hwæten* and *dūn*.

Waddon Croydon. *Waddone* 12th century, *Wadon* 1211, *Whaddon* 1241, *Woddon* 1279, that is 'hill where woad grows, or is grown', from Old English *wād* and *dūn*. Woad was widely cultivated in medieval times for its use as a blue dye, but by the 13th century most of that used in London was imported; the plant still grows wild in some areas. **Waddon Marsh** is low-lying near to the River WANDLE.

Walbrook City. *Walbrokstrate* 1292, *Walebrokstret* 1298. This street takes its name from a stream (covered over by c.1550) which ran into the River Thames at DOWGATE HILL, referred to as *Walebroc* in early 12th-century sources, that is 'brook of the Celts or Britons', from Old English *walh* (genitive case plural *wala*) and *brōc*. This interesting name suggests some survival of a native British element in the population into Anglo-Saxon times, *compare* WALLINGTON and WALWORTH. The brook also gives name to one of the ancient wards of the City.

Walham Green Hammersmith & Fulham. *Wendenegrene* 1386, *Wendenesgrene* 1397, *Wanam Grene* 1546, *Wallam Green* 1710, that is 'village green associated with a family called *(de) Wenden*', from Middle English *grene*. A family of this name is recorded in the parish of FULHAM from the 13th century; they probably came from Wendens (earlier *Wendene* 'the winding valley') in Essex.

Wallend Newham. Recorded thus c.1530 and marked as *Wall End* on the Ordnance Survey map of 1805, that is 'district (of EAST HAM) by the wall', from Middle English *wall* and *ende*. The 'wall' (perhaps an early riverside defence in this low-lying area by the River RODING) is referred to earlier in the surname of Semon *ate Walle* 1319, that is 'living at the wall', from Middle English *atte* 'at the'.

Wallington Sutton. *Waletona* c.1080, *Waletone* 1086 (Domesday Book), *Walton* c.1235, *Wallyngton* 1377, *Wallington alias Waleton* 1713, that is 'the farmstead or estate of the Britons', from Old English *wala* (genitive case plural of *walh* 'a Briton, a Welshman') and *tūn*. The relatively late development of medial *-ing-* (not found before the 14th century) is on the analogy of genuine *-ingtūn* names like BEDDINGTON and ADDING-TON. The name is of particular interest, since it implies the survival of an enclave of Britons here and their coexistence with the Saxons in this area in the centuries following the Anglo-Saxon settlement, *compare* WALBROOK and WALWORTH.

Wallwood Road (in Leytonstone) Waltham Forest. Preserves the old name *Wallewode* 1323, *Wallwood* 1589, that is 'the wood by the wall', from Middle English *wall* and *wode*. The 'wall' refers to Roman remains discovered here in the 18th century quite close to the course of the old Roman road, *see* LEYTONSTONE.

Walpole Park Ealing. Public park opened in 1898, named after Spencer *Walpole*, thrice Home Secretary during the period 1852–67, who lived at a property called *Elm Grove* near Ealing Common (*see* EALING).

Waltham Forest (borough). Now the name of a London borough (created 1965), but originally describing part of the vast royal hunting forest (later also known as EPPING FOREST) covering the south-west corner of Essex. It is recorded as *foresta de Wautham* 1261, *forest of Waltham* 1571, *Waltham Forest* 1654, and takes its name from Waltham (some 4 miles north of Chingford), which is *Waltham* in 1086 (Domesday Book) and means (significantly enough) 'homestead or village in a forest' from Old English *wald* and *hām*. Remnants of the forest still survive near CHINGFORD and WALTHAMSTOW (the latter not connected etymologically with the name of the borough in spite of its modern spelling).

Walthamstow Waltham Forest. *Wilcumestowe* c.1075, *Wilcumestou* 1086 (Domesday Book), *Welcomstowe* c.1120, *Walcumstowe* 1398, *Waltham-stowe* 1446, probably 'holy place where strangers or guests are welcome', from Old English *wilcuma* and *stōw*. Alternatively, 'holy place of a woman called Wilcume', if the first element is rather an Old English personal name. In either case the situation of Walthamstow and its 12th-century church of St Mary at an early crossroads on the route from London to Waltham Abbey in Essex (some 6 miles north from here) might suggest it was a place of hospitality and refuge in the

Anglo-Saxon period. The residential district of **Upper Walthamstow**
was developed from the end of the 19th century. The modern form of
the name, with *Waltham-* replacing the historical *Welcom-* or *Walcum-*, is
only common from the 16th century and is clearly in part due to
association with the name of Waltham Abbey, *see also* WALTHAM
FOREST which takes its name from this place.

Walworth Southwark. *Wealawyrth* 1001 (spurious Anglo-Saxon charter),
Waleorde 1086 (Domesday Book), *Wallewurth* 1196, *Walworth* 1354, that
is 'enclosed settlement of the Britons', from Old English *walh* (genitive
plural *wala*) and *worth* or *wyrth*. This name is particularly interesting
because it indicates the survival of a Celtic population in this area into
the Anglo-Saxon period, *compare* WALBROOK and WALLINGTON.

Wandle, River (rising near Croydon and flowing into the River Thames
at Wandsworth). A so-called back-formation from WANDSWORTH, first
recorded in a Latinized form *Vandalis riuulus* in 1586, and as *Vandal* or
Wandle in 1612. Its earlier name was *Hlida burnan* 11th century, *Ludeburne* 1255, that is 'stream called the loud one', from Old English **hlȳde*
and *burna*.

Wandle Park (near Waddon) Croydon. Named from the River WANDLE,
which flows through the park and rises near here.

Wandsworth (town and borough). *Wendleswurthe* 11th century, *Wandel-
esorde* 1086 (Domesday Book), *Wandesworth* 1200, *Wannesworth* 1393,
that is 'enclosed settlement of a man called **Wændel*', from an Old
English personal name and Old English *worth*. **Wandsworth Bridge**,
opened in 1940, replaced an earlier bridge built in 1870–3. **Wandsworth Common** is marked thus on the Ordnance Survey map of 1816.
Wandsworth Prison, originally known as the *Surrey House of Correction*,
was opened in 1851–2; it was here in 1895 that Oscar Wilde spent the
first six months of his sentence. The London Borough of Wandsworth
was created in 1965.

Wanstead Redbridge. *Wænstede c.*1055, *Wenstede* 1066, *Weneste da* 1086
(Domesday Book), *Wanstede* 1196, possibly 'place by a tumour-shaped
mound', from Old English *wænn* 'wen, lump' and *stede*; alternatively
'place where wagons are kept' if the first element is rather Old English
wæn 'wagon'. **Wanstead Flats**, marked thus on the Ordnance Survey
map of 1883, from *flat* 'stretch of level ground', are still called *Epping
Lower Forest* on the earlier map of 1805; this southern extremity of the

old forest is further indicated by nearby names like FOREST GATE and WOODGRANGE PARK. **Wanstead Park**, also marked thus on the 1883 map, incorporates part of the grounds of *Wanstead House* (demolished in 1824).

Wansunt Road (in Old Bexley) Bexley. Preserves the name of the old manor of *Wansunt* (marked thus on the Ordnance Survey maps of 1805 and 1905), which is recorded as *Wantesfonte* 1270, that is 'spring of a man called Want', from an Old English personal name and Old English **funta*. This place was near the River CRAY and within a mile of the old Roman road from London to Dover (WATLING STREET), and still had a pond in 1880; the 'spring' may have been a well sunk into the gravel here.

Wapping Tower Hamlets. *Wapping c.*1220, *Wappinges* 1231, *Wappyng* 1436, *Woppin* 1650, possibly '(settlement of) the family or followers of a man called *Wæppa', from an Old English personal name and *-ingas*, or '**Wæppa's place*', with singular *-ing*. Alternatively, 'marshy or miry place', from a derivative of a word related to Old English *wapol* 'pool, marsh, spring'. In medieval times (part of) it was also known as *Wappingge atte Wose* 1345 or *Wapping in the Woose c.*1510, that is 'at or in the muddy marsh' from Old English *wāse*. There is mention of *Wallemarshe alias Wapping Marshe* in 1562 and of *Wapping Walle* in 1611; the marsh was drained in the early 16th century, and the land later used for the *London Docks* (marked on the Ordnance Survey map of 1822) which opened in 1805 (but since the 1970s are filled in and redeveloped for housing). **Wapping High Street** (earlier simply *Wapping Street* 1703) was famous for its sailors' taverns, of which there were over 30 in the 18th century. The name is pronounced 'Wopping', already in use for several centuries as suggested by the 17th-century spelling.

Warren Farm (west of Romford) Havering. Marked as *Warren* on the Ordnance Survey map of 1883, earlier *Marks Warren* 1640, that is 'rabbit warren belonging to the manor of *Marks*', *see* MARKS GATE which lies just north of here. *Warren Stone* shown on a map of 1777 is a boundary mark of Hainault Forest (*see* HAINAULT).

Warren Street Camden. The street itself (from which the station takes its name) was so called in 1799 in honour of Anne *Warren*, wife of Charles Fitzroy (Baron Southampton), who inherited the manor of TOTTENHAM COURT from his grandfather the 2nd Duke of Grafton, *see* EUSTON.

Warwick Avenue & Gardens (in Maida Vale) Westminster. The street (which later gave name to the station) dates from the 1840s, but it was so called in honour of one Jane *Warwick* of Warwick Hall in Cumberland (now Cumbria) who married the heir to an estate here in 1778.

Warwick Lane & Square (off Newgate Street) City. The lane is *Werwyk Lane* 1475, *Warwyke lane* 1506, so named from the Earls of Warwick who had a tenement here in the 14th century and a town house known as *Warwick Inn* in the 15th. The lane was earlier called *Eldeneslane* 1257, *Oldeneslane* 1361, *Eldens lane alias Warwik lane* 1513, that is 'lane of the old dean' (probably referring to a dean of ST PAUL'S who once had a house here).

Water House (in Walthamstow) Waltham Forest. Marked thus on the Ordnance Survey map of 1805 and on an earlier map of 1777, so named because of its moat. This house, built *c.*1750 and the home of William Morris between 1848 and 1856, is now the William Morris Gallery with extensive displays of his textiles, wallpapers, and other works of art, *see* LLOYD PARK.

Waterloo, Waterloo Bridge Lambeth. Commemorating the famous battle of 1815, originally applied to the new bridge opened by the Prince Regent in 1817 and marked as *Waterloo Bridge* on the Ordnance Survey map of 1822, later applied to the main-line station (opened 1848) and to the locality. The present bridge dates from 1942.

Waterlow Park (near Highgate Hill) Camden. Named after Sir Sidney *Waterlow*, philanthropist and Lord Mayor of London (in 1872), who donated this part of his estate to the London County Council in 1889 for use as a public park.

Watling (at Burnt Oak) Barnet. 1930s residential estate named from its proximity to WATLING STREET, the old Roman road whose course is now represented by EDGWARE ROAD (A5).

Watling Street. Important old Roman road which ran from Dover in Kent via London and St Albans to Wroxeter in Shropshire. Its two alignments north and south of the River Thames may have originally converged at the lowest fordable point on the river near the site of what later became WESTMINSTER. It was called by the Anglo-Saxons *Wæclinga stræt* or *Wætlinga stræt* in the late 9th century, that is 'Roman road of the *Wæclingas* (the family or followers of a man called *Wacol)', from an Old English personal name with *-inga-* and *stræt*. The same folk name appears in *Wæclingaceaster* c.900, that is 'Roman fort of the *Wæclingas*', an early name for St Albans. It would seem then that the name *Watling Street* was applied to the stretch of the road between St Albans and London before it was extended to the whole length. The northern alignment (still followed by the course of the present A5 from MARBLE ARCH and now variously known as EDGWARE ROAD, MAIDA VALE, KILBURN High Road, SHOOT UP HILL, CRICKLEWOOD Broadway, BROCKLEY HILL, etc.) gives name to the modern district of WATLING, *see* previous name. Its alignment south of the Thames towards Dover crosses Greenwich Park (*see* GREENWICH) and runs east along the line of SHOOTERS HILL through BEXLEYHEATH and CRAYFORD (where it is still known as Watling Street) towards Dartford and the Kent coast. The small City street with the same name has a quite different origin, *see* next name.

Watling Street (near Cannon Street) City. Called *Watlingstrate* in 1307 and *Watheling streete* in 1603, but earlier *Aphelingestrate* c.1213, *Athelingstrate* 1289, *Athelingstrete* 1303, that is 'street of the prince or princes', from Old English *ætheling* (genitive case singular *-es* or plural *-a*) and *stræt*, *compare* ADDLE HILL. Even as early as the 14th century there was clearly confusion with the famous Roman road from Dover to St Albans called WATLING STREET, *see* previous name.

Waxwell Cottage & Lane (in Pinner) Harrow. Preserve the old name *Wakeswelle* 1274, *Waxwell* 1680, probably 'spring or stream of a man called **Wæcc*', from an Old English personal name and Old English *wella*.

Weald Brook (upper course of Ingrebourne River). Marked thus on the Ordnance Survey map of 1883, earlier *Weldeb(o)urne* 1297, so named with Old English *burna* 'stream' from South Weald in Essex (*Welde* 1062, Old English *weald* 'forest') by which it flows.

Wealdstone Harrow. Marked as *Weald Stone* on Rocque's map of 1754 and on the Ordnance Survey map of 1822, referring to a sarsen stone perhaps originally marking the boundary between HARROW WEALD and the rest of HARROW parish. The stone is mentioned in a document dated 1507–8 regarding the cleaning of a ditch 'lying between *le Weld* (i.e. Harrow Weald) and *le stone*', and may also be that referred to in the local surnames of John *atte Stone* ('at the stone') 1282 and John Stute de *Stone* 1548, from Middle English *atte* 'at the' and *stone*. It gives name to **Wealdstone Brook**, *le Weldebroke* in 1453, earlier *lidding* 767 (origin unknown). The growth of the district dates from the opening of the London & Birmingham Railway here in 1837.

Well Hall (near Eltham) Greenwich. Marked thus on the Ordnance Survey map of 1805, but earlier recorded as *Wellehawe* 1401, *Welhawe* 1446, that is 'hedged enclosure by a spring or stream', from Old English *wella* and *haga*. The original *hall* here was a Tudor mansion house dating from the early 16th century, rebuilt in the 18th century and finally demolished in 1931. On Bowen's map of *c*.1762 it is called *Well Place*.

Welling Bexley. *Wellyngs* 1362, *Wellynges* 1367, *Wellyng* 1370, *Well end* *c*.1762, possibly a manorial name from the family of Ralph *Willing* who held land in BEXLEY in 1301. However an alternative interpretation is '(place at) the spring(s)', from an Old English **w(i)elling* (a derivative with *-ing* of Old English *w(i)ella* 'spring, well, stream'), with reference to the springs in this vicinity, one being the source of the small stream feeding the lake in DANSON PARK. The *-s* in the 14th-century forms might then represent a plural (*wellings* 'springs') rather than a manorial possessive singular (*Welling's*), and of course the surname *Willing* may also derive from the place name and not vice versa.

Welsh Harp (Reservoir) (at West Hendon) Barnet. Popular alternative name for the Brent Reservoir (created 1835–9 by the damming of the River BRENT near its confluence with the SILK STREAM, *see* BRENT CROSS), transferred from the inn nearby called *Old Welsh Harp* (marked simply *The Harp* on the Ordnance Survey map of 1822, *The Old Welch Harp* on that of 1877), which was pulled down and rebuilt in 1937.

Wembley Brent. *Wembalea* 825 (Anglo-Saxon charter), *Wembanlea* 10th century, *Wembele* 1282, *Wemlee* 1387, *Wembley* 1535, that is 'woodland clearing of a man called *Wemba', from an Old English personal name and Old English *lēah*. The residential district of **North Wembley** is a 20th-century development. **Wembley Park** is marked as *Wembly Park* on the Ordnance Survey map of 1822 (then still describing a private estate of wooded parkland). After being acquired by the Metropolitan Railway Company in 1889 for leisure purposes the parkland later became the site of the British Empire Exhibition of 1924–5 for which **Wembley Stadium** was built in 1922–3. The nearby Wembley Arena was added in 1933–4.

Wennington (near Rainham) Havering. *Winintune* 1042–44, *Wemtuna* (*sic* for *Wenituna*) 1086 (Domesday Book), *Winintune c.*1100, *Weninton* 1190, *Wenyngton* 1324, that is 'farmstead or estate associated with a man called Wynna', from an Old English personal name with Old English medial connective *-ing-* and *tūn*. The spelling *Winintune* 969, sometimes cited as the earliest record for this name, is from a spurious charter. **Wennington Marshes** are marked *Wennington Marsh* on the Ordnance Survey map of 1805.

West Acton Ealing, *see* ACTON.

West Barnes Merton. *Westberne* 1290, *Westbarnes* 1538, *West Barns* 1819, 'the western barn(s)', from Old English *west* and *bere-ærn*; the place lies to the west of MERTON.

Westbourne Green Westminster. *Westborne Grene* 1548, *Wesborn Green* 1754, so named from a hamlet called *Westeburne* 1222, *Westbourne* 1294, that is '(place) west of the stream', from Old English *westan* and *burna*, with the later addition of Middle English *grene* 'village green'. The stream referred to, known as the **Westbourne Brook** (a later back-formation from the place name), rises in HAMPSTEAD and flows into the Thames at CHELSEA. It is now mainly covered in except where it flows through HYDE PARK and widens out (through damming) to form THE SERPENTINE. Rather more bizarrely, the brook is carried across the platforms at SLOANE SQUARE station in a huge 19th-century iron conduit! The station at **Westbourne Park** was opened in 1871.

West Brompton Kensington & Chelsea, *see* BROMPTON.

Westcombe Park Greenwich. Like the local street names Eastcombe Avenue and Westcombe Hill, preserves the name of the old manor of *Cumbe* 1044, 1226, shown on Bowen's map of *c.*1762 as divided into *East Combe* and *West Combe*, from Old English *cumb* 'valley'.

West Drayton Hillingdon. *Drægtun* 939 (spurious Anglo-Saxon charter), *Draitone* 1086 (Domesday Book), *Dreyton* 1314, *Westdrayton* 1465, from Old English *dræg* 'portage', 'sledge' and *tūn* 'estate', thus identical in origin with DRAYTON GREEN in Ealing, from which it is distinguished by the affix *West*. It lies near the River COLNE, to or from which loads were no doubt dragged across the marshy ground in early times.

West Dulwich Lambeth, *see* DULWICH.

West Ealing, *see* EALING.

West End (at Northolt) Ealing. Recorded thus in 1660 and also marked on Cary's map of 1786 and the Ordnance Survey map of 1816–22, earlier evidenced in the surname of Richard *atte* ('at the') *Westende* 1274, self-explanatory, this being the 'west end or district' of the parish of NORTHOLT, from Middle English *west* and *ende*.

West End, The Westminster. Term found from the beginning of the 19th century to describe that area of London lying west of CHARING CROSS and including the fashionable shopping district around OX-FORD STREET and REGENT STREET as well as MAYFAIR and the Parks, *compare* the parallel term EAST END.

West End Lane (at West Hampstead) Camden. So marked on Rocque's map of 1741–5, named from *West End*, earlier *le Westende* 1535, that is 'the western district (of HAMPSTEAD)', thus distinguished from NORTH END. The hamlet of *West End* (marked thus on the Ordnance Survey map of 1822) has now developed into the district of West Hampstead (*see* HAMPSTEAD).

Westferry Tower Hamlets. Station named from Westferry Road on the ISLE OF DOGS; a *ferry* across the River Thames from POPLAR to ROTHERHITHE is marked on the Ordnance Survey maps of 1876 and 1904.

West Green Haringey. *le Westgrene* 1502, *West Green* 1822, self-explanatory, 'western village green', from its situation on the west boundary of the parish of TOTTENHAM.

West Ham Newham, *see* HAM, EAST & WEST.

West Hampstead Camden, *see* HAMPSTEAD and WEST END LANE.

West Harrow, *see* HARROW.

West Heath Bexley. To be asociated with *Westheath House* marked on the Ordnance Survey map of 1888, thus named from the area of heathland west of LESSNESS HEATH.

West Hendon Barnet, *see* HENDON.

West Hill Wandsworth. Marked thus on the Ordnance Survey map of 1876, named from its situation to the west of WANDSWORTH.

West India Docks Tower Hamlets. Marked thus on the Ordnance Survey map of 1822 and opened in 1802, enabling the West India merchants to unload their ships in four days instead of the four weeks that had been needed previously. They were closed in 1980, but give name to the nearby **West India Quay** station, *see also* EAST INDIA DOCKS.

West Kilburn Westminster, *see* KILBURN.

West Lodge Park (near Hadley Wood) Enfield. Named from the *West Lodge* (recorded thus in 1702), one of three lodges originally built in 1399 around ENFIELD CHASE, the others being East Lodge (thus in 1609) and South Lodge (thus in 1750). West Lodge, now a hotel, was once the official dwelling of the Chief Ranger of the Chase, *see also* COCKFOSTERS.

Westminster (city and borough). Recorded as *Westmynster* in *c*.975, *Westminstre* in 1066, that is 'the west monastery', from Old English *west* and *mynster*, so called because it lay to the west of the City of London. An earlier spelling *Westmunster* occurs in an Anglo-Saxon charter dated 785 but the document is untrustworthy. The site of **Westminster Abbey** (originally a Benedictine monastic foundation certainly in existence by the 10th century) was earlier known as *Thorney* in 969, that is 'thorn-tree island', from Old English *thorn* and *ēg*, referring to a piece of land bounded by two branches of the *Tyburn* stream (for which, *see* MARYLEBONE) at its outfall into the Thames. **Westminster Bridge**, built 1854–62, replaced an earlier bridge opened in 1750. **Westminster Hall**, the only surviving part of the original royal *Palace of Westminster*, was built in 1097 by the Conqueror's son, William II. The present **Palace of Westminster** was built in the 1840s to be the new Houses of Parliament after the old *Palace* was destroyed in the disastrous fire of 1834.

West Norwood Lambeth. Formerly *Lower Norwood*, *see* NORWOOD.

West Ruislip Hillingdon, *see* RUISLIP.

West Smithfield City, *see* SMITHFIELD STREET.

West Wickham Bromley. *Wic hammes gemæru* 973 (Anglo-Saxon charter), *Wicheham* 1086 (Domesday Book), *Wicham* 1231, *Westwycham* 1284, probably 'homestead associated with a *vicus*, i.e. an earlier Romano-British settlement', from Old English **wīc-hām*. It is thus identical with EAST WICKHAM (some 10 miles north-east) from which 'west' later distinguished it: both names are likely to belong to the earliest stratum of Saxon names (see Introduction: 'The Anglo-Saxon Period').

West Wickham lay on the Roman road which formerly ran from Lewes to London; there are Roman settlement remains here. The first spelling (from a description of the Anglo-Saxon bounds of BROMLEY) contains the Old English word *gemǣre* 'boundary' and may also suggest confusion with the element *hamm* 'enclosure'. An even earlier reference, in another Bromley charter dated 862, is the phrase *Wichema mearcæ*, that is 'boundary of the people of Wickham', from Old English *hǣme* 'dwellers' and *mearc* 'mark, boundary'. The hamlet that became West Wickham town is named *Wickham Street* on the Ordnance Survey map of 1819, with *Wickham Green* nearby. **Wickham Court** (the manor house, now part of a school) is marked thus on the 1876 map; it was rebuilt as a fortified mansion in 1480.

Whalebone Lane (near Chadwell Heath) Barking & Dagenham. Like *Whalebone House* (marked thus on the Ordnance Survey map of 1805), so called from a pair of whale's jawbones once set up as an arch at the crossroads here (where the present-day Whalebone Lane North meets Whalebone Lane South) and referred to as *the Whalebone* in 1641.

Whetstone Barnet. *Wheston* 1417, *Whetstone* 1492, *Whetston* 16th century, from Old English *hwet-stān* 'a whetstone'. According to tradition there was once a large stone here used by soldiers to sharpen their weapons before the Battle of Barnet in 1471 (*see* HADLEY), but the name may rather have referred originally to a place where stone suitable for whetstones was to be found.

Whipps Cross (near Walthamstow) Waltham Forest. *Phyppys Crosse* 1517, *Fypps chrosse* 1537, *Phippes Cross* 1572, *Whipps Cross* 1636, that is 'cross or crossroads associated with the family called Phipp', from Middle English *cros*. There is record of a John *Phippe* in 1374. The dialectal sound development from F- to W- has led to the mistaken belief that the name relates to a whipping post set up in early times to punish offenders against the laws of the forest! The hospital here was built around the 18th-century *Forest House* (demolished 1964).

Whitchurch Gardens & Lane (at Stanmore) Harrow. Preserve the old parish name *Whitchurch* (shown on the Ordnance Survey map of 1822), earlier *Whyzt Churche* 1538, *Whytchurche* 1551, *Whitchurch alias Little Stanmer* 1590, 'the white church', i.e. probably 'the stone-built church', from Middle English *white* and *churche*. Its earlier name seems to have been *Little Stanmore*, which continued in use as an alternative, *see* STANMORE.

Whitechapel Tower Hamlets. *Whitechapele by Algate* 1340, *la White Chapel* 1344, *the paressh of the whitechapell* 1426, *parish of the Blessed Mary Matfelon of White Chapell* 1452, *parish of St Mary Matefelon alias Whitechappel* 1566, 'the white chapel', that is probably 'stone-built chapel', from Middle English *white* and *chapel*. The chapel from which the district came to be named was built in the 13th century and became the parish church of Whitechapel *c.*1338. The alternative spellings refer to the dedication of the chapel, the addition *Matfelon* being probably the name of a founder or benefactor to distinguish this church from others dedicated to St Mary.

White City Hammersmith & Fulham. So called from the white-stuccoed walls of the stadium and exhibition buildings opened here in 1908, originally as the venue for the Franco-British Exhibition and the 4th Olympic Games.

White Conduit Street Islington. Earlier *White Conduit Lane* 1735, named from a conduit which in the 15th century supplied water to CHARTERHOUSE.

Whitecross Street (near Barbican) City/Islington. *Whitecruchestrete* 1226, *Whitecrouchestrate* 1310, *Whitecrosse Strate* 1502, so named from a white stone cross (Middle English *crouch*) mentioned in the 13th century.

Whitehall Westminster. The present street takes its name from the former *Whitehall Palace*, otherwise known as *York Place* because it was the London residence of the Archbishops of York, which was burnt down in 1698 (only the Banqueting House survives). It is recorded as *Whitehale alias Yorke place* in 1530, and as *Whytthalle at Westminster that sometime was the bysshope of Yorkes place* in 1533. The Palace may have got its name 'the white hall' from the light-coloured stonework of the new Great Hall added to the original house in 1528 by Cardinal Wolsey, then Archbishop of York. However the name may have been given to the Palace (taken over by Henry VIII after Wolsey's fall) partly in imitation of the famous *White Hall* within the old *Palace* of WESTMINSTER. The street itself was extended in the 18th century, obliterating the north end of the old *King Street*, recorded as *Kyngestrete* in 1376 and as the *kings highway from Charyngcrosse to Westminster* in 1440.

White Hart Lane (at Tottenham) Haringey. The lane (also at a much later date giving name to the station) is recorded thus in 1600, and is so called after an early *White Hart* tavern. For the famous nickname of

Tottenham Hotspur Football Club whose ground is here, *see* NORTH-
UMBERLAND PARK which is nearby.

Whitehorse Lane & Road (at Selhurst/South Norwood) Croydon. Preserves an alternative name for the old manor of *Bensham* (*see* BENSHAM
LANE). This estate was held by Walter *Whithors*, the King's squire and
shieldbearer, in 1367, and is in fact referred to as *Bencham alias Whitehorse* in 1589. The last manor house here, built 1604, was pulled down
at the end of the 19th century. On the Ordnance Survey map of 1819,
the name is mistakenly represented as *White House Farm* and *White-
house Wood*.

White Lodge (in Richmond Park) Richmond. Marked thus on the
Ordnance Survey map of 1876, but shown as *New Lodge* on the earlier
map of 1816; the original Palladian villa (later much extended) dates
from the early 18th century and is now the Royal Ballet School.

Whitewebbs Park & Wood Enfield. Marked as *White Webbs Park* and
Whitewebbs Park Wood on the Ordnance Survey map of 1887, named
from *White Webbes* 1543, *White Webbs now called White Webbs place* 1610,
White Webbs 1822, that is 'estate of a family called *Whitewebb*'. The
surname is an occupational one meaning 'weaver of white cloth'.

Whitford Gardens (in Mitcham) Merton. Preserve the name of the old
manor of *Witford* 1086 (Domesday Book), *Wicford* 1199, *Wikeforde* 1200,
Wickford 1650, that is 'the ford by the trading settlement', from Old
English *wīc* and *ford*. The ford referred to was no doubt on the River
WANDLE. The change from *Wick-* to *Whit-* must be relatively recent (the
Domesday Book spelling *Wit-* is simply an error for *Wic-*).

Whitgift Hospital & School Croydon. Founded by John *Whitgift*, Archbishop of Canterbury in 1596–9, and originally part of the same complex of buildings of which only the almshouse remains. The present
school is sited at HALING PARK in a building dating from 1931. The
modern Whitgift Centre, developed from 1965, takes its name from
the same man.

Whittington Stone (at Highgate) Haringey. A stone (replacing earlier
ones and giving name to a public house) standing at the foot of Highgate Hill (*see* HIGHGATE) said to mark the spot where according to the
appealing legend Richard ('Dick') Whittington heard the sound of Bow
bells (those of St Mary-le-Bow in CHEAPSIDE) urging him to 'Turn
again, Whittington, thrice Mayor of London'. He was in fact four times

Lord Mayor of London (and a most effective one) during the period 1397–1420 and is also fittingly commemorated in the names of nearby **Whittington Hospital** and **Whittington Park**.

Whitton Richmond. *Wytton* 1274, *Whitton* 1352, *Whytton* 1357, probably 'white farmstead', from Old English *hwīt* and *tūn*, referring to stone buildings or to soil colour. Alternatively, the first element may be the Old English personal name *Hwīta*.

Whyteleafe (near Kenley) Croydon (partly Surrey). Residential district and station named from a field recorded as *White Leaf Field* in 1839, apparently so called from the aspens that grew there.

Wickham, East Bexley, *see* EAST WICKHAM.

Wickham, West Bromley, *see* WEST WICKHAM.

Widmore Bromley. *Withmere* 1226, *Wydemer* 1232, *Wythemere* 1313, *Widmere c.*1762, *Widmore* 1819, probably 'pool where withies (willow trees) grow', from Old English *wīthig* and *mere*. Confusion of the second element with Old English *mōr* 'moor, marshy ground' occurs from the late 16th century, when the place sometimes appears as *Wigmore*. The etymology is confirmed by references to a pond here, also the site of a cucking-stool, in 17th-century records; indeed the pond can still be seen on the Ordnance Survey map of 1819.

Wigmore Street (in Marylebone) Westminster. Recorded from 1792, earlier called *Wigmore Row* 1746, named after Edward Harley, 2nd Earl of Oxford, who also had the title of Baron *Wigmore* of Herefordshire, *see* HARLEY STREET.

Willesden Brent. *Wellesdone* 1086 (Domesday Book), *Wilesdune* 1185, *Wullesdon* 1248, *Wylsdon* 1563, that is 'hill with a spring or by a stream', from Old English *wiell* (genitive case *-es*) and *dūn*. The spellings *Wellesdune*, *Willesdone* 939 sometimes cited are from a spurious Anglo-Saxon charter. The usual spelling until *c.*1840 was *Wilsdon* (as on the 1822 Ordnance Survey map), but the unhistorical *Willesden* was adopted by the London & Birmingham Railway and appears on the later map of 1876 (*compare* NEASDEN). **Willesden Green**, formerly a distinct hamlet, is *Willesdone Grene* 1254, *Wilsdon grene* 1584, from Middle English *grene* 'village green'. **Willesden Junction** station, opened 1866, is marked thus on the 1876 map.

Wimbledon Merton. *Wunemannedune c.*950, *Wymmendona* 1154–61, *Wymendon* 13th century, *Wimeldon* 1202, *Wimbeldon* 1211, probably 'hill of a man called *Wynnmann', from Old English *dūn* and an Old English personal name. The change from medial *-en-* to *-el-* is probably due to Norman-French influence, and the *-b-* introduced from the 13th century is inorganic. **Wimbledon Chase** (station), so named when it was opened in 1929, like the nearby streets called The Chase and Chase Side Avenue, recalls the holding of a local stag hunt here during the 19th century. **Wimbledon Common**, recorded as *The common in Wymbyldon* 1490, is marked thus on the Ordnance Survey map of 1816; the windmill here, built in 1817 and now restored, is shown on the later map of 1876. **Wimbledon Park** is marked thus on the Ordnance Survey map of 1816; the All England Lawn Tennis & Croquet Club, host to the famous Wimbledon tennis championships, was moved here from WORPLE ROAD where it was founded in 1869. **South Wimbledon** is marked thus on the Ordnance Survey map of 1904, but is earlier called *New Wimbledon* on that of 1876.

Wimpole Street (in Marylebone) Westminster. Recorded as *Wimple Street* on Rocque's map of 1746, but in fact a transferred name from *Wimpole* in Cambridgeshire, where Edward Harley, 2nd Earl of Oxford, had other property, *see* HARLEY STREET.

Winchmore Hill Enfield. *Wynsemerhull* 1319, *Wynsmershull* 1395, *Wynsmorehyll* c.1530, *Winchmore Hill* 1586, possibly 'boundary hill of a man called Wynsige', from an Old English personal name with *mǣre* and *hyll*. The hamlet lay near the southern boundary of the ancient parish of EDMONTON. Alternatively, the second element may be Old English *mere* 'pool' with reference to a former pond here, drained c.1950.

Winn's Common (in Plumstead) Greenwich. So called from the family of Thomas *Winn* who held land adjacent to the eastern part of Plumstead Common (*see* PLUMSTEAD) in the mid-19th century.

Woodcock Hill & Park (near Preston) Brent. The former is *Woodcocks Hill* on Rocque's map of 1754, then *Woodcote Hill* (*sic*) on the Ordnance Survey map of 1822 and *Woodcock Hill* on that of 1877. Probably from the surname *Woodcock* of some local family. The 1822 spelling is no doubt an error, showing confusion with a different name.

Woodcote Croydon. *Wudecot* 1200, *la Wudecote* 1203, *Wodecote juxta Croydun* 1307, that is 'cottage(s) in or by a wood', from Old English *wudu* and *cot*. The same name occurs in Oxfordshire and other counties. **Little Woodcote** (in the borough of Sutton) is marked thus on the Ordnance

Survey maps of 1819 and 1876, in contrast with *Great Woodcote* (= Woodcote) on the 1876 map. **Woodcote Green** (also in Sutton) is near to *Woodcote Lodge* on the 1876 map, called *Woodcote Hall* in 1905.

Wood End (at Northolt) Ealing. Marked thus on the Ordnance Survey map of 1822 and as *Wood End Green* on Cary's map of 1786, recorded earlier as *Wodende* 1464, that is 'district (of the parish) by the wood', from Middle English *wode* and *ende*.

Wood End, Wood End Green Hillingdon. Marked on the Ordnance Survey map of 1880 as *Wood End* and *Woodend Green*, earlier *Wodehende* 1531, thus identical in origin with the previous name, here too with the later addition of *grene* 'village green'. The name may allude to part of the woodland for 400 swine mentioned in the description of the manor of HAYES in the Domesday Book of 1086.

Woodford Redbridge. *Wudeford, Wodeforda* 1062, *Wdefort* 1086 (Domesday Book), *Wodeforde* 1291, that is 'ford in or by the wood', from Old English *wudu* and *ford*. The original ford over the River RODING was replaced by a bridge before 1238 (a certain Thomas *de ponte de Wodeford* is recorded in that year); this is referred to as *Woodfordbrigge* in 1429 and gives name to the district of **Woodford Bridge** (marked thus on the Ordnance Survey map of 1805) which lies east of the river. **Woodford Green** is so marked on the 1883 Ordnance Survey map, but is called *Woodford Row* on the earlier map of 1805. **South Woodford** was developed from the end of the 19th century, and nearby **Woodford Side** is a recent name. **Woodford Wells** appears thus on the 1805 map, and is no doubt so called from springs here first mentioned in the surname of William *de fonte de Wodeford* 1285 (Latin 'of the spring') and later giving name to 'A dwelling House known by the sign of *the Wells*' 1722.

Woodgrange Park Newham. Named from *Woodgraunge* 1557, *Wood Grange* 1805, that is 'grange by the wood', from Middle English *wode* and *grange* 'an outlying farm (often belonging to a religious house) where crops are stored'. This estate belonged to the former abbey of *Stratford Langthorne* (for which, *see* STRATFORD). The 'wood' referred to was once at the southern end of Epping Forest, *see* FOREST GATE.

Wood Green Haringey. *Wodegrene* 1502, *Woodgreene* 1611, that is 'village green in or near woodland', from Middle English *wode* and *grene*. This was originally a hamlet at the edge of the extensively wooded area of ENFIELD CHASE.

Woodhall Drive & Gate (at Pinner) Harrow. Preserve the old name *Wodehalle* 1271, *la Wodehalle* 1274, *Wodhall* 1349, *Woodhall* 1573, that is 'hall or manor house by the wood', from Middle English *wode* and *hall*. It was near to Pinner Wood (*see* PINNER).

Woodlands Hounslow. Marked thus on the Ordnance Survey map of 1876, earlier *Wodelond* 1485, that is 'cultivated land by a wood', from Middle English *wode* and *land*.

Woodridings Avenue, Brook & Close (at Pinner) Harrow. Preserve the old name *Woodridings* marked thus on the Ordnance Survey map of 1877, earlier *Wodredynge* c.1530, *Woodreeding* 1733, *Woodready* 1822, that is 'clearing in the wood' from Middle English *wode* and *redyng*. It was near to Pinner Wood (*see* PINNER) and WOODHALL.

Woodside Croydon. *Woodesyde or Wodesyde* 1503, *Woodside* 1819, that is '(place at) the side of the wood', earlier simply *le Wode* 1452, and the home of Walter *ate Wode* 1332, 'at the wood', from Middle English *wode* and *side*. It lay on the southern edge of the once extensive woodland of NORWOOD.

Woodside Park (near North Finchley) Barnet. Named from *Woodside* 1686, *Woodside Farm & House* 1877, self-explanatory, 'place beside the wood', referring to the former woodland area north of FINCHLEY.

Wood Street City. *Wodestrata* 1157, *Wodestrate* c.1169, *Wudestrate* c.1171, that is 'street where wood was sold', from Middle English *wode* and *strete*. In early times this was one of several specialized market streets near to the main market of *Cheap* (for which, *see* CHEAPSIDE).

Wood Street (at Walthamstow) Waltham Forest. Once a hamlet to the east of WALTHAMSTOW, shown as *Wood Street* on the Ordnance Survey map of 1805 and recorded earlier as *Wodestrete* 1513, self-explanatory, 'hamlet by the wood', from its proximity to part of EPPING FOREST.

Woolwich Greenwich. *Uuluuich* 918, *Wulleuic* 964, *Hulviz* (sic) 1086 (Domesday Book), *Wulewic* 1227, that is 'trading settlement or harbour for wool', from Old English *wull* and *wīc*. Wool was an important and valuable commodity in medieval times. **Woolwich Arsenal** station is named from the Royal Arsenal, so called by George III in 1805 but established in the 17th century for the manufacture and testing of guns and other armaments; the Arsenal Football Club originated here in 1886, *see* ARSENAL. **Woolwich Common** is marked thus on the

Ordnance Survey map of 1805; part of it is Barrack Field, also shown on the 1805 map, so called from the Royal Artillery Barracks situated here. **Woolwich Dockyard** station is named from the Royal Dockyard (marked thus on the Ordnance Survey map of 1805) established here by Henry VIII in 1512 for the building of his flagship, the 'Great Harry'; the dockyard was closed in 1869 but some old features have been retained within the **Woolwich Dockyard Estate** started in 1969. **North Woolwich**, on the opposite bank of the River Thames from Woolwich itself in what was for 900 years a small detached part of Kent, is a name of 19th-century origin; possession of land on the north bank of the Thames may relate to early river crossings here (distant predecessors of the present-day Woolwich Free Ferry set up in 1889). The name Woolwich is pronounced 'Wullitch' or 'Wullidge', that is without sounding the medial *-w-*.

Worcester Park Sutton (but partly in Ewell, Surrey). So called on the Ordnance Survey map of 1819, named from *Worcester House*, residence of the Earl of Worcester who in 1606 was appointed Keeper of King Henry VIII's great Park of Nonsuch near Ewell. The Park itself remains but the magnificent Nonsuch Palace, built in 1538 on the site of the village of CUDDINGTON with stones from the dissolved Merton priory (*see* MERTON), was demolished in the late 17th century; its name, *Nonnesuche* in 1538, means literally 'none like it, without compare'.

World's End Enfield. A whimsical name for a dwelling or piece of land considered to be in a remote spot or one situated on the boundary of the parish (as this is). There is a much older example of the name in CHELSEA, recorded *c.*1670 and giving name to **World's End Passage**, so called in 1815; this was a tavern situated amid farmland at the western end of the old village, and therefore also considered remote! There is another **World's End** near CHELSFIELD, recorded on the Ordnance Survey map of 1819 and giving name to World's End Lane.

Wormholt Park (near Shepherd's Bush) Hammersmith & Fulham, *see* WORMWOOD SCRUBS.

Wormwood Scrubs Hammersmith & Fulham. Marked as *Wormholt Scrubbs* on Greenwood's map of 1819, and as *The Scrubs* on the Ordnance Survey map of 1822, named from *Wormeholte c.*1195, *Wermeholte* 1198, *Wormholtwode* 1437, *Wormewood* 1654, that is 'snake-infested thicket or wood', from Old English *wyrm* and *holt* (also *wudu*), with the later addition of *scrub* 'low stunted tree, brushwood'. The

original form of the name still appears on the Ordnance Survey map of
1822 as *Wormholt Farm* and survives as **Wormholt Park** near SHEP-
HERD'S BUSH. The prison here, built 1874–90 by the prisoners themselves, is known locally and colloquially as simply 'The Scrubs'.

Worple Road (in Wimbledon) Merton. Earlier *Warpelles* or *Warples* 1565,
*Worpole Lane c.*1745, from Old English **werpels* 'a path or track'. On the
Ordnance Survey map of 1816 there are two parallel lanes so called,
Middle Warpole Lane and *Lower Warpole*.

Worton Hall Estate (near Isleworth) Hounslow. Named from *Worton*
(marked thus on the Ordnance Survey map of 1816), which is earlier
Worton 1274, *Wortton* 1535, that is 'the herb or vegetable garden', from
Old English *wyrt-tūn*.

Wricklemarsh Road (near Kidbrooke) Greenwich. Preserves the name
of the old manor of *Wricklesmarsh* (marked thus on the Ordnance
Survey map of 1805), earlier *Witenemers* (sic) 1086 (Domesday Book),
Writelmerssh 1387, *Wrytelmersshe* 1388, *Whritelmershe* 1498, that is
'marsh by a babbling stream', from Old English **writol* and *mersc*. The
estate was bought in 1669 by Sir John Morden whose house here is
now Morden College.

Wrythe, The Sutton. *Rithe* 1229, *le Ryth* 1450, *la Rye* 1484, *Rye* 1819, that
is 'the small stream', from Old English *rīth*, referring to a branch of the
River WANDLE which rises near here. The modern spelling with unhistorical *W-* is first found on the Ordnance Survey map of 1867.

Wyck Gardens (at Brixton) Lambeth. Preserve the name of the old
manor of *le Wyk* 1271, *Wyck* 1291, *Wyk* 1329, that is 'the specialized
farm or trading settlement', from Old English *wīc*. Alternatively, it was
known as *Water Lambhith* 1495, *Waterlambeth* 1573, that is 'the LAM-
BETH manor by a pool or stream' (probably referring to the River
EFFRA which flowed just west of here). This manor was on the site of
Loughborough House, for which, *see* LOUGHBOROUGH JUNCTION & PARK.

Wyke Green (near Osterley Park) Hounslow. Marked thus on the
Ordnance Survey map of 1822, named from *la Wyke* 1238, *Wike* 1243,
that is 'the specialized farm or trading settlement', from Old English
wīc, with the later addition of *grene*.

Yeading (near Hayes) Hillingdon. *Geddinges* 716–57, *Geddingas* 793 (Anglo-Saxon charters), *Yeddings* 1325, *Yeddyng* 1331, that is '(settlement of) the family or followers of a man called Geddi', from an Old English personal name and Old English *-ingas*. This is therefore an Anglo-Saxon folk name of ancient type like BARKING and HAVERING. On the Ordnance Survey map of 1816–22 it is *Yedding Green*, earlier *Yedinge Grene* 1571, from Middle English *grene* 'village green'. In spite of the unhistorical modern spelling, the pronunciation of the name is 'Yedding'.

Yeading Brook (the upper course of the River Crane). Marked thus on the Ordnance Survey map of 1880, earlier *Yedding Brook* on the 1816–22 map, a late formation from YEADING. The earlier name of the river was *Fiscesburna*, 'the fish's stream', *see* River CRANE.

Yiewsley Hillingdon. *Wiuesleg* 1235, *Wyvesle* 1406, *Wewesley* 1593, *Yewsley* 1819, probably 'woodland clearing of a man called *Wifel', from an Old English personal name and Old English *lēah*. The development of the modern pronunciation and spelling from the more historical *Wewes-* is to be noted: the same loss of initial *W-* occurs in NORTH OCKENDON, UXBRIDGE, and UXENDON, but here a new prosthetic *Y-* has developed before the front vowel.

Glossary of the Elements Found in London Place Names

This list contains the words or elements that occur in the place names included in the alphabetical gazetteer, each element being followed by its meaning(s) and then by the name or names in which it is found. Place names no longer in current use are printed in italics, followed by the name (in brackets) under which they may be found in the gazetteer. The abbreviation OE stands for Old English, ME for Middle English, eModE for early Modern English, ModE for Modern English, and OFr for Old French. The Old English letter æ ('ash') represents a sound between *a* and *e*. The Old English letters 'thorn' and 'eth' have been rendered *th* throughout. Elements with an asterisk are postulated or hypothetical forms, that is they are words not recorded in independent use or only found in use at a later date.

abbeye *ME* abbey. Abbey Mills, Abbey Road, Abbey Wood (2), Westminster Abbey.

āc *OE*, **oke** *ME* oak tree. Acton, Honor Oak, Little Roke, Noak Hill.

adela *OE* dirty, muddy place. Addle Street.

adelphoi *Greek* brothers. Adelphi.

æcer *OE* plot of cultivated or arable land. Long Acre.

ætheling *OE* prince. Addle Hill, Watling Street.

æwell *OE* river spring, source. Carshalton.

æwelm *OE* river spring, source. River Cray.

ageines *ME* against, back. Turnagain Lane.

ald, eald *OE*, **olde, elde** *ME* old. Aldwych, *Eldedeneslane (earlier name for* Warwick Lane), Old Bailey, Oldchurch, Old Ford, Old Jewry, Old Oak Common, Old Street.

alder *ME* alder tree. Aldersbrook.

aley *ME* alley. Panyer Alley.

anerly *Scots dialect* solitary, lonely. Anerley.

apuldor *OE* apple tree. Aperfield.

arc, earc *OE* arc, chest, receptacle. Arkley.

ashe *ME* ash tree. Nash.

assise *OFr* seat, residence. Belsize Park.

āst *OE* oast, kiln. Limehouse.

atten *ME* at the. Nash, Noak Hill, Nower Hill.

atter *ME* at the. Little Roke.

*bæc-stān *OE* baking stone, stone used for baking. ?Baston Manor.

bǣr *OE* woodland pasture. ?Castlebar.

bærnet *OE* land cleared by burning. Barnet.

baille *ME* outwork or defensive rampart. Old Bailey.

banke *ME* bank, shore. Bankside, Millbank.

barbacane *OFr* outer fortification with watchtower. Barbican.

barne, *see* **bere-ærn**.

barre *ME* barrier, gate. Temple Bar.

bayard *ME* bay horse. ?Bayswater.

*b(e)alg *OE* smooth, rounded. Balham.

bēam *OE* beam of wood (*used as a footbridge*). Beam Bridge & River, Dagenham Beam Bridge.

bēan *OE* bean. Bandonhill, Benhilton.

beau *OFr* fine, beautiful. Beulah Hill, *Bewregarde* (*see* Sutton Court Road).

bece *OE* stream. ?Beech Street.

bēce *OE* beech tree. ?Beech Street.

beden, *see* **byden**.

bel *OFr* fine, beautiful. Belmont (4), Belsize Park, Belvedere.

belleyetere *ME* bellfounder. Billiter Square & Street.

beofor *OE* beaver. Beverley Brook.

beonet *OE* bent-grass. Bentley Priory.

beorg *OE* mound, rounded hill, barrow. Berrylands, Farnborough, Gosbury Hill, Romborough, Roxborough, Smallberry Green, Southborough (2).

*berdcherver *ME* beard-cutter, barber. ?Birchin Lane.

bere *OE* barley. Barwell Court.

bere-ærn *OE*, **barne** *ME* barn, store-house for barley. Barnes, Down Barns, West Barnes.

bere-tūn *OE* grange, outlying farm. Norbiton, Surbiton.

bere-wīc *OE* barley farm, outlying part of estate. Berwick Manor.

*bica *OE* pointed ridge. Bickley.

bigging *ME* building. Biggin Avenue, Biggin Hill.

bishop *ME* bishop. Bishopsgate, Bishop's Park, Bishopswood.

blæc *OE* black, dark-coloured. Blackbrook Lane, Blackfen, Blackheath, Blackwall.

boga *OE* bow, arch, arched bridge. Bow, Bow Lane, Bromley-by-Bow.

bon(e) *ME* bone. Bunhill Fields.

bord *OE* board, table, *also* border. ?Boston Manor, Langbourn.

borg-steall *OE* place of refuge or protection. Bostall.

borough *eModE* (from **burh** *OE*) suburb outside city wall. The Borough.

borow *ME* animal burrow. Broxhill Common & Road, The Burroughs.

bōt *OE* remedy. Botwell.

botm *OE* valley bottom. Locksbottom, Pratt's Bottom, Smithambottom.

bour *ME* bower, royal residence. Bower House, Havering-atte-Bower.

brād *OE*, **brade**, **brode** *ME* broad. Battle Bridge Road, Broad Green, Broad Street.

brade, *see* **brād**.

bræmbel *OE* bramble. Bromley.

breach *ModE* gap or break in river wall. Dagenham Breach.

bred *ME* bread. Bread Street.

*brigantiā *Celtic* holy one. River Brent.

brigge, *see* **brycg**.

brike *ME* brick, **brike-kiln** *ME* brick kiln. Brick Lane.

brōc *OE*, **broke** *ME* brook, stream. Aldersbrook, Blackbrook Lane, ?Brockley, Brook Green, Brook Street, Cranbrook, Eel Brook, Kidbrooke, Mayesbrook, Mutton Brook, Snaresbrook, Stamford Brook, Sudbrook, Walbrook, Wealdstone Brook.

brocc *OE*, **brok** *ME* badger. ?Brockley, ?Brockwell Park, Broxhill Common & Road.

brocc-hol *OE* badger hole. Brockley Hill.

brode, *see* **brād**.

brok, *see* **brocc**.

broke, *see* **brōc**.

brōm *OE* broom. Bromley, Brompton, Broomfield.

brycg *OE*, **brigge** *ME* bridge. Battle Bridge Road, Bollo Bridge, Greenford Bridge, Hackbridge, Knightsbridge, Lea Bridge, London Bridge, Mad Bridge, Phipps Bridge, Priests Bridge, Queen's Bridge, Redbridge, Risebridge, Stamford Bridge, Uxbridge, etc.

bugee, boge *ME* budge (a lambskin fur). Budge Row.

*****bula** *OE* bull. Bollo Bridge & Lane.

burh (*dative case* **byrig**) *OE* fortified place, **bury** *ME* manor, manor house (*see also* **borough**). Aldermanbury, Barnsbury, Bloomsbury, Brondesbury, Bucklersbury, Canbury, Canonbury, Claybury, Eastbury, Ebury, Edgware Bury, Finsbury, Gunnersbury, Highbury, Howbury, Kingsbury, Lothbury, Mapesbury Road, Newbury, Norbury, Ravensbury, St Paul's, Scadbury, Southbury, Sudbury.

burna *OE* stream. *Fiscesburna* (*earlier name for* Yeading Brook), *Heybourne* (*earlier name for* Deans Brook), Hideborne (*earlier name for* Falcon Brook), Holborn, Ingrebourne River, Kilburn, ?Langbourn, *Ludeburne* (*earlier name for* River Wandle), *Lurtebourne* (*earlier name for* Hogsmill River), Marylebone, Ravensbourne, Tyburn, Weald Brook, Westbourne Green.

burne-stede *OE* bathing place, watering place for cattle. Bursted Wood.

bury, *see* **burh**.

busshe *ME* bush. Bush Lane, Shepherd's Bush.

busshi *ME* bushy, covered in bushes. Bushey Mead, Bush Hill, Bushy Park.

butte *ME* archery butt. The Butts, Newington Butts.

byden, beden *OE* drinking vessel. East Bedfont.

*****byxe** *OE* box tree, box-tree thicket. Bexley.

cǣg *OE* key-shaped feature. ?Kew.

cærse *OE* watercress. Carshalton.

cald, ceald *OE* cold. Chadwell Heath, Chalk Farm, *Cold Harbour* (*see* Spring Park), Coldharbour (4).

camp *OE* enclosed land. Addiscombe.

candelwricht *ME* candle maker. Cannon Street, Candlewick.

canoun *ME* canon, member of religious order or cathedral chapter. Canbury, Cann Hall, Cannon Hill, Canonbury, Canons Park, ?Ken Wood.

cartere *ME* carter. Carter Lane.

castel *ME* castle, fortified or castellated mansion. Bruce Castle, Castlebar, Castle Baynard Street, Castle Green, Vanbrugh Castle (*see* Vanbrugh Fields).

catt *OE*, *ME* wildcat or domestic cat. Catford, *Cattestrete* (*here possibly* 'prostitute', *see* Gresham Street), Cattlegate.

caucie *ME* raised way across marshy ground. Newington Causeway.

cealc *OE* chalk, limestone. Chalk Wood, Chelsea.

ceald, *see* **cald**.

cēap *OE* market. Cheapside, Eastcheap.

*****cēd** *Celtic* wood. Penge.

*****ceg** *OE* tree stump. Cheam.

ceorl *OE* freeman, peasant. Charlton.

chace *ME* chase, tract of ground for hunting. Chase Cross, Chase Side, Enfield Chase, Wimbledon Chase.

change *OFr*, *ME* gold exchange, mint. New Change.

chapel *ME* chapel. Chapel End, Whitechapel.

chartrouse *OFr* house of Carthusian monks. Charterhouse.

chaunc(el)erie *ME* chancellor's office. Chancery Lane.

chockhole *ModE dialect* deep furrow or rut in a road. Chohole Gate.

churche, *see* **cirice**.

chute or **shoot** *ModE* place where debris is tipped. Mudchute.

cieping *OE* market. Chipping Barnet.

***c(i)erring** *OE* a turn or bend. Charing Cross.

***ciese** *OE* cheese. Chiswick.

***cingel** *OE* shingle. Chingford.

circus *eModE* circular open space at a road junction. Finsbury Circus, Oxford Circus, Piccadilly Circus, etc.

cirice *OE*, **churche** *ME* church. Abchurch, Church End, Church Hill, Fenchurch Street, Gracechurch Street, Hornchurch, Oldchurch, Whitchurch.

cisel *OE* gravel. Chislehurst.

clæg *OE*, **cleye** *ME* clay. Claybury, Clayhall, Clay Hill, Claysmore, Clay Tye Farm.

clam *ModE dialect* damp, cold and sticky. Clam Field.

clerc *ME* scholar, secretary, student. Clerkenwell.

cleye, *see* **clæg**.

clif *OE* bank, cliff. Ratcliff.

clink *eModE dialect* prison. Clink Street.

***clopp(a)** *OE* lump, hill. Clapham, Clapton.

cniht *OE* youth, young man, retainer, **knight** *ME* knight. Knighton Wood, Knightsbridge.

cnoll *OE* hillock. *Pinnesknol* (*earlier name for* Muswell Hill).

cnotta *OE* knot, lump. ?Notting Hill.

cocke *ME*, **cock** *eModE* (i) fighting cock. Cock Lane. (ii) leading, chief. Cockfosters.

cockpit *eModE* pit used for cockfighting. Cockpit Steps & Yard.

cockspur *eModE* steel spur fitted to fighting cocks. Cockspur Street.

col *OE* charcoal. Coldfall Wood.

***coleman** *ME* charcoal burner or seller. ?Coleman Street.

colier *ME* charcoal burner. Collier Row, Collier's Wood.

combe, *see* **cumb**.

comun *ME* common land, land belonging to the community. Barnes Common, Bow Common, Bromley Common, Clapham Common, etc.

coni *ME* rabbit. Coney Hall.

contesse *ME* countess. Counters Creek.

convent *ME* convent, monastery. Covent Garden.

copis *ME* coppice. Copse Hill & Wood.

coppede *OE* with a high peaked roof. Copthall.

cordewaner *ME* shoemaker. Cordwainer.

corn *OE* corn, grain. Cornhill.

corner *ME* angle, nook, corner (of parish), place where two streets meet. Amen Corner, Beddington Corner, Fallow Corner, Gallows Corner, Hawley's Corner, Hyde Park Corner, Padnall Corner.

corveiser *ME* shoemaker. Cordwainer.

cot (*plural* **cotu**) *OE* cottage. Chalk Farm, Eastcote, Woodcote.

court *ME* manor house, large mansion. Barons Court, Barwell Court, Earls Court, Hampton Court, Stonecot, Tottenham Court, Wickham Court, etc.

cran *OE* crane, *also probably* heron or similar bird. Cranbrook, Cranford.

crāwe *OE* crow. Cranham, Croham Hurst.

*crei *Celtic* fresh, clean. Crayford, River Cray.

creke *ME* creek, inlet. Barking Creek, Counters Creek, Creekmouth, Rainham Creek.

*crikeled *ME* indented, with an irregular outline. Cricklewood.

croh (*alternating with adjectival derivative* ***crogen**) *OE* wild saffron. Croydon.

crook *eModE* crooked, twisted. Crook Log.

cropp *OE* rounded hill. Crofton.

cros(s) *ME* cross, wayside crucifix, *also* crossroads. Brent Cross, Bulls Cross, Charing Cross, Cross Ness, Fair Cross, Fullwell Cross, New Cross, Whipps Cross.

crouch *ME* cross, wayside crucifix. Crouch End, Crouch Hill, Fair Cross, Whitecross Street.

crouched *ME* bearing or wearing a cross. Crutched Friars.

crypel-geat *OE* low gate in a wall. Cripplegate Street.

cū (genitive plural **cūna, cȳna**) *OE* cow. ?Kilburn.

cumb *OE*, **combe** *ME* coombe, valley (*especially used of a relatively short, broad valley*). Coombe (2), Hol(e)combe, Westcombe.

cwēn *OE* queen. Queenhithe, Queen's Bridge.

cyning *OE* king. Kensal Green, Kingsbury, Kingsland, Kingston.

cȳta *OE* kite. Kidbrooke.

dæl *OE* pit, hollow. ?Dawley.

dāl *OE*, **dole** *ME* share, portion of land in common field. ?Dawley, Dollis Brook.

dale *ModE* valley. Colindale, Holecombe Dale.

daneis *OFr*, **daneys** *ME* Danish, a Dane. St Clement Danes.

daneys, *see* **daneis**.

dell *ModE* hollow. Moorhall Dell.

dene (i) *ME* dean. Eldedeneslane (*earlier name for* Warwick Lane). (ii) *See* **denu**.

denn *OE* woodland pasture, especially for swine. Hockenden, ?Ramsden, Tubbenden, Turpington.

denu *OE*, **dene** *ME* valley (*especially used of a relatively long narrow valley*). Colindale, Croydon, Pripledeane (*see* Addington Hills), Smitham.

dēop *OE* deep. Deptford.

dēope *OE* deep place, valley. Colindeep Lane.

dīc *OE* ditch. Grim's Ditch, Houndsditch, Mardyke Farm, Shoreditch.

dile *OE* dill. Dulwich.

distaf *ME* stick that holds the bunch of flax or wool in spinning. Distaff Lane.

*dodd, *dodding *OE* rounded hill. ?Dudden Hill.

dok *ME* dock, wharf. Puddle Dock, St Katharine's Dock, St Saviour's Dock, Surrey Docks, etc.

dole, *see* **dāl**.

doun, *see* **dūn**.

dræg *OE* portage or slope for dragging down loads, *also* a dray or sledge. Drayton Green, West Drayton.

dūfe *OE* dove, pigeon. Dowgate.

dūn *OE*, **doun** *ME* hill, down. Bandonhill, Blendon, Brimsdown, Cannon Hill, Chessington, Coulsdon, Down Barns Farm, Downe, Downhills, Duntshill, Durnsford, Farthing or Fairdean Downs, Furzedown, Hackney

Downs, Hendon, Hillingdon, Horselydown, Horsenden, Islington, Langtons, Lyonsdown, Malden, Morden, Neasden, North Ockendon, Purley Downs, Riddlesdown, Rowdown, Selsdon, Stickleton Close (*see* Greenford), Tollington, Uxendon, Waddington, Waddon, Willesden, Wimbledon.

ēa *OE* river. River Colne, St Mary Overie.

eald, *see* **ald**.

ealdormann *OE* nobleman. Aldermanbury.

ealu *OE* ale. Aldgate.

*ēan *OE* lamb. ?Enfield.

ēar *OE* mud, gravel. Erith.

earc, *see* **arc**.

ēast *OE*, **est** *ME* east, eastern. *Æst geat* (*earlier name for* Aldgate), East Barnet, East Bedfont, Eastbury, Eastcheap, Eastcote, East End (2), East Hall, East Ham, East Sheen, etc.

ebb *ME* ebb, low tide. *Ebbegate* (*earlier name for* Swan Lane).

*efer, yfer *OE* bank, ridge. ?River Effra.

ēg *OE* island, land partly surrounded by water, dry ground in marsh. Battersea, Bermondsey, Ebury, Hackney, Horselydown, Rammey, *Thorney* (*see* Westminster), Upney.

ēgeth, īgeth, *see* **eyte**.

elfitu *OE* swan. ?Eltham.

elm *OE* elm tree. Barn Elms, Elmstead, Nine Elms.

embankment *ModE* length of river bank built up to carry a road. Albert, Chelsea & Victoria Embankments.

ende *ME* quarter or district of a parish, hamlet. Chapel End, Church End (2), Crouch End, East End (2), Elmers End, Hale End, Hatch End,

Hayes End, Hill End, Kingsend, Mile End, North End (3), Ponders End, Sands End, Southend, Wallend, West End (3), Wood End (2).

eowestre *OE* sheepfold. Osterley.

erl *ME* earl. Earls Court, Earlsfield, Earl's Sluice.

ersc *OE* ploughed land. Sundridge.

est, *see* **ēast**.

eyte, ayte *ME* (*from* **ēgeth, īgeth** *OE*) small island, islet. Brentford Ait, Chiswick Eyot, *Gose Eyte*, *Parish Ayte* (*earlier names for* Eel Pie Island), Isleworth Ait, etc.

faire *ME* fair, beautiful. ?Fair Cross.

faitour *ME* imposter, cheat. Fetter Lane.

falwe *ME* fallow, uncultivated. Fallow Corner.

*(ge)feall *OE* place where trees have been felled, i.e. woodland clearing. Coldfall Wood.

fearn *OE* fern. Farnborough.

feire *ME* a fair. ?Fair Cross, Fairlop, Mayfair.

feld *OE* open land, **feld** *ME* field. Aperfield, Broomfield, Chelsfield, East Smithfield, Enfield, ?Feltham, Greenford Green, Harefield, Leicester Fields, Lincoln's Inn Fields, London Fields, Mansfield Hill, Markfield Road, Millfields, Moorfields, Northfields, St Giles in the Fields, St Martin in the Fields, West Smithfield, Southfields, Spitalfields, Suffield.

felte *OE* mullein or similar plant. ?Feltham.

fenn *OE* fen, marsh. Blackfen, Fenchurch Street.

fēorthing *OE* a fourth part or quarter of an estate. Allfarthing, Farthing or Fairdean Downs, Farthing Street.

fery *ME* ferry. Horseferry Road, Westferry.

finc *OE* finch. Finchley.

fisc *OE*, **fishe** *ME* fish. *Fiscesburna* (*earlier name for* Yeading Brook), Fish Street Hill.

fishe, *see* **fisc**.

flat *eModE* stretch of level ground. Wanstead Flats.

flēot *OE* inlet, creek. Barking Creek, Creekmouth, Fleet (river), *Wythyflete* (*earlier name for* Paris Garden).

ford *OE*, *ME* ford, river crossing. Battle Bridge Road, Brentford, Catford, Chingford, Cranford, Crayford, Deptford, Durnsford, Greenford, Ilford, Longford, Loxford, Old Ford, Romford, Stamford Bridge, Stamford Brook, Stamford Hill, Stratford (2), Whitford, Woodford.

fore *OE* in front of. Fore Street.

forest *ME* forest, wooded area set aside for hunting. Epping Forest, Forest Gate, Forest Hill, Hainault Forest, Waltham Forest.

for(e)ster *eModE* forester. Cockfosters.

forth-ēg *OE* island of higher ground in marsh. Forty Avenue & Lane, Forty Hill.

fortune *eModE* luck, success, prosperity. Fortune Green, Temple Fortune.

fōt *OE* foot. ?Mossford Green.

fox *OE* fox. Foxgrove, Foxley Wood.

frere (plural **freren**) *ME* friar, brother. Blackfriars, Crutched Friars, Friary Park, Friern Barnet, Friern Road, Fryent.

frogga *OE* frog. Frognal (2).

fūl *OE* foul, dirty. Fullwell Cross, Fulwell.

*****funta** *OE* spring. East Bedfont, Wansunt.

furse *ME* furze, gorse. Furzedown, Motspur Park.

fyrhth(e) *OE* woodland, *often* sparse woodland or scrub. Frith Manor, Great & Little Thrift, Hamfrith Road, Monkfrith, Thrift Wood.

galga *OE* gallows. Galley Lane, Gallows Corner.

gāra *OE* wedge-shaped or triangular plot of ground. Kensington Gore, Pyrgo Park.

gardin *ME* garden. Covent Garden, Kew Gardens, Paris Garden.

garite *OFr*, *ME* watchtower. Garratt Green & Lane.

gār-lēac *OE* garlic. Garlick Hill.

gate, *see* **geat**.

geat *OE*, **gate** *ME* gate. Aldersgate Street, Aldgate, Barnet Gate, Billingsgate, Bishopsgate, Cattlegate, Dowgate, *Ebbegate* (*earlier name for* Swan Lane), Highgate, Ladderstile Gate, Lancaster Gate, Moorgate, New Cross Gate, Newgate Street, Oxgate, *Rederesgate* (*see* Pudding Lane), Southgate.

gidi *ME* foolish, crazy. Gidea Park.

gild-hall *OE* hall in which a guild met, guildhall. Guildhall Buildings & Yard.

*****gilt-spur** *eModE* gilt spur, spur overlaid with gold. Giltspur Street.

gōs *OE*, **gos** *ME* goose. Gooshays, Gosbury Hill.

græs *OE* grass. Gracechurch Street.

grāf(a) *OE*, **grove** *ME* grove, copse. Arnos Grove, Foxgrove, The Grove, Grovelands, Grove Park (2), Little Grove, Pratt's Grove.

grange *ME* outlying farm where crops are stored. Grange Park, Woodgrange.

grēne *OE*, **grene** *ME* (*adjective*) green, grassy. Greenford, ?Greenhill, Greenshaw, Green Street, Green Street Green, Greenwich.

grene *ME (noun)* grassy spot, village green, hamlet. Acton Green, Ardleigh Green, Barnes Green, Bell Green, Bethnal Green, Bounds Green, Broad Green, Brook Green, Camberwell Green, Colham Green, Drayton Green, Fortis Green, Fortune Green, Golders Green, Goulds Green, Greenford Green, Green Street Green, Hadley Green, Harrow Green, Haven Green, Hither Green, Kensal Green, Kingsbury Green, Leaves Green, Lee Green, Lisson Green, Mossford Green, Newington Green, Norwood Green, Page Green, Palmers Green, Parsons Green, Richmond Green, Roe Green, Rowley Green, Rushey Green, Rush Green, Slade Green, Smallberry Green, Stepney Green, Strand on the Green, Stroud Green (2), Turnham Green, Walham Green, Westbourne Green, West Green, Willesden Green, Wood End Green, Wood Green, Wyke Green, Yeading Green.

grete *ME* great, large, thick. Gutteridge Wood.

Grim *OE* probably a nickname for the heathen god Woden. Grim's Ditch.

grove, *see* **grāf(a)**.

grubbe *ME* grub, caterpillar, worm. *?Grubbestrete (earlier name for* Milton Street).

haca *OE* hook-shaped piece of land, a ridge or tongue of land. Hackbridge, ?Hackney, Hacton.

hache, *see* **hæcc**.

hæcc *OE*, **hache** *ME* hatch, hatch gate (*especially one giving access to woodland or forest*). Aldborough Hatch, Chingford Hatch, Colney Hatch, *Hachestrete (earlier name for* Royal Mint Street), Hatch End, Suffield Hatch.

hæg *OE*, **haye** *ME* enclosure. Gooshays, Hornsey/Harringay.

hǣme *OE* inhabitants, dwellers. Beckenham, Lewisham, Mottingham, West Wickham.

hǣm-styde, *see* **hām-stede**.

*****hær** *OE* rock, stone. ?Harwood Hall.

*****hǣs(e)** *OE* land overgrown with brushwood. Hayes (3), Heston.

hæsel *OE* hazel. Hazelwood.

hǣth *OE*, **hethe** *ME* heath, uncultivated land overgrown with heather. Ardleigh Green, Becontree Heath, Bexleyheath, Blackheath, Cambridge Heath, Chadwell Heath, Chafford Heath, Hadley, Hampstead Heath, Hatton, Heathrow, Hounslow Heath, Lessness Heath, Little Heath, Northumberland Heath, Pield Heath, Putney Heath, Squirrels Heath, Thornton Heath.

haga *OE*, **hawe** *ME* messuage, hedged enclosure. Basinghall Street, *Stæningahaga (see* Staining Lane), Well Hall.

hagge *ME* hag, old woman. *Haggelane (earlier name for* Bennet's Hill).

halh (dative case **hale**) *OE* nook or corner of land. Bethnal Green, Cattlegate, *Hale House (see* Cromwell Road), Frognal, The Hale, Hale End, ?Halliwick, Northolt, Padnall Corner, Southall, Tottenham Court Road, Tottenham Hale.

hālig *OE* holy. Holywell Lane.

halke *ME* nook or corner. The Hawk Wood.

hall *OE*, *ME* hall, manor house. Cann Hall, Clayhall, Coney Hall, Copthall, Cranham Hall, East Hall, Gidea Park, Hall Place, Leadenhall, Moor Hall, *Nakethalle (earlier name for* Aldersbrook), South Hall, Uphall, Vauxhall, Whitehall, Woodhall.

hām *OE* homestead, village, manor, estate. ?Beckenham, ?Bellingham,

?Bensham, Cheam, ?Clapham, ?Croham, ?Cudham, Dagenham, ?Eltham, ?Feltham, ?Hatcham, ?Higham, Ickenham, Lewisham, Mitcham, ?Mottingham, Peckham, Rainham, Streatham, ?Sydenham, Tottenham, ?Turnham Green, Waltham Forest.

hamm *OE* enclosure, land hemmed in by water or marsh, land in a river bend, river meadow. Balham, ?Beckenham, ?Bellingham, ?Bensham, ?Clapham, Colham Green, ?Croham, ?Cudham, East Ham, ?Eltham, ?Feltham, Fulham, Ham, Hampton, ?Hatcham, ?Higham, Layham's, Leigham, ?Mottingham, Petersham, ?Sydenham, ?Turnham Green, Twickenham, West Ham.

hamor *OE* hammer. Hammersmith.

hām-stede, hæm-styde *OE* homestead, site of a dwelling. Hampstead, Sanderstead.

hām-tūn *OE* home farm or settlement. Roehampton.

hana *OE* cock (of wild bird). ?Hanwell.

hangra *OE* wood on a steep slope. Hanger Hill & Lane, Pitshanger.

*****hāring** *OE* grey wood. ?Hornsey/Harringay.

haven *ModE* place of shelter or retreat, refuge. Haven Green.

hawe, *see* **haga**.

haye *ME* hay. Haymarket.

haye, *see* **hæg**.

hēah (*dative case* **hēan**) *OE*, **heghe** *ME* high. Hendon, Higham Hill, Highbury, Highgate, Highwood Hill.

healf *OE* half. Allfarthing.

hearg *OE* heathen shrine or temple. Harrow.

hecg *OE*, **hegge** *ME* hedge. Gutteridge Wood, Headstone, Osidge.

hegge, *see* **hecg**.

heghe, *see* **hēah**.

helde *OE* slope. Chalk Wood, Shooters Hill.

hell, *see* **hyll**.

here *OE* (invading) army. Harefield.

here-beorg *OE* shelter. *Cold Harbour* (*see* Spring Park), Coldharbour (4).

here-strǣt *OE* army road, i.e. main road suitable for the passage of an army, highway. Hare Street, *see also* Oxford Street.

herth *ME* hearth. Hart Street.

hethe, *see* **hǣth**.

hīd *OE* hide of land, amount of land for the support of one free family and its dependants (*usually about 120 acres*). Hideborne (*earlier name for* Falcon Brook), The Hyde, Hyde Park, North Hyde.

hīewet *OE* place where trees have been hewed or cut down, woodland clearing. Hewitts.

hill, *see* **hyll**.

hither *eModE* nearer. Hither Green.

hīwan *OE* plural (*genitive* **hīgna**) religious community. Hainault.

hlāf-mæsse *OE* Lammas. Lammas Park.

hlāw *OE* burial mound, tumulus. Hounslow.

*****hlēosn** *OE* burial mound, or shelter. ?Lessness.

hlinc *OE* ledge. ?Haling Park.

*****hlȳde** *OE* loud one, noisy stream. *Ludeburne* (*earlier name for* River Wandle).

hlȳp *OE* leaping place, i.e. place that can be crossed by leaping. Ruislip.

hōc *OE* hook-shaped spur of land. Hook.

hogge *ME* hog, pig. *Hog Lane* (*earlier name for* Middlesex Street and Petticoat Lane), *Hog moore lane* (*earlier name for* Gloucester Road), Huggin Hill.

hōh *OE* heel or spur of land, ridge. Cranham, Hoe Street, Howbury, Kew.

hol *OE* hole or hollow (*noun*), hollow or deep (*adjective*). Bollo Bridge & Lane, Holborn, Hol(e)combe, Holloway, Holwood, Kemnal Manor.

holt *OE* wood, thicket. Hainault, Kensal Green, Old Oak Common, Ruckholt, Shroffold Road, Wormwood Scrubs.

hon(o)ur *ME* renown, high rank, dignity. Honor Oak.

horn *OE* (i) horn-like projection, gable (*alternating with* **hornede** gabled). Hornchurch. (ii) projecting horn-shaped piece of land. Horn Park, Horns Green.

hors *OE* horse. Horseferry Road, Horselydown Lane.

hosiere *ME* hosier. Hosier Lane.

hous *ME* house. Kent House.

hrīs *OE* brushwood. ?Battersea Rise, Risebridge.

hrōc *OE*, **roke** *ME* rook. Roehampton, Ruckholt, ?Ruxley.

hrycg *OE* ridge. Plumridge, Totteridge.

hrycg-weg *OE* ridgeway, road along a ridge. The Ridgeway.

hrÿther *OE* cattle. *Rederesgate* (*see* Pudding Lane), Rotherhithe.

hull, *see* **hyll**.

hund *OE* hound, dog. ?Houndsditch, ?Hounslow.

huni *ME* honey. Honey Lane.

hurst, *see* **hyrst**.

hwǣten *OE* growing with wheat. Waddington.

hwet-stān *OE* whetstone. Whetstone.

hwīt *OE*, **white** *ME* white, light-coloured. Whitchurch, Whitechapel, Whitehall, Whitton.

hyll *OE*, **hill, hell, hull** *ME* hill. Benhilton, Biggin Hill, Broxhill, Bunhill Fields, Bush Hill, Cannon Hill, Child's Hill, Clay Hill, Coombe Hill, Cornhill, Dollis Hill, Downhills, Dudden Hill, Duntshill, Eel Brook, Friday Hill, Garlick Hill, Golders Hill Park, ?Greenhill, Harrow on the Hill, Herne Hill, Higham Hill, Highgate Hill, Highwood Hill, Hill End, Holders Hill, Knights Hill, Lambeth Hill, Marble Hill, Mill Hill (2), Muswell Hill, Noak Hill, Notting Hill, St Mary at Hill, Shooters Hill, Snow Hill, Stamford Hill, Stumpshill, Tower Hill, Winchmore Hill.

hyrne *OE* angle or corner of land. Herne Hill.

hyrst *OE*, **hurst** *ME* wooded hill. Barnehurst, Bayhurst Wood, Chislehurst, Croham Hurst, Hurst Road, Levehurst, Pickhurst, Selhurst, Tylers Common.

hÿth *OE* landing place on a river, harbour. Chelsea, Erith, Garlick Hill, Lambeth, *lundentunes hyth* (*see* London), Putney, Queenhithe, Rotherhithe, Stepney, *Tymberhethe* (*see* High Timber Street).

ile, yle *ME* island. Isle of Dogs.

-ing *OE suffix* place belonging to, place characterized by. ?Notting Hill, ?Wapping.

-ing- *OE medial connective particle implying* associated with or called after. Addington, Alperton, Beddington, Blendon, Cuddington, Danson, Dudden Hill, Edmonton, Harlington, Hockenden, Kennington, Kensington, Kenton, Kevingtown, Orpington, Paddenswick, Paddington, Teddington, Tokyngton, Tubbenden, Turpington, Wennington.

-inga- *OE (genitive case of* **-ingas**).
Bellingham, Mottingham,
?Rainham, Watling Street.

-ingas *OE plural suffix* people of,
family or followers of, dwellers at.
Barking, Ealing, Havering-atte-
Bower, ?Seven Kings, Tooting,
?Wapping, Yeading.

inn *OE, ME* residence, lodging.
Gray's Inn, *Hungerford Inne (see*
Hungerford Bridge), Lincoln's Inn,
Staple Inn.

inwode *ME* wood near the main
residence of an estate. Inwood Park.

ire(n)mongere *ME* ironmonger.
Ironmonger Lane.

ismongere *ME* ironmonger.
Ironmonger Lane.

iw *OE* yew tree. *Heybourne (earlier name
for* Deans Brook).

jack *eModE* smaller in size. Jack Wood.

juerie *ME* district occupied by Jews.
Jewry Street, Old Jewry.

junction *ModE* place where railway
lines meet. Clapham Junction,
Loughborough Junction.

key *ME* quay, landing place. ?Kew.

knight, *see* **cniht**.

*****knightridere** *ME* mounted knight,
knight who rode at tournaments.
Giltspur Street, Knightrider Street.

lacu *OE* small stream. Mortlake.

lady *eModE* Our Lady. Ladywell.

*****læge** *OE* fallow, unploughed.
Layham's, Leigham.

læs *OE,* **lese** *ME* pasture, meadowland.
?Lessness, Oxleas Wood.

lamb *OE* lamb. Lambeth, Lampton.

land *OE, ME* tract of land, estate, strip
of arable in common field.
Kingsland, Longlands, Maylands,
Newlands (2), Norland,

Northumberland Heath,
Shortlands, Woodlands.

lane *OE, ME* lane. Abchurch Lane,
Bartholomew Lane, Chancery Lane,
Fetter Lane, Leather Lane, Mark
Lane, Mincing Lane, etc. *(especially
frequent in City of London street names).*

lang *OE,* **long** *ME* long. Langbourn,
Langley Park, Langthorne,
Langtons, Long Acre, Longford,
Long Lane, Longlands.

laystall *ModE* place where refuse is
laid, rubbish dump. Laystall Street.

lēaden *OE* (with a roof) made of lead.
Leadenhall.

lēah *OE* wood, woodland clearing or
glade, *later* pasture, meadow.
Ardleigh Green, Arkley, Bentley
Priory, Bexley, Bickley, Brockley,
Bromley (2), Cowley, Dawley,
Finchley, Foxley Wood, Hadley,
Kenley, Langley Park, Lee, ?Marble
Hill, Mitchley, Osterley, Purley,
Riddlesdown, Rowley, Ruxley,
Shirley, Wembley, Yiewsley.

lese, *see* **læs**.

level *eModE* flat stretch of ground.
Eastbury Level.

lieu *OFr* place. Beulah Hill.

lim *OE* lime. Limehouse, Lime Street.

litel *ME* little. Little Grove, Little
Heath, Little Ilford, Little Stanmore,
etc.

log(g)e *ME* lodge. Bog Lodge, Queen
Elizabeth's Hunting Lodge, West
Lodge Park, etc.

log(ge) *ME* bulky piece of wood,
portion of felled tree. Crook Log.

lok *ME* lock, river barrier. Enfield
Lock, Pickett's Lock, Teddington
Lock.

long, *see* **lang**.

lop *eModE* lopped tree. Fairlop.

lordship *ME* manor, estate. Lordship
Lane (2).

*lort(e) *OE* dirt, mud. *Lurtebourne (earlier name for* Hogsmill River).

*lūce *OE* enclosure. ?Luxted.

ludgeat *OE* back gate, postern. Ludgate Hill.

lufu *OE* love. Love Lane, ?Lusted.

*lug- *Celtic* bright, light. ?River Lea or Lee.

mǣd *OE*, **mede** *ME* meadow. Bushey Mead, Mad Bridge, *Medeseye* (*earlier name for* Pymmes Brook).

mǣl *OE* cross, crucifix. Malden.

(ge)mǣne *OE* held in common. Mansfield Hill.

(ge)mǣre *OE*, **mere** *ME* boundary. Beckenham, Bellingham, Boxers Wood, Crofton, Keston, Mare Street, Mottingham, West Wickham, ?Winchmore Hill.

mansion *eModE* large and stately house. Mansion House.

market *ME* market. Haymarket, Shepherd Market.

may *ME* hawthorn. ?Maylands.

mearc *OE* mark, boundary. Beckenham, Bevis Marks, Farnborough, Keston Mark, Lewisham, Mardyke Farm, Markfield Road, Marks Gate, Mottingham, West Wickham.

mearth *OE* marten. ?Marble Hill, ?Mark Lane.

mede, *see* **mǣd**.

melle, *see* **myln**.

menouresse *ME* Franciscan nun. Minories.

meoluc *OE*, **milke** *ME* milk. Milk Street, Milkwood Road.

mēos *OE* moss, *also* marsh, bog. Muswell Hill.

mere *OE* pool. Merton, Stanmore, Widmore, ?Winchmore Hill.

mere, *see* **(ge)mǣre**.

mersc *OE*, **mershe** *ME* marsh. Figge's Marsh, Hackney Marsh, Lower Marsh, Rainham Marshes, Wennington Marshes, Wricklemarsh.

mershe, *see* **mersc**.

mew, mue *ME* cage for hawks. *King's Mews* (*see* Trafalgar Square).

micel *OE* large. Mitcham, ?Mitchley.

mile *ME* mile. Mile End.

milke, *see* **meoluc**.

mille, *see* **myln**.

monk (*plural* **monken**) *ME* monk. Monken Hadley, Monkfrith, Monkham's Avenue.

mont *OFr* hill, mount. Belmont (4), Moat Mount, Mount Pleasant, Richmond.

mōr *OE*, **more** *ME* moor, marshy ground. Bullsmoor, Claysmore, *Hog moore lane* (*earlier name for* Gloucester Road), Harefield Moor (*see* Harefield), Longfordmoor, Moor Bridge, Moorfields, Moorgate, Moor Hall, Moorhall, Moor Lane, Morden, Rushmore Hill, Uxbridge Moor.

more, *see* **mōr**.

*mort *OE* young salmon or similar fish. Mortlake.

mos *OE* moss. Mossford Green.

mote *ME* moat. Moat Mount.

mud *ModE* mud. Mudchute.

mue, *see* **mew**.

mūtha *OE* mouth, estuary. Creekmouth.

myln *OE*, **mille, melle** *ME* mill. Abbey Mills, Coppermill, Hogsmill River, Millbank, Millfields, Mill Hill (2), Mill Meads, Millwall, Temple Mills, Turnmill Street.

myncen *OE* nun. Mincing Lane.

mynster *OE* monastery, minster, large church. Upminster, Westminster.

næss, ness *OE* promontory, headland. Cross Ness, Gallions Point, ?Lessness, Margaret or Tripcock Ness.

naked *ME* bare, exposed, unoccupied. *Nakethalle* (*earlier name for* Aldersbrook).

nān-mann *OE* no man, nobody. Normand Park, ?Normanshire Drive.

neckercher *ME* neckerchief. Neckinger.

nedlere *ME* needler, maker of needles. *Nedlerslane* (*earlier name for* Pancras Lane).

*neosu *OE* nose, nose-shaped hill. Neasden.

ness, *see* **næss**.

newe, *see* **nīwe**.

nīwe *OE*, **newe** *ME* new. Newbury, New Cross, Newgate Street, Newington, Newlands (2), New River, Stoke Newington.

north *OE*, *ME* north, northern. Norbiton, Norbury, Norland, North Cray, North End (3), Northfields, North Hyde, North Ockendon, Northolt, Northumberland Heath, Northwood, Norton Folgate, Norwood (2).

oke, *see* **āc**.

olde, *see* **ald**.

ōra *OE* elongated, flat-topped hill. Nower Hill, Pinner.

ote *ME* oats. Oat Lane.

oxa *OE*, **oxe** *ME* ox. Oxgate, Oxleas.

oxe, *see* **oxa**.

pale *ME* land enclosed by a fence. Pale Well.

parke *ME* enclosed tract of land set apart for hunting, grounds of castle or mansion, *later* piece of ground for public recreation, or residential suburb. Beddington Park, Gidea Park, Grange Park, Green Park, Hampton Court Park, Hanworth Park, Havering Park (*see* Havering-atte-Bower), Hyde Park, Northumberland Park, Osterley Park, Park Wood (2), Pinner Park, Regent's Park, Richmond Park, St James's Park, etc.

paternostrer *ME* maker of rosaries. Paternoster Row.

*pĕac *OE* peak, hill. Peckham.

pealed *eModE* bare of vegetation. Pield Heath.

*penn *Celtic* head, end. Penge.

perie, *see* **pyrige**.

personage, *see* **persone**.

persone *ME* parson, **personage** *ME* parsonage. Parsons Green.

pety *OFr*, *ME* small. Petty France.

pīc *OE* point, peak. Pickhurst.

pightel *ME* small enclosure. Parson's Pightle, ?*Pigtail Farm* (*earlier name for* Crown Farm).

*pinc *OE* minnow. Pinkwell.

pinn *OE* pin, peg, point. Pinner, ?*Pinnesknol* (*earlier name for* Muswell Hill).

place *ME* residence, large house. Ely Place, Hall Place, Lower Place.

plaissiet *OFr* enclosure made with interlaced fencing, or **plaschiet** *OFr* marshy pool. Plashet.

pleg-stōw *OE* place where people gather for play or sport. Plaistow (2).

plūme *OE* plum tree. Plumridge, Plumstead.

point *ModE* promontory. Coldharbour Point, Cuckold's Point, Gallions Point, Maryland Point.

pōl *OE* pool, deep place in a river. The Pool, Pool River, Portpool Lane.

popler *ME* poplar tree. Poplar.

portsoken *ME* district outside a city over which jurisdiction is extended. Portsoken Street.

preble *eModE* gravel. *Pripledeane* (*see* Addington Hills).

prēost *OE*, **prest** *ME* priest. Preston, Priests Bridge.

prest, *see* **prēost**.

primerose *ME* primrose. Primrose Hill.

prior *ME* prior. Priors Farm.

puddel *ME* small dirty pool. Puddle Dock.

pudding *ME* bowels, entrails, guts. Pudding Lane.

pultrie *ME* poultry market. Poultry.

***putta** *OE* hawk. ?Putney.

pyrige *OE*, **perie** *ME* pear tree. Perivale, Perry Hill, Perry Rise & Vale, Perry Street, Purley, Pyrgo Park.

pyttel *OE* mousehawk. ?Pitshanger.

quaggy *eModE* boggy, marshy. Quaggy River.

ramm *OE* ram. Rammey Marsh.

rand, ***rend** *OE* boundary. Ravensbourne River.

reach *eModE* stretch of a river between two bends. Blackwall Reach, Gallions Reach, Limehouse Reach.

rēad *OE* red. Ratcliff.

***rede** *OE* clearing. Berry's Green.

redyng *ME* clearing. Woodridings.

regard *OFr* view. *Bewregarde* (*see* Sutton Court Road).

***rend**, *see* **rand**.

rewe, rowe *ME* (i) row of houses. Budge Row, Collier Row, Heathrow, Paternoster Row, Savile Row. (ii) row of trees. Rotten Row.

riche *OFr* strong. Richmond.

rill *eModE* small stream. Cranbrook.

***rippel** *OE* strip of land. Ripple Road, Rippleside.

rise *eModE* rising ground. ?Battersea Rise, Kensal Rise, Perry Rise.

rishe, *see* ***rysc**.

rīth *OE* small stream. Peckham Rye, The Wrythe.

rīthig *OE* small stream. Beverley Brook.

roke, *see* **hrōc**.

rood, *eModE* cross. Rood Lane.

rotten *eModE* extremely soft and friable. Rotten Row.

rowe, *see* **rewe**.

rūh *OE* rough. Rowdown Wood, Rowley Green.

rūm *OE* wide, spacious. Romborough, Romford.

rushe, *see* ***rysc**.

(ge)ryd(d) *OE* cleared of trees. Riddlesdown.

***rysc** *OE*, **rushe, rishe** *ME* rush. Ruislip, Rushmore Hill.

***ryscett** *OE* rush bed, place growing with rushes. Rushey Green, Rushett Farm.

***sæge** *OE* marsh stream. *Medeseye* (*earlier name for* Pymmes Brook).

safron *ME* saffron. Saffron Hill.

sanctuarie *ME* sanctuary, refuge. Broad & Little Sanctuary.

sand *OE*, *ME* sand. Sanderstead, Sands End, Stamford Bridge, Stamford Hill.

scatha *OE* robber, thief. Scadbury.

sceacol *OE* tether, shackle. Shacklewell.

***sceald** *OE* shallow. Shadwell.

scearn *OE* dirt, dung. Shernhall Street.

***scēo** *OE* shed, shelter. East Sheen.

***scēotere, *scȳtere** *OE* shooter, archer. Shooters Hill.

scīr *OE* (*adjective*) bright. ?Shirley.

scir *OE* (*noun*), **shire** *ME* shire, district, estate. Normanshire, Sherrick Green, ?Shirley.

scōhland *OE* land given to a monastic community to provide it with shoes. Shoe Lane.

*****scora** *OE* steep bank, slope. Shoreditch.

scræf *OE* cave, hovel. Shroffold Road.

scratch *eModE dialect* the Devil. Scratch Wood.

scrub *eModE* low stunted tree, brushwood. Wormwood Scrubs.

*****scȳtere**, *see* *****scēotere**.

sealh *OE* sallow willow. Selhurst.

sēath *OE* pit, hollow. Roxeth.

secole *ME* sea-coal (i.e. ordinary coal as opposed to charcoal). Old Seacoal Lane.

seething *eModE* bubbling or foaming as if boiling. Seething Wells.

sele *OE* hall. ?Selsdon.

*****sele** *OE* sallow copse. ?Selsdon.

*****sengel** *OE* burnt clearing. ?Single Street.

*****set-copp** *OE* seat-shaped or flat-topped hill. Sidcup.

seynt *ME* saint. St Clement Danes, St Giles in the Fields, St John's Wood, St Katharine's Dock, St Martin in the Fields, St Mary Cray, St Pancras, St Paul's, St Paul's Cray, etc.

shawe *ME* (*from* **sceaga** *OE*) copse, wood. Greenshaw, Roundshaw.

shire, *see* **scir**.

*****shite-burgh** *ME* (*****scite-burh** *OE*) privy. Sherborne Lane.

short *ME* short. Shortlands.

sīde *OE*, **side** *ME* side, street or district alongside. Bankside, Barkingside, Chaseside, Cheapside, Rippleside, Woodside (2).

*****sifethen** *OE* full of chaff or bran. Seething Lane.

slade *ME* valley, low-lying marshy land. Slade Green.

smæl *OE* narrow. Smallberry Green.

smēthe *OE* smooth, level. Smitham, Smithambottom, East Smithfield, West Smithfield.

smiththe *OE* smithy, forge. Hammersmith.

snare *ME* snare or trap for catching animals or birds. ?Snaresbrook.

*****snōr** *OE* road that curves across a gradient. Snow Hill.

southe, *see* **sūth**.

spanker *ModE dialect* something exceptional or striking, *also* fast moving horse. ?Spankers Hill Wood.

spa(w) *eModE* medicinal spring or well. Bermondsey Spa, Spa Fields.

spitel *ME* hospital, religious house. Spitalfields.

spring *eModE* spring. Springfield Park, Spring Grove, Spring Park.

square *eModE* open space surrounded by houses or buildings. Berkeley Square, Finsbury Square, Kensington Square, Russell Square, Sloane Square, etc.

*****stǣne** *OE* stony place. The Steyne.

stān *OE*, **stone** *ME* stone, standing stone, boundary stone. Brixton, ?Haggerston, Keston, Leytonstone, London Stone, Stamford Brook, *Stane Street*, Stanmore, Stonecot, Wealdstone.

*****stapled** *OE* built with pillars. Staple Inn.

stede *OE* enclosed pasture, place, site. Elmstead, Lusted, Luxted, Plumstead, Wanstead.

sticol *OE* steep. Stickleton Close (*see* Greenford).

stinkende *ME* stinking, smelly. *Stinking Lane* (*earlier name of* King Edward Street).

stocc *OE* tree stump. Stockwell.

stoccen *OE* by the tree stumps or made of logs. Stoke Newington.

stone, *see* **stān**.

stoop *ModE dialect* boundary post. Stoop Bridge.

stōw *OE* (holy) place. Walthamstow.

strǣt *OE* Roman road, paved road, **strete** *ME* urban street, street of houses, rural hamlet. Addle Street, 'Akeman Street' (*see* Great West Road), Bread Street, Broad Street, Cannon Street, *Ermine Street*, Farthing Street, Fish Street Hill, Green Street, Green Street Green, Lime Street, Mare Street, Milk Street, Old Street, Single Street, South Street, *Stane Street*, Stratford, Stratford Bridge, Streatham, Thames Street, Turkey Street, Watling Street (2), Wood Street (2), etc.

strand *OE* bank, shore. Strand, Strand on the Green.

strawberry *ModE* strawberry. Strawberry Hill, Strawberry House.

strete, *see* **strǣt**.

strōd *OE* marshy land overgrown with brushwood. Stroud Green (2).

stubb *ME* tree stump. Burnt Stub.

***stumbel** *OE* tree stump. Stumpshill Wood.

***stybba** *OE* stump, pile. ?Stepney.

sulh *OE* narrow gully. Silk Stream.

sundor *OE* separate, detached. Sundridge.

sūth *OE*, **southe** *ME* south, southern. Southall, Southborough (2), Southbury, Southend, Southfields, Southgate, South Hall, South Street, Southwark, Sudbrook, Sudbury, Suffield, Surbiton, Sutton (2), etc.

tēag, *see* **tye**.

tempel *ME* property of the Knights Templars. The Temple, Temple Bar, Temple Fortune, Temple Mills.

***tēo** *OE* boundary. Tyburn.

theef *ME* thief. *Theeving Lane* (*see* Globe Town).

thicke *ME* thick, dense. Greenshaw.

thorn *OE* thorn tree. Elthorne, Langthorne, *Thorney* (*see* Westminster), Thornton Heath.

tigel *OE* tile. Tylers Common.

timber *OE* timber. High Timber Street.

***tōt** *OE* lookout place. ?Tooting.

***tōt-hyll** *OE* lookout hill or mound. Tothill Street.

toun, *see* **tūn**.

town *eModE* (*from* **tūn** *OE*) newly developed residential area. *Agar Town* (*see* Agar Grove), Angell Town, Beckton, Camden Town, Canning Town, Cubitt Town, De Beauvoir Town, Globe Town, Kensal Town, Silvertown, Somers Town, Stratford New Town, Summerstown.

trēow *OE* tree. Becontree.

trille *ME* to turn, something that turns, wheel. Turnmill Street.

***trun**, ***turn** *OE* river bend. Turnham Green.

turne *ME* to turn. Turnagain Lane.

tūn *OE*, **toun** *ME* farmstead, estate, manor, village (*see also* **town**). Acton, Addington, Alperton, Beddington, Boston Manor, Brompton, Carshalton, Charlton, Clapton, Crofton, Cuddington, Dalston, Danson Park, Drayton Green, Edmonton, Hacton, ?Haggerston, Hampton, Harlesden, Harlington, Hatton, Headstone, Heston, Homerton, Hoxton, Kennington, Kensington, Kentish Town, Kenton, Kevingtown, Kingston, Knighton Wood, Lampton, Leyton, Lisson, *lundentunes hyth* (*see* London), Merton, Newington, Norton Folgate, Orpington, Paddington, Preston, Sipson, Stoke Newington,

Sutton (2), Teddington, Thornton Heath, Tokyngton, Upton (2), Wallington, Wennington, Whitton.

tur *ME* tower. The Tower, Tower Hamlets, Tower Hill.

*turn, *see* ***trun**.

*twicce *OE* river fork. ?Twickenham.

*twi-fyrde *OE* double ford. Twyford Abbey.

tye *ME* (*from* **tēag** *OE*) small enclosure. Clay Tye Farm, Corbets Tey.

upp *OE*, **up(p)** *ME* upper, higher. Uphall, Upminster, Upton (2).

uppan *OE* upon. Upney.

vale *ME* valley. Kingston Vale, Maida Vale, Perivale, Perry Vale, Putney Vale, Streatham Vale, Vale of Health.

vedeir *OFr* view. Belvedere.

ville *French* newly developed residential area. Pentonville.

viniterie *ME* wine store. Vintry.

wād *OE* woad. Waddon.

wǣn *OE* wagon. ?Wanstead.

wænn *OE* wen, lump, mound. ?Wanstead.

(ge)wæsc *OE* place that floods. Enfield Wash.

wald, weald *OE* woodland, forest. Harrow Weald, Waltham Forest, Weald Brook, Wealdstone.

walh *OE* Celt, Briton, Welshman. Walbrook, Wallington, Walworth.

wall *OE, ME* wall, bank. Blackwall, London Wall, Millwall, Wallend, Wallwood.

*wap(p)ing *OE* marsh, mire. ?Wapping.

wareine *ME* game preserve, especially for rabbits. Warren Farm.

wāse *OE* muddy marsh. Wapping.

water(ing) *ME* stream, ditch, pond. Bayswater, Freezywater, Seven Kings Water, Wyck Gardens.

weald, *see* **wald**.

weg *OE* way, road. Holloway.

welig *OE* willow. Wylys (*earlier name for* Paris Garden).

wella, wiell(a) *OE*, **welle** *ME* spring, well, stream. Barwell Court, Botwell, ?Brockwell Park, Camberwell, Chadwell Heath, Clerkenwell, Dormer's Wells, Fullwell Cross, Fulwell, Hanwell, Holywell, Ladywell, Maswell, *Milkewell* (*see* Milkwood Road), Monkwell Square, Muswell Hill, Pinkwell, Sadler's Wells, Seething Wells, Shacklewell, Shadwell, Shernhall Street, Stockwell, Waxwell, Well Hall, Willesden, Woodford Wells.

welle, *see* **wella**.

wende *ME* to turn. Turnagain Lane.

wente *ME* path, way. Four Wantz, Four Wents.

(ge)weorc *OE* defensive work or fort. Southwark.

wer *OE* weir, fishing enclosure. Edgware.

*werpels *OE* path, track. Worple Road.

west *OE, ME* west, western. West Barnes, Westcombe, West Drayton, West End (3), West Ham, Westminster, West Wickham, etc.

westan *OE* (*adverb*) west, west of. Westbourne Green.

wharfe *ME* wharf. Puddle Dock, St Katharine's Dock.

white, *see* **hwīt**.

wīc *OE* specialized farm or building, trading or industrial settlement, port or harbour. Aldwych, Chiswick, Greenwich, Hackney Wick, Halliwick, Hampton Wick, *Lundenwic* (*see* Introduction: 'The

Anglo-Saxon Period'), Outwich Street, Paddenswick, Sherrick Green, Whitford, Woolwich, Wyck Gardens, Wyke Green.

*wic·hām *OE* homestead associated with an earlier Romano-British settlement. East Wickham, West Wickham.

wiell(a), *see* **wella**.

*w(i)elling *OE* (place at the) spring. ?Welling.

wilcuma *OE* welcome guest or stranger. ?Walthamstow.

wisc *OE* marshy meadow. Dulwich.

wīthig *OE* withy, willow. Widmore, *Wythyflete* (*earlier name for* Paris Garden).

Wixan *OE* tribal name. Uxbridge, Uxendon.

worth, wyrth *OE* enclosure, enclosed farmstead or settlement. Baber Bridge, Batsworth Road, Bonner Hill Road, Chafford Heath, Hanworth, Harmondsworth, Isleworth, *Lolsworth* (*see* Spitalfields), Tolworth, Walworth, Wandsworth.

*writol *OE* babbling stream. Wricklemarsh.

wro *ME* nook or corner of land. Roe Green.

wudu *OE*, **wode** *ME* wood. Bishopswood Road, Brownswood, Colliers Wood, Cricklewood, Elmstead Wood, *Hangar Wood* (*see* Hanger Hill), Harold Wood, Harwood Hall, Hazelwood, Highwood Hill, Holwood, Ken Wood, Kings Wood, Milkwood Road, Northwood, Norwood (2), Petts Wood, St John's Wood, Wallwood, Woodcote, Wood End (2), Woodford, Woodgrange, Wood Green, Woodhall, Woodlands, Woodridings, Woodside (2), Wood Street (2), Wormwood.

wull *OE* wool. Woolwich.

wyrm *OE* snake, reptile. Wormwood.

wyrth, *see* **worth**.

wyrt-tūn *OE* herb or vegetable garden. Worton.

yfer, *see* **efer**.

yle, *see* **ile**.

Select Bibliography

Bebbington, G., *Street Names of London* (London, 1988).

Cameron, K., *English Place Names* (London, 1996).

Coates, R., 'A new explanation of the name London', *Transactions of the Philological Society*, 96: 2 (1998), 203–29.

—— 'The first American place-name in England: Pimlico', *Names*, 43.3 (Sept. 1995), 213–27.

Ekwall, E., *Street-Names of the City of London* (Oxford, 1954).

Fairfield, S., *The Streets of London: A Dictionary of the Names and their Origins* (London, 1984).

Field, J., *Place-Names of Greater London* (London, 1980).

Gelling, M., *Signposts to the Past*, 3rd edn. (Chichester, 1997).

—— *The Landscape of Place Names* (Stamford, 2000).

Glover, J., *The Place-Names of Kent* (Rainham, 1982).

Gover, J. E. B., Mawer, A., and Stenton, F. M., *The Place-Names of Hertfordshire*, English Place-Name Society, Volume XV (Cambridge, 1938).

—— with Bonner, A., *The Place-Names of Surrey*, English Place-Name Society, Volume XI (Cambridge, 1934).

—— with Madge, S. J., *The Place-Names of Middlesex (apart from the City of London)*, English Place-Name Society, Volume XVIII (Cambridge, 1942).

Harben, H. A., *A Dictionary of London* (London, 1918).

Inwood, S., *A History of London* (London, 1998).

Lobel, M. D. (ed.), *The City of London to c.1520*, Historic Towns Atlas III (Oxford, 1989).

Mills, A. D., *A Dictionary of English Place-Names*, 2nd edn. (Oxford, 1998).

Parsons, D., and Styles, T., with Hough, C., *The Vocabulary of English Place-Names*, Part 1 (others to follow) (Nottingham, 1997).

Pointon, G. E. (ed.), *BBC Pronouncing Dictionary of British Names*, 2nd edn. (Oxford, 1983).

Reaney, P. H., *The Place-Names of Essex*, English Place-Name Society, Volume XII (Cambridge, 1935).

Room, A., *The Street Names of England* (Stamford, 1992).

Rumble, A. R., 'Place-names and their context, with special regard to the Croydon Survey Region', *Proceedings of the Croydon Natural History & Scientific Society*, 15: 8 (1976), 161–84.

Smith, A. H., *English Place-Name Elements*, English Place-Name Society, Volumes XXV, XXVI (Cambridge, 1956).

Spital, J., and Field, J., *A Reader's Guide to the Place-Names of the United Kingdom* (Stamford, 1990).

Stow, J., *A Survey of London* (1598, 1603), ed. C. L. Kingsford (Oxford, 1908).

The Survey of London (various editors), Volumes I–XLIV (in progress).

Victoria County History (various editors), volumes for *Essex*, *Hertfordshire*, *London*, *Middlesex*, and *Surrey* (in progress).

Wallenberg, J. K., *Kentish Place-Names* (Uppsala, 1931).

—— *The Place-Names of Kent* (Uppsala, 1934).

Weinreb, B., and Hibbert, C., *The London Encyclopaedia*, revised edn. (London, 1995).